Tom Woerner-Powell
Another Road to Damascus

Tom Woerner-Powell

Another Road to Damascus

An Integrative Approach to ʿAbd al-Qādir al-Jazāʾirī (1808–1883)

DE GRUYTER

ISBN 978-3-11-050055-4
e-ISBN (PDF) 978-3-11-049951-3
e-ISBN (EPUB) 978-3-11-049769-4

Library of Congress Cataloging-in-Publication Data
A CIP catalog record for this book has been applied for at the Library of Congress.

Bibliografic information published by the Deutsche Nationalbibliothek
The Deutsche Nationalbibliothek lists this publication in the Deutschen Nationalbibliografie; detailed bibliografic data are available on the Internet at http://dnb.dnb.de.

This volume is text- and page-identical with the hardback published in 2017.
Cover image: Jean Baptiste Huysmans, Abd-el-Kader. Gros et Delettrez, Paris/wikicommons
Printing and binding: CPI books GmbH, Leck

♾ Printed on acid-free paper
Printed in Germany

www.degruyter.com

Contents

Foreword — 1

Introduction — 2
The Many Lives of ʿAbd al-Qādir al-Jazāʾirī — **2**
Aims and Methods — **4**
An Overview of Sources — **8**
Chapter Outline — **12**

1.0 Chapter One – *Sīrah Sayfiyyah:* ʿAbd al-Qādir in North Africa, 1833–1848 — 15
1.1 First Steps and Interpretive Framework — **15**
1.2 Origins — **21**
1.3 ʿAbd al-Qādir's Internal Policy — **27**
1.4 ʿAbd al-Qādir's Relations with France — **37**
1.5 ʿAbd al-Qādir's Relations with Morocco — **49**
1.6 Conclusion — **58**

2.0 Chapter Two – ʿAbd al-Qādir's *Risālah on Hijrah* — 62
2.1 Style and Presentation — **65**
2.2 Sources — **67**
2.3 Forms of Inference and Argumentation — **70**
2.4 Further Themes: Sincerity and Hypocrisy — **73**
2.5 Faith, Nation, and Legitimation – The secondary literature in light of the *Risālah on Hijrah* — **78**

3.0 Chapter Three – Exile and Imprisonment on the Road to Damascus; 1848–1852 — 95
3.1 Imprisonment — **96**
3.2 Trial and Tribulation — **100**
3.3 Release — **104**
3.4 A 'Road to Damascus' Moment? — **107**
3.5 Continuity — **115**

4.0 Chapter Four – From Istanbul to Damascus, 1853–1864 — 120
4.1 An Algerian Island off the Sea of Marmara — **120**
4.2 A Reminder to the Reasonable and an Admonishment to the Negligent — **125**

4.3 The *Dhikrā* and a European Conversion — 131
4.4 Arrival in Damascus, 1855 — 140
4.5 Riot, Rescue, and Representation — 145

5.0 Chapter Five – *Sīrah Ṣūfiyyah:* Sufism, Suspicion, and the *Kitāb al-Mawāqif*; 1864–1883 — 155
5.1 Major Themes in the *Kitāb al-Mawāqif* — 163
5.2 ʿAbd al-Qādir's Later Life and Politics: Reading Conversion into the *Kitāb al-Mawāqif* — 171
5.3 ʿAbd al-Qādir's Conversion to Pluralism: Investigating the Evidence — 178
5.4 The Western Roots of ʿAbd al-Qādir's Spiritual 'Conversion' — 187

6.0 Conclusion — 198
6.1 Another Road to Damascus — 198
6.2 Reflections on the Road Onward — 206

Afterword — 219

Bibliography – Archival Sources — 227
Texts by ʿAbd al-Qādir al-Jazāʾirī — 229
Additional Primary Sources — 230
Secondary Sources — 231

Appendix A – ʿAbd al-Qādir's Risālah on Hijrah — 239

Appendix B – ʿAbd al-Qādir's Mawqif #254 ('He Is [Like] That') — 251

Index — 255

Author Index — 259

Foreword

I would very much like to thank all of the people and institutions which have made this work possible. I would like to thank Oxford University and the Arts and Humanities Research Council for arranging and funding my doctoral studies, as well as to the Fondation Ousseimi's *Prix de la Tolérance* for funding further research which has also enriched the present work. Special thanks must be given to my supervisors Ronald Nettler and Michael Willis.

Most of all, I would like to thank my parents, Ricca and Markus, my brother Christopher, and most especially Abby, my wife.

In this book, transliteration will broadly follow the conventions of the *Encyclopaedia of Islam* – with the exceptions that *qāf* will be represented by *q*, *jīm* by *j*, and *shīn* by sh (hence *ʿAbd al-Qādir al-Jazāʾirī* rather than *ʿAbd al-Ḳādir al-Dshazāʾirī*). 'Sun' and 'moon' letters will not be distinguished. In some cases, conventional spelling will be retained where the word in question has entered into sufficiently wide usage in English to justify this, or so as to reproduce the source material.

In what follows, all translations from German, French, and Arabic (unless otherwise stated) are my own – with the exception of Qur'ānic excerpts, which are from the Yūsuf ʿAlī version.

All errors are my own.

DOI 10.1515/9783110499513-001

Introduction

The Many Lives of ʿAbd al-Qādir al-Jazāʾirī

A great deal has already been said about ʿAbd al-Qādir al-Jazāʾirī. He was and is a figure of remarkable historical significance, popular enthusiasm, and scholarly interest. Yet doubts remain. While all agree that he was a fascinating figure, disagreement reigns over why this is the case. We are told both that he was a pioneer on the cusp of modernity, and that he was a romantic, bent on returning to a long-gone past. We learn that he was a cosmopolitan Francophile, and that he was the pioneer of Algeria's struggle for independence from France. He is described as a selfless and ascetic man of God, and as an ambitious manipulator of others for the sake of personal advancement. He is presented to us as an innovative metaphysician who embraced modern European philosophies, and as the unerringly faithful spokesman for a Muslim mystic some eight centuries dead.[1] A great deal has been said about ʿAbd al-Qādir al-Jazāʾirī, and all too much of it has been paradoxical and contradictory.

That so much has been written about him is only right. His influences, direct and indirect, deliberate and accidental, practical and symbolic, are manifold. In the 1830s and 1840s he was the foremost leader of Algerian resistance to French colonialism, often named alongside Shamyl (Imām Shāmil) as the age's foremost *mujāhid:* a holy warrior in the cause of *jihād.* Sympathisers saw a chevalier, opponents a fanatic. His heroic defence of thousands of Christians during the Syrian sectarian riots of 1860 justly made him a *cause célèbre* across the western world. In between, his name had become a potent political tool in contestations between Moroccan centres of power, between French monarchists and republicans, between English, French, and Ottoman imperialists, and between all of these and new varieties of cosmopolitans. Many still draw inspiration from his memory today.

ʿAbd al-Qādir has come to be many things to many people. Yet the panoply of radically differing images now confronting us share a common theme. It is with this theme that this book will concern itself. This study will aim to question a crucial narrative structure imposed on ʿAbd al-Qādir's life even by perspectives which seem irreconcilably opposed. Remarked or unremarked, yet invariably unchallenged, it forms the most fundamental presupposition assumed by his many

1 These pairs of opposing views are respectively to be found in, for instance, in the work of John Kiser [2008] and Peshah Shinar [1965]; Bruno Étienne [2003] and Badīʿah Al-Ḥasanī al-Jazāʾirī [2000]; ʿAbd al-Razzāq Al-Bayṭar [1963] and Raphael Danziger [1977]; and Itzchak Weismann [2001] and Michel Chodkiewicz [1995].

DOI 10.1515/9783110499513-002

biographers. What the broad gamut of accounts of his life share is a dramatically bipartite structure. Two starkly contrasting images of the man are typically presented: the first and second halves of his life are separated by a 'Road to Damascus' narrative of dramatic conversion – typically related to his period of captivity in France. Not only is his memory fractured by the competing perspectives which have reflected it, each in their own image, but it is dichotomised within each account. ʿAbd al-Qādir, whose body was twice buried, seems also to have lived twice: once in Damascus[2] and once in Algeria.[3]

No matter which perspective on ʿAbd al-Qādir one examines, this pattern manifests itself. It is less an argument than a discursive formation, the unquestioned structure within which the overwhelming majority of writing on the subject operates. It shows itself both implicitly, through the presumption that only one half of his life is worth discussing in lieu of the other, and explicitly, through overt periodic juxtaposition and psychological accounts of personal transformation. It arises as the result of overt authorial intention, and as an unintended product of convention. Every telling of ʿAbd al-Qādir's story naturally has its own strengths and its weaknesses, its own inspirations, interpretations, and ellipses. Yet the presumption that his life is best understood in two separate halves – one Algerian, one Damascene – has played an unexamined role in a deeply unhelpful hermeneutic circle, needlessly detracting from the many insights of past accounts. The narrative of conversion encourages us to over-state individual characteristics of his earlier and later lives, hardening subtle distinctions into black and white contrasts, contemplating actualities less than archetypes.

This 'mythology of incoherence'[4] needs to be questioned by developing a more continuous and life-like account of the man. An account supported by a broad gamut of argumentation, primary textual analysis, and archival evidence. This account will engage with reception- and *Wirkungsgeschichte*[5] to redress lingering effects of European colonialism on ʿAbd al-Qādir's life's representation up

---

2 His initial burial is recorded by, for example, *Tuḥfah*, p. 857; Al-Bayṭār, 1963, p. 903.

3 The re-interment took place on the 5th of July 1965 [King, 1997, p. 72]. A statue in Algiers had already been erected in 1962, soon after Algeria gained its independence [Abun-Nasr, 2007, p. 205].

4 This reversal of the Skinnerian construction ('mythology of coherence') is borrowed from Mark Hulliung's commentary on Quentin Skinner's interpretation of Machiavelli. 'As a corrective… Skinner's point is well-taken. It is to Skinner's apparent reversal of an *a priori* assumption of unity into an *a priori* assumption of disunity that we must object.' [Hulliung, 1983, p. 230]. That debate is mentioned not to take sides with respect to the interpretation of Machiavelli, but rather to illustrate the degree to which assumptions about the structure of a life's history can influence one's interpretation of its contents.

5 Particularly with respect to the manner in which susequent interpretations shape, absorb, and iterate upon one another [Gadamer, 2003, *passim*].

to the present. It will throw new light on his character, intentions, ambitions, and limitations, as well as re-formulating his relationship with enduring questions of faith and politics, war and peace, spirituality and legalism, and the tension between confident faith and inter-religious toleration. Finally, it attempts thereby to deliver the long called-for 're-evaluation of his life that integrates the various facets and stages of his career'.[6]

To this end, the shifting array of accounts brought by successive waves of biographers will be compared to their primary sources, and shown to have been shaped by the pressure of this appealing narrative arc. The 'Road to Damascus' narrative will be compared to a less fractured reading of ʿAbd al-Qādir's life and revealed as an artificial imposition, whose mainsprings can be traced back to specific developments in European colonial and cultural history. In the absence of such potentially misleading narrative impositions, context and continuity will be brought to the fore, replacing conflict and contradiction.

A more conventional, more conservative, more human figure will be described as a result of this interrogation than is reflected in previous accounts – yet one who is no less remarkable for all of that. ʿAbd al-Qādir's path was not that of severe Saul of Tarsus, whose journey transformed him into loving St Paul: no blinding light, no great conversion. ʿAbd al-Qādir, it will become apparent, took another road to Damascus.

Aims and Methods

While this study will draw on a wide range of primary materials, it does not seek to simply replace previous accounts with its own. Rather, ʿAbd al-Qādir's path through life will be traced in partnership with previous biographies – particularly the most recent. It will offer this perspective as a corrective to the narrative of conversion's effects on previous scholarship. The aim is constructive, both in offering a new departure of its own and in presenting critiques of earlier scholarship. This will both enhance our understanding of ʿAbd al-Qādir's life as he lived it, and contribute meaningfully to debates surrounding his life and ideas.

This effort will be integrative in the sense of resisting the essential separation or elimination of significant elements of ʿAbd al-Qādir's thought and action, and will be concomitantly wary of reductive approaches. The goal is to explain without explaining away.

6 Commins, 1988, p. 131.

ʿAbd al-Qādir's life has been addressed by scholars working to very different sets of methodologies. In order to engage constructively with the gamut of work on him, it will be necessary both to meet these on their own terms and, where possible and appropriate, to bring them into dialogue. This attempt must unavoidably, therefore, have a multi-disciplinary character, representing both a challenge and an opportunity. Every effort will be made to avoid over-reliance upon the terminology and internal debates which are the preserve of one discipline rather than another. Instead, issues will be dealt with as and when they arise within the study's chronological progression, and in as broadly intelligible a lexicon as possible.

Archival research, textual analysis, and the description and comparison of theological and philosophical positions as they are presented by varying perspectives are crucial to this effort. Each facet of its subject is approached with the conceptual toolset best suited to the task at hand and most widely reflected in the secondary literature. In the broadest terms, this study draws primarily on scholarship in political history and in Islamic studies – disciplines which have tended to focus on the pre- and post-conversion halves of ʿAbd al-Qādir's life, respectively.[7] As a result, he has acquired two distinct biographies which this work aims at harmonising: those of the Algerian soldier and of the Syrian Sufi, a *sīrah sayfiyyah* and *sīrah ṣūfiyyah*, in the words of Pessah Shinar.[8]

Previous accounts of ʿAbd al-Qādir have confined themselves to smaller and smaller subsets within this range. This very fact makes necessary an integrative, inter-disciplinary approach, attempting a holistic presentation of the man. It cannot, though, aim to compete with the sum total of individual detail in all more narrowly-focused studies. This is an unavoidable consequence of interdisciplinary work. Nevertheless, benefits brought by an integrative approach should more than compensate for this – both in generating a less fractured impression of ʿAbd al-Qādir and in laying bare systematic assumptions in some more methodologically constrained work. Many of these assumptions have origins external to their ostensible subject matter; their sources can be located in their authors' cultural worlds rather than that inhabited by ʿAbd al-Qādir.

In all of this, this study follows in the long tradition of orientalism, which has always combined elements of historical, political, theological, and philosophical discussion within a context heavily informed by philology and textual study. It began, after all, as a doctoral thesis in Oriental Studies at Oxford Uni-

---

7 This fact is pointed out by the pre-eminent scholar of ʿAbd al-Qādir's thought during his time in Damascus [Chodkiewicz, 1995, p. 5] – who himself fits the same pattern by ignoring the Algerian decades and denigrating ʿAbd al-Qādir's earlier writing.

8 Shinar, 1965, p. 160.

versity's Oriental Insitute. Yet this is a work of orientalism undertaken since Edward Said's eponymous application of Foucauldian power/knowledge analysis to European constructions of the 'orient'.[9] As such, it will make accounting for the distorting effect of European interests and expectations a central concern. It will do so both in its approach to the history of ideas and interpretation, and in its selection of sources, which have been chosen for their salience in the development of European ideas about ʿAbd al-Qādir. This will decidedly be a work of post-*Orientalism* orientalism.

A chronological progression is followed here. Each chapter will begin with a successive period in ʿAbd al-Qādir's life, leaning heavily on primary sources – particularly archival evidence and ʿAbd al-Qādir's own writing. Each such account will be accompanied by engagement with secondary literature, particularly pre-eminent western scholarship of recent decades.[10] In each instance, it will be argued beyond reasonable doubt that the presumption of an acute inflection point, a dramatic conversion event contemporaneous with ʿAbd al-Qādir's defeat and imprisonment by France, has distorted our view of the facts. The resulting account will synthesise the many significant insights of the secondary literature with the account developed here. The cumulative result of this dialogue will be a continuous and integrated account of ʿAbd al-Qādir's life and thought, a case study in the history of ideas based on a systematic and circumspect critique of the present state of scholarly research.

The disciplinary dynamics arising from the 'Road to Damascus' narrative are such that a chronological progression naturally imposes a certain thematic structure. The first half of ʿAbd al-Qādir's life has interested political historians to a greater extent than scholars of Islamic thought, and the latter vice versa. This is not to say that all political historians denigrate the significance of religion, nor is it to claim that students of Islamic thought invariably oppose historical contextualisation.

---

9 Said, 1978.

10 A study dedicated to more general use of of ʿAbd al-Qādir as a symbol or trope might focus on ʿAbd al-Qādir's representation in 19th-century France, or Europe, alone. It might describe his changing significance in 19th and 20th-century Algeria. It might compare any and all of the above. The present study is primarily concerned with the scholarly literature on ʿAbd al-Qādir, however. This has been overwhelmingly western in origin and in character. Even writing in Arabic tends to take European studies as its basis [pointed out by Danziger, 1977, p. 295 and Achrati, 2007, p. 147, *inter alia*]. Similarly, one might choose to study popular attitudes to ʿAbd al-Qādir, not least in Algeria, where he is most famous and most beloved. Many have remarked upon the same dichotomous interest in one half of ʿAbd al-Qādir's life to the exclusion of the other reflected in Algerian attitudes to ʿAbd al-Qādir and his ideas (e.g. Fatima-Zohra Imalayen/Assia Djebar [quoted in McDougall, 2006, p. 178] and Bruno Étienne's [2008, p. 11] bemoaning the lack of interest in Algeria in ʿAbd al-Qādir's later decades or their poetic and theological output), but these are not the focus of this study.

This book will ultimately challenge both of those misapprehensions. It is rather that this division (however deliberately or otherwise) reinforces the presumption of a change of heart on ʿAbd al-Qādir's part, widely taken to justify such a separation. It is hoped that the alternative narrative developed here will add to our understanding both of the religious dimensions of his political career, and of the political dimensions of his spiritual life, without effacing either aspect.

The approach taken here will be informed, in both its more political and more theological analyses, by a hermeneutically-sensitive form of 'soft' social constructivism, influenced by writers such as Charles Taylor, Talal Asad, and Richard King.[11] In particular, it will draw on such writers' combination of attention both to the interpretive specificities of individual texts, and to the implicit boundaries placed on individual thought by collective social imaginaries. These writers' accounts of secular[12] modernity and its development will particularly inform the perspective taken here, though in the event discussion of specific issues will be favoured over general characterisation of (Multiple) Modernity(ies). Against this general perspective, ʿAbd al-Qādir's religious thought and its political effects will have to be related to each other; his self-understanding will be compared with systematic divergences in the secondary literature, and the almost-incommensurable methodologies applied by differing scholars to ʿAbd al-Qādir's biography will need to be brought into accord. This will demand a consciousness of the social history of ideas and imagination, and their power to constitute lived realities.

Such a multi-faceted awareness will also be brought into harmony with a secular point of departure in research dealing with largely theological and religio-political issues. None of this is to argue for relativism or a disregard for empirical evidence. Rather, this approach enjoins an insistence on close analysis, not only of ʿAbd al-Qādir's biography and its historical contexts, but also of the texts he authored. Imagination does not take the place of fact, but does constitute part of its (re)construction; 'trying to reconstruct this imagination without

---

11 Particularly Taylor, 2007; Asad, 1993; and King, 2008, respectively.

12 Throughout this study, secularism is taken to refer to that family of approaches to social and political arrangements which systematically separate institutions identified as religious from those seen as political. The latter, secular political authorities, take it upon themselves to remain neutral with respect to religion, while religious leaders facilitate such neutrality by avoiding political engagement. The manner and degree to which these parallel processes take place vary significantly from culture to culture. One might contrast the United States and France, for instance. While both are secular states, religious language and symbolism permeates American political discourse, while French *laïcité* strictly prohibits it. Associated with this range of social structures, one might also refer to the range of philosophical, cultural, and theological justifications and rationalisations for such phenomena as secular or as constituting the property of secularity [see for instance Taylor, 2007, *passim*].

recourse to the texts in which it is inscribed is like trying to interpret a poem in a language one does not read.'[13] In its engagements with textual evidence, this study will offer a more rounded impression of ʿAbd al-Qādir's life and thought, trace mis-interpretations of and mis-attributions to him to their (European) roots, and return something of his own voice to discussions in which later commentaries have almost drowned it out.

An Overview of Sources

A wide range of primary sources in both Arabic and European languages will be brought to bear here, including a substantive engagement with ʿAbd al-Qādir's own writing. This will include several significant texts authored by ʿAbd al-Qādir in both Algeria and in Damascus, as well as his letters to be found in the archives. Specifically, we shall analyse a text written during his conflict with France and its Algerian partisans;[14] his essay on the subordination of the intellect to divine revelation, the *Dhikrā al-ʿĀqil*;[15] and his posthumously-published collection of lecture notes, the *Kitāb al-Mawāqif*.[16] Each of these will be seen to have substantial biographical significance, and each has been either neglected (in the first instance) or mis-represented (in the latter instances) by accounts in the secondary literature. ʿAbd al-Qādir's less influential writings will not be analysed so closely – these include his poetry; an apologetic tract prefiguring the *Dhikrā*;[17] his military regulations;[18] a 'multiple authored, composite text'[19] dating from the early months of his imprisonment in France[20] (presented as an autobiography in its partial French translation),[21] and his chapter on the virtues of the Arabian horse.[22] This is for reasons of brevity and focus rather

13 Munson, 1993, p. 4.

14 This text is reproduced in his son's biography [*Tuḥfah*, pp. 411–422].

15 *Dhikrā' al-ʿĀqil wa tanbīh al-ghāfil* [al-Jazā'irī, 1966]. This text is referred to as *Dhikrā* throughout this book.

16 *Kitāb al-Mawāqif fī al-taṣawwuf wa al-waʿz wa al-irshād* [al-Jazā'irī, 1867]. This text is referred to as *Mawāqif* throughout this book.

17 *Al-Miqrāḍ al-Ḥādd li-qaṭʿ lisān muntaqis dīn al-islām bil-bāṭil wa al-ilhād* [al-Jazā'irī, 1973].

18 al-Jazā'irī (Patroni, F., trans. and Benachenhou,Y., ed.), 2009.

19 Brower, 2011, p. 50.

20 al-Jazā'irī, 2007; several letters authored by ʿAbd al-Qādir during this period, as well as his son's and companions' accounts of the time will be brought to bear, however, as these have played a greater role in framing our understanding of the man to-date.

21 al-Jazā'irī (trans. Benmansour, H.), 1995.

22 Daumas, 1865; Al-Bayṭār, 1963, p. 903.

than any denigration of their intrinsic value. ʿAbd al-Qādir's life gave rise to a very considerable quantity of writing, and this study's aims require the limiting of its ambit to those texts which have been most salient in the secondary literature, and which are most directly implicated in European accounts of ʿAbd al-Qādir's life and character. We shall also draw on biographical material in Arabic written by ʿAbd al-Qādir's contemporaries – particularly the historical texts containing biographies of ʿAbd al-Qādir authored by his son Muḥammad[23] and his student ʿAbd al-Razzāq al-Bayṭar[24] (the latter based largely on the former).[25]

In addition to these Arabic texts, a broad range of primary sources in European languages will inform this research. In addition to biographical texts authored by ʿAbd al-Qādir's European contemporaries, chiefly Alexandre Bellemare (whose work was supported by the French government which employed him in Algeria),[26] and Charles Henry Churchill,[27] but generally avoiding the 'discredited'[28] memoires of the colourful 'renegade'[29] Léon Roches. A wide range of archival evidence will be included. Military and diplomatic despatches by French, British, American, and Austrian agents will be examined, drawn from archives in Paris,[30] Nantes,[31] Aix-en-Provence,[32] London,[33] Washington D.C.,[34] and Vienna.[35] This body of materials also contains many letters written by ʿAbd al-Qādir, as well as captured correspondence between himself and the Sultanate of Morocco. It will provide insights into the manner in which the earliest European accounts

23 *Tuḥfaht al-Zā'ir fī tarīkh al-jazā'ir wa al-amīr ʿabd al-qādir,* [al-Jazāirī, M, 1964]. In some printings (such as the 1903 Alexandria edition) the order of the subtitle is altered, though the main title remains the same. This text is referred to as *Tuḥfah* throughout this book.
24 *Ḥilyat al-bashar fī ta'rīkh al-qarn al-thālith ʿashar* [Al-Bayṭār,1963].
25 Al-Bayṭār, 1963, p. 889.
26 Ministry of Foreign Affairs to Consul Hecquard, *Damas/Consulat/69,* 17-09-1862.
27 1863 and 1878, respectively. The French translation of the latter (which plagiarises the former) would become a symbol of nascent Algerian independence in the work of Kateb Yacine (particularly *Nedjma*).
28 Emerit, 1947, pp. 81–105; Julien, 1964, p. 180. This figure, known to ʿAbd al-Qādir as ʿOmar following his fraudulent conversion to Islam, is mainly reflected in this book through his official capacity as French interlocutor with the Moroccan Sultanate in the late 1840s.
29 Bennison, 2002, p. 127
30 Centre des Archives Diplomatiques de La Courneuve; references will begin 'Correspondance Politique...'
31 Centre des Archives Diplomatiques de Nantes (CADN); references will begin 'Damas/Consulat... or Constantinople/Ambassade...'
32 Archives Nationales d'Outre Mer (ANOM); references will begin 'FR ANOM...'
33 British National Archives; references will begin 'FO...'
34 United States National Archives; references will being 'A2 Cab....'
35 Haus-, Hof- und Staatsarchiv; references will begin VII/2 ... or PA XIII ...'

of the man were mediated by European interests and perspectives, as well as how European ideas have shifted over time. Finally, the personal archives of the Marquess of (later Lord) Londonderry[36] will contribute an understanding of ʿAbd al-Qādir's times, particularly as they relate to his period of imprisonment in France and campaigns for his liberation. While it does not include a survey of all private records, nor Moroccan, Ottoman, or other archival materials (which would certainly also be pertinent),[37] except through contacts between those states and European powers, secondary literature developed from such material will also be taken into account – most notably Amira Bennison's careful and important work on the Moroccan Royal Archives in Rabat.

Some reflections on ʿAbd al-Qādir by his contemporaries with little or no personal contact with the man – such as those of Alexis de Tocqueville, Johann Carl Berndt, and others – will be drawn upon to a lesser extent. So also will be earlier biographies postdating his death – such as those of Paul Azan and Jawād al-Murābiṭ. In keeping with the aim of engagement with the current state of research, however, the main focus in the secondary literature will be on late 20th and early 21st century scholarship – which divides itself quite markedly between Algerian and Damascene periods.

The major studies of ʿAbd al-Qādir's Algerian period on which this study will draw, and with which it will enter into dialogue, are those of Raphael Danziger, Amira Bennison, Pessah Shinar, and Bruno Étienne. The first two bodies of work, in particular, are substantial products of systematic archival research, and offer compelling illustrations of ʿAbd al-Qādir's roles as state-builder, war-leader, and propagandist. They will consequently be the main reference points for engagement with the literature on ʿAbd al-Qādir's Algerian period. None overlaps perfectly with the other's concerns, of course. Amira Bennison's study focuses on polemics within Morocco, and is not exclusively concerned with ʿAbd al-Qādir alone, for instance, whereas Raphael Danziger's study of his Algerian career largely ignores his later years in Moroccan territory – a lacuna substantially addressed in his later articles. Whereas Raphael Danziger's work does argue explicitly for ʿAbd al-Qādir's mid-life transformation, it should also be noted, Bennison's does not do so. Shinar's writing, while lesser in scale and influence, is in turn indispensible for the adroitness with which it approaches the religio-political complexities of ʿAbd al-Qādir's career as Algerian leader. With the work of

36 Durham County Records Office; references will begin 'D/Lo...'

37 It is also likely that Spanish and Portuguese archives contain materials relevant to ʿAbd al-Qādir, given his economic and diplomatic contacts with those countries. These, too, have not been examined during the preparation of the present study, and have received only very limited attention elsewhere (see, for instance, Bū ʿAzīz, 2004, pp. 410 – 411).

Amira Bennison and David Dean Commins, it is a significant inspiration for the integrative approach undertaken here.

The writing of Bruno Étienne, however, is simultaneously more influential (in Francophone contexts), and more inherently problematic. The product of decades of research and an unmistakable personal passion, it rarely references its (actually very extensive) sources and frequently makes controversial and hermetic claims, including deeply subjective comparisons between Sufism, Freemasonry, and East-Asian martial arts,[38] and interpretations based on numerology and sacred geometry.[39] Overtly based on personal conviction, Étienne's major account of ʿAbd al-Qādir's life presents itself as an 'authorised biography' through the mystical dialogues its author claims to have experienced with ʿAbd al-Qādir. In these séances, which might recall Louis Massignon's intense personal 'communion' with the departed Manṣūr al-Ḥallāj,[40] ʿAbd al-Qādir reportedly offered Étienne both special insights and demands to keep certain unspecified secrets.[41] Such claims are as insuperably problematic to secular scholarship as they may be profoundly significant to those who make them. Nevertheless, Étienne's remains a pre-eminent account of ʿAbd al-Qādir's life in French, and makes its own, however idiosyncratic, attempt at a religio-political account of ʿAbd al-Qādir (even while insisting that his 'kingdom was not of this world').[42] It simply cannot be ignored, notwithstanding the advisability of avoiding what Bernd Radtke has called the 'mystification of the study of the mystical'.[43]

When Étienne engages with the Sufi teaching of ʿAbd al-Qādir's Damascene years, he does so through the writing of Michel Chodkiewicz – even attributing an unacknowledged passage from Chodkiewicz's translation to ʿAbd al-Qādir's

---

38 E.g. Étienne, 2003, pp. 12–13; Étienne, 2008, *passim*. Étienne has signed his books with a *soi-disant* name derived from a pot-pourri of these influences: 'Sho Dan [indicating in this case a first-degree or 'beginner' black belt in Karate. The term is widely used in Japanese for any activity using a *Kyu/Dan* grading system (such as the boardgame *Go*), but not traditionally employed as part of a person's name] Stephanus [indicating Masonic initiation] ibn al-Awal [indicating Sufi initiation].' It is, significantly, also by this eclectic 'multi-initiatic' epithet that the spirit of ʿAbd al-Qādir reportedly addresses him directly [Étienne, 2003, p. 12].

39 Étienne, 2003, pp. 91, 196, 280, 312, 314.

40 *C.f.* Massignon, 1994.

41 Étienne, 2003, 12–13.

42 Étienne in Geoffroy et al., 2010, p. 79.

43 Radtke, 1992, p. 71: 'To put it simply: the opinion of some scholars is that since the object of mysticism is mystical, it is acceptable to mystify it. This position is justified by the assumption that mysticism is in itself incapable of rational explanation. More seriously, this latter opinion may be rooted in a concern that the study of Islamic mysticism lies on a frontier between scholarship and belief, a frontier too easily overlooked and overstepped...'

ghost. This dependence on the seminal work of Michel Chodkiewicz is shared by most writers who concentrate on ʿAbd al-Qādir's Damascene period. The latter's partial translation of the *Kitāb al-Mawāqif* was the first to introduce ʿAbd al-Qādir's Sufi thought to a western audience. Even though more comprehensive translations have recently become available,[44] it is Chodkiewicz's account of ʿAbd al-Qādir's ideas in Damascus, and their 'perfect identity of views'[45] with 12/13th century Murcian mystic Ibn al-ʿArabī, which informs almost all scholarly engagements with his later life.[46] With the more recent work of Itzchak Weismann in tracing ʿAbd al-Qādir's role in the development of Syrian Salafism, it will form a major point of engagement with the secondary literature on ʿAbd al-Qādir's later life. While both writers concentrate on the history and development of Islamic thought, elements of the work of David Commins and Linda Schatkowski Schilcher[47] provide additional contextualisation in terms of political economy. So also do studies of the period not focused on ʿAbd al-Qādir, such as those of Eugene Rogan,[48] and a plethora of other texts.[49]

Chapter Outline

Chapter One will begin with an account of ʿAbd al-Qādir's rise to political power in what is now Algeria, following the invading French army's destruction of the old Ottoman order. It will conclude with his 'surrender' to the French army under Lamoricière and d'Orsay; thus it covers the period between 1803 and 1848. After a brief discussion of ʿAbd al-Qādir's youth, it will analyse his career as putative *amīr al-mu'minīn* ('Commander of the Faithful') from multiple inter-related perspectives. While broadly chronological, it will describe ʿAbd al-Qādir's organisa-

44 That of Michel Lagarde is the most complete, but as it has not had the chance to influence the broader literature on ʿAbd al-Qādir to any significant degree it will not be discussed in depth by the present study.

45 Chodkiewicz, 1995, p. 217

46 This is explicitly recognised by Berque, 1978, pp. 506, 520; Weismann, 2001, p. XI; Étienne, 1994, p. 428, *inter alia*.

47 1988 and 1981, respectively.

48 E.g. Rogan, 2004.

49 This brief account of major sources used here is not exhaustive. We might also touch, for example, on the narrative biographies by Ahmed Bouyerdene [2008], Yaḥyā bū ʿAzīz [2004], John Kiser [2008], Vista Clayton [1975], and Wilfrid Blunt [1947], or an excellent chapter by Jacques Berque [1978], or numerous article-length discussions, or more general supporting literatures (see bibliography). But it is intended to offer some indication of the study's main foci in both primary and secondary sources.

tion of his own state; his relations with the French presence; and his relationship with the Sultanate of Morocco. The chapter will also include engagements with the major qualitative conclusions drawn in the secondary literature, particularly when they encourage 'Road to Damascus' narratives of conversion in their approach to ʿAbd al-Qādir's life story. It will provide an historical and political overview of his earlier years which begins to call into question some past representations. This will set the stage for evidence in subsequent chapters intended to substantiate an integrated interpretation of ʿAbd al-Qādir's biography.

Chapter Two will attempt to elucidate some of the themes resulting from this exploration of ʿAbd al-Qādir's aims and methods. Specifically, it will analyse a text he composed in the early 1840s, mid-way through his career as Algerian leader. This untitled text, which has gone un-studied by western scholars, will be referred to throughout as the *Risālah on Hijrah*, as the obligation to migration is its primary theme and *Leitmotif*. The text will be analysed in terms of its political aims, its intellectual background, and its rhetorical character.

The chapter will close by connecting the inferrences drawn from this text to debates in the secondary literature on ʿAbd al-Qādir's Algerian career, particularly as they pertain to dichotomous 'Road to Damascus' accounts of his life. It will reveal the gulf between his self-representation and his reflection in secondary literatures, while simultaneously uncovering details of his thoughts on religio-political questions whose relevance to his own decisions would only increase with time.

Chapter Three will take up the chronological thread of ʿAbd al-Qādir's life where it was last left: with his passing into the hands of the French army. It will end with his release from captivity and his transfer to the Ottoman Empire; it covers the years 1848–1853. It will discuss ʿAbd al-Qādir's imprisonment in a series of chateaux across France from multiple connected perspectives. This period will be described in terms of the nature of his imprisonment; the trials to which he was subjected while captive, particularly as they relate to his own views as evinced previously; and finally the circumstances of his release.

This chapter will also engage with the scholarly accounts of this period, particularly with attempts to situate ʿAbd al-Qādir's putative conversion event during these years. It will show through reference to primary sources that the conventional dichotomous account of this period fails to deal adequately with a number of significant facts, and will suggest that this account can be largely understood in terms of specifically European political and cultural concerns.

Chapter Four will trace ʿAbd al-Qādir's journey to Istanbul, then Bursa, and finally to Damascus. It will describe his reception by and conflicts with Ottoman and French authorities; his role as patron of an émigré state-within-a-state; his writing of the *Dhikrā al-ʿĀqil*; and finally his mobilising of an armed militia on behalf of the imperilled Christians of Damascus. The chronological focus here will lie between the years 1853 and 1864. The chapter will question scholarly attempts to adduce the final two events listed above – his writing of the *Dhikrā* and his heroism during the 1860 Riots – as further evidence for a putative conversion experience or radical change of heart. In casting more doubt on these efforts, it will also argue for the greater plausibility of alternative interpretations.

Chapter Five will delve deeper into the theological teachings of ʿAbd al-Qādir during the years leading up to his death in 1883, as well as the context of their composition. Its main focus will be upon the *Kitāb al-Mawāqif*, assembled from records of his lessons in a distinctly Sufi exegesis of Qur'ānic verses. It will attempt to provide an overview of this voluminous but fractured text, relying as much as possible on extended quotations of ʿAbd al-Qādir's own words in lieu of speculative interpellation. Thereafter, scholarly characterisations of the *Kitāb al-Mawāqif* which have been used as evidence for a radical transformation in his thinking will be called into question by comparing them with their own primary sources. It will be argued that the apparent disjuncture between the character of these later writings and ʿAbd al-Qādir's earlier words and deeds result from the influence of 20th-century French cultural developments and persistent 'Road to Damascus' tropes. Alternative interpretations will be developed in tandem, further integrating ʿAbd al-Qādir's Sufi teachings within his broader biography.

The Conclusion will draw together the various strands of the previous chapters' accounts of ʿAbd al-Qādir's life, analyses of his writings, and engagements with their representation in the secondary sources. It will illustrate the common themes and challenges which this study, and writing on ʿAbd al-Qādir more broadly, has encountered. It will also synthesise the insights developed here to form a new, continuous and coherent, perspective on ʿAbd al-Qādir. Besides functioning as a critique of problematic inferences in aspects of earlier accounts, this new perspective will also uncover compelling new avenues for research. As well as throwing new light on ʿAbd al-Qādir's views on such perennially pertinent issues as the limits of human understanding, the place of faith in society, and the nature of inter-religious toleration, it will provide opportunities to build bridges within the academy, highlighting overlapping concerns and potentially synergistic approaches across disciplines.

1.0 Chapter One – *Sīrah Sayfiyyah:* ʿAbd al-Qādir in North Africa, 1833–1848

'Despite their poor appearance, the marabouts[1] should no less be considered the most influential members of Arab society [in Algeria]... It is generally the marabouts who re-establish peace among the tribes and who secretly direct the mainsprings of their politics. You should note, sir, that Abd-el-Kader [al-Jazā'irī], whom you have heard mentioned, belongs to one of the foremost families of marabouts in the regency and that he himself is a marabout. This explains a great deal.'
-Alexis de Tocqueville[2]

'It is as though there were an object within the grasp of a person, yet if he does not cast his eye from side to side many times he will not spot it. So is the reasoning mind. If the mind does not move from conception to conception, it will not perceive the reality of a thing.'

-ʿAbd al-Qādir al-Jazā'irī[3]

1.1 First Steps and Interpretive Framework

ʿAbd al-Qādir's early decades in North Africa prior to his imprisonment in France and migration to the eastern Mediterranean are our first concern. Discussing this period will call both on archival evidence and the secondary literature with which it enters into dialogue. It will describe his early life, his rise to power, and his role as putative *amīr al-mu'minīn* or 'commander of the faithful'. His career will be examined in terms of his nascent state's internal organisation, his relations with France, and his relationship with the Morocco of Sultan ʿAbd al-Raḥmān. In the process, it will be argued that recent scholarship has developed accounts of ʿAbd al-Qādir's motivations intimately bound up with the 'Road to

1 *Marabout*, via French from the Arabic *Murābiṭ*, is the term generally used to refer to North African Sufis of standing.

2 Tocqueville, 2001, p. 9.

3 *Dhikrā*, p. 38

DOI 10.1515/9783110499513-003

Damascus' narratives of conversion which are challenged here. This tendency will be most clearly identified in the work of Raphael Danziger and Amira Bennison, authors of the most substantial 20th-century archival studies published on this period of ʿAbd al-Qādir's life,[4] but also connected to other writers and broader methodological issues. This is not to impugn the remarkable achievements of these scholars, nor their indispensable contributions to our understanding of ʿAbd al-Qādir's life made on the basis of considerable archival research and interpretive energy. Rather, it is the very fact of their being so substantial that makes them natural landmarks and points of reference.

Before we embark on this chapter's historical account of ʿAbd al-Qādir's early decades in North Africa, an impression will be given of the current state of Anglophone scholarship on the *amīr*, and how the present work relates to that body of writing. During exploration of ʿAbd al-Qādir's rise to power and eventual surrender to the French, a case will be made for the deeper engagement with ʿAbd al-Qādir's religio-political ideas that will be attempted in subsequent chapters.

Late-20th-century analyses of ʿAbd al-Qādir's career in North Africa have reacted against his characterisation as a 'Muslim bigot'[5] in French colonial-era sources.[6] This necessary response has not been without its own difficulties, however. This is most crucially the case with respect to the role – or otherwise – of ideals, ethics, and jurisprudence in our accounts. ʿAbd al-Qādir's French contemporaries found it easy to paint him as motivated by fundamentally irrational religious sentiments: for them, his opposition to France was the product of religious fanaticism, not legitimate grievance. This view flattered colonial chauvinisms toward foreign religions and those who practised them, while simultaneously justifying the use of force in overcoming irrational and therefore

---

4 The writing of the late Bruno Étienne is the only comparably researched work published in recent decades, though it concentrates more heavily on ʿAbd al-Qādir's later life. As noted in this book's introductory literature review, however, its lack of systematic referencing, creative mixing of factual and fictionalised elements, and highly idiosyncratic perspective (including appeals to séances, gematria/numerology, and sacred geometry) would demand specific discussion beyond the ambit of the present study. As a pre-eminent writer on ʿAbd al-Qādir in French, however, his work will be referred to repeatedly in the course of this book.

5 Azan, 1925, p. 125.

6 Such stereotypes were hardly limited to French writers and proponents of colonialism, of course. They are to be found also in his more laudatory treatments by English authors. One example: '[ʿAbd al-Qādir] could not brook such a glaring violation of the clear and unequivocal injunctions of the Koran. That sacred volume neither countenanced nor admitted the principle of expediency. To conquer or to die, sword in hand, for the Faith, was its uncompromising and inexorable dogma' [Churchill, 1867, p. 41].

irreconcilable differences between coloniser and colonised.[7] The rejection of such caricatures, and the rehabilitation of ʿAbd al-Qādir's leadership role as both rational and comprehensible, has led to radical re-evaluations of the role of ideas in his thought and action. The results of this project have been mixed, however, and have given rise to a grave hermeneutic problem.

The rejection of colonial caricatures of a religious fanatic has increasingly led to questioning the nature and significance of the Algerian ʿAbd al-Qādir's putatively religious motivations *per se*. But as he consistently expressed himself in religious language (no alternative secular political or moral discourse being available to him), such scepticism radically undermines his self-expression. Moreover, in doing so it automatically privileges the interpretive models, presumptions, and conclusions of those scholars who study him. This occurs with a range of degrees of explicitness. Raphael Danziger's work, as well as being the foremost discussion of ʿAbd al-Qādir's Algerian state and its development available in any language, the product of concentrated and systematic archival research, is most salient in this regard. It stands out both in the force with which it relegates 'religion' as motivation and analytic category, and in the degree to which it does so as a reaction to early French writing.

A refutation of ʿAbd al-Qādir's religious motivation is the central theme of that study, which frequently reiterates the view that ʿAbd al-Qādir was a 'political, not a religious' leader.[8] Meanwhile, a religiously-motivated reading of ʿAbd al-Qādir is repeatedly attributed to early French authors as though they had invented it out of whole cloth in order to serve their political ends; '[t]his [religious] interpretation was first espoused by French writers who openly favoured France's colonial policies.'[9] Both are highly problematic assertions, which demand deeper discussion than they have yet received. Both, moreover, flow from and contribute to narratives of the conversion of 'political' Algerian ʿAbd al-Qādir into his 'religious' Damascene incarnation. This is, after all, a narrative which Raphael Danziger's study explicitly endorses, describing accounts of ʿAbd al-Qādir's spirituality *prior* to his time in France (after which it is unquestioned) as 'merely an attempt to increase his prestige among his followers'.[10]

It is certainly not intended, here, to invert the above formulation by arguing that ʿAbd al-Qādir was 'a religious, not a political leader', with all the opacities this would involve. No attempt will be made to defend demarcation criteria be-

---

7 These attitudes are salient in de Tocqueville's writing on ʿAbd al-Qādir and the Algeria of his day [2001, *passim*], for example – and not unconnected to his support of for the colonial project.

8 Danziger, 1977, pp. 183, 212.

9 Danziger, 1977, p. XIII (emphasis added). See also *op. cit.*, pp. 46, 182–4.

10 Danziger, 1977, p. 181.

tween the religious and the political as discrete categories in human affairs, still less to establish the priority of one over the other. Rather, issue is taken with the dismissal of ideas expressed through an ostensibly theological vocabulary as non-cognitive, irrational, and contingent. It is taken, too, with the specific kinds of secular explanatory models which have been chosen to replace them, or imbue them with radically new meanings. We shall not deny that both ʿAbd al-Qādir, and the religious discourses through which he communicates, are implicated in systems of power and social organisation. On the contrary, it will repeatedly be shown that they certainly are so implicated – not only during his Algerian years but throughout his lifetime, including his supposedly apolitical Damascene years. What should be questioned here are the related tendencies of presenting his ideas as reducible to certain models of such systems, and consequently as instrumentally-applied rhetorical strategies intended to obfuscate what are considered to be his true intentions.

The early ʿAbd al-Qādir's self-expression has increasingly been replaced through his re-imagining not as irrational fanatic, but as a variety of *homo economicus*. That is, as the calculating utility-maximiser theorised by certain schools of 20th-century social science (particularly microeconomics and rational choice theory). Employing this approach in economics focuses on determining explicit values of specific goods to a given actor, whereas in ʿAbd al-Qādir's case a more nebulous attribution of 'ambition' towards 'power' has come to serve this critical purpose. This, we shall argue, is a function for which such broad, polysemic, and contested concepts are quite unsuitable without a depth of elaboration they have not received in the literature on ʿAbd al-Qādir.

The ironic result is not only an unsatisfying account of his intentions, but an inadvertent reproduction of 19th-century assumptions which recent scholarship was intended to remedy. Just as some recent writing has reproduced 19th-century caricatures of the essentially irrational and non-cognitive status of (Islamic) religion, so it has approximated another feature of that century's historiography: the 'Great Man' model of history. Most strikingly expressed by Carlyle, this view sees history as dominated by the biographies of those few titanic figures whose personalities are seen as having directed its course. Historical actors, on such a view, are divorced from and dominant over the social contexts out of which they themselves arose.

This approach to historiography unsurprisingly dominated the early writing on ʿAbd al-Qādir by Europeans who admired his power and sophistication, but could not bring themselves to respect his civilisation. ʿAbd al-Qādir and his Algerians had always to be distinguished as of two fundamental types, cut from different cloth.[11] "Abd al-Qādir may have been a nobleman and a hero, but he was part of (even an exception to) a stagnant, savage society.'[12] His rule, it followed from this, depended on his manipulation of 'the latent fires of fanaticism which slumber in every Muslim breast'.[13]

A similar tendency exists today, developed through a convergent evolution more indebted to Clifford Geertz's seminal depiction of marabouts as 'vivid' and 'contriving' manipulators[14] of their fellows than to the bigotry of the age of empire. The Algerian ʿAbd al-Qādir's argumentation and self-presentation is approached in recent histories through an instrumental conceptual framework that implies the conscious manipulation of the ruled by the ruler, where ethics and ideals are used and employed rather than appealed to and internalised.[15] In this context, it is worth recalling the observations of Talal Asad on the anthropology of political religion:

> '[A]ttempts by social scientists at rendering such [religo-political] discourses as instances of local leaders manipulating religious symbols to legitimise their social power should be viewed sceptically. This is not simply because "manipulation" carries a strong sense of cynical motivation, even in cases where evidence for such imputation is not forthcoming, but more broadly because it introduces the notion of a deliberative, rationalistic stance into descriptions of relationships where that notion is not appropriate. For the same reason, the metaphor of 'negotiation' – with its overtones of calculation – seems to me equally suspect. Although these familiar metaphors are central to market transactions everywhere and to politics in liberal societies, this fact does not make them suited to explicating every kind of practice in all societies.'[16]

Again, it is entirely reasonable to suppose that ʿAbd al-Qādir's self-expression and -presentation were bound up with structural power relations, and that his attempts to convince and influence others were just that. His power cannot be envisaged as independent of such relations and such influence. It will not be argued here that ʿAbd al-Qādir was an unusual paragon of honesty and consistency, with no interest in how his words were received or to what effect. Nor do we intend to question the usefulness of broadly structuralist or functionalist analyses. But the signal contribution of such perspectives lies in describing power re-

11 E.g. Bellemare 1863, p. 455.
12 Achratī, 2007, p. 148.
13 Churchill, 1867, p. 31.
14 Geertz, 1971, p. 8.
15 E.g. Danziger, 1977, pp. 43, 46, 47, 59, 71, 79, 80, 84, 96, 116, 118, 124, 130–1, 159, 181–4, 213, 215. Instances of this tendency in the work of other writers will be included below.
16 Asad, 1993, pp. 210–211.

lationships *irrespective* of the intentions of their constituents,[17] not in supplying privileged accounts of their inner life.

Analysis of socio-cultural structures was never intended to function as a substitute for individual psychology. Yet in ʿAbd al-Qādir's case, this is precisely what has occurred in recent scholarship. Not stopping at (correctly) observing that he exerted influence through such structures, his biographers have come to assert that this is all that he did, and that he did so knowingly. This methodological bridge too far, taken on numerous occasions, adds little to our understanding of his structural function in Algeria, to which it is strictly speaking irrelevant. It plays a central role, however, in justifying the 'Road to Damascus' narratives of ʿAbd al-Qādir's 'conversion' between contrasting (Machiavellian) Algerian and (devout) Damascene incarnations.

While the work of Raphael Danziger presents the clearest examples of this interpretive tendency, he is not alone. Even the work of Amira Bennison, preeminent with Danziger among recent archival studies of ʿAbd al-Qādir's Algerian career, for instance, is open to being (mis-)read in a similar vein. This is in spite of the lengths to which her sober and sensitive studies go towards reconstructing the opposing perspectives of multiple actors of the time, and doing so informed by genuine documentary evidence. These set out from the assertion that ʿAbd al-Qādir was 'neither a proto-nationalist nor a simple fighter for the faith but an ambitious man hoping to politicise his religious prestige as a *sharīf* and a Sufi scholar by performance in the *jihād*'.[18] ʿAbd al-Qādir is described as having 'manipulated a central tenet of Moroccan religio-political discourse in his struggle'[19] through a scholarly lexicon focused on the political effects of such ideas as an 'ideological umbrella'[20] legitimating dynastic rule, 'using a variety of tactics involving language, ritual, and space'.[21] It is such legitimation, rather than private conviction or otherwise, which is the object of her perspective on ʿAbd al-Qādir's followers seeing him as 'represent[ing] an ideal – altruistic commitment to the jihad devoid of personal ambition – an illusion he fostered'.[22]

17 This very fact, of course, forms a central plank of common post-structuralist and decontructionist critiques of structuralism as paying too little attention to individual agency in reimagining such relations.
18 Bennison, 2000, p.1.
19 Bennison, 2011, pp. 69–70.
20 Bennison, 2002, p. 143.
21 Bennison, 2004, p. 597.
22 Bennison, 2002, p. 143.

Such language may lead some readers (following Talal Asad, quoted at length on this semantic and interpretive topic above)[23] to infer implications of dishonesty where perhaps none are intended. It is a sometimes unfortunate fact that we write under discursive conditions as they exist rather than as we might choose them: a fact as true in this case as it is with respect to the narrative of conversion challenged by this text. The unfortunate result here would constitute further support for that dichotomous division of ʿAbd al-Qādir's life into earlier 'political' and later 'religious' halves, between manipulation and sincerity, pragmatism and authenticity.

Nevertheless, the work of Amira Bennison distinguishes itself by also containing means for overcoming the excesses of such reductive tendencies. The first of these is a systematic effort at reformulating Islamic ethico-political categories so as to make them more commensurable with the toolset of secular social science. The second lies in a call for greater recognition of the reciprocal character of such ideas (particularly if not understood as the 'negotiation' criticised by Asad, above). Both insights, and the range of methodological alternatives they illustrate, will be drawn upon here in the hope of rendering ʿAbd al-Qādir comprehensible without applying secular presumptions so abrasively as to polish his image into a mirror revealing only our own reflections. In so doing, they will help us to move beyond an image of ʿAbd al-Qādir's life defined by 'Road to Damascus' narratives of conversion from cynic to saint, foe to friend, Algerian to Damascene.

1.2 Origins

ʿAbd al-Qādir bin Muḥyī al-Dīn bin Muṣṭafā al-Ḥasanī, now generally known as ʿAbd al-Qādir al-Jazā'irī,[24] was born in Guetna (al-Qayṭanah), near Mascara, in or

---

23 Asad, 1993, pp. 210–211.

24 ʿAbd al-Razzāq al-Bayṭār, in his *Ḥilyat al-bashr fī tārīkh al-qarn al-thālith ʿashar* [1963, p. 884], gives ʿAbd al-Qādir's full name, title, and sharifian ancestry (*nasab*) as 'The Amīr ʿAbd al-Qādir al-Maghrebī al-Jazā'irī bin al-sayyid Muḥyī al-Dīn bin al-sayyid Muṣṭafā bin al-sayyid Muḥammad bin al-sayyid al-Mukhtār bin al-sayyid ʿAbd al-Qādir bin al-sayyid Aḥmad al-Mukhtār bin al-sayyid ʿAbd al-Qādir bin al-sayyid Aḥmad bin al-sayyid Muḥammad bin al-sayyid ʿAbd al-Qawīy bin al-sayyid ʿAlī bin al-sayyid Aḥmad bin al-sayyid ʿAbd al-Qawīy bin al-sayyid Khāled bin al-sayyid Yūsuf bin al-sayyid Aḥmad bin al-sayyid Bashār bin al-Sayyid Muḥammad bin al-sayyid Masʿūd bin al-sayyid Ṭāwūs bin al-sayyid Yaʿqūb bin al-sayyid ʿAbd al-Qawī bin al-sayyid Aḥmad bin al-sayyid Muḥammad bin al-sayyid Idrīs al-Aṣghar bin al-sayyid Idrīs al-Akbar bin al-sayyid ʿAbd Allah bin al-sayyid Ḥasan al-Muthnā bin al-sayyid Ḥasan al-Ṣibṭ bin ʿAlī bin Abī Ṭālib and Fāṭima al-Zahrā the daughter of the *sayyid al-ʿālamīn*,

around the year 1807.[25] He was born into the most prominent family of one of the most widespread Sufi *ṭuruq*[26] in the region. His father, Muḥyī al-Dīn, was himself the local head of the Sufi *ṭarīqah Qādiriyyah*,[27] a position he had inherited from his own father and founder of the *ṭarīqah*'s compound (or *zāwiyah*)[28] in that town.[29] Muḥyī al-Dīn was 'not only in charge of the religious, political, and economic affairs of Guetna, but also acted as a judge for disputing parties from as far as 100 miles away and as arbiter among warring tribes.'[30] In addition, as was not unconventional for members of most Sufi groups, Muḥyī al-Dīn received *ijāzahs*[31] from at least four other *ṭuruq:* the Naqshbandiyyah, Suhrawardiyyah, Kubrawiyyah, and Chishtiyyah[32] – though these lacked a comparable following in Algeria.[33]

---

foremost of the Prophets and Messengers, Muḥammad, may God bless him and grant him peace and honour and greatness and dignity.'

25 This date is also sometimes given as 1808 (e. g. Serauky, 1990, p. 51) or 1805 (e. g. *The Times*, Wednesday, Jan 14, 1846, p. 8).

26 Plural of *ṭarīqah*; 'path' or 'way', sometimes rendered as 'order'. The Arabic term will be retained throughout so as to avoid misunderstandings arising from too-direct analogy with Christian monastic orders. While some aspects are similar – such as a founding figure who gives the order its name, and a specific rule – others are decidedly dissimilar. It has long been common for Sufis including 'Abd al-Qādir and his father to have affiliations with numerous *ṭuruq* throughout their lives (notwithstanding the more exclusive *Tijāniyyah*), for instance – whereas a Benedictine will not also be a Dominican or Franciscan. Sufis are not compelled to celibacy, tend to stress involvement within the wider community rather than cloistering, and of course espouse a different – Islamic rather than Christian – theology, ethics, and set of devotional practices.

27 The *ṭarīqah* founded in Baghdad by 'Abd al-Qādir al-Jīlānī (d. 1166), stressing conformity with and obedience to the message of Muḥammad.

28 Though *zāwiyah* (pl. *zawāya*; corner, nook) was also a term for the monastic cells of arabophone Christianity, in the context of post-Marinid North Africa the term designates an entire complex used by a given Sufi order, usually including a shrine (serving as a place of pilgrimage), a school, and facilities for boarding, frequently to be found on trade routes. This term can sometimes also be used as synonymous with *ṭarīqah* in North Africa [See Blair, Katz and Hamès, *EI2* article on *zāwiyah*]. Julien describes these as 'at the same time monastaries, schools, and hostels' (Julien, 1964, p. 15).

29 Abun-nasr, 2007, p. 203.

30 Danziger, 1977, p. 53.

31 Essentially certificates of competence within a given field, typically authorised familiarity with a given text, permitting the recipient to pass on his or her understanding of that text. These licences were and are sometimes granted for other ['fictional' – *EI2* entry on *ijāza*] reasons, however, and it is not *necessarily* altogether clear what degree of education is signified in this instance.

32 Shinar, 1965, p. 144 ff.

What is more, he and his family laid claim to descent from the Prophet Muḥammad, claiming the *sharīf* status of descent from the Prophet Muḥammad whose significance has been seen as particularly salient in pre-colonial North Africa.[34] There has been some difference of opinion over the degree of this last connection's significance. Clayton, for instance, argues that ʿAbd al-Qādir and his father deliberately played down such status,[35] while Bennison has suggested that sharifianism (broadly understood in her case as a statist ideology of aristocratic legitimation through descent and warfare) was at that time largely confined to the ʿAlid sultanate of Morocco.[36] The family name al-Ḥasanī, indicating descent through the Prophet's grandson Ḥasan ibn ʿAlī, relates to this, as does ʿAbd al-Qādir's use of the sharifian title *sayyid*. While the number of such Prophetic 'descendants' is both large and difficult to verify, it has been observed that 'the vast majority of Algerians'[37] accepted ʿAbd al-Qādir's family's status as *sharīfs*. Whatever specific ramifications this had, such status can only have added to their prestige. The integration of North African religio-political categories such as *sharīf* into secular scholarly analyses will be taken up again in this chapter, as well as later on. Suffice it at this juncture to observe that ʿAbd al-Qādir was born into a major Sharifian and Maraboutic family of 'regional significance'.[38]

The young ʿAbd al-Qādir received the bulk of his education at his father's *zāwiyah* and in Mascara. Yet his education also included a brief period at an Ottoman school – in part as 'hostage to his father's good behaviour'.[39] The Ottoman administration quite intelligibly feared that Muḥyī al-Dīn was plotting against it; he was an influential figure who held them in disfavour, while they had already endured several marabout-led insurrections during the early 19th century. So pronounced was the tendency of the Sufi confraternities to become channels

---

33 The major sufi confraternities of the time in this area were the Qādiriyyah, the Darqāwiyyah, the Tijāniyyah, and the Raḥmāniyyah [Julien, 1864, p. 16].

34 While *shurafā'* (sharīfs) were generally respected throughout the Islamic world (indeed the term itself might be translated as 'noble' or 'honourable', and is employed as such in other contexts), North Africa is often singled out among Sunni regions for the prevalence in it of linking Prophetic lineage to religio-temporal ascendancy. This tendency is still very much to be found in present-day Moroccan royal legitimation.

35 Clayton, 1975, p. 39.

36 Bennison [2000 and 2002] presents the spread of 'sharīfian ideology' to Algeria as a central aspect of ʿAbd al-Qādir's career in that country, and his relative success as evidence of Algeria's location in a Moroccan rather than Ottoman periphery.

37 Danziger, 1977, p. 52.

38 Serauky, 1990, p. 51.

39 King, 1997, p. 63.

for popular unrest that by this time 'insurgent and *darqāwī* (Sufi) had for the Turks become synonymous.'[40] The Ottoman authorities did not imagine for a moment that ostensibly religious notables would limit their ambitions to otherworldly issues. It is also for this reason that, between 1824 and 1826, 'Abd al-Qādir and his father were subjected to a lengthy period of house arrest.[41]

The precise content of 'Abd al-Qādir's education is not attested to in detail in the historical sources, though the analysis of his writing in subsequent chapters will give a fair impression; it is certainly said that he had memorised the *Ṣaḥīḥ* of al-Bukhārī,[42] while exposure to Sufi ideas and practices would have been absolutely unavoidable for him. A testament to his religious upbringing, which would become a source of moral authority for the young ruler, presents itself between 1826 and 1828. During this time 'Abd al-Qādir travelled east on pilgrimage to Mecca with his father – not least to evade the suspicious Ottoman authorities.[43] On their journey they are said to have met Muḥammad 'Alī in Egypt, and spent time performing Sufi devotions with Shaykh Khāled al-Naqshbandī[44] in Damascus, as well as each receiving certification from Shaykh Maḥmūd al-Qādirī in Baghdad (both *naqīb al-ashrāf*[45] and chief of their own chief *ṭarīqah* the Qādiriyyah).[46] It is clear from this episode that 'Abd al-Qādir was a practising Sufi after his father's tradition, and similarly open to embracing a wide range of Sufi practices and learning. It has also been suggested, albeit without any direct evidence, that he may have come into contact while in the Hejaz with followers of Muḥammad bin 'Abd al-Wahhāb.[47]

By the time of their return to Algeria, 'Abd al-Qādir and his father had performed the pilgrimage to Mecca twice,[48] received the blessings of Sufis and Sharīfs of international repute, and thereby substantially bolstered their own credentials. This was a fact with palpable political significance. This is emphasised by

---

40 Julien, 1964, p. 17.
41 Churchill, 1867, pp. 8 – 9, Danziger, 1977, p. 57.
42 Abun-Nasr, 2007, p. 203; Al-Bayṭār, 1963, p. 887.
43 As suggested in his obituary in the *Times* [*The Times*, May 28, 1883; p. 8].
44 Abun-Nasr, 2007, p. 203; this connection will be revisited later in this book, as it forms a significant if somewhat ambiguous element of 'Abd al-Qādir's presentation by Weismann. Commins [1988, p. 127] notes that they did not spread Shaykh Khāled's *Naqshbandiyya* on their return to Algeria.
45 'The marshal of the noble [descendants of the Prophet]', the nominal head of the Prophet's descendants (*ashrāf*). For discussion of the origins and functions of this office, see Havemann, *EI2* article on *naqīb al-ashrāf.*
46 Danziger, 1977, p. 57; Shinar, p. 144.
47 Commins, 1988, p.128.
48 Bellemare, 1863, p. 23.

Muḥyī al-Dīn's clairvoyant visions of the time, which predicted ʿAbd al-Qādir's ascendancy as a leader of the Muslim community.[49] As well the more personal benefits the long journey brought to the father and to the son, they returned from it with 'immense prestige'.[50]

Soon after their return home to North Africa, their society would be shaken to its foundations. The collapse of the ailing and unpopular Ottoman regime run by a minority of Turks,[51] and the arrival of the conquering French (ultimately colonial)[52] presence in 1830, heralded the beginning of ʿAbd al-Qādir's public career. By 1831 Muḥyī al-Dīn had been approached by several tribes as a potential leader to fill the vacuum created by the collapse of Ottoman rule brought about by the French invasion and refusal to accept anything but total submission from the remaining Ottoman presence.[53] This position was natural both because of his own eminence and because of his involvement with abortive Moroccan attempts at extending rule in lieu of the Ottomans (touched on again in the section on Moroccan affairs below). The aging Muḥyī al-Dīn soon put forward young ʿAbd al-Qādir as potential leader in his stead – while recounting another vision to explain and justify the decision.[54] The 25 year old ʿAbd al-Qādir was accepted in 1832 – also the year of his marriage to Khayrah bint ʿAlī Abū Ṭālib.

On the 22nd of November in 1832, ʿAbd al-Qādir's investiture as *amīr al-mu'minīn* ('commander of the faithful') took place through several tribes'[55] elders' pledge of allegiance (*bayʿah*) to him under an elm tree in Oran. This setting was evidently intended to recall the tree under which Muḥammad addressed his followers during his conflict with the pagans of Mecca (the so-called 'Pledge of the Tree' or *bayʿah al-riḍwān*).[56] ʿAbd al-Qādir was by no means the first North

---

49 Bellemare, 1863, p. 22.
50 Julien, 1964, p. 179.
51 Julien, 1964, p. 1.
52 The extent of French ambitions in Algeria was not initially apparent, and it is not clear that the French colony which was ultimately established was the original aim [Danziger, 1977, pp. 137–8]. The first five years of the French precedence were to be described in the Chamber of Deputies in the following terms: 'It is not colonisation... It is not occupation on a large scale; its is not occupation on a small scale. It is not peace; it is not war. It is war badly made' [Churchill, p. 78].
53 Danziger, 1977, p. 81.
54 Bellemare, 1863, p. 37; Daumas to military command, Oran, FR ANOM GGA1E116, 03-09-1838.
55 Namely the Hāshim, the Banū ʿAmir, and the Gharābah.
56 Ibn Hishām, 2005, pp. 551–2; *Tuḥfah*, p. 97; Shinar, 1965, p. 145. One might with the benefit of hindsight imagine that the symbolic intention was to identity the French with the Meccan polytheists, with whom (like Muḥammad) the commander of the faithful might treat but would ultimately overcome. While registering such overtones is not unreasonable, it is not necessary to take too literal-minded an approach to this symbolic allusion; this gesture is not tantamount

African ruler to invoke these Prophetic precedents, of course – the 'Mahdī' Ibn Tumart, founder of the Almohad dynasty, did just the same, for instance.[57] ʿAbd al-Qādir's first speech to his new followers insisted on cleaving to the Qur'ān and Islamic law to pacify and edify the land, up to the point that should his 'brother forfeit his life according to the Qur'ān, he should die':[58] both a statement of commitment to Shariah-based governance and another Prophetic echo.[59] It is worth noting that this claim of absolutely disinterested and self-abnegating devotion to the Islamic law, however well or otherwise it reflected ʿAbd al-Qādir's true intentions, is the inverse of that relationship reflected in recent historical scholarship. The tendency there, as this chapter's engagement with the scholarly analyses will show, has increasingly been to present religion and law as handmaidens to his personal political ambition.

This chapter will plot ʿAbd al-Qādir's subsequent career as Algerian *amīr al-mu'minīn*, during which he also adopted the epithet Nāṣir al-Dīn[60] ('protector of the religion'), 'a title of particular resonance in the Maghribī political past, associated as it was with both 'Abd al-Raḥmān III of Cordoba and with Yūsuf b. Tāshfīn'.[61] It appears reasonable to approach the period falling between the years 1832 and 1848 through three broad and interrelated themes: (1) the internal organisation of ʿAbd al-Qādir's state, (2) his relations with France, and (3) his relations with the Sultanate of Morocco under ʿAbd al-Raḥmān. The result will provide a factual account of ʿAbd al-Qādir's North African career, as well as a basis for drawing more systematic inferences about his actions, intentions, and representation by others. This will also make it possible to start sketching the contours

to a manifesto. One may simply understand this scene as designed to convey the message that ʿAbd al-Qādir intended to uphold the Islamic tradition in a style modeled on the Prophet and *al-salaf al-ṣāliḥ* (the 'righteous forebears' following the Prophet) – a reading consistent with his subsequent self-presentation, and arguably with his policy. His state seal bore the names of the *rāshidūn* caliphs and in his later poetry he refers to himself as having 'trodden the path of [Caliph] 'Umār bin al-Khaṭṭāb' [Shinar, 1965, p. 145].

57 Munson, 1993, p 48. Shinar [1965 p. 144] also compares Muḥyī al-Dīn's prior prognostications of ʿAbd al-Qādir's ascendance to 'al-Ghazalli's prediction of the overthrow of the Almoravids by his alleged disciple Muḥammad Ibn Tumart, the future Mahdi'.

58 Daumas to Military Command, Oran, *FR ANOM GGA1E116*, 03-09-1838; Bellemare, 1863, p. 37; Clayton, p. 50; Blunt, 1947, p. 35; Julien, 1964, 179.

59 This utterance refers to a well-known *ḥadīth* narrated by al-Bukhārī [*al-ṣaḥīḥ*, vol. 4, book 56, no. 681] in which the Prophet insists on the equal application of the law, even to his own relatives – a tradition with obvious relevance also to the discussion of genealogical 'sharifianism' above. 'By Allah, if Fatima, the daughter of Muḥammad stole, I would cut off her hand,' the Prophet is recorded as concluding.

60 Al-Bayṭār, 1963, p. 889.

61 Bennison, 2011, p. 83.

of the 'Road to Damascus' narrative's role in his later representation – both in relation to his internal policy and, not un-coincidentally, to his relations with European powers. These inferences will begin to be drawn below, and subsequently developed with reference ʿAbd al-Qādir's own acts and writings.

1.3 ʿAbd al-Qādir's Internal Policy

The crucial political process which brought ʿAbd al-Qādir to power was the collapse of Ottoman rule.[62] The anarchy its passing presaged was arguably the main threat to which he would oppose himself as leader – perhaps more even than the threat of conquest by France, which was initially slow to manifest itself. This was evidenced in his first speech as leader, which focused on enforcing the Shariah (even upon his own family) more than combatting the French.[63] 'Anarchy gave birth to his power,'[64] observed Alexis de Tocqueville with characteristic acuity. This is not to say, however, that ʿAbd al-Qādir harboured nostalgia for the old order. He began his career with an unwillingness to protect the vestiges of the Ottoman *ancien régime*, neglected to ally himself with its successors in Constantine (who were similarly disinclined to trust him, given his lack of Turkish heredity),[65] and would ultimately harass and disperse a large number of notables of Turkish extraction.[66] The comprehensiveness of his assault on the previous regime is contestable, however. It is true that he was inclement to the representatives of the collapsed Ottoman regime (including a fugitive Bey, whom he convinced his father to deny succour)[67] and cold toward Aḥmad Bey and the vestigial 'Ottoman' presence in eastern Algeria (arguably a grave error in strategic terms). Yet ʿAbd al-Qādir was prepared both to employ figures who had held posts under the Ottomans, and to follow the broad outline of Ottoman policy towards the tribes. In fact, this continuity has been presented by recent scholars as evidence of a certain kind of calculated pragmatism at odds with his stated ideals. This question will be explored shortly – for the time being, suffice it to say that his organisational policy evinced a significant degree of continuity with its precedents.

---

62 Bellemare, 1863, p. 30.
63 Daumas to military command, Oran, FR ANOM GGA1E116, 03-09-1838; Bellemare, 1863, p. 37.
64 Tocqueville, 2001, p. 18.
65 Julien, 1964, p. 147.
66 Daumas to military command, Oran, FR ANOM GGA1E116, 30-09-1839.
67 Blunt, 1947, p. 29; Churchill, 1867, pp. 16–17; Danziger, 1977, p. 59.

That policy, not unlike the system employed in the Kingdom of Morocco and throughout the region in previous centuries, revolved around a shifting balance of tribal powers. Centralising organisation was ultimately enforced by a privileged minority of more loyal (or co-opted) tribes collectively referred to as the *makhzan*.[68] This policy was broadly continued by ʿAbd al-Qādir,[69] albeit with the novel addition of a small standing professional (*nizāmī*) army[70] and a homogenisation of tax burdens which stripped *makhzan* tribes of special exemptions in favour of greater 'fiscal equality'.[71]

Tribal arrangements remained significant subdivisions of ʿAbd al-Qādir's 'loose federation',[72] his 'collection of [eight][73] khalifaliks'.[74] He appointed regional governors through a hierarchy of khalifas, aghas, qā'ids and shaykhs – tying tribal allegiances into a superstructure centred on himself.[75] Each tribe's allegiances vacillated over time between degrees of loyalty and hostility towards him, and the methods used to keep them in line varied from the legal and spiritual to the plainly coercive. Eugène Daumas (later director of Algerian Affairs and Senator), while captain and consul[76] to Mascara, remarked that 'while Abd el-Kader is present, all tremble and obey. But when he is absent none can dominate the tribes.'[77] '[W]hen things were going well, the Arabs flocked to [ʿAbd al-Qādir's] banner, but at the smallest sign of defeat they vanished into the mountains;'[78] '[t]ribes which left his sphere of authority did so as a mat-

---

68 Julien, 1863, p. 4.
69 Bellemare, 1863, pp. 6 – 7.
70 Amira Bennison [2004] has devoted an article to this development, particularly its ideological legitimation and function as an arm of the state: 'nizāmī corps were more frequently used to preserve and extend the reach of central government than to wage warfare against European adversaries, exposing them to accusation of being un-Islamic innovation, which their opponents were quick to make' [Bennison, 2004, p. 591]. It seems to have been the employment of this corps against Muslims, rather than its existence as such, which was controversial: 'Many questioned the validity of ʿAbd al-Qādir's mission, his right to assume power, and his motivation, but they did not criticize his introduction of 'infidel' military organisation or employment of Europeans...' [*op. cit.*, p. 597].
71 Julien, 1964, p. 184.
72 Danziger, 1977, p. 186.
73 Bellemare, 1863, p. 220.
74 Blunt, 1947, p. 140.
75 Bellemare, 1863, p. 220.
76 Bellemare, 1863, pp. 219, 348.
77 Daumas to Montpezat, FR ANOM GGA1E116, 28-07-1838.
78 Blunt, 1947, p. 39; 'three times abandoned by his troops, ʿAbd al-Ḳādir immediately regrouped them' – de Cossé-Brissac, *EI2* article on *ʿAbd al- Ḳādir b. Muḥyi al-Dīn al-Ḥasanī.*

ter of self-interest.'[79] Again, this situation is reflected in the previous Ottoman experience, where violence was often found necessary even to extract taxation.[80]

It has already been remarked that the broad continuities of tribal-based '*makhzan* politics' between ʿAbd al-Qādir's state and the Ottoman regime which preceded it (not to mention earlier and neighbouring states) has become significant in recent studies. More specifically, it has been seen by Raphael Danziger as demarcating a dividing line between principle and pragmatism, and between religion and politics. This perception is supportive of the Road to Damascus narrative of ʿAbd al-Qādir's life, but is culturally inappropriate to the context of early-19th-century North Africa. The decision to continue Ottoman policies, that is, has been presented as a pragmatic one of rational utility-maximisation – and concomitantly as a betrayal of other-worldly religious morality. Aside from the immense theological and sociological questions such stark dichotomies beg, Ernest Gellner points also to the role of anachronistic false premises in this approach: 'Danziger talks as if ʿAbd-al-Qādir could, had he chosen, have abolished the tribal system. What else was there, and how could it conceivably have been abrogated at that stage, and with the means at his disposal?'[81] For Danziger it is a central thesis that 'it is in pragmatism, rather than the inflexible observance of Islam, that the key to Abd al-Qadir's political conduct lies,'[82] but bearing in mind the entrenched continuity of (not self-evidently 'un-Islamic') tribal dealings at this time begins to shed a different light on his conduct.

Tribal politics continued. Sometimes recalcitrant tribes were attacked[83] or menaced – as when in 1835 a coalition formed against ʿAbd al-Qādir only to dissipate as he marched on them.[84] There were also occasions where he himself was overtaken and abused by members of rebelling groups – such as some of the Hāshim, Gharābah, and Benī ʿĀmir who ran amok in Mascara.[85] On other occasions, historical tensions and vendettas led to tribes under ʿAbd al-Qādir's nominal command turning on or pillaging one other. The inter-tribal aspect of the society at whose head ʿAbd al-Qādir found himself, that is to say, was far from consistently subordinated to the state institutions set up to govern the region. This, in turn, narrowed the alternatives to taking recourse to a unifying reli-

79 King, 1997, p.73.
80 Julien 1964, p. 14.
81 Gellner, 1979, p. 224.
82 Danziger, 1977, p. 183.
83 Danziger, 1977, p. 95, 128.
84 Danziger, 1977, p. 104.
85 Danziger, 1977, p. 121–2; ironically, these were also among the first tribes to pledge allegiance to ʿAbd al-Qādir.

gio-legal discourse which cut across and superseded both formal and informal allegiances.

Ethnic and tribal allegiances (including inter-tribal leagues or *ṣaffs*) were by no means the only sub-state level structures in ʿAbd al-Qādir's Algeria, however. Perhaps most salient, especially given his family background, were the Sufi *ṭarīqahs* ('paths' or brotherhoods) with which most Algerians were in some way connected. 'The Algerian tribes left to fend for themselves had no agency of cohesion and coordination other than the Sufi orders… [his *ṭarīqah*, the Qādiriyyah] were the most influential Sufi order in the country.'[86] Qādirī affiliation seems to have been a significant factor also in ʿAbd al-Qādir's dealings with the tribes of the Moroccan *Rīf*,[87] among whom he would spend the final years of his time in North Africa.

This '*Qādirī*' aspect of ʿAbd al-Qādir's career in Algeria has seen a range of interpretations. 19th-century sources portray a generalised 'fanatical Maraboutism' as essentially identical with his supposedly irrational hostility toward 'civilising' France, while some more recent writing has played down this aspect of his career significantly. Jamil Abun-Nasr presents ʿAbd al-Qādir as a mere 'upstart'[88] in the eyes of the wider Qādiriyyah, for instance, while Danziger goes further: 'I have not come across a single document attesting to [ʿAbd al-Qādir's] use of the Qādiriyyah as an instrument for domination.'[89] This demand that Sufism's socio-political significance be demonstrated by evidence of outright 'domination', of course, conflicts with the most common modes of influence historically exerted by Sufis (or indeed political figures more generally). These have tended towards mediation, persuasion, and indoctrination – a fact of which Alexis de Tocqueville, quoted at the opening of this chapter, was well aware over a century earlier.

In contrast with Raphael Danziger's demand for 'hard' evidence, Amira Bennison's approach is more nuanced. It offers a way forward by recognising that political influence can be symbolic, ideological, and psychological as well as physical. She assimilates the Algerian Qādiriyyah as part of a wider anti-colonial moment and the development of indigenous 'statist' politics. 'Qādirī ideology resembled that of other religious brotherhoods and Sufi-inspired jihad movements [of the time] in West Africa and further afield.'[90] This view is broadly repeated in

86 Abun-nasr, 1971, p. 241.
87 Bennison, 2002, p. 125.
88 Abun-nasr, 2007, p. 202.
89 Danziger, 1977, p. 196.
90 Bennison, 2002, p. 78.

different terms by Martin's *Muslim Brotherhoods in 19th Century Africa*.[91] Moreover, Qādirī affiliation has been suggested as a root cause of ʿAbd al-Qādir's embarrassing and costly campaign against the rival *ṭarīqah* Tijāniyyah stronghold of ʿAin Māḍī ruled by Muḥammad al-Ṣaghīr al-Tijānī (along with tribal politics, pride, and poor military strategy).[92]

During the latter half of 1838 and early 1839 ʿAbd al-Qādir besieged Muḥammad al-Ṣaghīr al-Tijānī's headquarters at ʿAin Māḍī. Muḥammad al-Ṣaghīr al-Tijānī, the leader of the local Tijāniyyah, had his own rival claims to authority as against those of ʿAbd al-Qādir. Both as a marabout and as a sharīf, al-Tijānī asserted that he need submit to none in the country[93] – though he was already expressing his preparedness to submit both to Moroccan Sultan ʿAbd al-Raḥmān[94] and to the French[95] (a position he would maintain in subsequent decades, ultimately becoming a 'docile instrument of French colonial policy').[96] In spite of support from the Moroccan Sultanate, which both supplied ʿAbd al-Qādir[97] and later commanded al-Tijānī to make peace with him,[98] this campaign was an almost unmitigated debacle for ʿAbd al-Qādir. The siege dragged on month after month with little result[99] other than the demoralising of his troops and the emptying of his coffers. The siege appears to have become a 'matter of pride'[100] for ʿAbd al-Qādir. Archival reports record that rumours even circulated that he was displaying signs of madness.[101] It is also from this period, however, that the most famous description of ʿAbd al-Qādir at prayer originates: Léon Roches' depiction of an 'ecstatic' amīr sighted alone in 'mystical transport... as the great saints of Christianity must have prayed.'[102]

91 Martin, 1976, p. 66.

92 Abun-Nasr [1971, p. 243] relates the origins of this conflict to a quarrel between the Tijāniyya and ʿAbd al-Qādir's Hāshim tribe dating back to 1827, as well as the Tijāniyya's ambitions and relative preparedness to deal with France. Daumas's reports from Mascara, for their part, also point to ʿAbd al-Qādir's '*amour-propre*' as a causal factor: FR ANOM GGA1E116, 09-09-1838 and 25-11-1838.

93 Daumas to military command, Oran, FR ANOM GGA1E116, 15-07-1838.

94 Julien, 1964, p. 82.

95 Daumas to military command, Oran, FR ANOM GGA1E116, 31-12-1838.

96 Abun-nasr, 2007, p. 218; Michot, 2006, pp. Xii-xiii.

97 Ben Jelloun to ʿAbd al-Qādir, FR ANOM GGA1E211,—09 – 1838.

98 DeNion to the Ministry of Foreign Affairs, Correspondance Politique/Maroc/9, 22-04-1843.

99 Daumas to military command, Oran, FR ANOM GGA1E116, 07-10-1838.

100 Daumas to military command, Oran, FR ANOM GGA1E116, 25-11-1838.

101 Daumas to military command, Oran, FR ANOM GGA1E116, 14-10-1839.

102 Roches, 1904, pp. 140 – 141.

By the time al-Tijānī was finally forced to give up his defence of 'Ain Māḍī, 'Abd al-Qādir was left almost bankrupt,[103] forced to increase taxation[104] in the face of general unwillingness on the part of his subjects to pay[105] – even were it to finance a revived *jihād* against France. Before setting out from Tagdempt to canvass support around the country, 'Abd al-Qādir asserted,

> 'My intention is to renew the holy war against the enemies of God... to chase out the impious... I will not deceive you as to the strength and power of the Christian, whom we can only overcome if we are united. Decide now, and if you have not the courage to fight, then supply me with money.'[106]

All of this is hardly without precedent, in the region and elsewhere. Differences of opinion have already been remarked upon with respect to the overall novelty or otherwise of 'Abd al-Qādir's state structure. This question comes together with debates on the role of the Sufi *ṭarīqahs* in the matter of 'Abd al-Qādir's appointments. 'In the choice of his ministers, governors and administrative staff, the Emir leaned heavily on the religious element,'[107] substantially raising the profile of marabouts and religious scholars from the relatively lower status they had enjoyed under Turkish rule. Danziger, on the other hand, reminds us of the limits of this less than totally revolutionary change, pointing to 'Abd al-Qādir's contravening tendency to 'retain men who had a local power base...rather than introduce men of his own marabout background who had no administrative experience'.[108]

Danziger then goes further, however, concluding from the fact that not all senior figures were marabouts that it is reasonable to describe the degree of maraboutic occupation of 'top positions' as 'relatively minor'.[109] 'A reliable source', he writes elsewhere, 'confirms that in the early part of Abd al-Qadir's rule, there was no transfer of power to the marabouts.'[110] If the role of marabouts was relatively minor, one must ask: relative to what? It is not at all clear what the presumed point of comparison may be. It cannot be either the previous or subsequent governments of that region, neither of which had a comparable maraboutic element.

103 Daumas to military command, Oran, FR ANOM GGA1E116, 29-07-1839.
104 Daumas to military command, Oran, FR ANOM GGA1E116, 02-03-1839.
105 Daumas to military command, Oran, FR ANOM GGA1E116, 06-04-1839.
106 Daumas to military command, Oran, FR ANOM GGA1E116, 07-09-1839.
107 Shinar, 1965, p. 147.
108 Danziger, 1977, p. 77.
109 Danziger, 1977, p. 195.
110 Veuillot, 1873, *Les Français en Algérie: souvenirs d'un voyage fait en 1841*, pp. 275, 280; quoted in Danziger, 1977, pp. 77–8.

A parallel question arises in the case of the other salient religio-political aspect of ʿAbd al-Qādir's state. His establishment of salaried *qāḍīs* or Islamic judges to standardise the rule of sharīʿah law across his territory has been described as his 'greatest achievement'.[111] This system replaced a historical situation where a judge's variable wealth (and sometimes concomitantly variable opinion in matters on which he would adjudicate) derived from more local sources. Under the new system, all judges were assigned a fixed salary,[112] as well as having their numbers increased and efforts overseen by a chief jurist (*qāḍī al-quḍāt*) and advisory council composed of eleven religious scholars or *ʿulemā'*.[113] As such, this policy allowed both for a greater degree of independence from local politics by the judiciary, and a greater homogenisation of legal practice over the whole state. Along with ʿAbd al-Qādir's creation of a standing army and moves toward a uniform system of taxation, moreover, this development represents perhaps the most substantive effort in state institution building attributable to him.

This, too, has been questioned by recent writers, who point out that the authority of these judges was not in all cases paramount, indeed was in some areas overridden by ʿAbd al-Qādir himself and the council of eleven leading religious scholars appointed to oversee the courts.[114] Objections to the 'Islamic' character of ʿAbd al-Qādir's state on the basis of executive privilege may however be levelled at most, if not all, historical 'Islamic states' which preceded it, which shared such practices to greater and lesser extents. [It is also the case that local judges' decisions are sometimes overridden by the legal hierarchy in modern Western states following both Napoleonic and Common Law.] This objection must also be considered in light of the historically integrated role of customary law [*ʿurf*] in Islamic states.[115] All relate to more general debates about the role of Islam (however conceived) in Muslim societies. In ʿAbd al-Qādir's case, however,

111 'The transfer of justice to salaried qadis, judging in accordance with the Shari'a, has been described by some historians as one of Abd al-Qadir's greatest achievements,' Danziger, 1977, p. 192.

112 Shinar, 1965, p. 149.

113 Abun-nasr, 2007, p. 204, 5; Shinar, 1965, p. 149.

114 Shinar, 1965, p. 149.; Danziger, 1977, pp. 192–3.

115 Ayubi, 2007, p. 120; this does not seem to have been extremely controversial, as even the redoubtable Ibn Taymiyya praised the Mamluk state's defence of Islam in spite of its application of codes drawn from the non-Islamic Mongol *yasa* [Ayubi, 2007, p. 144]. 'Eventually, in the 16th century, [customary law] gained something close to formal recognition; but before that time attempts were made to incorporate custom in the law without granting it formal recognition... Essentially, Islamic law up to the 16th century resolved the tension between theory and practice by *de facto* recognition of the role of custom'... [Lisbon, G., *EI2* entry on *ʿurf*].

these difficult anthropological and jurisprudential questions have frequently been begged in favour of a simple power-maximising motive.[116]

Once more, it is asserted that pragmatism wins out over principle – the same questionable dichotomy still unsupported by sufficient evidence. In Raphael Danziger's defence, these are vexed and complex issues, and he is far from alone in questioning ʿAbd al-Qādir's orthodoxy on the basis of over-simplified understandings of the relevant Islamic norms. Serauky, for instance, presents ʿAbd al-Qādir's reference to the (perfectly conventional and Qur'ānic)[117] 'wines of paradise' as scandalously un-Islamic[118] proof that his Sufi mysticism led him to deny the tee-totalling Shariah.[119] Even Amira Bennison's outstanding treatment puzzlingly characterises ʿAbd al-Qādir's preparedness to negotiate with France as a 'contrave[ntion of] the ethics of *jihad*'.[120] The ethics of *jihād* certainly do permit peace treaties to be signed between Muslim leaders and non-Muslims,[121] and there exists considerable precedent for this in the actions not only of supreme rulers themselves but also by 'commanders in the field'.[122] The intention here is not to defend ʿAbd al-Qādir's ideas or actions. Rather it is to illustrate that, as in Danziger's work, the tendentious implication in each case is that some 'other' form of thought is latently at work rather than the (how-

---

116 Danziger, *ibid.*

117 Qur'ān 47:15.

118 Serauky, 1990, p. 56.

119 This is a theme which will be more developed during later chapters' discussion of the later ʿAbd al-Qādir's depiction by writers on Islamic thought.

120 Bennison, 2002, p. 81.

121 The ethical possibility of peace treaties with non-Muslims is supported by both Qur'ān (typically verse 9:7) and *sunnah* – including a *ḥadīth* in Tabarī ('The Byzantines will be making a secure peace with you' [quoted in Khadduri, 1955, p. 203]), and the Prophet's peace-treaty with the Meccan polytheists. Other writers on ʿAbd al-Qādir have recognised this: the legal possibility of negotiated peace, originally modelled on the Prophet's *ṣulḥ* with the pagans at Ḥudaybiyyah, is directly related to ʿAbd al-Qādir's decision for example by Shinar [1965, p. 156]. Where ʿAbd al-Qādir's contemporary coreligionists questioned his application of the laws on warfare, it was not by ruling out settlements (as western scholars have suggested), but by questioning whether he held sufficient authority to make decisions for war or peace as such, and whether warfare was practically possible. For an example of both, see the letter of the Qa'id of Oujda to Sidi Hamza Ben Taïeb [Correspondance Politique/Maroc/10, 22-02-1844], in which it is argued that ʿAbd al-Qādir should abandon his *jihād* on the grounds that '*jihād* is obligatory, but it is not a Muslim's only obligation, to be discharged only when situations permit.' The qā'id urges that these situations are to be identified only by the Sultan of Morocco, who has decided that they do not obtain, and 'when two evils arrive, one must always choose the lesser of them.'

122 Khadduri, 1955, p. 203.

ever idiosyncratic) understanding of Islamic ethics which informed ʿAbd al-Qādir's discourse and those of his followers.

As Shinar has argued, moreover, even the overriding of judicial opinion in ʿAbd al-Qādir's state was itself expected to be held accountable to both Qur'ān and customary law.[123] It seems to be as a consequence of this that John King correctly observes that 'the rule of law was in theory supreme,' a fact whose significance he relates to 'modernity' as opposed to the 'medieval'.[124] Again, the question of the degree to which ʿAbd al-Qādir envisaged a rule of law or a rule by law (that is, the extent to which his decisions were constrained by laws extrinsic to rather than issuing from his own immediate political intentions) is highly significant to attempts at portraying the 'pre-Damascene Conversion' ʿAbd al-Qādir as motivated by a certain notion of material utility. The latter, it is contended here, is principally the product of a narrative superimposition: it overrides sensitivity to the context of the times in favour of the narrative of ʿAbd al-Qādir's conversion from belligerent worldliness to other-worldly pacifism, from politician to saint, from enmity towards France to its cosmopolitan embrace.

There seems good reason to give credence to ʿAbd al-Qādir's pious convictions well before his supposed 'conversion' by France. Beyond the significance of his judicial system with respect to the creation of the institutions characteristic of modern states, many sources attest both to ʿAbd al-Qādir's personal asceticism and to that enforced on his countrymen. It seems to have been the case that none of the money he collected in taxes was 'intended for self-enrichment, [rather] it was all designated for the community'[125] (a fact interpreted by Danziger in terms of its political expediency in aiding tax-collection).[126] ʿAbd al-Qādir 'lived according to the laws and manners prescribed in Islam,'[127] 'his costume... so simple, that one can hardly distinguish him from the labourers'.[128]

His fellow Algerians, meanwhile, witnessed a marked increase in the religio-legal censure and (often corporal) punishment for religiously proscribed practices such as prostitution, gambling, the consumption of alcohol,[129] and even the use of precious metals in clothing.[130] Muḥammad al-Jazā'irī relates that people

123 Shinar, 1965, p. 149.
124 King, 1997, p.73.
125 Danziger, 1977, p. 182.
126 *Ibid.*
127 Berndt, pp. 62–63.
128 Churchill, 1867, p. 126.
129 Shinar, 1965, p. 150.
130 Bellemare, 1863, pp. 240–241.

found working in their shops during prayer times were beaten, apparently in an attempt to enforce the observance of the five daily prayers.[131] More charitably, ʿAbd al-Qādir broke with earlier traditions of paying bounties, encouraging his men to take their enemies alive, and not mutilate corpses; he 'pays more for whole bodies than for heads.'[132]

ʿAbd al-Qādir's traditional piety was also evinced in his love of learning and the importance he seems to have attached to the collection and preservation of texts. '[A]ll persons found guilty of damaging manuscripts were severely punished, and those who brought him fine copies were sure to be well rewarded.'[133] He had intended to form a central library in Tagdempt,[134] though in the event his library travelled with him – only to be largely destroyed by a French attack on his camp in 1843.[135] As we shall see, he would take up similar projects again in his later life.

Similarly abortive was ʿAbd al-Qādir's initial intention to develop Tlemsen into a commercial centre.[136] To this end, he employed numerous Europeans, including Frenchmen, Germans, Italians and Spaniards to help establish modern industrial methods.[137] His life-long interest not only in learning, but in openness to the technical innovations being developed in Europe is worth establishing clearly and early on. It will be remarked upon again many times in the course of this study – though it, too, has been represented as a product of his mid-life imprisonment among and 'conversion' to French ways [see Chapters Three and Four]. In spite of Europeans' assistance, however, projects such as ʿAbd al-Qādir's arms foundry at Tagdempt[138] met with very little success, due largely to chronic shortages of raw materials. Even his attempts at industrialising textile production proved unsuccessful.[139] When it came to arming his tribal levees and

131 *Tuḥfah*, p. 310; Commins, 1988, p.127; such penalties do have juristic precedence, especially in the Hanbalī *madhhab.*

132 Bugeaud to the Ministry of War, Correspondance Politique/Maroc/4, 31-12-1836. Also recorded by Scott, 2010, p. 29; Julien, 1986, p. 183.

133 Blunt, 1947, p. 141; Churchill, pp. 144–147.

134 Bellemare, 1863, p. 238; Julien, 1964, p. 181.

135 *Ibid.*; this incident among the many acts of the French colonial forces has in more recent Arab nationalist literature been compared to the intolerance of the Spanish *Reconquista* [Bū-ʿAzīz, 1964, p. 144] – a major theme of ʿAbd al-Qādir's *Risālah on Hijrah* presented in the following chapter.

136 Bugeaud to the Ministry of War, FR ANOM GGA1E113, 13-08-1837.

137 *Ibid.*

138 DeNion to the Ministry of Foreign Affairs, Correspondance Politique/Maroc/6, 04-08-1840.

139 Scott, 2010. p. 49.

nascent *nizāmī* professional soldier corps, he would have to rely on trade and assistance from Morocco and from Europe.

ʿAbd al-Qādir's relations with the wider world, and particularly with Morocco, would become increasingly crucial during the 1840s. With his territory in Algeria lost to the overwhelming force of the French army, he and his remaining followers were forced to flee toward the territory of Sultan ʿAbd al-Raḥmān. During those final years one cannot speak of ʿAbd al-Qādir's state, which had largely ceased to exist, but must understand his position in relation to the great powers of the area – most particularly the Moroccan Sultanate. Before tracing the path of that relationship from amity to enmity, and ultimately to defeat and imprisonment, we must first address its major cause: the French invasions and conquest of Algeria.

1.4 ʿAbd al-Qādir's Relations with France

The state into which ʿAbd al-Qādir emerged as leader in succession to his father was one of chaos and conflict. The French had arrived as a conquering army, and it was to be three years before their status was made subject to the terms of treaty. Muḥyī al-Dīn had made his first assault on French forces seven months before ʿAbd al-Qādir's taking his place in late 1832. His first treaty with France was signed on the 26th of February 1834, apparently on their initiative. In it, France recognised his sovereignty over Oran and the interior, away from French coastal power-centres. This recognition was never reciprocated.

This treaty – or rather treaties, as addenda were kept secret – was signed by ʿAbd al-Qādir and the then-head of the French presence, General Desmichels.[140] Its first article declared a cessation of hostilities, while its second recognised the inviolability of Muslim religion and customs. The third and fifth articles concerned the exchange of prisoners and the handing over of deserters to the French army, and all wanted Muslims to ʿAbd al-Qādir's state. The fourth condition made a gesture toward freedom of trade, albeit in such a way as to be essentially meaningless.[141] The final condition was that Europeans travelling into the interior of the country would require official authorisation from ʿAbd al-Qādir. Among those conditions which were kept secret are additional notes on trade and still further recognition of ʿAbd al-Qādir's power over the Muslims of Alge-

140 The texts of ʿAbd al-Qādir's treaties with France are conveniently available as appendices to Raphael Danziger's study [1977, pp. 241–260].

141 Both through vague phrasing and the numerous exceptions stipulated.

ria – specifically prohibiting France from hindering any Muslim from leaving towns under their sway for those of ʿAbd al-Qādir.

The issue of fundamentally differing conceptions of sovereignty and jurisdiction between ʿAbd al-Qādir on the one hand, and the French (as well as most western scholars, for that matter) on the other, will be a recurrent issue here. For their part and for the time being, the attitude of the French authorities of the time was equivocal – not least because informants led them to believe that ʿAbd al-Qādir saw the 'deplorably lax'[142] Desmichels Treaty as an opportunity to consolidate his position against them.[143] Other western diplomats similarly doubted the treaty's durability, especially given the strength of Arab antipathy towards the invading French.[144]

The peace was indeed short-lived, breaking into hostilities the subsequent year. Throughout this and later conflicts with the French military, ʿAbd al-Qādir's tactics were broadly those of *karr wa farr*, the (literally) 'hit and run' strategy common both to the tribal warriors[145] who preceded and the guerrilla fighters who were later to draw inspiration from him. This tactic reflected both the traditional practice of the bulk of ʿAbd al-Qādir's tribal supporters, and the exigencies of what might today be called 'asymmetrical warfare'.[146] In spite of the obvious difficulty of combatting such a strategy in the long term, the French military typically gained the upper hand in armed engagements. The French army was vastly superior to the soldiers at ʿAbd al-Qādir's command in terms of training and equipment. Even his greatest 'triumphs' had a pyrrhic quality – like the vaunted June 1835 battle (or from the French perspective 'Disaster') of Macta, which nevertheless ended with many times more deaths on his own side than on that of the French soldiery.[147] In spite of contemporary sources comparing him to Saladin and Napoleon[148] (largely through juxtaposition with what were assumed to be his less competent or impressive countrymen and coreligionists), it has often

142 Bellemare, 1863, p. 77.

143 Abdallah to Desmichels, FR ANOM F80/1071, 18-07-1834.

144 Dalton to the State Department, A2 Cab. 14/8, 15-04-1834.

145 Some effort was made under ʿAbd al-Qādir to create a more western-style professional army, as has already been touched upon. The only pitched battle of the conflict in which it was involved was that of Sikkak in 1836, where ʿAbd al-Qādir's side proved unsuccessful [Danziger, 1977, p. 126].

146 Julien [1964, p. 176] calls his strategy 'bush warfare'.

147 Danziger, 1977, p. 117.

148 See for instance ʿAbd al-Qādir's obituary in the *Times* of London: "Marshal St Arnaud once said unthinkingly to Napoleon III, 'if he were a Frenchman we should have another Napoleon.' 'Perhaps it is as well for me then that he is an Arab', was the not very gratified reply" [*The Times*, May 28, 1883; pg. 8]. This was also related by his French contemporaries [Clayton, 1975, p. 5].

been remarked that in the final analysis ʿAbd al-Qādir 'owed his success in part to French incompetence.'[149]

Be that as it may, the French military occupied Mascara in 1835. As a result, ʿAbd al-Qādir offered his resignation to the tribes under his authority – an offer which was rejected, as such offers will tend to be under such circumstances.[150] Nonetheless, he was forced to flee, moving the headquarters of his government with his camp[151] (a practice which he would continue in later years through the creation of a mobile 'tent city')[152] and practising a readiness to cede territory it would be too costly to hold. This last can be considered a characteristic feature of ʿAbd al-Qādir's strategy when dealing with the expansionist French presence. Churchill records ʿAbd al-Qādir as giving a military justification for this approach: 'Let the French keep the towns... Will the towns give them food? So long as I hold the country, and can attack and intercept their convoys my position will be superior to theirs.'[153] This strategic analysis is also supported by current historical scholarship on the basis of contemporary French archives;[154] 'we can only conclude that he was more interested in people than land.'[155] More contemporary French sources also point out the amenability of such tactics to the pillage of his subject populations, however.[156] Again, it is worth pointing to the distinction between the (perfectly legitimate) *Realpolitik* premises of these interpretations and the more principled manner in which political leaders will explain themselves to their followers – as did ʿAbd al-Qādir, as the next chapter will show.

A new peace was concluded between ʿAbd al-Qādir's state and the French presence through the Tafna treaty of 1837, signed by himself and General Bugeaud. The negotiations were considerably complicated by competition between Damrémont and Bugeaud over who held the authority to negotiate – giving rise to numerous recriminations from the latter in particular.[157] The former, mean-

---

149 Blunt, 1947, p. 56; Danziger, 1977, pp. 106, 123, 127, 129, 164–5.

150 Churchill, 1867, pp. 82–3

151 Abun-nasr, 2007, p. 205.

152 The so-called *smala* or *zmala* (from *zamālah* or *fellowship*) captured by the French army on the 16th of May, 1843 only to be reformed on a smaller scale as the *dāʾirah* (the *circle*)

153 Churchill, 1867, p.198.

154 Bennison, 2002, p. 138: '...he therefore began to appeal to the population to abandon the jihad and migrate to Muslim territory to render the French possession of their land worthless by depriving them of taxable subjects and labour.'

155 Danziger, 1977, p. 205.

156 Bellemare, 1863, p. 121.

157 See correspondence between Bugeaud and the Ministry of War, GGA1E113, between 21-04-1837 and 02-07-1837.

while, derided the eventual treaty as 'neither honourable, nor advantageous, nor necessary'.[158] This agreement, like that with Desmichels before it, was widely viewed at the time as 'invit[ing] dispute from both parties to it,'[159] albeit with the French expectation was that it would ultimately weaken ʿAbd al-Qādir's position.[160]

The signing was completed after an often-noted scene in which ʿAbd al-Qādir's comportment towards Bugeaud, like his earlier 'haughty'[161] comportment towards Desmichels, has been described as 'studied insolence'.[162] Danziger[163] interprets ʿAbd al-Qādir's comportment as a (feigned) hostility to Christians in general, rather than as a gesture designed to emphasise that his stature and that of the French representative were not of an equal nature or degree – a more natural reading bestowed on the episode by Bellemare.[164] Nevertheless, this incident has come to play a significant role in recent attempts at eliminating any ostensibly religious element from our accounts of ʿAbd al-Qādir.

Danziger castigates 'erroneous interpretations' of ʿAbd al-Qādir's 'inner thoughts' based on paying too much attention to his 'self-proclaimed intentions... the amir's piety is a case in point.'[165] The signing of his treaties with France has been presented as evidence that his desire to observe the precepts of Islam' is 'problematic',[166] and better understood as dissimulation. His friendliness toward individual Christians has been painted as evidence of his difficulty in observing his own religious precepts, with his coldness toward the ruthless Bugeaud interpreted as evidence of his insincerity and duplicity in the public sphere.[167] [It is worth noting that Danziger makes the same argument with respect to the Sultan of Morocco, explicitly presenting it as a general model for

158 Bellemare, 1863, p. 189.
159 St John to Palmerston, FO 3/42, 20-01-1839.
160 St John to Palmerston, FO 3/43, 30-05-1840.
161 Bellemare, 1863, p. 63.
162 Blunt, 1947, p. 100.
163 Danziger, 1977, pp. 182–3.
164 Bellemare, 1863, p. 178.
165 Danziger, 1977, p. 183.
166 Danziger, 1977, p. 182.
167 Danziger, 1977, pp. 182–3: 'In addition to demonstrating that Abd al-Qādir's resistance was not motivated by a blind hatred of all Christians, these expressions of a relaxed, jovial attitude toward individual Christians on private occasions, which form a striking contrast with the rigid formality displayed by the amir toward General Bugeaud during their official meeting, illustrate the gap between the amir's personal attitudes and his public image.'

the interpretation of Muslim rulers' relationships with Europe.][168] ʿAbd al-Qādir's decision to abandon those Muslims inhabitants of Mostaganem who decided to remain under French rule is presented as further evidence for the relegation of religious motives[169] – even though he had secured them passage to Muslim territory and called on them to migrate. Neither respect for individual Christians, coldness towards invading generals, nor the abandoning of willing defectors is obviously problematic from the point of view of Islamic law, however. ʿAbd al-Qādir himself argued as much in the text discussed in next chapter. Yet more still remains to be said here about his treaties with the French.

It must be recalled that none of ʿAbd al-Qādir's treaties with France recognised French sovereignty. Similar to the earlier compact between the two sides in many other respects, the Tafna agreement also consisted of both openly published and secret terms. Again, France recognised ʿAbd al-Qādir's sovereignty over most of what is now called Algeria. Also like its predecessor, this treaty guaranteed the right of Muslims to leave French-controlled areas for ʿAbd al-Qādir's state, though it also allowed them to make the reverse journey (Article 4). Its secret terms included a French commitment to exile certain recalcitrant tribes and their elders to lands under his control. This substantially undermined the provisions of Article 4 with respect to Muslims wishing to move away from (as opposed to into) ʿAbd al-Qādir's territory, and once more asserted his authority over the Muslims of the region. In addition to the exchange of prisoners and the cessation of hostilities, this agreement also contained various stipulations relating to trade – perhaps most notably the French commitment to supply arms to ʿAbd al-Qādir in exchange for trade commodities.

ʿAbd al-Qādir's position during negotiations of the Tafna Treaty was consistent with his earlier assertion of the separateness of French and Muslim political regimes; 'If you wish to become the ruler of the Arabs, this shall not come to pass. If you desire to make commerce, [however], this can be done... This shall occur when you no longer have authority over the Muslims.'[170] The Muslim population, ʿAbd al-Qādir wrote to Bugeaud, 'will respect only the authority of Islamic law, and anyone who tells you otherwise is lying to you.'[171] It was under-

168 Danziger, 1983, pp. 45–47. Danziger presents ʿAbd al-Raḥmān's referring to the Treaty of Tangier as a *ṣulḥ sharʿī* as conflicting with his description of the French as unbelievers [p. 45], in spite of the model for *ṣulḥ* in Islamic thought being supplied by Muḥammad's treaty with (archetypical unbelievers) the Meccan polytheists, and his politeness to French diplomatic representatives as a sign of conflicting religious beliefs and political pragmatism [pp. 46–47].

169 *Ibid.*

170 ʿAbd al-Qādir to Damrémont, GGA1E113, 25-05-1837.

171 ʿAbd al-Qādir to Bugeaud, GGA1E113, 29-09-1837.

stood that 'Abd al-Qādir's state would constitute the structure within which such Islamic law would be practised. Such would also be one of the duties of his representative agent (*wakīl*) to the French, Hadj el-Habeb ben al-Maher, in the event of dispute between two Muslims in French territory (in the case of disputes between Muslims and Christians, the claimants were to decide on their arbitrator between themselves).[172]

Unsurprisingly, 'Abd al-Qādir's armistice with France coincided with a sustained campaign aimed at encouraging the Muslims in French-ruled areas to migrate to his own territory.[173] This process of population transfer, though never of a momentous scale, began just as the Tafna treaty had been signed. 'Abd al-Qādir carried out numerous secret negotiations with tribes in French territory,[174] which the French authorities attempted to contain by exiling offending chiefs. Whatever his motivations for such a movement of Muslim populations, they seem to have been widely shared among those populations themselves.

Again, while France recognised 'Abd al-Qādir's sovereignty by treaty and overt policy, he did not reciprocate; Bugeaud reported during negotiations that 'Abd al-Qādir wanted sovereignty over the entire region, with French rights 'illusory'.[175] He would negotiate and trade with the French as a power, but never unequivocally recognised their right to govern a Muslim population. As well as obviously extending his influence at the expense of a (French) competitor, this situation also illustrates fundamentally different conceptions of polity, sovereignty, and international relations. 'Abd al-Qādir and his state did not grow from the same intellectual soil as the French: Hugo Grotius, the Peace of Westphalia, and nation-state sovereignty within formal borders were as foreign to him as the long history of Islamic political thought was to his European interlocutors. 'Abd al-Qādir and his French counterparts were both literally and figuratively speaking different languages. The resultant misunderstandings made apparent agreement more achievable, but ultimately undermined its durability.

Though the French translation of the Tafna agreement recognised French sovereignty over the coastal regions already under French control, the official Arabic version did not. [Negotiations were conducted in Arabic, and only the Arabic version was signed, it should be noted.] Rather, it spoke of 'Abd al-Qādir 'being aware of' rather than 'granting recognition to'[176] French 'power (*sulṭah*) in Africa'. The distinction, clear in Arabic, was also evident to informed

---

172 'Abd al-Qādir to Bugeaud, GGA1E113, late-08 – 1837.
173 St John to Palmerson, FO 3/42, 07-04-1839.
174 Daumas to the Ministry of War, FR ANOM GGA1E116, 12-05-1839.
175 Bugeaud to the Ministry of War, FR ANOM GGA1E113, 05-05-1837.
176 *Ya'rifu* rather than *yu'atarifu bi...*

French commentators of the time, including Alexis de Tocqueville,[177] who denounced the treaty on these very grounds. This matter was not to prove the sticking point, however, so much as an infamous phrase in Article 2, wherein spheres of influence were demarcated. With respect to the eastern limit of French presence, the phrase 'to the edge of Oued Khadra *wa ilā quddām*' ('and in front of it' or 'and before it') was used. In the French text, however, this apparently superfluous phrase was rendered '*et au delà*' ('and beyond that'). What seemed a fairly unambiguous border in the official text became, in the unofficial French version, *carte blanche* for further expansion.

That opportunity was taken two years later in late 1839 when a French expeditionary corps of 20,000 was dispatched to take Constantine from Aḥmad Bey, whom ʿAbd al-Qādir had failed to support in spite of his strategic importance as a bulwark against French expansion. This invasion marked a dramatic expansion of French influence and ambition, establishing a 'bridgehead in the interior of Algeria... [and thereby] a fundamental change in ʿAbd al-Qādir's policy toward France'.[178] Preparations for war against France were stepped up, arms procured, and prospective foreign allies courted. By 1839, with French influence gradually expanding, the decision was reached to declare war if the French marched through the province of Hamza. On the 27th of September 1839 the Duc d'Orléans and Governor General Valée led a march through the Bībān pass from Constantine to Algiers through ʿAbd al-Qādir's territory,[179] and the latter declared war. His relationship with France would remain a belligerent one from this point until his final removal from North Africa.

It is at this point worth turning once more to the recent scholarship on ʿAbd al-Qadir's Algerian career, as both recent archival studies have engaged with the nature of the war – or *jihād* – declared by ʿAbd al-Qādir. Amira Bennison offers the more substantive account, which presents an elegant structural model, intimately related with the state-building project. In Bennison's analysis, *jihād* is explained in terms of power-legitimacy,[180] systematically related to three other concepts which together form a closed feedback system. *State* relies upon *jihād*, which in turn relies upon identification of *kufr/fasād* [unbelief and corruption], themselves defined by the *state*.[181] The latter pair of sometimes-contested 'dy-

177 Tocqueville, 2001, p. 50.
178 Danziger, 1977, p. 154.
179 Julien, 1964, p. 151.
180 Bennison, 2002, p. 143.
181 See also Bennison, 2011, p. 78. Compare Bennison, 1996 [pp.1–5] for an earlier and less developed version of this abstraction, based on a dichotomy between *imāmah* and *fisād*, building

nastic constructs'[182] are distinguished as representing non-Muslim foreign opponents and Muslim domestic dissidents, respectively: foreign and domestic challenges to the *state*. The great elegance of this analytical device and its parsimony in describing many historical developments need not necessarily represent an exclusive perspective on history, however – still less an insight into the psychology or motivations of individuals involved.

While preparedness to wage war has certainly been no less significant in North African social history than elsewhere, it is an exaggeration to represent warfare as the pre-eminent 'imperative for state formation'.[183] It has not in all circumstances proved an attractive option; in ʿAbd al-Qādir's time Sultan ʿAbd al-Raḥmān and Muḥammad al-Ṣaghīr al-Tijānī respectively saw peace rather than war with France as means to protect and construct their own 'states'. ʿAbd al-Qādir himself spent years at peace with France, consistently representing its rupture as the result of French treaty breaches. A range of complex and intersecting values, judgements, and perceptions underlie the tendencies both to live in communities and to fight other groups – in North Africa as everywhere else. The model developed by Bennison is an elegant description of political events on a structural level, then, but not necessarily informative as to the subjective experiences and intentions of our subjects. It should also be praised for its attempt at rendering the phenomenon of North African *jihād* comprehensible to audiences unfamiliar with the concept's long and complex history as an Islamic ethical, spiritual,[184] and jurisprudential category.

Raphael Danziger's account of *jihād*, however, lacks these virtues. *Jihād*, as part of a religious lexicon, is given little attention considering his study's detailed and informative engagement with military strategy. It is presented as an essentially non-cognitive phenomenon, 'a sentiment'[185] – the irrational desire for war against the other. Edmund Burke has rightly remarked that Danziger's understanding of *jihād* as 'holy war, unrelenting and continuous, with no truces and no negotiations...[is] a stereotyped view.'[186] But while Danziger's work has been focused upon here because of its pre-eminence in the secondary literature,

---

upon Raphael Danziger's attempt at using *jihād* as a demarcation criterion in makhzan-siba relations [Danziger, 1981, pp. 30–34].

182 Bennison, 2002, p. 12. This seems slightly exaggerated, and Bennison points out that the dynasty could not maintain a monopoly on these terms, even assuming that they had created them [*ibid.*].

183 Bennison, 2002, p. 83.

184 The spiritual role of *jihād* is discussed in this book's chapter on ʿAbd al-Qādir's *Kitāb al-Mawāqif.*

185 E.g., Danziger, 1977, p. 215.

186 Burke III, 1978, p. 294.

this reductive view of (ʿAbd al-Qādir's attitude to) just warfare in Islam is widely in evidence among other recent and influential writers. Abun-Nasr's account of these events, for instance, simply asserts without explanation that 'the religious character of ʿAbd al-Qādir's state excluded peace with the French,'[187] a sentence which could have been written a century earlier.[188] While Bennison offers an alternative account of *jihād* to that presented by Islamic thought, as described above, no other writer on ʿAbd al-Qādir has attempted so thorough and thoughtful a project. Many short-cuts have been taken. More broadly, the habit of analysing religio-political power in North Africa without thoroughgoing recourse to the concepts it comprises goes back at least as far as Clifford Geertz's seminal *Islam Observed.*[189]

What Burke has called a 'stereotypical view' of *jihād* and its place in Islamic political thought is not only an over-generalisation, but often a wildly inaccurate one. So, for instance, we find dismissive attributions of the idea that *jihād* is an 'automatic response' to the conquest of Muslims by non-Muslims to 'French scholars'[190] – when it in fact represents one of the most long-standing and uncontroversial legal criteria for *jihād* within the Islamic tradition.[191] It is worth noting in this context that the term most often associated with ʿAbd al-Qādir, *murābiṭ* or marabout,[192] so often a generic term for North African Sufis of standing, shares its roots with the defensive *ribāṭ* – 'fortified monasteries'.[193] This fortified frontier outpost, manned by the *murābiṭ*, was devoted to the

> 'safeguarding of the frontiers of the *Dār al-Islām* [Muslim world] by stationing forces in the harbours and frontier-towns (*thughūr*) for defensive purposes. This type of *jihād*, although based on a Qur'ānic injunction, developed at a time when the Islamic state was on the defensive... But the jurists, especially the Mālikī jurists of Spain and North Africa (whose frontiers had become constantly the targets of attack from European forces [and whom the next chapter of this book will demonstrate ʿAbd al-Qādir explicitly quoting]), emphasised the de-

---

187 Abun-Nasr, 1971, p. 214.

188 As indeed it was, for instance by de Tocqueville [2001, p. 65] and Churchill [1867, p. 41].

189 For a trenchant criticism of Geertz's approach, focusing specifically on a dearth of engagement with the content of Islamic ideas, see for instance Munson, 1993, *passim.*

190 Danziger, 1977, p. 46.

191 Khadduri, 1955, pp. 69,94–95.

192 Including the Moroccan Sultan ʿAbd al-Raḥmān, who addressed ʿAbd al-Qādir as a '*murābiṭ mujāhid*' in their correspondence [ʿAbd al-Raḥmān to ʿAbd al-Qādir, FR ANOM GGA1E211,—10–1839].

193 Julien, 1964, p. 15.

fensive purpose of the *ribāṭ*... [A *ḥadīth* in Bukhārī states] that spending one night in a *ribāṭ* is worth more than a thousand in prayer.'[194]

It should also be noted that the defensive principle is one which the Islamic elaboration of ethical warfare shares with most other religious and secular formulations of *jus ad bellum* – from Catholic Just War doctrine to the writing of Hugo Grotius or the Nuremberg Charter. Notably, Article 51 of the United Nations Charter classes defence as the only pretext for war which requires no UN authorisation. By contrast, it is relatively difficult to imagine any systematic formulation of the right to war which does not argue for self-defence – still less that it would have to wait a millennium for foreign scholars to artificially introduce it.

The failure of some authors to account for the conceptual complexity of Islamic thought when discussing ʿAbd al-Qādir's actions in North Africa is not simply the matter of under-developed categories pointed out by Burke, however. Rather, it also derives from theological, moral, and ideological preconceptions, all of which cast light on the manner in which stereotypes arise. In the first instance, it may be the product of anachronism, either accidental or (for some believers) deliberate; enthusiastic or unreflective embrace of secular distinctions in the present may lead one to project them into the past. In the second instance, it may be more directly moralising; the refusal to recognise appeals to religion may simply embody a rejection of the moral claims or spiritual authority these might imply.[195] Thirdly, however, the staunch rejection of 'religion' as an explanatory factor in the political lives of non-secular groups,[196] such as those which ʿAbd al-Qādir led, also results from a reductive interpretative agenda. Rather than investigating culture, ethics, and ideology, writers advancing this perspective urge their readers to focus instead on 'the issues'[197] of territory and material economics. Culture and politics are thereby presented as epiphenomena dependent on

194 Khadduri, 1955, pp. 81–82. ʿAbd al-Qādir (said to have memorised al-Bukhārī's *ḥadīth* collection) seems to be alluding to such traditions when, for instance, he writes to Bugeaud that time spent opposing him is more meritorious than longer years in Mecca [Julien, 1964, p. 195].
195 This is more common in relation to ʿAbd al-Qādir's context during the 19th century – e.g. de Tocqueville's apology for French colonialism and condemnation of resistance movements on the grounds that '[e]xperience has shown us a thousand times that, whatever the fanaticism and the national spirit among the Arabs, personal ambition and greed have always animated them even more powerfully... The same phenomenon has always occurred among half-civilised men' [Tocqueville, 2001, pp. 68–69].
196 That is to say, groups which do not espouse a separation between religious and non-religious realms which are not to interfere with one another, and which lack separate or parallel insitutions to embody such a divison.
197 Danziger [1977, p. 46] makes this assertion explicitly.

underlying material processes – a simplistic view which has already been thoroughly questioned by the economic sciences out of which it arises.[198]

It would be an error, therefore, to adopt either the theologically or the morally judgemental positions entailed by the first two functions of the 'rejection of religion' as an explanatory factor for ʿAbd al-Qādir's North African actions. We may hold views which differ from those of our subjects without insisting that the latter secretly agree with us. Caution is also required towards any starkly reductive models of *Realpolitik* implied by the third, ideological, function. What all three grounds for rejecting ʿAbd al-Qādir's 'religious motivation' share, however, is their contribution to the narrative of conversion from material to spiritual incarnations that is challenged here. All three set the scene, in ways we shall continue to explore, for his transformation by French captivity – be it on a spiritual, moral, or intellectual plane.

Whatever one's interpretation of its biographical or spiritual significance, the fact of violence erupting once more in 1839 remains inescapable. A second, lengthier, and ultimately decisive, period of conflict had begun, with ruinous consequences for the population of Algeria and for the career of ʿAbd al-Qādir. This time, the gloves were most decidedly off. While he had developed a reputation in Europe for tolerance, 'probity and fair treatment of captives',[199] the more powerful French army's tactics escalated in violence through 'scorched earth' policies of collective punishment. There were many publicised incidents of French officers ordering the mass slaughter of soldiers and civilians 'even after they offered to surrender'.[200] The British press, in particular, was full of condemnation (as well as pride in the mistaken assumption that British colonial exploits had never involved such violence); *Punch* was withdrawn from sale in France

---

198 This has long been the case, from Gramscian reformulations of Marxian ideas to more Neoclassical developments in Cultural and Behavioural Economics.

199 Abun-nasr, 1971, p. 244; Churchill, 1867, p. 208; Danizger, 1977, p. 182; an example was his writing to the Bishop of Algiers, asking him to send a priest to attend to the religious needs of his Christian captives [Clayton, 1975, p. 221]. Berndt makes similar observations, adding that ʿAbd al-Qādir 'proves himself in all circumstances most tolerant and unprejudiced against those who think differently [from himself]' [Berndt, 1840, p. 63]. *The Times* of the day related that ʿAbd al-Qādir 'often interfered to prevent cruelties by the Arabs on the Christians, and when his army has taken any prisoners they were uniformly treated with humanity' (*The Times*, Wednesday, Jan 14, 1846, p. 8). On his eventual surrender, twenty-one European women were found among his group, all but one of whom insisted in remaining with the Algerians, with whom they had built families [Julien, 1964, p. 207]. The only significant incident of ʿAbd al-Qādir's captives being killed or mistreated occurred at the order not by his order but that of a lieutenant during his absence [Bennison, 2002, p. 140].

200 Abun-nasr, 1971, p. 246.

after its satirical attacks on French policy (some of which were authored by William Makepeace Thackeray).[201] Critical attitudes were not restricted to Britons with a penchant for imperial competition, however. Friedrich Engels wrote that '[t]hrough this barbaric approach to the waging of war, the French have taken a stand against all laws of Humanity, of Civilisation, and of Christianity.'[202] The relatively conscientious underdog ʿAbd al-Qādir, by much the same token, had by now become something of a *cause célèbre* in presses hostile to French imperialism.

In this notoriety, the initial seeds of a 'Road to Damascus' narrative had already been sown. ʿAbd al-Qādir was a thorn in France's side, and a blot on her honour. It was politically imperative for France that he be either neutralised or (better yet) converted by what would become known as the *mission civilisatrice.*[203] Subsequent chapters will illustrate some of the strategies which were employed by the French state to foster the latter impression. For his part, General Bugeaud was forced to resign in 1847, not least because of the shame he was bringing on his country in the international arena, after an expedition to loot Grand Kabylia 'in spite of the French Chamber of Deputies and Minister of War denouncing the plan'.[204] He would land many crushing blows before that time, nonetheless.

As the 1840s progressed, ʿAbd al-Qādir found his support in the region increasingly eroded by insuperable French military and diplomatic pressure. By the end of 1842, Bugeaud was confident enough to declare that 'the serious war is over.'[205] The final years of war were characterised largely by flight (often to Morocco, particularly the relatively lawless *Rīf*) on ʿAbd al-Qādir's part, failed attempts at gaining Spanish mediation,[206] and eventual suing for peace through his erstwhile ally Léon Roches[207] at the end of the year 1847.

---

201 Abdel-Jaouad, 1999, p. 196.

202 Serauky, 1990, p. 56

203 This phrase itself (like its English counterpart in Kipling's 'White Man's Burden') is of course anachronistic, coming into common use through Jules Ferry some fifty years later. Even then, however, it was not always intended to describe a new invention, and its characteristic combination of magnanimity, arrogance, and imperialism is easily divined throughout the history of empire. The phrase has been used repeatedly by Amira Bennison, moreover, specifically to describe French attitudes towards the invasion of Algeria [Bennison, 1998, *passim* and 2000, p. 8].

204 Abun-nasr, 1971, p. 246.

205 Julien, 1964, p. 194.

206 Des Bois to the Naval Ministry, FR ANOM GGA1E215, 15-11-1847.

207 Included in Chasteau to the Ministry of Foreign Affairs, Correspondance Politique/Maroc/19, 06-01-1848.

His cessation of hostilities against France came on the condition that he be allowed to exit the country for the Muslim states to the east,[208] an offer which France had made before.[209] This guarantee was immediately violated, however, and ʿAbd al-Qādir was instead transported to France, where he remained confined with his retinue of about one hundred people in a succession of chateaux (at Toulon, Pau, and ultimately Amboise) until 1852. This imprisonment, its representation, its resolution, and its critical role in the 'Road to Damascus' historiographical tendency, will be the main topic of Chapter Three. The present narration, on the other hand, must now turn to the role of Morocco, often underrepresented in accounts of ʿAbd al-Qādir's early decades which focus more exclusively on his significance to Europe. It is in nominally Moroccan territory where ʿAbd al-Qādir would spend the bulk of his final half-decade at war with the French conquest of North Africa.

1.5 ʿAbd al-Qādir's Relations with Morocco

Under-estimating the dynamism and influence of ʿAbd al-Qādir's tumultuous relationship with the Morocco of Sultan ʿAbd al-Raḥmān simultaneously exaggerates the Francocentrism of his biography while obscuring the way it would have appeared to the colonised as opposed to the coloniser. In both of these respects, it contributes to the variously Francocentric 'Road to Damascus' narratives surrounding ʿAbd al-Qādir. This relationship demands a lengthier treatment than it can be given here. Bennison's work in drawing out salient themes in the developing polemic between ʿAbd al-Qādir and 'Abd al-Raḥmān is particularly praiseworthy in this respect.

ʿAbd al-Qādir's connection with the Sultan of Morocco ʿAbd al-Raḥmān began even before the former's emergence as putative *amīr al-mu'minīn*. The border between what we now know as Morocco and Algeria was in the early 19th century far more fluid and ambiguous than has since become the case. This change has been effected both through treaties and through the ideological absorption of the European concept of the 'nation-state' along with technologies leading to a marked increase in state control during the 20th century. As we have already begun to see, many misunderstandings of ʿAbd al-Qādir's motives that need to be challenged here derive from an over-hasty attribution to him of

208 ʿAbd al-Qādir planned to travel to 'Constantine, or Acre, or Alexandria', the last of which was accepted as reasonable by France [*Tuḥfah*, p. 526].
209 Julien, 1964, p. 195.

alien and anachronistic conceptions of state, nation, and sovereignty. In his time, the Moroccan sultanate had for the previous century claimed authority as far into 'Algeria' as Tafna, overlapping with the supposedly Ottoman sphere of influence.[210] Indeed, a Moroccan annexation of much of contemporary Algeria might eventually have occurred had it not been for French involvement.

Sultan ʿAbd al-Raḥmān was quick to extend his influence as Ottoman power receded – establishing ʿAbd al-Qādir's father Muḥyī al-Dīn as his local representative (*khalīfah*) in 1831 soon before the end of that 'disaster[ous]'[211] intervention and its failed attempt to establish the Sultan's nephew[212] seeing French warships sent to Tangiers in response.[213] This brief role was one which ʿAbd al-Qādir was during the subsequent years to claim passed to him. His deference to the Moroccan Sultanate was generally of a symbolic or rhetorical nature, however, and their alliance was neither as firm nor as lasting as either party would pretend.

By 1834, French military reports on contact between ʿAbd al-Qādir and the Sultan remark pointedly on ʿAbd al-Raḥmān's 'equivocal'[214] attitude towards his supposed subordinate, opining however that the Sultan was nonetheless keen to make use of him so as to augment his own influence. By the following year, French agents in Tangiers were suggesting that the Sultan hoped to play France and ʿAbd al-Qādir off against one another – not least for fear that ʿAbd al-Qādir might have designs on his own imperial throne.[215] This worry would never leave the Sultan, and was encouraged to great effect by French diplomats so as to drive a wedge between ʿAbd al-Raḥmān and ʿAbd al-Qādir[216] – though, in spite of some assertions in the secondary literature, at no time would ʿAbd al-Qādir attempt to usurp the Sultan in point of fact. No single factor, except for the increasingly real possibility of French military reprisals against Morocco, would do more in the subsequent decade to incline the Sultan against ʿAbd al-Qādir – and ultimately to turn him against the Algerian *amīr* with force of arms.

In spite of such mounting suspicions, however, the Sultanate maintained a considerable degree of clandestine support for ʿAbd al-Qādir for many years –

210 Bennison, 2002, p. 128 calls the 'concept of a border-line anomalous'.

211 Bennison, 1996, p. 9.

212 Bellemare, 1863, p. 31.

213 Danziger, 1980, p. 64; Danziger, 1983, p. 42.

214 Desmichels to the Ministry of War, Correspondance Politique/Maroc/4, 19-08-1834. Notably, Danziger's account of this relationship is very different, portraying it as starting very amicably and only deteriorating into 'deep antagonism' during 1846 [Danziger, 1980, pp. 64–67].

215 Méchain to the Ministry of Foreign Affairs, Correspondance Politique/Maroc/4, 02-02-1835.

216 E.g. DeNion to the Pasha of Tangier, Correspondance Politique/Maroc/6, 12-07-1840; St John to the Foreign Office, FO 3/45, 25-04-1842.

providing volunteers, materiel, and trade routes to European arms suppliers. Aside from his utility as a buffer to French expansion toward his realms and (in the event of French withdrawal) a source of prestige in defending Muslim lands in the Sultan's name, ʿAbd al-Raḥmān was also motivated by a combination of a natural Muslim solidarity, by the views of his court, and by popular opinion.

Among ʿAbd al-Qādir's most powerful partisans in the imperial court were the Sultan's influential first wife (rumoured to have had contacts with many marabouts sympathetic to ʿAbd al-Qādir and to have harboured an intense distrust of France)[217] and his Minister of Finance (discussed below). ʿAbd al-Qādir's 'immense'[218] popularity among the Moroccan people – particularly those of the eastern Rīf – was perhaps as great a motivating factor for the Sultan as was his support from the elite class, and concomitantly also a source of justifiable anxiety. ʿAbd al-Qādir's status as both a marabout *mujāhid* (a long-established model of authority in the region, recognised in the Sultan's correspondence with him)[219] and *ʿālid* sharīf (like ʿAbd al-Raḥmān's ruling dynasty) amplified both popular support and elite suspicion; ʿAbd al-Qādir was clearly a potential rival. Only his relative success in war and peace during the 1830s (and by extension, his patron's) prevented this issue from coming to a head as it would in the subsequent decade.

The resumption of hostilities between ʿAbd al-Qādir and the French army after their breach of the Tafna treaty in 1839 was greeted with great excitement by the Moroccan population at large, among whom ʿAbd al-Qādir was widely regarded as 'destined to revive the Islamic religion'.[220] ʿAbd al-Raḥmān's correspondence with him ('a man fighting for his faith and for his country')[221] in the immediate aftermath of the 'Iron Gates Expedition' (a French military march through the *Bībān*, and ʿAbd al-Qādir's territory – seen as a *casus belli*, as already described) hailed ʿAbd al-Qādir as sherif, marabout, *mujāhid*, and reviver of religion,[222] while identifying his struggle as 'our cause' against 'the unbelievers' – even when denying ʿAbd al-Qādir supplies he requested.[223] As he was pushed out of expanding French territory, however, he found himself more and more often in Morocco, bringing with him both the threat of French

217 Méchain to the Ministry of Foreign Affairs, Correspondance Politique/Maroc/5, 01-08-1839.
218 Julien, 1964, p. 186.
219 E.g. ʿAbd al-Raḥmān to ʿAbd al-Qādir, FR ANOM GGA1E211,—10,1839.
220 Delaporte to the Ministry of Foreign Affairs, Correspondance Politique/Maroc/5, 19-07-1839.
221 ʿAbd al-Raḥmān to DeNion, Correspondance Politique/Maroc/6, 13-03-1840.
222 ʿAbd al-Raḥmān to ʿAbd al-Qādir, Correspondance Politique/Maroc/9, 21-03-1840.
223 Delaporte to the Ministry of Foreign Affairs, Correspondance Politique/Maroc/5, 21-02-1840.

reprisals against the Sultanate and the potential of becoming a focal point for domestic disorder which might threaten the imperial throne.

From the beginning of ʿAbd al-Qādir's campaign, the Sultanate of Morocco used the ambiguous nature of North African boundaries, and the inconsistencies in areas of control, as a cloak for supporting ʿAbd al-Qādir. The Moroccan response to French remonstrations over Moroccan volunteers joining ʿAbd al-Qādir was typified by the US consul in 1836 as invariably pointing to the 'lawless and indomitable character' of the border peoples of the Rīf, 'rarely recognising the authority of the Emperor and not to be restrained by him.'[224] The same pattern of evasion would be continued for many years subsequently, with the Sultan professing himself powerless to close 'the infinity of routes' into Algeria and the commerce of traders 'great and small' who travel them.[225] By the eve of the Franco-Moroccan war of 1844, the Moroccan court went so far as to attempt to argue that it lacked authority over ʿAbd al-Qādir on the grounds that he was an Ottoman rather than Moroccan subject,[226] his homelands in what is now Algeria 'the domain of the Turk'.[227] This view was quite widely held at the time, including by the US consul[228] and some in the Ottoman court itself – a fact which would occasion some consternation on ʿAbd al-Qādir's appearance before the Porte a decade later.[229] With his move westward into the Moroccan Rīf during the 1840s, this ambiguity had become increasingly hazardous to the Moroccan state.

The year 1842, in particular, marked a multiple fracture of the always ambivalent relationship between ʿAbd al-Qādir and the Moroccan court – the same year in which Bugeaud had declared that 'the serious war is over.'[230] That year saw the departure of one of ʿAbd al-Qādir's most influential supporters, a strategic *faux-pas* on his part, and a diplomatic failure by his emissaries – all within the context of steadily mounting French diplomatic and military pressure on the Sultanate. 1842 marked the death of the aged Ben Jelloun,[231] ʿAbd al-Raḥmān's Minister of Finance. It was he who had overseen the Sultanate's campaign of clandestine military and financial support for ʿAbd al-Qādir,[232] and who had con-

224 Lieb to the State Department, A2 Cab. 38/3, 24-08-1836.

225 ʿAbd al-Raḥmān to DeNion, Correspondance Politique/Maroc/5, 20-01-1840; ʿAbd al-Raḥmān to DeNion, Correspondance Politique/Maroc/6, 13-03-1840.

226 Bousellam to DeNion, Correspondance Politique/Maroc/10, 03-03-1844.

227 Bendris to Drummond Hay, Correspondance Politique/Maroc/11, 20-07-1844.

228 E.g. Carr to the State Department, A2 Cab. 38/8, 15-10-1840.

229 See Chapter Four.

230 Julien, 1964, p. 194.

231 DeNion to the Ministry of Foreign Affairs, Correspondance Politique/Maroc/8, 22-08-1842.

232 E.g. Ben Jelloun to ʿAbd al-Qādir, FR ANOM GGA1E211, Ben Jelloun to ʿAbd al-Qādir, FR ANOM GGA1E211—09 – 1838, Ben Jelloun to ʿAbd al-Qādir, FR ANOM GGA1E211—05 – 1839, Ben

sistently been identified as foremost among his intermediaries with the court.[233] His death was described by French agents as having 'dealt a fatal blow' to ʿAbd al-Qādir's cause.[234] Before six months were out, the Sultan was already reneging on agreements made with ʿAbd al-Qādir, seizing supplies bound for him, and arresting agents he sent to claim them[235] – drawing inflammatory accusations of capitulation to the Christians from the emir.[236]

Meanwhile, the Sultan of Morocco had by early 1842 granted ʿAbd al-Qādir's request to sue for peace with France. This was to occur on condition, ʿAbd al-Raḥmān wrote, that ʿAbd al-Qādir secured British mediation – on the curious grounds that 'the English help the Muslims.'[237] It seems unlikely that this stipulation was intended as a stumbling block, but such was its result – due both to British unwillingness to intercede for ʿAbd al-Qādir and to the performance of his representative. ʿAbd al-Qādir's recently-recruited[238] diplomatic agent, Colonel Scott,[239] was at that time travelling Europe and North Africa, where he would attempt without success to gain the sympathies of first the British, and then the French governments.[240] It is clear from Scott's memoirs that he had little command of Arabic,[241] and less sympathetic understanding of North African culture.[242] So maladroit were his efforts that far from influencing foreign powers

Jelloun to ʿAbd al-Qādir, FR ANOM GGA1E211—10 – 1839, Ben Jelloun to ʿAbd al-Qādir, FR ANOM GGA1E211—11 – 1839.

233 E.g. DeNion to the Ministry of Foreign Affairs, Correspondance Politique/Maroc/6, 16-05-1840; DeNion to the Ministry of Foreign Affairs, Correspondance Politique/Maroc/6, 09-08-1840; memorandum of Marius Garcin, Correspondance Politique/Maroc/6, 26-07-1840.

234 DeNion to the Ministry of Foreign Affairs, Correspondance Politique/Maroc/8, 27-09-1842.

235 DeNion to the Ministry of Foreign Affairs, Correspondance Politique/Maroc/9, 06-03-1843.

236 DeNion to the Ministry of Foreign Affairs, Correspondance Politique/Maroc/9, 06-09-1843.

237 ʿAbd al-Raḥmān to ʿAbd al-Qādir, FR ANOM GGA1E211, early 1842. This view contrasts with ʿAbd al-Raḥmān's later writing to his son Muḥammad that all Christians are in league with one another against Islam [quoted in Danziger, 1983, p. 44].

238 Drummond Hay records Scott's arrival from Spain (where he had seen military service) in early 1841 – Hay to the Foreign Office, FO 99/7, 23-03-1841.

239 While having military experience in Spain, it seems that Scott's primary usefulness to ʿAbd al-Qādir was diplomatic rather than martial, ʿAbd al-Qādir having been particularly lacking in English-speaking subordinates (cf Bennison, 2004, p. 597: 'Scott, whose own contribution was presumably military').

240 E.g. Scott to Aberdeen, FO 3/45, 10-04-1842; FO to Scott, FO 3/45, 14-04-1842; St Aulaire to Guizot, Correspondance Politique/Angleterre/659, 24-02-1842; Bugeaud to St John, FO 3/45, 29-08-1842.

241 E.g. Scott, 2010, pp. 13, 31, 72, 77, 87.

242 Scott informs his readers, for instance, that 'Marabout signifies Saint, and the qualification necessary for canonisation is being a simple fool, or one who contents himself with saying and

to support 'Abd al-Qādir, he managed only to cause offence – both among Europeans[243] and in the Maghreb. By the end of his calamitous campaign, Scott had openly reproached and indirectly threatened the Moroccan Sultan (whose sceptre should pass, he wrote, 'into more active hands').[244] He made this misstep in spite of being aware that the French were attributing such threats to 'Abd al-Qādir's camp in a strategy of divide and rule.[245] To make matters worse, 'Abd al-Qādir chose this moment to compound his agent's political blundering by establishing friendly relations with rebels against the Moroccan Sultan at Tafilit[246] – heaping fuel on the long-smouldering fire of 'Abd al-Raḥmān's suspicions about his designs on the throne.

With the relationship between 'Abd al-Qādir and 'Abd al-Raḥmān already at low ebb, the brief Franco-Moroccan War of 1844, largely precipitated by 'Abd al-Qādir's practice of raiding French territory from Morocco,[247] would put the final nail in the coffin of his campaign. Bellemare divides 'Abd al-Qādir's post-Tafna war with France into two periods – the latter beginning in 1845.[248] Though he would struggle on for two more years, it must have been clear to 'Abd al-Qādir at this point that victory on his terms was impossible – a fact which he himself would later admit.[249] That brief but decisive conflict made clear that open support for 'Abd al-Qādir would have been suicidal to the Moroccan regime, and lead only to conquest by France. Article 4 of the settlement signed

acting the greatest absurdities' [Scott, 2010, p. 25], while the inhabitants of Fez are 'sunk into such a state of barbarism, that they are little superior to a New Zealander' [*op. cit.*, p.10].

243 The British representative in Algiers, for instance, 'experienc[ed] difficulty in repressing [his] indignation' [St John to Aberdeen, FO 3/45, 30-08-1842] with this 'most impudent utterer of falsehoods' [St John to the Foreign Office, FO 3/45, 01-09-1842] – Scott, in turn, threatened legal actions against him, alleging partisanship in favour of France [Scott to the Foreign Office, FO 3/45, 18-09-1842]. 'Abd al-Qādir's earlier European emissary to the western powers, (against whom he had already been warned [Garavini to 'Abd al-Qādir, FR ANOM GGA1E211, – 1837]), had faired similarly poorly: Gibraltar's Governor, Sir Alexander Woodford, terminated contact with the agent Manucci, resolving that on future visits to the exclave, the later would 'simply be asked to leave' [Woodford to the Foreign Office, FO 3/43, 03-12-1840.].

244 DeNion to the Ministry of Foreign Affairs, Correspondance Politique/Maroc/9, 10-02-1843. Scott 2010, p. 3.

245 Scott to the Foreign Office, FO 3/45, 25-04-1842.

246 DeNion to the Ministry of Foreign Affairs, Correspondance Politique/Maroc/8, 02-06-1842.

247 The demand for 'Abd al-Qādir's capture or expulsion featured prominently in the pre-war French ultimatum; 'Abd al-Qādir's actions formed part of the French *casus belli*. Guizot to Glücksberg, Correspondance Politique/Maroc/12, 09-08-1844. Danziger [1983, p. 42] describes 'Abd al-Qādir as 'the principal irritant to Franco-Moroccan relations'.

248 Bellemare, 1863, p. 269.

249 Bellemare, 1863, p. 318.

by Morocco and France obliged the Sultanate to take steps against ʿAbd al-Qādir (now styled as the common enemy of France and Morocco), confining him to the west coast and away from French territory.[250] ʿAbd al-Qādir's presence on the French frontier, meanwhile, would be considered 'a commencement of hostilities',[251] the French army threatening to pursue into Morocco should he retreat. Discussions began as to which city on the seaboard would be best suited for his detention,[252] while the Sultan went so far as to offer him a place in his court as an inducement to end his *jihād* against the French – proposals ʿAbd al-Qādir rejected out of hand.[253] From early 1845, with the Sultan ordering that ʿAbd al-Qādir be driven from his lands and 'wherever he may go, find only misery and suffering',[254] rumours proliferated that the people of the Moroccan Rīf were preparing to declare ʿAbd al-Qādir their Sultan in place of ʿAbd al-Raḥmān.[255]

The Sultan of Morocco's disbursal of large sums of money among the Moroccan elite to induce them to deliver ʿAbd al-Qādir 'if not by force, then by some ruse'[256] proved ineffective, as did periodic waves of arrests of those notables of Fez believed to sympathise with him.[257] Over the final years of his time in North Africa, a game of cat and mouse was played out between ʿAbd al-Qādir's encampment and armies loyal to the Sultan, in an attempt to intimidate him into surrender or flight. The Sultanate evidently wished to avoid direct confrontation – not least given ʿAbd al-Qādir's popularity in Morocco and the Sultan's damaged prestige following his capitulation to France. Some even predicted that Imperial troops would change sides should they be ordered to attack the great *mujāhid* ʿAbd al-Qādir, 'who is widely regarded as supernatural'.[258] Popular interpretations at the time, the archival evidence suggests, took for granted that his polit-

250 Glücksberg to the Ministry of Foreign Affairs, Correspondance Politique/Maroc/12, 16-09-1844.
251 Bugeaud to the Qā'id of Oujda, Correspondance Politique/Maroc/12, 04-08-1844.
252 DeNion to Bugeaud, Correspondance Politique/Maroc/12, 11-09-1844.
253 Mauboissin to the Ministry of Foreign Affairs, Correspondance Politique/Maroc/12, 13-12-1844; Lamoricière to the Ministry of War, Correspondance Politique/Maroc/12, 30-12-1844.
254 Bousellam to Mauboissin, Correspondance Politique/Maroc/13, 18-02-1845.
255 De la Rue to the Duc de Dalmatie, Correspondance Politique/Maroc/13, 12-03-1845; Hay to the Foreign Office, Correspondance Politique/Maroc/13, 17-03-1845; Roches to the Ministry of Foreign Affairs, Correspondance Politique/Maroc/14, 03-09-1845. (Hay also attributes this view to the Lieutenant Governor of Tangier, and Roches to Bendris.)
256 Chasteau to the Ministry of Foreign Affairs, Correspondance Politique/Maroc/15, 13-11-1845.
257 DeNion to the Ministry of Foreign Affairs, Correspondance Politique/Maroc/11, 25-07-1844.
258 Chasteau to the Ministry of Foreign Affairs, Correspondance Politique/ Maroc, 13, 19-04-1845.

ical and military life was of one piece with his religious convictions. With ʿAbd al-Qādir increasingly abandoning faith in the Sultan,[259] however, the latter accused him[260] of being a cursed imposter and unworthy of the name of Muslim,[261] indeed 'no Muslim, but a rebel, impious, and a sower of discord',[262] a vile scourge and a godless man: 'neither Christian, nor Muslim, nor Jew'.[263]

In spite of the rancour of ʿAbd al-Qādir's relations with ʿAbd al-Raḥmān during his final months in North Africa, ʿAbd al-Qādir never took the step of declaring himself against the Sultan. His position remained that he would not take up arms against the Sultan,[264] whose authority (unlike his moral character and decision-making) he never questioned. He was prepared to defend himself, however. 1847, ʿAbd al-Qādir's final year in Morocco, would provide two opportunities for such action. In June, he overran the camp of Al-Aḥmar, newly appointed governor of the Rīf – killing him and many of his men.[265] The attack was a pre-emptive one, as local informants confirmed: [266] ʿAbd al-Qādir's spies had discovered the governor's plan of attack prior to the assault. Rīf tribal elders, hoping to contain the volatile situation, wrote to the Sultan, re-affirming their allegiance to him while euphemistically noting that 'God has punished Qā'id al-Aḥmar for his hostile intentions.'[267] Like them, ʿAbd al-Qādir continued to profess his friendship with ʿAbd al-Raḥmān[268] in the face of increasingly dangerous reality, attempting to square the circle of submitting to ʿAbd al-Raḥmān's authority while opposing his will and condemning his actions. ʿAbd al-Qādir's final clash with Imperial forces would come at by end of the year.

By that time, the stakes had been raised still further. Since early 1847, Benī ʿĀmir and Hāshim tribes had made known to the French their desire to leave ʿAbd al-Qādir's camp and the dominion of the Sultan of Morocco for French-con-

---

259 Mullowny to the State Department, A2 Cab. 38/8, 09-02-1845.

260 The war of words between ʿAbd al-Qādir and ʿAbd al-Raḥmān is best described in the work of Amira Bennison drawn upon by this study.

261 Chasteau to the Ministry of Foreign Affairs, Correspondance Politique/Maroc/16, 13-06-1846.

262 Chasteau to the Ministry of Foreign Affairs, Correspondance Politique/Maroc/19, 07-11-1847.

263 Chasteau to the Ministry of Foreign Affairs, Correspondance Politique/Maroc/18, 10-02-1847.

264 De Bar to Bugeaud, Correspondance Politique/Maroc/19, 25-04-1847.

265 Chasteau to the Ministry of Foreign Affairs, Correspondance Politique/Maroc/18, 21-06-1847.

266 Chasteau to the Ministry of Foreign Affairs, Correspondance Politique/Maroc/18, 22-06-1847; an unnamed marabout of the Benī Saʿīd to Roches, Correspondance Politique/Maroc/19, 25-06-1847.

267 Chasteau to the Ministry of Foreign Affairs, Correspondance Politique/Maroc/19, 05-07-1847.

268 Chasteau to the Ministry of Foreign Affairs, Correspondance Politique/Maroc/19, 25-11-1847.

trolled Algeria.[269] Bugeaud balked at this, expressing trepidation over the danger they might pose.[270] Having been refused, the defecting Algerians set out for ʿAbd al-Qādir's encampment once more – only to be ambushed by Moroccan tribes loyal to the Sultan *en route*. Their severed heads were displayed in several cities as a warning to any who might support ʿAbd al-Qādir.[271] By the Autumn of 1847, ʿAbd al-Qādir and his companions had every reason to expect further attacks from the Sultan's camps. ʿAbd al-Qādir would later write of his last month in Morocco that

> 'The ruler of Marrakesh moved upon me and manifested such anger as he had… I was more at my guard from the wild tribes of the *Rīf* than the French, whose power grew day by day along with my fear and worry.'[272]

Even as some of ʿAbd al-Qādir's followers began to seek refuge in, or safe transit through, French-controlled Algeria,[273] a final effort was made to avert military confrontation with the Sultanate.[274] In the face of ʿAbd al-Raḥmān's implacable insistence that ʿAbd al-Qādir disarm and surrender, the latter dispatched his lieutenant and brother-in-law Bouhamedi (Abū Ḥamīdī) at the head of a contingent of chiefs and marabouts to plead his case before the Sultan.[275] He brought with him a gift of two horses for the Sultan, requesting ʿAbd al-Raḥmān's chaplet and prayer-book as tokens of *amān* or guarantee of ʿAbd al-Qādir's safe passage.[276] The Sultan's reception, however, was hostile and accusatory, imprisoning him and reportedly ordering an attack on ʿAbd al-Qādir.[277]

The year 1847 closed with ʿAbd al-Qādir launching a night attack to push through the encircling Imperial forces before striking out towards French territory. Instead of ʿAbd al-Raḥmān's chaplet, ʿAbd al-Qādir accepted the sabre of French general Lamoricière as token of *amān* – a guarantee that, like some of his followers before him, [278] he would be permitted safe passage beyond French

269 Chasteau to Bugeaud, Correspondance Politique/Maroc/18, 22-03-1847; Thiéry to Bugeaud, Correspondance Politique/Maroc/18, 05-04-1847.
270 Bugeaud to Chasteau, Correspondance Politique/Maroc/18, 08-04-1847.
271 Chasteau to the Ministry of Foreign Affairs, Correspondance Politique/Maroc/19, 04-09-1847.
272 From a letter written by ʿAbd al-Qādir and reproduced in the *Tuḥfah al-Zāʾir* (p. 525).
273 E. g. Bellemare, 1863, pp. 315, 319; Chasteau to the Ministry of Foreign Affairs, Correspondance Politique/Maroc/19, 03-10-1847.
274 Chasteau to the Ministry of Foreign Affairs, Correspondance Politique/Maroc/19, 25-11-1847;
275 Chasteau to the Ministry of Foreign Affairs, Correspondance Politique/Maroc/19, 04-12-1847.
276 Chasteau to the Ministry of Foreign Affairs, Correspondance Politique/Maroc/19, 26-11-1847.
277 Chasteau to the Ministry of Foreign Affairs, Correspondance Politique/Maroc/19, 12-12-1847.
278 Al-Barki to numerous, FR ANOM GGA1E218,—02–1848.

Algeria to Alexandria and further east. 'Abd al-Qādir's battle against the French conquest had come to an end, and he finally abandoned it for lands still ruled by Muslims.

For his part, 'Abd al-Raḥmān ordered national celebrations, with condemnation of 'Abd al-Qādir in the mosques. French sources record that only the loyal Makhzan showed much enthusiasm for these festivities, while the general Moroccan population felt the defeat of 'the most fervent Muslim of this age' as 'a terrible blow to their religion and their nation'.[279] This epilogue aptly illustrates the great contradictions in 'Abd al-Qādir's relationship with Morocco, and the degree to which his once-vital ties to its ruling elite had been severed.

In spite of the 'Road to Damascus' narrative of 'Abd al-Qādir's conquest by, surrender to, and ultimately conversion in France – it was arguably Morocco which defeated him, and most definitively ended his hopes in the Maghreb. The story of his time as leader of the people who would come to call themselves Algerians is at least as much one defined by their neighbour to the west as by their conqueror from across the sea to the north. While the French drove him from his homelands, it was the Sultan of Morocco, whose support had been so invaluable during 'Abd al-Qādir's years of plenty, who had delivered the *coup de grâce* to his *jihād*.

1.6 Conclusion

This chapter has offered a firm historical grounding for the present study. Beginning with an account of 'Abd al-Qādir's youth, it has analysed the structure of his state and his relations with France and Morocco, culminating in the end of his *jihād* and his removal to France. In doing so, it has drawn both upon primary sources including archival records, and upon secondary literatures in French, English, and German. Besides providing us with a detailed impression of 'Abd al-Qādir's early decades, this chapter has been concerned to call into question interpretations by European observers which cannot be sustained in the light of further research. Many of these have been highlighted and explained, particularly as they arise in the most recent Anglophone studies.

It has been important to highlight 'Abd al-Qādir's situatedness in a distinctly North African context – in terms of cultural tradition, historical practices, and political realities. These have been shown to have been distinct from, and sometimes incomprehensible to, his European counterparts. It has also been impor-

---

[279] Chasteau to the Ministry of Foreign Affairs, Correspondance Politique/Maroc/19, 09-01-1848.

tant to point out that his concerns with scholarly learning, theological reflection, and technological development are clearly in evidence in his early years, prior to his having meaningful experience of French civilisation – in spite of suggestions that will later arise to the contrary.

In all of this, it has begun to become clear why the narrative of a converted ʿAbd al-Qādir would initially prove so attractive to French political interests. He was an immensely troublesome opponent possessing enormous prestige both in North Africa and, increasingly, in the west. There were strong incentives (conscious or otherwise) to try and neutralise his symbolic power. From the point of view of his French contemporaries, it would have been relatively difficult to appreciate as serious his motivations in the years prior to his defeat by French forces and putative 'conversion' to Francophilia. By the same token, there would also have been a strong incentive to downplay the crucial Moroccan role in his downfall. For them, to see him as an honourable and beneficent man would be to see him as having grown to be very like a Frenchman. Reasons for maintaining the narrative of conversion in the 20th century which pertain to this period have been quite different, of course, depending on more generalised methodological scepticisms about the religious motivations of political actors.

The aim here has no more been to defend ʿAbd al-Qādir's piety, probity, or orthodoxy than to argue for or against the wisdom or justice of his cause. Still less has it been to divorce his ostensibly religious appeals from his overtly political projects. Rather, a specific interpretative turn in the secondary literature on ʿAbd al-Qādir's Algerian career has been problematised. It is one which demands that we see his Algerian incarnation as profoundly different from its Damascene counterpart – a difference so stark as to demand a dramatic inflection point to account for the disjuncture.

An integral part of the 'Road to Damascus' narrative imposition on ʿAbd al-Qādir, it rests on privileging dynamics invisible to our subjects' consciousness but readily accessible to the modern historian through the application of a suitably reductive methodology. The prominent anthropologist of political religion, Talal Asad, calls this

> 'the sociologism according to which religious ideologies are said to get their real meaning from the political or economic structure, and the self-confirming methodology according to which this reductive semantic principle is evident to the (authoritative) anthropologist and not to the people being written about... I regard this position as untenable.'[280]

---

280 Asad, 1993, pp. 189–90.

If such a process is 'untenable' with respect to ʿAbd al-Qādir's followers, how much more problematic is it when writers such as those quoted in this chapter attempt to make the our primary subject complicit in such 'sociologism'? Perhaps Asad shows too little sympathy with the project of discovering structures and relations in social formations of which their constituents are unaware. But a line must be drawn far in advance of the point where we allow ourselves to assert that figures such as ʿAbd al-Qādir not only conformed to our theoretical models, but secretly did so knowingly.

The desire to rehabilitate ʿAbd al-Qādir's political biography from the obscurity of projected 'fanaticism' has in the most recent studies rendered him hyper-rational. Political histories of ʿAbd al-Qādir's early life have fallen victim to a variety of the dogma of *homo economicus.* Ambition and interest-seeking have been recent keys to understanding his actions, as we have seen his recent biographers insist time and again. Yet 'ambition' or 'interests' are in themselves no less mystifying and uninformative as explanatory factors than 'fanaticism' was in its turn. All are contingent upon other factors (particularly the question of what constitutes a Good) which render their expressions wildly heterogeneous.[281] One does not have interests in the abstract, but rather interests in particular things or states of affairs. To assert that someone is motivated by their interests in itself tells us no more than that they are concerned with what concerns them, notwithstanding any implicit suggestion of bad faith.

Such analysis demands contextual elaboration to rise above the level of tautology. If such contextualisation is to avoid the 'sociologism' castigated by Asad, it must include engagement with the ways in which our subjects themselves see our world. In ʿAbd al-Qādir's case, this means engagement with his ideas, including his religious ideas, not only as epiphenomena of underlying realities but also as historical facts in themselves. Hence, it seems appropriate to render ʿAbd al-Qādir's actions rationally comprehensible, but to do so within an approach based on bounded and embedded rationality, contextualised within and conditioned by an idiosyncratic cultural milieu.

Such a project has been most notably carried forward by Amira Bennison among recent scholars of ʿAbd al-Qādir. At its best, her account of the role of religious discourses in ʿAbd al-Qādir's rule calls our attention to the dynamic and reciprocal[282] 'dialectics'[283] between ruler and ruled. ʿAbd al-Qādir ruled a 'system

281 This problem is one which besets many attempts at applying 'rational choice' economic theory in the social sciences – see, for instance, the discussions in Green and Shapiro [1994].
282 Bennison, 2002, p. 163.
283 Bennison, 2002, p. 9.

whose head was perpetually on trial'.[284] The central focus of her study of ʿAbd al-Qādir is a testament to this insight: it is at its heart an analysis of the propaganda war between ʿAbd al-Qādir and the Sultan of Morocco. Each participant is presented as attempting to justify himself in terms meaningful to the population at large, even if this might appear more externally instrumental than (pre-)psychologically subjectifying or interpellating.[285]

Despite those aspects of Bennison's presentation of ʿAbd al-Qādir with which issue has been taken above, this insight remains a critical one, and points the way towards a deeper contextual understanding. This is particularly true if, following the warning by Talal Asad cited earlier[286] in this chapter's introduction, we are careful not to interpret the reciprocity and dialogue between ruler and ruled pointed to by Bennison as a conscious, deliberate processes of negotiation rather than as an emergent phenomenon. Synchronic and diachronic, structural and psychological elements of past studies must be distinguished, as this chapter has tried to do. But more is needed than a reappraisal of past secondary literatures on the basis of archival research. We need to pursue a deeper engagement with ʿAbd al-Qādir's own account of his motivations as he made them known to his fellows.

This project will now be developed through analysis of a substantial text authored by ʿAbd al-Qādir in the heart of his Algerian career. This text was clearly intended by its author to provide explanation and justification for his policies with respect to both the 'external' and 'internal' threats of the French colony and to rival or recalcitrant Muslims. It will provide an eloquent impression of ʿAbd al-Qādir's self-understanding and presentation to his countrymen and co-religionists in a manner combining religious and political elements – the removal of any of which would empty it of significance and coherence. What is more, a closer reading of this text will allow us to draw numerous inferences about ʿAbd al-Qādir's cultural and intellectual background. It will provide an additional milestone on his life's journey, permitting us to discover a degree of continuity which obviates the need to rely upon tendentious and Eurocentric 'Road to Damascus' narratives of dramatic conversion in our accounts of ʿAbd al-Qādir's life.

284 Bennison, 2002, p. 163.
285 These terms are borrowed from Foucault and Althusser, respectively, but are used here to refer to ways of seeing ʿAbd al-Qādir's socio-political context and enculturation as fundamentally constitutive of his own experience of himself and of the world.
286 Asad, 1993, pp. 210–211.

2.0 Chapter Two – ʿAbd al-Qādir's *Risālah on Hijrah*

'The People of the States [*ahl al-aḥwāl*][1] have said that there are five necessities which must be preserved: religious duty [*dīn*], [2] one's self, reason, kin, and wealth. Every one of these must be preserved, and all accepted that does not conflict with them. Wealth is the last of these in ranking, and religious obligation [*al-dīn*] the first, with priority over all others.'

-*ʿAbd al-Qādir al-Jazā'irī*[3]

We have now explored aspects of the relationship between political and religious thought and action in ʿAbd al-Qādir's early life. To substantiate this exploration, it will be necessary to interrogate the degree to which ʿAbd al-Qādir's political thinking during his Algerian period was conditioned by long-established traditions of thought, inference, and judgement. This will allow us to offer a deeper contextualisation of his Algerian career, which will in turn elucidate his rise to

1 *Ḥāl* (literally state, mode, or circumstance), while used in the context of discursive theology (in the sense of 'predicate' [Wolfson, 1976, p. 183]), is also a central Sufi preoccupation: a (transient) psycho-spiritual state. The phrase 'People of the States' has consequently also been used to indicate Sufis (*'ahl al-aḥwāl wa al-ḥaqā'iq wa al-taṣawwuf'*). The Sufi usage is commonly related to the term *maqām* [Al-Ḥakīm, 1981, p. 330], also referring to distinctions in (less transient) spiritual states, which is evoked by the title of ʿAbd al-Qādir's posthumous *Kitāb al-Mawāqif.* The term has been used in this sense by Sufis as early as Ḥārith al-Muḥāsibī in ninth century Baghdad; '*aḥwāl* can there be defined as modalities of activation, realities essentially "instantaneous" and trans-temporal, which seize the "state" of the subject in the act of "encounter" with an internal "favour" (*fā'ida*), received from God' [Gardet, L., *EI2* article on ḤĀL]. See also al-Ḥakīm, 1981, pp. 329 – 334.

2 'It is usual to emphasize three distinct senses of *dīn* : (1) judgment, retribution; (2) custom, usage; (3) religion...Arabic philologists freely derive *dīn* from *dāna li-* "submit to". *Dīn* henceforth is the corpus of obligatory prescriptions given by God, to which one must submit... [T]he concept indicated by *dīn* does not exactly coincide with the ordinary concept of "religion", precisely because of the semantic connexions of the words. *Religio* evokes primarily that which binds man to God; and *dīn* the obligations which God imposes on His "reasoning creatures"' [Gardet, *EI2* entry on *dīn*]. See also the discussion in Smith, 1991, especially pp. 80 – 119.

3 *Tuḥfah*, p. 414. This five-fold scheme, attributed to the great 12th-century Sufi and Shāfiʿī juridical scholar Abū Ḥāmid al-Ghazālī, is common in *maqāṣid al-sharīʿah* ('the intentions of the Shariah') literature and influential in the Mālikī approach of *iṣtiṣlāḥ* (deriving rulings for the public benefit when no clear scriptural text is available).

DOI 10.1515/9783110499513-004

power and his ability to influence his countrymen. At the same time, it will provide a specific ideological issue by which to judge his actions in his later life – particularly the crucial period of his imprisonment in France which will be the subject of the subsequent chapter.

Specifically, we shall analyse a significant text composed by 'Abd al-Qādir in the early 1840's,[4] which is to say, approximately two-thirds through his Algerian career. The main focus of this text, faithfully[5] reproduced by his son, is the question of migration or *hijrah* from territory controlled by non-Muslims, based primarily on the perspective of Mālikī jurisprudence. It has previously received the scantest attention in the western scholarly literature: a brief mention to the effect that it exists and concerns *hijrah*, to be found in Martin's *Muslim Brotherhoods in 19th Century Africa.*[6] It will be referred to here as the *Risālah on Hijrah.*

'Abd al-Qādir was focused during this period on overcoming both the French army (following their breach of the Tafna treaty) and Arabs either aligned with France or resistant to him. The state he ruled was in a somewhat parlous condition at this point, given the reluctance of many tribes to pay taxes, and the emergence of rival centres of religio-political power (particularly the increasingly pro-French 'Aīn Māḍī Tijāniyyah of Muḥammad al-Ṣaghīr). It has also become evident that, from the earliest days of 'Abd al-Qādir's rule, he insisted on claiming sovereignty through Islamic law over all the Muslims of the region, including those living in areas within the French sphere of influence[7] (whose own sovereignty, as de Tocqueville rightly indicated,[8] he never formally recognised). The *Risālah on Hijrah* arises from this political context. Its goal, briefly stated, is to rally the region's Muslims under 'Abd al-Qādir's banner by warning them of the sinfulness of life under non-Muslim rule. The manner by which this goal is achieved, however, conveys far more than *Realpolitik*. The *Risālah on Hijrah* is highly illustrative of 'Abd al-Qādir's intellectual and cultural background, his style of rhetoric and argumentation, and his historical view of the world. It casts remarkable light on what be believed and what motivated him to act.

---

4 *Tuḥfah*, p. 422. This text is also discussed in an article in *Studia Islamica* by the present author.

5 Even Badī'ah al-Ḥasanī, who goes furthest in questioning the attribution of texts to 'Abd al-Qādir, considers the attribution of the *Tuḥfah al-Zā'ir* and its contents to be (in spite of some typographical errors) 'correct beyond doubt' [2000, p. 230]. The text itself is reproduced in the Appendices below.

6 'The main theme in the *Risālah* is the separation of Muslims from alien invaders,' Martin, 1976, p. 66.

7 E.g. 'Abd al-Qādir to Damrémont, GGA1E113, 25-05-1837, 'Abd al-Qādir to Bugeaud, GGA1E113, 29-09-1837.

8 Tocqueville, 2001, p. 50.

The interpretation of this text will offer a reasoned counterbalance to the impressions given in some recent scholarship that ʿAbd al-Qādir's 'use of religion' is unproblematically reducible to a 'black box' of mysterious 'charisma'.[9] 'To explain the 'amir's rise by invoking such sponge concepts as "religious character" or "charisma" is simply to evade the question.'[10] Rather, the substantive structure and 'thickness' of the traditions in which ʿAbd al-Qādir is engaged are such as both permit and demand their deeper discussion in any comprehensive analysis of his political life. It yields evidence of the religious lens through which ʿAbd al-Qādir saw his political situation as much as it illuminates the character of his rhetorical self-presentation.

The text itself consists of about a dozen pages, presented in the *Tuḥfah al-Zā'ir* under the title 'that which the Amīr [ʿAbd al-Qādir] wrote in answer to a question put to him by some notable persons of distinction'.[11] An almost identical text is held in Rabat,[12] under another title.[13] The text contains no subheadings, but is rather a continuous piece of prose, punctuated by two lines of poetry. Its central concern is with (condemning) those who submit to the rule of the impious *[al-dākhil taḥta dhimmat ahl al-būwār]*,[14] while exhorting all faithful Muslims to remember their obligation to migrate into the Muslim community. The text will be approached via the overlapping concerns of its 1) style and presentation; 2) sources; 3) forms of inference and argumentation; 4) discussion of sincerity and hypocrisy. We shall then begin to integrate the observations which arise into discussions on ʿAbd al-Qādir in the secondary literature.

---

9 E.g. Abun-Nasr, 2007, p. 180: 'The many works written on the Sufi brotherhoods since the 1960s… unable to explain the nature of this spiritual authority [of their shaykhs], the authors of these works often refer to it as 'charisma'. This term was made fashionable by Max Weber's monumental work *Wirtschaft und Gesellschaft…* [which] defines it not so much by what it is, but by what it is not… Thus the description of the spiritual authority exercised by Sufi Brotherhoods' shaykhs as charisma tells us nothing more about it than what the Sufis have long recognised, namely that it is a mystery.'

10 Christelow, 1980, p. 139.

11 *Mā kataba al-amīr jawāban ʿan su'āl qaddama ileyhi baʿḍ al-aʿyān min al-khawwāṣ: Tuḥfah*, pp. 411–422.

12 ʿAbd al-Karīm, 1981, p. 41.

13 '*Ḥusām al-dīn li-qaṭʿi shaym al-murtaddīn.*'

14 *Tuḥfah*, p. 411.

2.1 Style and Presentation

> 'God the Most High said: Oh ye who believe, do not take my enemies or yours as confederates nor behave cordially toward them.[15] This to the point that He says: whosoever of you has done this, by whatever means, has gone astray.[16] Truly God has forbidden you from [amity with] him who opposes your religion, who casts you out of your homes, or who conquers you, and they who submit to the authority of the conqueror are themselves doers of injustice.[17] He said: preach to the hypocrites that [there await them] grievous punishments...[18] All glory be to God. God the Most High has specified his intention toward the hypocrites in the following verse: those who take unbelievers as confederates in lieu of believers, are hypocrites.[19] [This also in other] verses and sound, clear and unambiguous *ḥadīths* which bear no re-interpretation [on the matter].'[20]

Perhaps the most salient characteristic of ʿAbd al-Qādir's rhetoric in this text is its apparent self-effacement. ʿAbd al-Qādir presents himself as entering only with reluctance, compelled by his questioner's need, into a discussion which he claims he will carry out through relaying already-established truths. Only out of compassion does he pass on 'what has been related to us about the matter'[21] in the authoritative sources. The attitude he adopts in this respect is clearly congruent both with pre-existing conventions of good scholarly manners and with his interest throughout his Algerian career in what one might call the rule of law (as we have seen above). Yet this style serves to magnify the author's status as much as diminish it. An ambiguity is automatically established as to the genesis of the treatise's arguments – are these the words of ʿAbd al-Qādir (the individual), or of the (ultimately Divine) Islamic tradition? In these and other respects, this language represents both an ethical perspective and a rhetoric of power and influence.

The words and phrases ʿAbd al-Qādir uses are frequently a composite of multiple Qur'ānic and *ḥadīth* quotations. These are sometimes quite extended, and occasionally foreshortened in such a way as would assume his audience's conversance with the Qur'ānic text.[22] ʿAbd al-Qādir quite literally speaks through

15 Qur'ān 60:1.

16 *Ibid.*

17 Qur'ān 60:9.

18 Qur'ān 4:138.

19 Most likely a reference to Qur'ān 3:28; 4:139; 4:144; 9:23; 60:1.

20 *Tuḥfah*, p. 415.

21 *Tuḥfah*, p. 411.

22 An example of this is to be found on page 412, where ʿAbd al-Qādir includes an indirect threat by writing of God's saying [Qurʿān 16:106]: 'Anyone who, after accepting faith in Allah utters Unbelief – except under compulsion, his heart remaining firm in his faith – but such

the Qur'ān, and in so doing forcefully invokes its authority on behalf of such views as he advances. Some pages in fact contain less text authored by himself than run-together sections of different Qur'ānic verses and excerpts from the authoritative *ḥadīth* collections of Abū Dāwūd and al-Bukhārī. Page 412 of the text as presented in the *Tuḥfah*, for instance, is composed almost entirely of some dozen unattributed quotations which his audience would immediately recognise as Qur'ānic.[23]

In spite of this rhetoric of tradition, authority, and obedience, any lack of active reason is also lambasted.[24] Indeed, the text's main 'political' aim requires the active engagement of its readers' faculties. It contains almost no direct discussion of the political situation in which it was written, even though every page clearly reflects on that situation in quite literally life-or-death terms. Almost all of the historical narrative contained in this text refers overtly to events already centuries past. Even the armies of France and their Muslim allies are referred to only occasionally and in extremely general terms (for instance as 'the Nazarenes', 'the people of perdition', 'the Christianised', 'the Mudejars', or 'the hypocrites'). The reader is left to form his own opinions on the Maghrebī politics of the day – their own opinions, that is, decisively predetermined by the facts as 'Abd al-Qādir has presented them. The resulting tone is highly moralistic, giving the impression of informing the reader as to their general obligations as good Muslims rather than invoking Islam as a reason to follow one policy or another. He does not urge Muslims to leave French territory for his own, but rather describes the duties of a Muslim in such a way that failing to leave the French sphere for his would appear unthinkably immoral.

It would be over-hasty to see these characteristics of 'Abd al-Qādir's writing as simple manipulation. He does hope to influence his readership into co-operating with him, that much is obvious. Yet his approach is also the product of long-established traditional styles of exposition, of inference, and of commitment to the truth of what are taken to be historical facts – primarily the Qur'ānic revelation, and secondarily the experience of Muslims under Spanish Christian rule. Such an expository style has not always commended itself to commenta-

---

as open their breast to Unbelief – on them is Wrath from Allah, and theirs will be a dreadful penalty.'

23 In addition to two *aḥādīth* – one from each of the aforementioned collections (though only Bukharī is named), that page of text contains unattributed excerpts from Qur'ān 7:155, 48:23, 29:3, 2:214, 3:142, 2:246, 4:77, 5:24, 16:106, 12:55, and close paraphrases of Qur'ān 63:1–5, 12:18, and 12:83.

24 *Tuḥfah*, p. 418; also through a *ḥadīth* quoted from Al-Bukhārī on the folly of imitating the mistakes of one's forbears [*Ṣaḥīḥ* of al-Bukhārī, Book 56, number 662, quoted in *Tuḥfah*, p. 412].

tors; post-Marinid Malikism in general has been described as being 'long on authority and short on personal initiative'.[25] Yet, whether attractive to us or not, this rhetoric cannot be assigned the non-cognitive status implied by those political histories of ʿAbd al-Qādir which treat religious discourse simply as an epiphenomenon of *Realpolitik* or as a sentimental product of mystical personal charisma.

2.2 Sources

> 'Know this: that this tragedy, that is the conquest of Muslims by unbelievers and their entry under the protective compact [of the unbelievers] occurred not in the first, nor second, nor third, nor fourth century [after the Prophet's *hijrah*] – but has occurred since the fifth. For this reason, there is not to be found a [Prophetic] utterance, nor unambiguous decisive text [*naṣṣ*] from anyone in the Community (may God be pleased with them!) as it had not yet occurred. It came to pass that the question was [later] asked, and analogical reasoning was employed by our most authoritative theoreticians and adjudicators [*ahl al-naẓar wa al-ijtihād*] with respect to him who accepts Islām but does not migrate. [*Qāḍī al-jamāʿah*][26] Ibn Rushd has said that this analogical reasoning was sound [though] the community differed in their opinions of him who accepts Islam and does not migrate…'[27]

The most significant and most frequently quoted sources for this text are of course the Qur'ān and major *ḥadīth* collections. In addition to these, however, the text contains direct references to over two dozen authorities of varying degrees of fame in North Africa and the wider Islamic world. As ʿAbd al-Qādir himself remarks, the issue of obligations incumbent upon Muslims conquered by non-Muslims is one neglected by the most universally recognised of early Muslim sources.[28] Martin, in his brief note on this text, remarks that this text 'makes a valuable contribution to a part of Islamic theory untouched by the classical writers on this subject… [of] Muslim populations stranded under Christian or other governments.'[29]

What Martin does not remark on is the history of this question among the legal scholars of the Islamic world subsequent to the earliest sources but significantly prior to ʿAbd al-Qādir's writing. There exists, in fact, a substantial quantity of writing on this topic, particularly in ʿAbd al-Qādir's Mālikī jurisprudential

---

25 De Jong and Radtke (eds.), 1999, p. 213.

26 That is to say, holder of the highest post in the Iberian judiciary; Latham, J.D., EI2 entry on 'Ibn Rushd, Abu 'l- Walīd Muḥammad b. Aḥmad'.

27 *Tuḥfah*, pp. 418–419.

28 *Tuḥfah*, pp. 418–419.

29 Martin, 1976, p. 66.

school (*madhhab*). ʿAbd al-Qādir himself points out that 'it came to pass that the question was [later] asked, and analogical reasoning [*qiyās*] was employed'[30] to address the problem. This interest arose from the fact that the Mālikī *madhhab*, most prevalent in the Islamic west, experienced centuries of conquests by Christian kingdoms, particularly as part of what came to be called the *Reconquista*.[31] This period of overthrow of Muslim states in the Iberian Peninsula, frequently followed by purges of Jews and Muslims through forced conversion, the infamous Inquisition, exile, or death, is repeatedly evoked by ʿAbd al-Qādir in this text.

It is primarily on this Mālikī tradition, with which ʿAbd al-Qādir remained connected until his death,[32] that this text draws – as do others of the period (for example, his letter to the jurists of Fez).[33] Its authorities include the 'most famous'[34] Almoravid ruler Yūsuf bin Tāshfīn and the judge Ibn Rushd,[35] once holder of the highest office in the Andalusian judiciary.[36] (The latter was also grandfather to the Ibn Rushd known in Europe as Averroes and famed for his commentaries on Aristotle, consequent influence on Thomas Aquinas, and appearance in Dante's *Divine Comedy*.) The Imām al-Mālik, eponymous founder of ʿAbd al-Qādir's jurisprudential school, makes repeated appearances in the text so as to urge the reader to 'journey and migrate from the lands of injustice [*arḍ al-ẓulm*] and enemies',[37] as 'no one should remain in any place where the practice of the people is based on anything other than the correct truth [*yuʿmal fīhi bi-ghayr al-ḥaqq*]'[38]

Those mentioned by name who are neither Mālikīs, nor above or outside *madhhabī* distinctions, are Shāfiʿīs. This is also the case in his letter to the jurists of Fez.[39] What is more, the Shāfiʿīs quoted share notoriety in the areas of *ḥadīth*

---

30 *Tuḥfah*, p. 419.
31 Abou el Fadl, 1994, p. 163.
32 ʿAbd al-Qādir gave instruction on Mālikite law throughout his later years in Damascus [Goldziher, 1981, p. 242; Weisman, 2001a, pp. 198, 222].
33 *Tuḥfah*, p. 384–5.
34 Munson, 1993, p. 40.
35 *Tuḥfah*, pp. 420, 419.
36 *Qāḍī al-Jamāʿah* [J. D. Latham, "Ibn Rushd, Abu 'l- Walīd Muḥammad b. Aḥmad" in the Encyclopaedia of Islam, 2nd ed.]. See above.
37 *Tuḥfah*, p. 414.
38 *Tuḥfah*, p. 417; *al-ḥaqq* encompasses meanings from 'real' to 'true' to 'correct' to 'right' (as resulting in obligation). It seems that it is more the later (normative) than the former (ontological) sense which is intended here.
39 *Tuḥfah*, p. 385.

scholarship, Qur'ān exegesis, and *uṣūl al-fiqh* (al-Nawwawī,[40] Ibn Ḥajar,[41] al-Suyūṭī,[42] al-Bayḍāwī,[43] al-Rāfiʿī[44]). In his study of post-Marinid North African Islam, Vincent Cornell consistently identifies the influence of Shāfiʿism in that area specifically with these interests,[45] which he describes broadly as an interest in what he terms '*uṣūl*'.[46] On the other hand, ʿAbd al-Qādir's persistent lack of interest in the Hanafī[47] juridical tradition of the former Ottoman colony, while suggestive given his lifelong anti-Turkish attitudes, might largely be explained by the conservative pace with which Mālikism integrated external influences.

ʿAbd al-Qādir's most quoted source throughout (aside from the Qur'ān) is al-Wansharīsī's *al-Miʿyār al-mughrib ʿan fatāwa ʿulamaʾ Ifrīqiya wa al-Andalus wa al-Maghrib*, a compendium of writings on Malikite jurisprudence. This is still recognised as one of the most significant texts on the subject, while its author has been connected with the milieu of what Scott Kugle calls 'juridical Sufism' – sharing his master with the noted 'legist' Sufi Aḥmad Zārrūq.[48] The fifteenth century *Miʿyār* of al-Wansharīsī has been described by Abou el Fadl as 'a resounding condemnation of Muslims who accepted Mudejar [Christian subject minority] status in al-Andalus [previously Muslim-ruled Iberia]'.[49] Commenting on this text during a relatively recent Arabic study of the question of *hijrah* in Algerian Islamic thought, Muḥammad Ibn ʿAbd al-Karīm remarks repeatedly on the indebtedness of ʿAbd al-Qādir's reasoning to al-Wansharīsī's juridical collection.

> 'ʿAbd al-Qādir relied on [al-Wansharīsī's writing], as its author exceeded him in knowledge and preceded him in history. And why should he not? Ibn Ghāzī has described al-Wansharīsī as a mountain of knowledge astride the earth.'[50]

Abou el Fadl's survey of the question of *hijrah* in Māliki law (which does not mention ʿAbd al-Qādir) provides numerous direct parallels with the positions taken by ʿAbd al-Qādir in this treatise. Many of the same Qur'ānic verses,[51]

---

40 *Tuḥfah*, p. 418.
41 *Tuḥfah*, p. 421.
42 *Tuḥfah*, p. 414.
43 *Tuḥfah*, p. 417.
44 *Ibid.*
45 Cornell, 1998, *passim.*
46 Cornell, 1998, p. 124.
47 A passing reference is made [*Tuḥfah*, p. 420] to the agreement of 'the Kufans' with a Mālikī view. It seems likely that the Ḥanafīs are intended here, owing to Abū Ḥanīfa's Kufan origins.
48 Kugle, 2006, p. 56.
49 Abou el Fadl, 1994, p. 154.
50 ʿAbd al-Karīm, 1981, p. 8.
51 E.g. 4:97–100. [Abou el Fadl, 1994, p. 144, *Tuḥfah*, p. 414].

ḥadīths,[52] and juridical writings[53] he draws upon have been presented by Abou el Fadl as typical of pre-Modern Mālikī reasoning on the question of migration from territory ruled by non-Muslims. Other studies focusing on earlier periods of this debate, during the Iberian *Reconquista*, also identify views similar to those represented by ʿAbd al-Qādir in this text as held at that time.[54] Broad comparisons might also be drawn with comparable pro-*hijrah* positions famously taken by Malikis more contemporary with ʿAbd al-Qādir, such as 18th century fellow Qādirī and 'accomplished scholar of religious law'[55] Usman dan Fodio of the Sokoto Caliphate, another religo-political state founder who drew on texts also taught by ʿAbd al-Qādir.[56] While the positions he takes do not represent a unanimous body of opinion, he is drawing from the mainstream of a substantive legal tradition, elaborated over many centuries.

2.3 Forms of Inference and Argumentation

> 'They are in this respect like the tribe of Israel, also, when they said to Moses – peace be upon him! – '*Go thou, and thy Lord, and fight ye two, whilst we sit here (and watch).*'[57] Then, after this, they were despoiled by the unbelievers, in both their wealth and their very lives, save those who held fast to the bonds of Islām.'[58]

The traditional character of ʿAbd al-Qādir's thought manifests itself too in the manner in which he selects and connects arguments and assertions. His 'speaking through the Qur'ān' has been remarked on above – the manner in which he also 'thinks through the Qur'ān' calls for further elucidation. As the eternal and inerrant word of God and His final and most perfect revelation to humanity, the scripture's interpretation presents for ʿAbd al-Qādir (as for many other Muslims throughout history) the highest and purest case of all understanding. For him, that is to say, his approach to the text of the Qur'ān is in many respects paradigmatic.

52 E.g. 'Whoever associates with an infidel and lives with him, he is like him' [Abou el Fadl, 1994, p. 144; *Tuḥfah*, p. 415].
53 Particularly the abovementioned *Miʿyār* of Al-Wansharīsī and quotations from al-Mālik, the centrality of which to ʿAbd al-Qādir's case is apparent throughout the text.
54 E.g. Miller, 2000, *passim*.
55 Abun-Nasr, 2007, p. 192.
56 E.g. the *Ṣughrā* of al-Sanūsī, taught by ʿAbd al-Qādir at Amboise [*EI2* on Yūsuf al-Sanūsī; *Tuḥfah*, p. 529]
57 Qur'ān 5:24.
58 *Tuḥfah*, p. 412.

This approach may be characterised in a number of ways. It is thematic rather than chronological, concerned more with cases than with causality. History and the world, like the text of the Qur'ān, are for ʿAbd al-Qādir intrinsically meaning-bearing messages or *signs* (*āyāt* – also the standard term for a Qur'ānic verse) directed by God to the human consciousness. The Qur'ān itself does not cleave to a chronological narrative. The result is that ʿAbd al-Qādir sees no more difficulty in leaping from one historical epoch to another than he does in running together thematically connected verses from different chapters of the Qur'ān (as above).

Like generations of Muslim scholars before him (and indeed many pre-modern non-Muslim scholars, such as the European Schoolmen), ʿAbd al-Qādir's favoured form of inference is very much the analogical – called *qiyāṣ*[59] in the Islamic tradition. The result here is a weaving together of Qur'ānic verses, reported utterances of the Prophet, and a variety of historical anecdotes, on the basis of their thematic commonalities and similarity as cases. The centrality of this 'analogical' approach has been remarked on in the discussion of style above; this text itself invites its readers to draw analogies between the narratives it contains and their own contemporary political environment.

The result is that ʿAbd al-Qādir presents five historical periods scattered over more than three millennia more or less concurrently. This may appear anachronistic from the more historicist perspectives in some modern academic history writing, but results from ʿAbd al-Qādir's greater interest in case and analogy than cause and chronology. This occurs to the extent that it is sometimes not immediately clear which period is being discussed. These historical periods are the Maghreb of the early 19th century;[60] the Islamic Iberian Peninsula (*al-Andalus*) during the period now known as the *Reconquista*;[61] the time of the Prophet and *Rāshidūn*, particularly during the *hijrah* from Mecca to Medina;[62] and the time of the Israelites in the days of Moses[63] and Samuel[64] as presented in the Qur'ān. There is no sense of pluralism in ʿAbd al-Qādir's references to events

---

59 *Tuḥfah*, pp. 418, 419, 420. This term is also the traditional Arabic translation (for instance in Ibn Khaldūn) of the Greek term *syllogismos* [Wolfson, 1976, p. 7], though the *fiqh*-based sense of reasoning by analogy based on Qur'ān and Sunnah (employed here) is broader than true syllogism. *Qiyāṣ* may however be understood as stricter than the related *enthymeme* (called *qiyāṣ nāqiṣ* or 'incomplete or defective *qiyāṣ*' by al-Ghazālī, for instance – see Ward Gwynne, 2004, pp. 150–155).

60 E.g. *Tuḥfah*, p. 411.

61 E.g. *Tuḥfah*, p. 418.

62 E.g. *Tuḥfah*, pp. 411, 422.

63 E.g. *Tuḥfah*, p. 412.

64 E.g. *Tuḥfah*, p. 412; this prophet is not explicitly named.

prior to the life of Muḥammad. Like the Qur'ānic text, ʿAbd al-Qādir sees Islām not just as a historical religious formation so much as godly religiosity as such. So, for instance, pious pre-Muḥammad Jews are described as having 'held fast to the bonds of Islam'.[65] All instances, moreover, are characterised by a situation of threat to the community of believers.

In this, ʿAbd al-Qādir writes in a style more reminiscent of his predecessors' than of those often more monovocal 'modernists' and 'Islamists' who would follow him in the subsequent century. On more than one occasion, he recognises differences and ambiguities in interpretation or transmission. He does this, however, without ever questioning the inerrancy of the Qur'ān, the authority of the *ḥadīth* literature, or the example of the early caliphs (*al-rāshidūn*) and pious forbears such as the Imām Mālik. Differing phrasings of reported sayings of the Prophet are repeatedly mentioned,[66] and related to established debates in Islamic thought, and differences of legal opinion are recognised (though views dissenting from his own are relatively downplayed). In spite of the obvious political significance of this text, ʿAbd al-Qādir presents, and presumably understands, himself to be engaged not in political theorising but in traditional exegesis.

His most detailed engagement with differences of opinion occur with respect to the legal status of Muslims who remain under the rule of non-Muslims – the same topic on which he had consulted the jurists of Fez and Cairo. The first distinction is between those who actively support the non-Muslim order and those who do not. With respect to the latter, ʿAbd al-Qādir invokes the judgements of figures including Qāḍī Ibn al-Ḥājj al-Tajīnī al-Andalūsī and Imām al-Mālik to the effect that 'their wealth is to be seized, and they are to be fought against, even if they read the Qur'ān.'[67] Finally, an analogy is drawn from the Prophet's rewarding of ʿUthmān, Ṭalḥa, and Saʿīd bin Zayd for their support of the battle of Badr, despite their having held back from the actual fighting.[68]

With respect to the wives, children, and property of 'turncoat' Muslims, ʿAbd al-Qādir then presents a number of opinions. The origin of the dispute, according

---

65 *Ibid.*

66 For instance in his quoting the alternative receptions: 'him whom He gives succour through knowledge [*man ajārahu bil-ʿilm*]' or 'through His knowledge [*biʿilmihi*]', according to another reception' (*Sunan Abī Dāwūd; 35:4230, 35:4246, 35:4249*). Another example is ʿAbd al-Qādir's recognition of competing views on the abrogation of *hijrah* after the conquest of Mecca [*Tuḥfah*, p. 416], mentioned also by Abou el Fadl in his survey of Malikite reasoning on *hijrah* and ultimately rejected by ʿAbd al-Qādir on the basis of ḥadīth and a quotation from Ibn al-ʿArabī [*Tuḥfah*, pp. 413, 416].

67 *Tuḥfah*, p. 419.

68 *Tuḥfah*, p. 419–20.

to the Sufi Qāḍī Abū Bakr bin al-ʿArabī, is the question 'why is the unbeliever killed – for his unbelief, or for his fighting [against the Muslims]?'[69] ʿAbd al-Qādir informs us that where Abū Bakr bin al-ʿArabī argues for the return of wealth to the repentant, Ibn Shaʿbān argues that it retains the status of spoils.[70] In a similar vein, the views of Ibn Wahb and Ibn Baṭṭāl (via Ibn Ḥajar's commentary on the *ʿArbaʿīn*) are contrasted over views of 'the Mālikīs, and a great many of the Shāfiʿīs' with respect to the capture of apostates. Finally, the contrasting treatment of captives' families by caliphs ʿAlī Ibn Abī Ṭālib, Abū Bakr, and ʿUmar are discussed. ʿAbd al-Qādir's conclusion is somewhat ambiguous, recognising conflicting cases. There is 'no gainsaying' benevolence, he says, yet '[i]f the invasion kills the women or children of those Christianised [Muslims], those who are under the protective compact [*dhimmah*] of the Christians, then their killers should not be oppressed or [considered] sinners.'[71] The grave political relevance of this conclusion is clear.

Throughout the above, ʿAbd al-Qādir pursues arguments from religious authority[72] through analogy based on exemplary cases.[73] The fact that he is aware of, and prepared to repeat, differing or ambiguous opinions on this subject gives the impression that his requests for *fatāwa* (legal rulings) from other scholars should not necessarily be dismissed as insincere rhetorical posturing and ex-post-facto rationalisation.[74] The question of sincerity is in fact a central question put by ʿAbd al-Qādir himself in this text.

2.4 Further Themes: Sincerity and Hypocrisy

> 'God – the Most High – does not excuse dwelling under the protective compact of the unbeliever [*taḥta dhimmat al-kāfir*], except for him who is unable to escape and who cannot take to any road, such as a blind man who can find no-one to guide him or the invalid with none to bear him away. [Nonetheless] their intention is very much that of the migrant, and were they to abandon that intention, they should not behave as true believers – there are many [Qur'ānic] textual bases for this assertion.'[75]

69 *Tuḥfah*, p. 421.
70 *Ibid.*
71 *Tuḥfah*, p. 422.
72 Principally through the Qur'ān and *ḥadīth* texts, and secondarily through the Mālikī sources evident throughout this chapter.
73 Examples are given above, e.g. at *Tuḥfah*, pp. 418, 419, 420, 421.
74 The view taken, for instance, by Danziger, 1977, p. 130 – 1.
75 *Tuḥfah*, p. 415.

The major theme of this text is of course the inescapability of the obligation on all able-bodied Muslims to migrate from territory governed by non-Muslims. We are presented not only with rulings on a specific question (whether or not to migrate), however, but also with a typology of righteousness and backsliding more nuanced than a simple dichotomy of right and wrong action. This typology is based on a particular understanding of the nature of human consciousness; it is through this that ʿAbd al-Qādir more meaningfully reveals his Sufi background and its role in his moralising perspective.

While this is not a Sufi text in the sense used in textual scholarship, it is undoubtedly a text authored by a Sufi. Given the salience of ʿAbd al-Qādir's maraboutic lineage and upbringing, the paucity of appeals to Sufism here might come as a surprise – but is itself a telling feature. It does not mobilise Sufi claims to divine favour, still less that of its author, in order to convince its audience (not all of whom will have been Sufis, nor adherents to the same orders). Rather, the text is concerned with religio-legal obligation, but takes for granted the integration of Sufis within the Muslim community. Sufi groups are equally addressed by a Shariah-based rhetoric which cut across tribal, ethnic, and confraternal lines to maximise the effectiveness of ʿAbd al-Qādir's political message.

No Sufi exemptions from legal obligations are recognised. ʿAbd al-Qādir does cite noted Sufis – not as authorities in themselves but as conventional sources on jurisprudential questions. The most notable of these is Sufi and jurist Abū Ḥāmid al-Ghazālī, a continual presence throughout all of ʿAbd al-Qādir's writings, and giant of Islamic thought more broadly. His reference to al-Ghazālī's seminal formulation of the *maqāṣid al-sharīʿah* (which opens the present chapter) is a salient example, not least because it takes him as spokesman for Sufism in general while having him pronounce on a legal matter in a mainstream manner. ʿAbd al-Qādir also draws on other notable Sufi scholars, including al-Ghazālī's student[76] Qāḍī Abū Bakr Ibn al-ʿArabī[77] and al-Suyūtī.[78]

It is not only in this evocation of the right path that we are interested, however; the text condemns deviation more than it sets out to pronounce definitively on right action. ʿAbd al-Qādir attributes such deviation to a variety of moral, intellectual, and spiritual failings. The causes in least need of comment are simple timorousness or moral weakness – like the greedy and foolish or those who fear that they might starve to death should they embark on the rigours of *hijrah*. Next mentioned is the avaricious worldly man [*al-mutakālib ʿala al-dunyā*] who de-

76 Cornell, 1998, p. 46.
77 *Tuḥfah*, p. 421.
78 *Tuḥfah*, p. 414.

sires the things of this world by any means – 'be they those of Islam or of unbelief'.[79] Neither of these two types is given any lengthy treatment, and 'never will hopes or expectations of the reform to righteousness nor the salvation of either such men be raised.'[80]

A more telling discussion of error, however, comes soon after, and offers us a deeper insight into the younger ʿAbd al-Qādir's attitudes to morality and knowledge which will become critical in understanding his later life. This new distinction is presaged by the opening lines' reference to trials and dilemmas 'both evident and concealed' (*ẓāhiran* and *bāṭinan*). As well as being readable as censuring tribal leaders' secret negotiations with the French along with open connivance, these terms hint at a more spiritual significance. In this vein, ʿAbd al-Qādir enters into a second discussion of immoral behaviour, this time divided between the simply ignorant and those who have true knowledge but refuse to act upon it – and 'it is firstly through this one that the fires [of hell] are fed.'[81] This discussion both widens his condemnation to include ostensible religious authorities and sets the stage for a protracted condemnation of hypocrisy which plays a major role in his polemic and the justification of his policies.

One immoral character is the ignorant would-be *ʿālim*. He

> 'had read a few chapters of jurisprudence... [and] knows some of the rules for prayer, marriage, and trade, reckoning that he has reached an end qualifying him to be called an *ʿālim* ... He seeks guidance from [Qur'ānic' verses], traditions of the Prophet, and the words of the Imams [though] he does not excel at [the traditional linguistic and exegetical sciences of] correct reading and verbal morphology which are the premises [of such exercises]. How then might he delve into their [true] meanings?'[82]

The other immoral person is one who knows the truth with certainty, '*ʿarafa al-ḥaqq*', echoing that intimate and fully-internalised knowledge (*maʿrifat al-ḥaqq*) which is a goal of Sufi practice, but does not put its legal commands into practice. Even aside from the suggestive lexical opposition between the verbs *ʿalama* and *ʿarafa* (which is asymmetrically exclusive; both are used of the second 'knower', but only the first of the former), it is clearly Maraboutic and clerical opposition to ʿAbd al-Qādir's policies which is the target of this condemnation. Such opposition had at the time of his writing come both from the Tijāniyyah

79 *Tuḥfah*, p. 411.
80 *Ibid.*
81 *Tuḥfah*, p. 413.
82 *Tuḥfah*, p. 413.

order at 'Aīn Māḍī and from marabouts of Abd al-Qādir's own Hāshim tribe.[83] Even the most ostensibly respectable religious authorities are not to be trusted, 'Abd al-Qādir contends, if they fail to observe their legal obligation to flee the French influence under his banner. The seniority of his critics, that is, is negated by their disobedience to the political course which his presentation of the law advocates – a nomocratic argument at odds with the treatment of religious law as a tool of potentates in some historical accounts. The person who knows the truth yet does not obey its demands, he writes, is like

> 'some who were present at the time of the Prophet (peace be upon him) and who witnessed his inimitable acts [yet did not heed the message of Islam]. God the Most High said of them: '*It is not thee they reject: it is the Signs of Allah, which the wicked condemn*'.[84] This is the greatest of goings-astray and virulent obstinacy of him whom '*Allah has, knowing him (as such [one who takes as god his own vain desire]) left him astray, and sealed his hearing and his heart (and understanding), and put a cover over his sight.*''[85]

From this brief exposition of error we may infer its corollary: 'Abd al-Qādir's prescriptions for the correct functioning of knowledge. Discursive knowledge, *'ilm*, requires the authoritative sources and the linguistic and exegetical competences fostered by the *uṣūl* disciplines to avoid error in grasping God's laws. Meanwhile, fully realised knowledge of the truth, *ma'rifah al-ḥaqq*, obliges the knower to put his or her knowledge into sincere action – or face the deepest damnation [this is also a theme of 'Abd al-Qādir's later writings, from the *Miqrāḍ al-Ḥādd* to the *Kitāb al-Mawāqif*].[86] One must be well educated, that is, and one must be obedient to the strictures of the revelation, no matter how profound one's knowledge of it may be. While unproblematic from the perspective of Islamic thought in general, this is a common position for legist Sufism,[87] to be found for instance in al-Ghazālī's *fayṣal al-tafriqah bayna al-islām wa al-zindaqah*,[88] as well as in 'Abd al-Qādir's 'mystical' writings discussed below. He demands *ṣidq*, 'honestly doing the right thing for the right reasons', a goal of all devout Muslims and the

---

83 E.g. Daumas to Military Command, Oran, FR ANOM GGA1E116, 01-09-1838; see also Chapter One.
84 Qur'ān 6:33.
85 *Tuḥfah*, p. 413. Quoting Qur'ān 45:23, and paraphrasing of Qur'ān 2:7.
86 See Chapters Three to Five.
87 E.g. Karamustafa's discussion of the attitudes of *ṭarīqah* Sufis to antinomian 'dervishes' [Karamustafa, 2006, *passim*]. See also Kugle's discussion of Aḥmad Zārrūq's dictum 'be a jurist first and then a Sufi' and its wide support by Muslim governments [Kugle, 2006, pp. 61, 130] – which Zārrūq himself uses to gloss Al-Shāfi'ī.
88 Jackson (*trans.*), 2003, p. 115.

'state most directly related to the affirmation of Sufism as a normative framework for social action'.[89]

Characterisations of fractured or imperfect piety, conversely, find wider resonance in the treatise's persistent concern with those who are referred to by the antonym of *ṣidq:* 'the hypocrites' (*al-munāfiqūn*).[90] 'Roughly speaking, *nifāq* (the verbal noun form of *munāfiq*) consists in professing faith with the tongue while secretly disbelieving in the heart;'[91] the *munāfiq* is a 'hypocrite' or 'waverer'.[92] The Qur'ānic usage of this term originates with those Medinese fresh converts to Islam who had not proved their commitment through the *hijrah* from Mecca, and whose commitment to Islam vacillated. This was particularly apparent when Muḥammad suffered misfortunes or they were called upon to go to war[93] – a scenario repeatedly described by ʿAbd al-Qādir in this text and which he himself experienced while trying to marshal the tribes under his nominal sovereignty. Given our account above of the vacillations of ʿAbd al-Qādir's supporters, the political relevance of this theme is only too obvious. He accuses those who fail to support him of *nifāq*,[94] invoking the great opprobrium heaped on *al-munāfiqūn* by the Qur'ān,[95] which has sometimes led them to be considered a variety of unbeliever (*kuffār*).[96]

ʿAbd al-Qādir reminds his readers that they, the present inhabitants of Algeria, have come to refer to those Mudejar Muslims[97] who remained under Christian rule in Spain as hypocritical *munāfiqūn*. They are those 'Muslims who entered under the compact of the Christians, whom the people of Algeria called hypocrites.'[98] Not only is submission the product of hypocrisy, he goes on, but also productive of hypocrisy and ultimately apostasy.

---

89 Pinto in Heck (ed.), 2007, p. 128.

90 This term is used specifically on several occasions (e. g. *Tuḥfah*, pp. 415, 416, 420), and is a recurrent subtext.

91 Izutsu, 2002, p. 178.

92 *EI2* entry on *al-munāfiḳūn*.

93 Izutsu, 2002, pp. 180, 182–3; Qur'ān 63; *EI2, ibid.*

94 *Tuḥfah*, p. 415 quotes Qur'ān 4:138, though many other Qur'ānic passages similarly condemn *al-munāfiqūn* (for instance 4:144/145, and the 63rd *sūrah*, '*al-munāfiqūn*').

95 For instance at Qur'ān 57: 13–14, 61: 2–3, 63:1–5, 66:9.

96 Izutsu, 2002, p. 179.

97 *Tuḥfah*, p.416; *ahl al-dajn*, hence *mudajjan* hence *Mudejar* – the word can be literally translated as 'people of remaining' but carries also the connotation of domestication and servitude, and is often used in that sense of animals.

98 *Tuḥfah*, p. 416.

> 'The Nazarenes do not honour their agreements unless the word of Islam is most exalted and its power most prominent. God – the Most High – says: they will not cease in fighting against ye until they have driven ye from your religion, if they can.'[99]

These hypocrites, ʿAbd al-Qādir warms, will lose touch with their religion, forgetting the month of Ramadan, and sending their alms into the coffers of the enemies of Islam. They will be Muslims in name only; 'Those who live under the compact of the Christians will not have none of their prayers recognised – nor their fasting, nor their pilgrimage, nor their *jihād*.'[100]

So, the symbolism of sincerity and hypocrisy ties together ʿAbd al-Qādir's condemnation of the common man, the religious authority, and the Christians who seek power over them both. It does so, what is more, through repeated invocation of the Prophet's biography and of the experience of Muslims under the *Reconquista*. This approach constitutes a very powerful and resonant rhetoric, and it is not difficult to imagine why so many North Africans continued to be swayed by it even when the fortunes of war turned against ʿAbd al-Qādir – as they had already begun to do as this text was being written.

2.5 Faith, Nation, and Legitimation – The secondary literature in light of the *Risālah on Hijrah*

Throughout this discussion of the form and content of ʿAbd al-Qādir's wartime *Risālah on Hijrah*, we have noted certain general characteristics, including an 'ahistorical' Qur'ānic focus, promotion of education in *uṣūl al-dīn* and obedience to *sharīʿah* law, the use of analogical reasoning, a Sufi background, Shāfiʿī and especially Mālikī juridical influences. Perhaps the most remarkable aspect of this work, however, is simply how unremarkable it is. ʿAbd al-Qādir promotes ethics and standards which are, for his time and place, decidedly conservative. This is not to denigrate the text or its author for a lack of originality, but rather to emphasise the evidently traditional aspects of his thought and its exposition. ʿAbd al-Qādir is not obviously innovating; it is the appeal to tradition, in various forms, which lends this text its voice of authority. Given the chaotic political context of its composition, moreover, one can readily imagine the reassuring appeal of such traditionalism among his countrymen.

How can discussion of ʿAbd al-Qādir's *Risālah on Hijrah* be related to his representation in the political histories of his Algerian career? Many connections

---

99 *Tuḥfah*, p. 418, quoting Qur'ān 2:217.
100 *Tuḥfah*, p. 415.

can be drawn – some supportive of existing literature, and some opposed to it. Relevant reflections will need to touch on ʿAbd al-Qādir's relationship to Sharifianism, Maraboutism, Sufism, and to non-Muslims, particularly with regard to questions of treaty, war, and peace with Christians.

At the start, however, a more fundamental point should be made. Attempts to categorically divide political and religious aspects of ʿAbd al-Qādir's career, remarked upon above in connection with the secondary literature, are cast into doubt by texts like this. This is true for many reasons. First, the text itself recognises no such division, and lacks the conceptual resources to conceive of it, coming as it does from a different historical trajectory. Secondly, the text's content is overwhelmingly religious, yet its intent is blatantly political. It employs distinctions which cut across typical secular distinctions in both directions, however: not only is politics moralised and imbued with cosmic religious significance, but its closest equivalent of secularity is a poor match for the modern phenonomenon. When ʿAbd al-Qādir castigates 'the avaricious worldly man' [*al-mutakālib ʿala al-dunyā*] who desires the things of this world by any means – be they those of Islam or of unbelief',[101] he does not imply that this world is secular and the next divine. Rather, the corollary of his distinction is that 'the things of this world' may be pursued using either the means of unbelief *or* those of an Islam which permits and governs such pursuits. Where several writers in the secondary historical literature[102] have analysed ʿAbd al-Qādir on the basis of an opposition between practical effect and spiritual affect, pragmatism and principle, ambition and piety, this world and the next, in order to model his motivations, this passage alone demonstrates such an approach's incompatibility with ʿAbd al-Qādir's world-view. As analysis of his actions such tools may find purchase, but as insights into his character and motivation they are doomed to fail. This is not to argue that ʿAbd al-Qādir acted only on the basis of high-minded principles, still less that all points of view informing his decisions were correct.

The existing discussions of his military and political strategy note his propensity for strategic withdrawal: the abandoning of towns to the French may be taken as a case in point. Tactical reasons for this policy, subject to the demands of what we would today call asymmetric warfare, have been widely adduced in the secondary literature.[103] These are absolutely valid – and remarked upon in passing by ʿAbd al-Qādir in the *Risālah* itself.[104] What those accounts

101 *Tuḥfah*, p. 411.
102 See Chapter One.
103 E.g. Bennison, 2002, p. 138; Danziger, 1977, pp. 130, 205.
104 *Tuḥfah*, p. 415.

have not mentioned is his view, put throughout this text on the authority of major juristic luminaries, that the adequate functioning of Islamic life – from personal prayer to the administration of justice to the community's status as Muslims per se – demands freedom from non-Muslim rule. This is the central message of his exhortation to migrate from the French sphere of influence, and it was evidently one which resonated with his people.[105] There is no necessary conflict between these observations, and all must be taken seriously if we are to form a fully rounded impression of our subject; ideas, including many religious ideas, are part of the political landscape.

The ideas drawn upon by ʿAbd al-Qādir are broadly mainstream ones; the comforting (if reactionary) appeal of familiar signs and habits during times of chaos and crisis has already been noted, and evidenced throughout ʿAbd al-Qādir's *Risālah on Hijrah.* This encourages the view that ʿAbd al-Qādir's modernising efforts (such as the standing *niẓāmī* corps and limited industrialisation) represent technical rather than conceptual modernisation. His importing of organisational and technological novelties was not necessarily 'conducive to heightening his regard for western civilisation or to any desire to import any of it into his country', as Shinar points out.[106]

This should not be too surprising, given that even the great 'Moderniser'[107] Muḥammad ʿAlī, by whose Egypt the youthful ʿAbd al-Qādir was reportedly impressed,

> 'issued no new statement of principles which might be, or seem to be, in contrast with those of the Sharīʿah [... as his] innovations were mainly in the spheres of economic life and administration, about which the Sharīʿah says little, rather than the basic institutions of society or the realm of personal status, about which it says much.'[108]

The (for westerners) seductive presumption that adopting western technical innovations necessarily entails an embrace of 'western values' is, conversely, discouraged by ʿAbd al-Qādir's experience.

Julia Clancy-Smith's description of ʿAbd al-Qādir's state as 'a classical tribal-based theocracy',[109] on the other hand, might be in danger of understating the significance of such structural novelty as was intended and implemented: (how-

105 Large-scale migration from the country continued throughout the period examined by this study (e.g. Berque, 1978, pp. 411–415, 315).
106 Shinar, 1965, p. 157.
107 E.g. Gellner, 2000, p. 225.
108 Hourani, 2008, p. 83.
109 Clancy-Smith, 1997, p. 71.

ever hesitant) projects of industrialisation, centralisation, and professionalisation of military and judiciary (see above).[110] Similarly, Shinar's conclusion from ʿAbd al-Qādir's intentions that the 'state he set about to organise...[was] patterned after the Medinese *ummah* of Muḥammad and his immediate successors'[111] might understate the continuity between his state and that which preceded it,[112] not to mention the previous centuries' political experience reflected in his *Risālah on Hijrah.*

The Andalusian experience, in particular, is one which – while sometimes remarked upon in the Arabophone literature[113] – is largely unrepresented in western studies of ʿAbd al-Qādir's Algerian career. It does not come naturally to western historiographical habits to relate the falls of Grenada and of Algiers, separated as they are by some four centuries. ʿAbd al-Qādir's invoking of the spirit of lost al-Andalus is at least partly sentimental. Aside from the subjective resonance of such parallels – which itself constitutes a social reality for our subject which we cannot ignore even if we ourselves are unmoved by it – the connection between the *Reconquista* and the French colonisation of Algeria is more than symbolic. Through the marks left on Mālikite juridical reasoning by the experience of the Christian re-conquest of the Iberian peninsula, the Reconquista and its aftermath have a direct and detectable influence on ʿAbd al-Qādir's politics. The *Risālah on Hijrah* provides textual evidence of the manner in which Andalusian experiences shaped the legal frameworks through which he interpreted his circumstances, and by appeal to which he mobilised his followers.

The significance of Mālikī jurisprudence to ʿAbd al-Qādir's political worldview extends further than his opposition to the French invasion. It includes also his conception of his own sphere of influence. Far from being a nationalist in the Romantic sense, as he has often been depicted by both western and Arab writers, his *Risālah on Hijrah* goes so far as to say that those who cleave to their *terroir*, their *waṭan* (region, latterly nation)[114] in disobedience of the Divine imperative to migrate idolatrously misattribute the role of the Divine Name *al-Raz-*

---

110 It might also be noted that ʿAbd al-Qādir's contemporary Alexis de Tocqueville repeatedly observed that the ʿAbd al-Qādir's state was considerably more centralised and institutionally powerful than the Ottoman regime which preceded it [de Tocqueville, 2001, pp. 18, 39, 66, 67–68].

111 Shinar, 1965, p. 145.

112 Gellner, 1979, pp. 108–9 and Gellner, 2000, p. 224; Danziger, 1977, pp. 76–78, 185–187.

113 E.g. Bū-ʿAzīz, 1964, p. 144.

114 Shinar, 1965, p. 154: 'In Turkish administrative parlance, *waṭan* applied to a district or canton, or in most cases, to an area inhabited by a given tribe and co-extensive with it: often it would simply designate the tribe itself. Hence its frequent occurrence in the plural form, *awṭān*, when obviously referring to different tribal areas, not countries.' See also Julien, 1964, p. 5.

zāq, the Provider or Sustainer,[115] to their soil. For him, it is not land, but religious jurisdiction which is crucial – the basic position of pre-Modernist Islamic law.[116] This is also a typical Mālikite legal position. 'Most Mālikī jurists were inclined toward territoriality, but only at the theological level. Islam can exist only in territory formally ruled by Muslims.'[117] It is Muslims and non-Muslims who are to have their own distinct spheres of governance, rather than the inhabitants of particular geographic zones thought to define identity, ideally distinct enough that 'they will not see one another's [cooking] fires'.[118]

For Muslim scholars, jurists, and judges to perform their crucial function, ʿAbd al-Qādir argues, it is necessary that they be free to exercise their functions independently of coersion from outside the Islamic tradition. This might more readily be construed as a claim to 'sovereignty' than one might his more ambiguous references to *waṭan*. This view is also a long-standing Mālikī one, taken by many of the eminent jurists quoted by ʿAbd al-Qādir.[119] This argument furthermore has a historical dimension, in that the example of al-Andalus is held up as proof that Christians, as a result of their less perfect submission to the divine will, are more likely to renege on their commitments, break their promises, and overstep their limits,[120] ultimately interfering intolerably with the Muslim community they rule over. This view is also to be found in al-Wansharīsī's *Miʿyār*,[121] though ʿAbd al-Qādir does not attribute it to him. [The relative propensities of Christians and Muslims to keep their words forms the major theme of ʿAbd al-Qādir's apologetic tract the *Miqrāḍ al-Ḥādd*, as well as a constant refrain in his communication with his captors in France – see Chapter Three.]

115 *Tuḥfah*, p. 411.

116 'Furthermore, the Muslim law of nations was ordinarily binding on individuals rather than territorial groups. For Islamic law, like all ancient law, had a personal rather than a territorial character and was obligatory upon the Muslims, as individuals or as a group, regardless of the territory they resided in… It has only been in modern times, especially under the pressure of modern material civilisation and culture, that the observance of law has been attached to people in relation to the territory they live in rather than in relation to the group they belong to.' Khadduri, 1955, p. 45.

117 Abou el Fadl, 1994, p. 183.

118 *Tuḥfah*, p. 414.

119 Abou el Fadl, 1994, p. 146: 'Saḥnūn (d. 2401/854) reports that Mālik (d. 1791/796) strongly disapproved of Muslims travelling to the lands of non-believers for purposes of trade because they might become subject to the laws of unbelievers. The operative legal cause in Mālik's view is that Muslims will be forced to submit to non-Muslim law, an issue that later became a crux of legal discussions.' This view is also taken by Qāḍī Abū Bakr Ibn al-ʿArabī and Qāḍī Ibn Rushd [*op. cit.*, pp. 146, 150 – 1], both of whom are drawn on by ʿAbd al-Qādir in this treatise.

120 *Tuḥfah*, p. 418.

121 Abou el Fadl, 1994, p. 155

This recollection is also connected to ʿAbd al-Qādir's insistence on the traditional relationship between the Islamic system and its non-Muslim *dhimmī* subjects – as indeed had been practised in his own state.[122] The experience of the Andalusī Muslims is explicitly invoked in connection with the assertion that

> 'the Nazarenes do not honour their agreements unless the word of Islam is most exalted and its power most prominent. God – the Most High – says: *they will not cease in fighting against ye until they have driven ye from your religion, if they can.*[123] And He says – *How* [can there be such an agreement with unbelievers] *if they get the upper hand over you, they do not respect the bonds of kinship or covenant* [*dhimmah*],[124] for they are proud and self-important.'[125]

Non-Muslims, in short, are tolerable subjects but not acceptable rulers. This view, again with Qur'ānic endorsement, is repeated elsewhere in the *Risālah.*[126] Jews and Christians, the text reminds us after all,[127] are guilty of *taḥrīf:*[128] the alleged adulteration and alteration of God's revelation to suit their own ends.

Awareness of ʿAbd al-Qādir's conservative attitude towards the relationship between confessional communities offers an elegant resolution to a prevalent tension in the secondary literature. From his contemporaries to his most recent biographers, most have presented him as both obliging toward individual Christians while evincing 'studied insolence'[129] towards French military commanders. This is a 'contradiction' which some political historians, particularly Raphael Danziger, have interpreted as evidence of ʿAbd al-Qādir's manipulative duplicity and opportunism.[130] Yet both this interpretation and its attendant psychological inference are unjustified. The qualitative 'gap', in ʿAbd al-Qādir's terms, is not

---

122 Scott, 2010, p. 5.
123 Qur'ān 2:217.
124 Qur'ān 9:8.
125 *Tuḥfah*, p. 418.
126 For instance, at *Tuḥfah*, p. 416's quoting of Qur'ān 3:28.
127 *Tuḥfah*, p. 412, quoting the *Ṣaḥīḥ* of al-Bukhārī, Book 56, number 662.
128 *Taḥrīf* is understood as 'change, alteration, forgery; used with regard to words, and more specifically with regard to what Jews and Christians are supposed to have done to their respective Scriptures, in the sense of perverting the language through altering words from their proper meaning, changing words in form or substituting words or letters for others... Muslim authors understood the falsification as either *taḥrīf al-maʿnā*, distortion of the meaning of the text, or *taḥrīf al-naṣṣ*, falsification of the text itself' [Lazarus-Yafe, *EI2* entry on '*taḥrīf*'].
129 Blunt, 1947, p. 100.
130 Danziger, 1977, pp. 182–3; '...[T]hese expressions of a relaxed, jovial attitude toward individual Christians on private occasions, which form such a striking contrast with the rigid formality displayed by the amir toward General Bugeaud during their official meeting, illustrate the gap between the amir's personal attitudes and his public image.'

between individual Christians and Christian communities, but rather between submissive and domineering Christians. God's plan for the world, as revealed to ʿAbd al-Qādir through his mainstream Mālikite reading of Qur'ānic injunctions, includes Christians as a protected population but warns against their ruling over Muslims.

This also explains why ʿAbd al-Qādir never recognised French sovereignty – a fact which previous studies have tended to relate only to the (genuine) propaganda value of appearing powerful to his subjects, or his (arguable) reluctance to make peace. Where political historians have remarked that ʿAbd al-Qādir's treaties with France resemble those between 'sovereign states',[131] this characterisation draws on a political concept quite distinct from the religious territoriality ʿAbd al-Qādir invokes in the *Risālah*. Sovereignty is not an ahistorical universal concept with a single unavoidable significance. While the law of nations that developed in Europe after the Thirty Years' War is predicated on reciprocal recognitions of sovereignty, the same cannot be said for the Islamic juridical tradition on which ʿAbd al-Qādir has been shown to draw. ʿAbd al-Qādir's failure to recognise French sovereign equality with himself need not indicate a reluctance on ʿAbd al-Qādir's part to enter into 'genuine' treaties. Rather, it is the product of a different conception of the nature of such treaties, informed more by the *ṣulḥ* of Ḥudaybiyyah than the Treaties of Westphalia.[132]

While the *ṣulḥ* tended to be understood by Muslim jurists as being based on the ten-year moratorium Muḥammad placed on his treaty with the Meccans, this convention has not historically been observed as it can be renewed indefinitely.[133] Nowhere in ʿAbd al-Qādir's treaties is a hard time-limit set, nor does he at any point claim that lasting peace with Christian powers is impossible. As such, assertions by other historians, such as Abun-Nasr, that 'the religious character of the Amir's leadership excluded permanent co-existence'[134] are not obviously justified. Since such inferences cannot appeal to any textual evidence, they

131 E.g. Kedourie, 1980, p. 3.

132 The 1648 Peace (or Treaty, or Treaties) of Westphalia established order through a new international regime in Europe following the 30 Years and 8 Years Wars, and is conventionally seen as marking the basis for modern western conceptions of international community. The Peace [*ṣulḥ*] of Ḥudaybiyyah, concluded between Muḥammad and the Mekkan polytheists, is a conventional model for international settlement in the Islamic tradition. Khadduri's survey of the history of Islamic thought in relation to international affairs makes this comparison explicitly, distinguishing post-Westphalian international law from Islamic law by the former's foundational conception of 'legal equality among nations...a community of states enjoying full sovereign rights and equality of status' [Khadduri, 1955, pp. 43–44].

133 Khadduri, 1955, pp. 54, 134, 273.

134 Abun-Nasr, 1971, p. 214.

must rely on psycho-cultural generalisations about ʿAbd al-Qādir and the people who followed him. But these run the risk of reproducing the discredited essentialisms of 19th-century observers who wrote incessantly about the inherently warlike nature of North African 'fanatical hordes'. Specifically, this mischaracterises the nature of ʿAbd al-Qādir's commitment to *jihād* as part of his religio-political project, and exaggerates its inevitability. It is true that making war on the French was a source of political status and economic rents for ʿAbd al-Qādir (as well as being the direct cause of his quite predictable downfall, it must be noted). *Mutatis mutandis*, the same could also be said of the French army and the nobility which led it. Yet speculations about the implausibility of lasting peace with an expansionistic military empire are not to be found in political biographies of ʿAbd al-Qādir's which attribute to him an insatiable appetite for *jihād*. In neither case are such simplistic accounts of the role of questions of war and peace in political legitimation especially helpful.

The historical literature on ʿAbd al-Qādir's Algerian career has tended to represent his calls for *jihād*, perhaps more than any other of his invocations of Islamic categories, as a political tool rather than an expression of genuinely-held political beliefs. Engagement with the secondary literature here has already begun to critique this tendency. *Jihād* is not a simple or homogenous idea; western writers from ʿAbd al-Qādir's French contemporaries to some more recent are rightly castigated for perpetuating stereotypes[135] in place of disinterested description. Nor are political ideas, however simple or complex, normally adequately described through the metaphor of the tool used by the powerful agent upon the powerless and passive mass. This chapter's analysis of ʿAbd al-Qādir's *Risālah on Hijrah* demonstrates something of the degree to which he was the product of the culture in which he was psychically, intellectually, and culturally embedded. His temporary position of political power did not raise him above his fellows' plane into an abstracted realm of utility maximisation inhabited only by the crystalline rationality of *homo economicus*. Rather, socially constructed, culturally and spiritually-effective ideas and imaginaries which shape thought and define interests emerge from broader sections of society than a small leadership's deliberate cogitation – as the contemporary social sciences generally recognise.[136] Moreover, it has frequently been argued in the fields of political philosophy and economic anthropology that ideologically- and cul-

135 See for example the criticism of Raphael Danziger's work in Burke III, 1978, p. 294.

136 E.g. 'Power comes from below; that is, there is no binary and all-encompassing opposition between rulers and ruled at the root of power relations and serving as a general matrix – no such duality extending from the top down and reacting on more and more limited groups to the very depths of the social body.' Foucault, 1978, p. 94.

turally-embedded culturalist or substantivist approaches are far more appropriate to the analysis of non-Western pre-industrial settings than are the neo-classicist materialism of 'rational choice' theories.[137] Many representation of ʿAbd al-Qādir's early life in recent scholarship would benefit from such an approach.

Indeed, recognising the socially-constituted limitations on leaders' freedom to act is clearly an aim of Bennison's approach to ʿAbd al-Qādir – acknowledging a 'system whose head was perpetually on trial'.[138] In turn, her approach to the role of jihad is intended as a move away from 'the more or less passive subject "flocks" of the past'.[139] Not only is the leader's freedom to act delimited and determined by social constructs (such as a given understanding of *jihād* – part of 'a complex and contantly mutating discourse'[140] we must be wary of essentialising, Bennison reminds us), however, but so also is the leader's ability to imagine, to conceive, to choose to act. That is: not only are rulers rarely free to do as they will, as Schopenhauer might have said, but they are never free to will as they will. Recognising the significance of 'dialectics'[141] between ruler and ruled does offer a central insight into 'dynamism and reciprocity'.[142] This insight would be undermined by envisaging ideology as close to propaganda or negotiation rather than as a mutually-constitutive discourse – a warning we have already seen delivered by Talal Asad. The present chapter's analysis of the *Risālah on Hijrah* illustrates not only of the propagandistic function of the text – which is certainly one aspect of it – but also the forms culturally imposed on ʿAbd al-Qādir's thought by his community and intellectual tradition. It is rhetorical in both the Greek and the Latin senses: it is discourse aimed at understanding as well as at convincing.

It is through recognition of the content of ideology as well as its effects that the imposition of a propagandistic 'ruler-ruled' binary might be avoided – an approach increasingly urged by anthropologists of North Africa.[143] This study is therefore in full agreement with Bennison's view that ʿAbd al-Qādir's attempt at the 'creation of a new Sharīʿah-based regime and resistance to infidel encroachment were thus two sides of the same coin,'[144] but suggests this connection might usefully be taken further. One need not consider those 'sides' as

137 E.g. Plattner, 1989, p. 212; Polanyi, 2001; Bourdieu, 2005; Gudeman, 1986.
138 Bennison, 2002, p. 163.
139 Bennison, 2002, p. 164.
140 Bennison, 2011, p. 70.
141 Bennison, 2002, p. 9.
142 Bennison, 2002, p. 163.
143 This is the central plank of Munson's [1993, *passim*] critique of Clifford Geertz, for instance.
144 Bennison, 2002, p. 78.

equal, let alone see the former simply as a means toward the latter. Rather, the suggestion here is that the former – Sharīʿah as understood by ʿAbd al-Qādir and his compatriots – has significantly greater cultural, conceptual, and ideological significance. *Jihād* is a special case and subset of Sharīʿah, not an extra-legal counterpart to it. It is to be found discussed in the great *ḥadīth* collections as one chapter-heading among many.

> 'Finally, the Muslim law of nations [of which *jihād* forms an element] is not a separate body of Muslim law; it is merely an extension of the law designed to govern the relations of the Muslims with non-Muslims... [While i]n the Muslim legal theory, the divine law preceded both society and the state.'[145]

To see *Jihād* and Shariah as standing in any relation other than that of a part to a whole, then, would have struck most Muslim thinkers of ʿAbd al-Qādir's time and before as a simple category error. We must assume he would have found it similarly perplexing.

ʿAbd al-Qādir's views as evinced by his *Risālah on Hijrah* certainly encourage such a view. It does not argue for *hijrah* because *hijrah* is a good in itself – on the contrary, he assumes that it will occasion hardship, while refusal to migrate might provide greater material wealth. Rather, he insists that the pious must migrate because it is enjoined by God as part of an overall plan for humanity which is itself good [ʿAbd al-Qādir explicitly makes the same argument in relation to warfare in a chapter of his *Kitāb al-Mawāqif* which has since been misrepresented as pacifistic; see Chapter Five.] His world-view, centred as it was on the Qur'ānic revelation as interpreted by Mālikī jurisprudence and Qādirī Sufism, could not have helped but measure the rightness or wrongness of a policy by its congruence with the divine law as he understood it. The fact that his casuistic approach to moral reasoning might meet with disfavour in the western world[146] di-

---

145 Khadduri, 1955, pp. 46, 23.

146 Casuistic forms of moral reasoning are not entirely without their secular defenders [e.g. Jonsen and Toulmin, 1989], though the popular disrepute into which they were first brought by Pascal's *Provincial Letters* has been the general rule. This not least in Oriental Studies, where casuistry has often been blamed for a perceived decline in later Islamic thought [e.g. Goldziher, 1981, pp. 44, 53]. Such scepticism is also to be found in Islamic Modernism, at least since Muḥammad ʿAbduh, many of whose proponents identified casuistry with what they see as the *jumūd*, the ossification or freezing up of an Islamic tradition which should be flexible and dynamic. For additional discussion of the place of casuistry in Islamic law and moral thought, as well as its under-representation in western research, see for instance Johansen, 1995.

minishes neither its meaningfulness to him and his peers, nor obviates the scrupulous historian's obligation to recognise and understand its contents.

This note of caution applies similarly with respect to the significance of ʿAbd al-Qādir's 'marabout' status. While sometimes exalted as pious 'friends' or 'confederates' of God (*awliyāʾ allah*),[147] even the most venerated Sufis are not considered lawgivers in the true sense – hence also their presence in the legal discussion above in their capacities as juridical interpreters rather than sources of law. ʿAbd al-Qādir himself argues this point explicitly in the course of a discussion in his later *Kitāb al-Mawāqif* on the distinction between 'saintly'[148] and legislative prophecy (*nubūwwah ʿāmmah* and *nubūwwah khāṣah* or *tashrīʿīah*),[149] congruent with the views of the likes of Ibn al-ʿArabī[150] and al-Jīlī[151] (to whose conception of the 'perfect man' ʿAbd al-Qādir evidently subscribes). While a Sufi 'saint' may gain the most perfect understanding of the nature of God and the world, he must obey and embody rather than make or change the Law.[152] In this context we might again recall from the *Risālah on Hijrah* ʿAbd al-Qādir's damning of those 'knowers of the truth' who fail to observe the Law scrupulously and by whom 'the fires of hell are fed', as well as the typical anti-(and intra-)Sufi polemical charge of *bidʿah* [innovation], against which countless historical Sufis have argued.

Transmitting God's law to creation (as opposed to understanding, applying, or symbolically embodying it) remains the inviolable prerogative of the prophets culminating in Muḥammad. In terms of 'legitimation', then, such roles as *sharīf* and marabout function as conduits for or magnifiers of other legitimating factors in their social reality. They rely on a range of social and symbolic networks without which they are only words. In the text here, the proud *sharīf* and marabout

---

147 A term taken from Qur'ān, 10:62: *inna awliyāʾ allah lā khawfa ʿalayhim wa lā humma yaḥzanūn* ('Behold! verily on the friends of Allah there is no fear, nor shall they grieve'). The term is often translated into English as 'saint'.

148 As throughout this study, the word saint is applied following common convention. The Christian conception of sainthood is nonetheless diguishable from Muslim concepts such as *walī* (as here) – not least by the Islamic possibility of 'living sainthood' in the absence of miracles (whereas Catholic beatification occurs only posthumously, and requires the presence of miracles). This debate will not be entered into by the present study.

149 'General Prophecy' and 'Specific or Legislative Prophecy'. *Mawqif* #255 [*Kitāb al-Mawāqif*, vol. 2, pp. 769–711] is explicitly concerned with this question, using the Qur'ānic figures of Moses and al-Khiḍr as exemplars of prophetic and 'saintly' varieties, respectively. [See also Chapter 4].

150 For a discussion of these terms in Ibn ʿArabī see Al-Ḥakīm, 1981, pp. 1039–1047.

151 Nicholson, 2003, p. 141.

152 *Kitāb al-Mawāqif*, vol. 2, p. 711.

ʿAbd al-Qādir makes no legal arguments on the basis of the authority conferred by this status. This seems significant: a position congruent with the quantitative studies of Vincent Cornell establishing the indispensible '*sine qua non*' role of socially-understood orthopraxy in North African 'living sainthood'[153] – notwithstanding debates about the advent of so-called 'Neo-Sufism' in the 18th and 19th centuries.[154] These views distinguish themselves from the more Weberian assertions in Bennison and elsewhere that such 'charismatic' figures' authority flowed more simply from their personal spiritual powers, genealogical *barakah*, and martial success[155] (though, especially on a psychological level, they are not mutually exclusive).

While ʿAbd al-Qādir's sharifian and maraboutic aspects are clearly significant to his status and identity, neither is discrete or foundational. 'It is clear from recent anthropological studies on Morocco that the "maraboutic phenomenon" was by no means a uniform one, in which all cases fit nicely into one clearly defined concept.'[156] 'Maraboutism is in perpetual creation.'[157] Like 'sharifianism', 'Maraboutism' is after all 'a western term',[158] encompassing a range of social phenomena whose practitioners did not identify by either substantive. Both are embedded in and ultimately owe their meaningfulness to broader systems of value, meaning, and signification. This is in fact an argument implicitly demonstrated by ʿAbd al-Qādir himself in the course of the *Risālah on Hijrah:* he employs his (sharīf, marabout) status to argue from law and morality, rather than using his status in itself as the 'instrument of domination'[159] expected by Danziger. This subordination of privileged status to ethico-religious criteria was also explicitly stated by ʿAbd al-Qādir as he first accepted the allegiance of the Algerian tribes: he would 'cut his own brother's throat', he claimed, if the Shariah demanded it.[160] We must be wary of under-interpreting the *barakah* of sharīf and marabout by 'reducing it to one of its social (and political) correlates, the fact that specific individuals are believed to possess it.'[161] The symbolic and conceptual place of divine law in both ʿAbd al-Qādir's writing and in the or-

153 Cornell, 1998, p. 94.
154 See for instance O'Fahey, 1990 and O'Fahey and Radke, 1993.
155 Bennison, 2002, p. 5.
156 Christelow, 1980, p. 139.
157 Julien, 1964, p. 15.
158 Munson, 1993, p. 2.
159 Danziger, 1977, p. 196.
160 Daumas to Military Command, Oran, *FR ANOM GGA1E116*, 03-09-1838; Bellemare, 1863, p. 37; Clayton, p. 50; Blunt, 1947, p. 35; King, 1997, p.73.
161 Munson, 1993, p. 6.

ganisation of his state is both institutionally and ideologically foundational. In ʿAbd al-Qādir's thought, as in so much of the Islamic tradition, 'law and religion form a unity.'[162]

It is to this divine law, however rightly or wrongly, formally or informally conceived, that the roles of marabout and sharīf are inevitably related – both as expressions of virtue (naturally seen as *sharʿī*) and as social realities; 'to be a *sayyid* was not necessarily to be a legal specialist oneself, but it was, so to speak, to have a lawyer in the family.'[163] Analyses of ʿAbd al-Qādir or his state which take either sharifianism or maraboutism as foundational and abstracted conceptual constructs or discrete political factors are unhelpfully reductive, unduly privileging the perspective of the (western) academic observer.

Alternative approaches, such for instance as that offered by Michael Freeden's morphological approach to political ideology,[164] might more effectively recognise the contextual and interpellated character of these concepts. It also permits us to see their connections to other ideas as not diminishing but rather expanding and explaining their own ideological significance. Relating such phenomena to other social imaginaries has the advantage both of better reflecting their meaningfulness to our subjects and also of generating political insights. In the *Risālah on Hijrah*, ʿAbd al-Qādir attempts to draw on a maximal reservoir of legitimacy and meaning neither within nor interstitial to the tribal subdivisions of his country, but cutting across all of these. It does so for precisely the same reason he has recourse to it *in extremis:* it is an elevated discourse, embodying as well as demanding recognition of its own gravitas, but also one with deep roots in the lived experience of its audience. It is therefore both for reasons of conviction and of practicality that he naturally addresses his countrymen through the language of Islamic law. He had already insisted to Bugeaud that 'the Arabs will respect only the authority of Islamic law, and whosoever tells you otherwise is lying to you.'[165] That authoritative discourse, in turn, provides rich material for scholarly analysis.

Recognising the symbolic and ideological significance of categories like 'sharīf' and 'marabout' without reductively rendering them discrete or foundational has the additional merit of obviating the need to deal with other quandaries currently found in the secondary literature. One instance is Raphael Danziger's questioning of the 'maraboutic' character of ʿAbd al-Qādir's state on the basis that, while it empowered more marabouts than the previous Ottoman

162 Khadduri, 1955, p. 59.
163 Christelow, 1980, p. 143.
164 Freeden, 1998, *passim.*
165 ʿAbd al-Qādir to Bugeaud, FR ANOM GGA1E113, 29-09-1837.

and subsequent French regimes, it was not limited to marabouts.[166] This seems founded on the view that the label 'marabout' is a source rather than an expression of legitimacy, whose binary character can be either present or absent. Every failure to promote a marabout thus seems a betrayal of 'maraboutism'. If 'marabout' status is understood as one expression rather of legitimacy or social capital rather than as uniquely constitutive of it, of course, then this apparent quandary need not arise in the first place. It did not seem to do so for ʿAbd al-Qādir or his countrymen.

Another case might relate to the disjuncture between Danziger's downplaying of the significance of the Qādirī *ṭarīqah* to ʿAbd al-Qādir's state (since it was not employed as 'an instrument of domination'),[167] and Bennison's converse assertion that ʿAbd al-Qādir aspired in fact to fuse state and *ṭarīqah*,[168] 'plac[ing] the discourse of Islamic revival... at the service of the state'.[169] The contrast between their accounts might rather be explained by the differing degrees to which these authors arrogate broader forms of religio-political legitimation to certain (Sufi) practices which embody them, than by any inherent contradictoriness or mysteriousness in the role of the Qādiriyyah in particular or (maraboutic) Sufism in general.

The minimal role of Sufism in the *Risālah on Hijrah* suggests its intertwining and interpellation with its surrounding cultural, moral, and theological traditions. There is no sense that Sufism is a competitor or substitute for the Qur'ānic ethics understood to be embodied in Islamic law. In spite of a scattering of references to 'the people of states', and typically Sufi concerns with levels and degrees of understanding, certainty, and sincerity, the text does not invoke Sufism – still less Qādirism in competition with other *ṭuruq* – as a source of authority. Similarly, the symbols of ʿAbd al-Qādir's state, while employed in pursuit of a certain understanding of legal and historical precedent, are adorned with Sufi and pietistic overtones. The loaded term *muḥammadī*[170] (which would be central to his

166 E.g. Danziger, 1977, pp. 77, 195.
167 Danziger, 1977, p. 196.
168 Bennison, 2002, p. 78.
169 Bennison, 2002, p. 161.
170 Potentially interpreted as a synonym for 'Islamic' (an adjective which has enjoyed differing degrees of use), this term has many more specific connotations. These range from the post-Jīlī Sufi metaphysics of the 'Muhammedan Reality' (*ḥaqīqah muḥammadiyyah*) to the *ṭarīqah muḥammadiyyah* which gave the title to an eponymous Ottoman pietistic work and which the local Tijāniyyah attempted to claim for itself [Abun-Nasr, 2007, p. 132]. 'Gran describes the *ṭarīqah muḥammadiyyah* as the ideological superstructure for deep-rooted economic changes, but his interpretation is, alas, vitiated by the absence of any sources which support this view... In contrast with Gran's totally unsubstantiated assertions... in 18th and 19th century Suf-

Damascene *Kitāb al-Mawāqif*),[171] for instance, was applied to 'Abd al-Qādir's army,[172] his banner,[173] and his currency.[174] This was part of a gamut of more or less 'popular' or 'intellectual' Sufi symbols. Hands of Fatima[175] were used as symbolic embellishment alongside Qur'ānic verses typically chosen by Sufis (including 'Abd al-Qādir)[176] hoping to demonstrate their equivocal views on the basic ontological status of man: 'you did not throw when you threw, but [God] threw' was the fatalistic motto of 'Abd al-Qādir's artillery corps.[177] Once more, however, relationship appears to have been one of part to whole, not the opposition of discrete alternative religious expressions. This does not mean, however, that the role of Sufism in his rule was a purely harmonious one.

Though there were no forced conversions and no 'Sufi brigades', most of 'Abd al-Qādir's subjects would have had some connection or other to a major local *ṭarīqah*, such as the Qādiriyyah or Raḥmāniyyah. Intra-*ṭariqah* violence did occasionally embarrass 'Abd al-Qādir,[178] as did his protracted inter-*ṭarīqah* conflict with the Tijāniyyah. While perhaps not an 'instrument for domination', as Danziger points out, it is clear that Sufism played a significant role in 'Abd al-Qādir's state. Bennison's more nuanced approach, on the other hand, may be in danger of overstating its case by privileging a certain form of political analysis at the expense of other approaches which might be more attuned to the task at hand precisely because of the sorts of facts alluded to by Danziger.

Given these accounts of what 'Abd al-Qādir believed he defended, we may ask against what he felt he defended it, and what light the *Risālah on Hijrah* throws on the question? This question, too, arises from developments in the secondary literature. While 'Abd al-Qādir's conflict with France has recently been anachronistically depicted in the secondary literature as a battle against en-

---

ism, *ṭarīqah muḥammadiyyah* meant, not one or more specific brotherhoods, but a mystical way, a mystical discipline, in order to come into direct contact with the Prophet' [Radtke, 1992, p. 73].

171 This will be seen in Chapter Five.

172 *Al-Jaysh al-Muḥammadī* – *Tuḥfah*, p. 199.

173 *Al-Rāyah al-Muḥammadiyyah* – *Tuḥfah*, p. 201.

174 'The larger coin was called a *muḥammadiyyah*' [Martin, 1976, p. 59]; Shinar [1965, pp. 146–7].

175 *Tuḥfah*, p. 195.

176 'Abd al-Qādir quotes this verse in its ontologically equivocal Sufi sense during the initial chapter of the *Kitāb al-Mawāqif.*

177 Qur'ān 8:17; Shinar [1965, p. 146] remarks on this fact, though he does not mention its significance in Sufi thought. By contrast, Penot [2008, p. 47] for example, remarks on its significance to 'Abd al-Qādir's ideas on Sufism, but does not mention his applying it also to his artillery corps.

178 E.g. Clancy-Smith, 1997, p. 79; Shinar, 1965, p. 148; *Tuḥfah*, pp. 185–188.

croaching French secularism,[179] this text offers no such suggestion. There is no hint here that ʿAbd al-Qādir was even aware of developing European concepts such as laïcism or the religiously neutral secular state. It must be remembered that it would be another half-century before those concepts enjoyed wide currency in Europe itself. Whenever he refers to the French, on the contrary, it is in moral or religious terms.

One might certainly assume that ʿAbd al-Qādir's theocratic political inclination would have led him to oppose secularism in the modern sense,[180] were he thoroughly conversant with the notion. Historically, however, the development of European secularism has been seen as the main factor in undermining precisely the traditional Islamic arguments in favour of *hijrah* from non-Muslim territory that he expounded in the *Risālah on Hijrah.*[181] Were ʿAbd al-Qādir to experience the freedom of religion offered by a modern secular state of the 21st century, it might be anticipated that he might see no more need for the arguments brought in that text than do the millions of Muslims currently happily at home in Europe and North America. Such speculation, however, is not the purpose of this study. His attitudes toward 'the religions' will nevertheless be returned to once more in this book's closing chapters.

For the time being, we can observe that the analysis of ʿAbd al-Qādir's *Risālah on Hijrah* has revealed his intellectual background, his deliberative toolset, and the methods he chose to convince others of the rightness of his decisions. Moreover, its central political theme is also significant beyond the immediate circumstances of its writing. ʿAbd al-Qādir's conservative attitude to the obligation of Muslims to live in Muslim-ruled communities, governed by Islamic law and imbued with Islamic morality, had been a theme since first he came to power. In 1834 he had written to Desmichels that '[French] protectors and [Muslim] protected are all my enemies, and all those in the province of Oran who live under you are bad believers who are ignorant of their duty.'[182] This attitude persisted during his North African rule, and buttressed his political authority, and where conviction and material interest coincide they are often difficult to disentangle. The subsequent decades of ʿAbd al-Qādir's life, however, would demonstrate that both were indeed present. Coming chapters will demonstrate his con-

---

179 For instance in Heck (ed.), 2007, pp. 12–13.

180 That is, the systematic separation of religious insitutions from political institutions; state endorsement of religious neutrality; religious disavowal of political involvement; the development of non-religious discources of public reason and so on [see for instance, Taylor, 2007, *passim*].

181 Waardenburg, 2003, p. 265.

182 Bellemare, 1863, p. 62.

tinued adherence to the principle that Muslims should live under Muslim rule, even when it prevented him from making more materially attractive choices. This in turn makes clear that personal power-maximisation was not his only motivation for holding such views in Algeria, if it was a motivation at all. It also elucidates an aspect of his relationship with France to which past studies have failed to draw enough attention. This failure, it will be argued, is intimately related to the perpetuation of 'Road to Damascus' narratives surrounding ʿAbd al-Qādir's life.

In the next chapter, the thread of ʿAbd al-Qādir's biography will be taken up once more where the last chapter left it: with his 'surrender' to the armies of France. It will track his time in captivity until his release by Louis Napoleon. During those years, ʿAbd al-Qādir would find himself faced with a very similar quandary to that addressed by his *Risālah on Hijrah*. His convictions, in this and in other regards, would be put to a new and difficult test. Where previous studies have seen the coming period as one of disjuncture and transformation, the basis provided by our reading of ʿAbd al-Qādir's wartime writing will illuminate the continuity of his convictions as he travelled his own road toward Damascus.

3.0 Chapter Three – Exile and Imprisonment on the Road to Damascus; 1848–1852

From his earliest contacts with the French, ʿAbd al-Qādir had insisted that it was a violation of religious obligation for a Muslim to live under Christian rule.[1] In the midst of his campaign against the French conquest, he had presented his *Risālah on Hijrah* as part of a campaign to encourage Muslims to abandon French territory, while damning those who failed to do so. His arguments would take on a new significance half a decade later still with his surrender to the armies of France. Having been forced to abandon his holy war against the French conquest of Algeria and in danger for his life in Morocco, he chose migration. Where before he had abandoned towns and cities to the insuperable powers of the French army, he would now quit the Maghreb as a whole. The result of his choice, however, would deliver him into French hands, where he would be tested in his determination to practise what he had preached for over a decade. The degree to which he did so, for its part, will become crucial to the framing of his broader biography – particularly those 'Road to Damascus' narratives which see ʿAbd al-Qādir as undergoing a momentous change at this time.

The terms of his 'surrender' to the French, like those of some of his less prestigious followers before him,[2] were an immediate cessation of hostilities in return for a guarantee of safe passage from the disputed area. Abandoning the lands of Algeria to the French after fifteen years of political and military resistance, ʿAbd al-Qādir requested passage to Alexandria and beyond to the Levant and Hejaz. While these terms were accepted by Lamoricière and the Duc d'Aumale in the name of King Louis Philippe, France would take several eventful years to honour its side of the bargain.

In the interim, ʿAbd al-Qādir and about one hundred of his family and followers would be tested repeatedly in their determination to migrate eastward. The years of communal captivity in the forts and chateaux of Pau, Toulon, and Amboise would challenge the small community he still led, as would French attempts at settling them permanently in France. Those years would also present opportunities – both for ʿAbd al-Qādir himself and for the French who imprisoned him. The denouement to this period of captivity would result both in a markedly changed relationship between ʿAbd al-Qādir and the French throne,

1 As ʿAbd al-Qādir wrote to Desmichels in 1834 [e.g. Bellemare, 1863, p. 62].
2 E.g. Bellemare, 1863, pp. 315, 319.

DOI 10.1515/9783110499513-005

and in the genesis of a mythologised narrative of his conversion to and endorsement of French culture more broadly.

3.1 Imprisonment

As ʿAbd al-Qādir and his companions prepared to board the French vessel which would take them into captivity, all expected to find themselves delivered to the east. Writing on the eve of his embarkation, he reiterated to his brothers the encouraging exhortations expounded in his wartime text on migration. 'God's Earth is vast', he reminds them again in Qur'ānic terms, exhorting them 'not to be restrained by their love of their lands' nor to make other excuses for avoiding the obligation to *hijrah.*[3] 'Wheresoever he may turn', the Sufi ʿAbd al-Qādir reminds those closest to him, 'he sees the face of God.'[4] The evidence of his companions' letters[5] show that the group expected to be delivered to Alexandria, even as the days of their detention in southern France grew into weeks – but all must have suspected the truth. A country caught up in the turmoil of 1848's 'Year of Revolution'[6] had more pressing business; the Algerians were to be detained indefinitely.

ʿAbd al-Qādir's attitude to this increasingly apparent development remained consistent throughout his entire imprisonment. He maintained that he had not surrendered outright to France, still less 'place[d] myself, my women, and children, in your hands to be delivered into your shadow.'[7] Rather, he had received a guarantee (*amān*)[8] of free passage toward the Levant. The archival material makes clear that again and again, he 'insisted in the most energetic terms that he was the victim of a betrayal.'[9] Incensed by this mendacity, he spurned his captors' initial attempts at paying him honours, refusing to acknowledge 'even a single word of French'.[10]

To make matters worse, on their arrival in France, ʿAbd al-Qādir's sizeable group was divided into two contingents of about three dozen each, held sepa-

3 ʿAbd al-Qādir to various, FR ANOM GGA1E217, 08-01-1848, *cf. Tuḥfah*, pp. 411, 414.
4 ʿAbd al-Qādir to Bou Hamedi, FR ANOM GGA1E217, 08-01-1848, quoting Qur'ān 2:115.
5 E. g. El-Barki to various and Aga Muḥammad to various, FR ANOM GGA1E218,—02–1848.
6 1848 saw a variety of revolutions take place in many European states, including France.
7 ʿAbd al-Qādir to Governor General of Algeria, FR ANOM GGA1E218, 11-02-1848.
8 *Ibid.*; and ʿAbd al-Qādir to Louis Philippe, FR ANOM GGA1E219,—01–1848; ʿAbd al-Qādir to the Minister of War, FR ANOM GGA1E219, 11-01-1848.
9 L'Heureux to the Ministry of War, FR ANOM GGA1E219, 29-03-1848.
10 L'Heureux to the Ministry of War, FR ANOM GGA1E219, 09-01-1848.

rately at the Forts Lamalgue and Malbousquet. He protested this separation, while commending 'patience and resignation to the will of God' to his companions.[11] While the decision to divide the Algerians was swiftly reversed,[12] other sorrows were soon to inflict themselves upon the captives. An infant died[13] soon after their arrival, while a former Aga of 'Abd al-Qādir's infantry asphyxiated through having used too many braziers in an enclosed room.[14] The latter misfortune particularly affected 'Abd al-Qādir, greatly preoccupying him during the tours of Toulon and its naval yards organised for him by his handlers l'Heureux and Daumas.[15]

In a letter to Lamoricière, reminding the latter of his obligation to live up to his agreement to permit the Algerians passage to the Muslim east, 'Abd al-Qādir asserted that even death would be preferable to his current predicament.[16] He would even warn of the potential for suicides among his group should their detention be prolonged, in spite of the fact that it is 'a great sin in his religion'.[17] Poetic hyperbole is a salient feature of his official correspondence, and characteristic of the idioms of power and politesse upon which he draws; in the event no suicide attempts would take place. Nevertheless, these dire warnings demand recognition both of the great unease among 'Abd al-Qādir's group, and of his patriarchal concern for their wellbeing.

His role as leader and inspiration for his followers certainly continued during their captivity. In addition to settling disputes and arranging affairs (including marriages)[18] among them, he gave classes on *ḥadīth* and Mālikī jurisprudence to his fellow Algerian captives.[19] He also produced both a body of poetry and a short polemical text. The prose *al-Miqrāḍ al-Ḥādd*, was a brief 'apologetic essay'[20] defending Islamic ethics – hence its title: 'the sharp scissors for cutting the tongue of those who would defame Islam with falsehood and faithlessness'. The text's prologue concerns the reasonable character of Islam, and most is incorporated into his later and more significant *Dhikrā al-'Āqil*,

11 L'Heureux to the Ministry of War, FR ANOM GGA1E219, 14-01-1848.
12 L'Heureux to the Ministry of War, FR ANOM GGA1E219, 19-01-1848.
13 *Ibid.*
14 L'Heureux to the Ministry of War, FR ANOM GGA1E219, 07-02-1848.
15 L'Heureux writes to the Ministry of War, FR ANOM GGA1E219, 20-02-1848.
16 'Abd al-Qādir to Lamoricière, FR ANOM GGA1E219, 17-03-1848.
17 Daumas to the Ministry of War, FR ANOM GGA1E219, 29-03-1848.
18 L'Heureux to the Ministry of War, FR ANOM GGA1E219, 19-01-1848.
19 'Abd al-Qādir's lessons focused on the *Ṣughrā* of al-Sanūsī, the *Risālah* of Ibn Abī Zayd al-Qayrawānī on Mālikī *fiqh*, the Ṣaḥīḥ of al-Bukhārī, and the *Shifā'* of Imām 'Ayyāḍ [*Tuḥfah*, pp. 529–530].
20 Shinar, 1965, p. 151.

which will be explored more deeply in coming chapters. In it, ʿAbd al-Qādir defends his religion from Christian proselytisers' claims that it was morally retrograde, 'not forbid[ding] or consider[ing] wrong deception and breaking treaties'.[21] In effect, he defends Muslims from the charges his *Risālah on Hijrah* had previously brought against his French Christian opponents.[22] In doing so, he challenges the dangerous implication that alleged Muslim infidelity might invalidate agreements made with Muslims – such as that reached with his own group. As such, this text can also be understood on multiple and inter-related theological, moral, and political levels. His parlous position will doubtless also have motivated him to defend the honour and boost the morale of his followers. ʿAbd al-Qādir felt obliged to speak for his people, and called his readers to piety and truth to one's word: both as an exhortation to his captors and as an encouragement to the community of followers for whom he was responsible.

Though 'he appears calm and resigned,' Daumas observed, and 'in spite of his immense facility for dissimulation, he could not hide his anxiety.'[23] That anxiety remained centred on achieving his group's release, and all of ʿAbd al-Qādir's words and actions during his years in France must be understood as oriented toward that goal. He fashioned his existence into 'a sort of permanent protest against his detention'.[24] His means for achieving his goal of freedom were few, however. Aside from reminding the French authorities of their own duty, he had nothing of value to offer them other than to re-iterate his abandonment of North Africa as a field of action, forswearing all future hostility toward France.

Rather than appearing as a final concession or change of heart, as it has overwhelmingly been depicted since, this assurance was made immediately. It did not appear as a result of the years he would spend in France – neither through awe, nor enlightenment, nor acculturation, nor even gratitude to his eventual liberator. The archives show that this concession was made consistently, both by ʿAbd al-Qādir and by his companions, from the very first days of their imprisonment[25] – often accompanied by emollient flattery of the French king and

---

21 Commins, 1988, p. 122.

22 'The Nazarenes do not honour their agreements unless the word of Islam is most exalted and its power most prominent. How? God – the Most High – says: *nor will they cease fighting you until they turn you back from your faith if they can.* [Qur'ān 2:217] And He says – *how (can there be such a league), seeing that if they get an advantage over you, they respect not in you the ties either of kinship or of covenant* [*dhimma*]?, [Qur'ān 9:8] for they are proud and self-important." *Tuḥfah*, p. 418.

23 Daumas to the Ministry of War, FR ANOM GGA1E219, 23-01-1848.

24 Bellemare, 1863, p. 379.

25 ʿAbd al-Qādir to Louis Philippe, FR ANOM GGA1E219, 21-01-1848; L'Heureux to the Ministry of War, FR ANOM GGA1E219, 11-02-1848.

government. When the French governments changed during the turbulence of 1848, ʿAbd al-Qādir immediately renewed his offer, declaring his further troubling of French interests 'impossible', and claiming to desire only a peaceful and pious life of quiet study in the Muslim east.[26] In a letter signed by himself and seventeen of his companions, mere weeks into their long captivity, the Algerians swore 'by Muḥammad, Abraham, Moses, and Jesus; by the Torah, the Gospels, the Zabour,[27] and the Qur'ān; by [*ḥadīth* collectors] Bukhārī and Muslim'[28] to renounce any future interference in French affairs if they were released.[29]

Under the circumstances, it is difficult to imagine what other option was open to ʿAbd al-Qādir and his companions if they were to hold out any hope of a return to their people. They were, in a sense, simply extending the terms of the agreement of safe passage out of the Maghreb which he had reached with Lamoricière: an end to warfare in exchange for passage beyond French territory. It is similarly difficult to imagine less pacific assurances being acceptable to any French government which might contemplate their release. The obviousness and necessity of these gestures will not have lent them credibility, still less so when accompanied by the evident insincerity of ʿAbd al-Qādir's flattery for figures such as the 'Sultan of Sultans'[30] Louis Philippe, for whom ʿAbd al-Qādir harboured considerable contempt,[31] and a Republican revolution he did not obviously understand,[32] and would ultimately cast the only vote of his life... against.[33]

Official suspicion over his designs on French power and possessions would persist throughout his imprisonment, and indeed throughout the remainder of

---

26 ʿAbd al-Qādir to the French Provisional Government, FR ANOM GGA1E219, 15-03-1848.

27 A revelation mentioned in the Qur'ān alongside those enumerated by ʿAbd al-Qādir here, which is sometimes taken to refer to the Book of Psalms.

28 It is worth noting that this litany does not represent, as it has sometimes been taken to do, a religiously pluralist gesture. Rather, it is a list of major revelations, prophets, and hadith scholars from a Sunni Muslim perspective – hence also the inclusion of the *Zabour* (see preceeding footnote).

29 ʿAbd al-Qādir et al. to the French Provisional Government, FR ANOM GGA1E219, 15-03-1848.

30 ʿAbd al-Qādir to Louis Philippe, FR ANOM GGA1E219, 21-01-1848.

31 The Ottoman Sultan would remark after meeting ʿAbd al-Qādir in 1853 that he had never heard anyone speak so negatively about another as ʿAbd al-Qādir about Louis Philippe [Lane to the Foreign Office, FO 195/385, 11-01-1853].

32 ʿAbd al-Qādir's letter to the French Provisional Government [FR ANOM GGA1E219, 15-03-1848] opens with very vague praise for equality, brotherhood, and the protection of the weak (as applicable to the Code of Hammurabi as to the Second Republic's political philosophies) before returning to the themes of his unjust imprisonment, which the 'wise *ʿulemā*'' [*ibid.*] of the new government should end.

33 During the plebiscite on Empire [Extract from *Le Mubacher*, FR ANOM GGA1E235, 01-12-1852].

his life. At this point, however, he evinced no aspiration greater than to return to Muslim lands in peace. He would 'throw without regret all the treasures of the Christian countries into the blue sea' if only to be permitted to leave for the Hejaz, he told Daumas.[34] There is reason to believe him – for in spite of the Algerians' fear of separation from their families, communities, and coreligionists, the French also expended some effort in wooing the captive amīr.

3.2 Trial and Tribulation

ʿAbd al-Qādir's companions in their French captivity record the pomp with which they were received in Toulon. Cannons were fired in the 'very beautiful'[35] town to mark their arrival, where the authorities and local notables received them 'with benevolence and generosity',[36] including gifts and Arab clothes procured for them from Morocco. In spite of his uncommunicativeness, ʿAbd al-Qādir was instantly of great interest to local society.[37] France also exerted efforts, partly motivated by security concerns and partly by benevolence, to gather his relatives in North Africa (with Léon Roches, whom ʿAbd al-Qādir knew as Omar,[38] assigned as mediator with Morocco).[39] Much of his remaining capital in North Africa, including livestock and books,[40] were either transferred to him or sold, with the proceeds being held in trust for him until his release.[41] The series of chateaux in which the Algerians were housed, meanwhile, were relatively gilded cages: certainly cages, but nevertheless more agreeable prisons (in which the occupants were afforded a greater luxury, freedom, and consideration) than less esteemed captives might have expected. ʿAbd al-Qādir's captivity was not a purely vindictive action, and so the carrot was employed as well as the stick.

Long before the prospect of release back into the Muslim world would become realistic, ʿAbd al-Qādir was repeatedly[42] approached with the option of settling, instead, in France – and in great comfort. He would be given a sizeable

34 Daumas to the Ministry of War, FR ANOM GGA1E219, 21-01-1848.
35 Abdallah al-Barka bin Muḥammad to several, FR ANOM GGA1E218,—02–1848.
36 Aga Muḥammad to several, FR ANOM GGA1E218,—02–1848.
37 L'Heureux to the Ministry of War, FR ANOM GGA1E219, 14-01-1848.
38 ʿAbd al-Qādir persisted in this, and in professing amity, even after Roches' being exposed [ʿAbd al-Qādir to Roches, Correspondance Politique/Maroc/17, 04-11-1846].
39 D'Aumale to the Ministry of War, FR ANOM GGA1E218, 23-01-1848.
40 E.g. Ministry of War catalogue to D'Aumale, FR ANOM GGA1E218, 21-02-1848; L'Heureux to the Ministry of War, FR ANOM GGA1E219, 17-03-1848.
41 E.g. L'Heureux to the Ministry of War, FR ANOM GGA1E219, 21-04-1848.
42 Bellemare, 1863, p. 374.

estate, comprising 'all that he might need', including cultivable land, hunting grounds, baths, and a mosque.[43] When presented with a choice between this salubrious prospect and continued imprisonment, albeit in Egypt, ʿAbd al-Qādir immediately opted for the latter.[44] He chose Egyptian discomfort over French opulence, Muslim captivity over Christian freedom, that is. The offer was of course intended to induce ʿAbd al-Qādir to stay in France and away from mischief; no resultant transfer to Egypt was to take place. His response is telling, however: both in rejecting the French offer, and moreover in the justification he gives for doing so. Repeating an assertion made in his wartime *Risālah on Hijrah*,[45] ʿAbd al-Qādir maintains to Daumas that it is obligatory for him as a Muslim to live among Muslims – repeating that Friday prayers are invalid unless offered within a Muslim majority community.[46]

The same concern is echoed once more in his letter to King Louis Philippe, in which he rejects the offer of lands and property in France. ʿAbd al-Qādir, he says, wishes only to return to the lands of the Muslims and their scholars (*ʿulemā'*), the lands of 'Community and [Friday] Congregation' (*al-jamāʿah wa-l-jumʿa*),[47] again manifesting the religio-political character of his faith. For him, personal devotion did not exist separately from the socio-political context in which it takes place. It is worth noting that on the rare occasions that this episode has been noted by recent histories, it has been as evidence of ʿAbd al-Qādir's love of that republican virtue of *'liberté'*,[48] rather than as evidence of religio-political conservatism: a rejection of France is thereby transformed into an embrace of its values. That he preferred confinement in Egypt over freedom in France, as evidenced above, belies this re-interpretation.

While offers to settle in Christendom could only have presented themselves to ʿAbd al-Qādir as tests of his faith and of his determination to leave, one need not assume that they were motivated by malevolence. The political goal of these offers is clear: to keep him on a short leash far from Algeria, where he might once more become a symbol of resistance. The Frenchmen assigned to monitor ʿAbd al-Qādir, for their part, were clearly interested in his wellbeing, however. They often praised his virtues, interceded for his benefit, and pressed for his ambigu-

---

43 Daumas to the Ministry of War, FR ANOM GGA1E219, 03-02-1848.
44 Julien, 1964, p. 208.
45 'Those who live under the compact of the Christians will not have their prayers recognised' [*Tuḥfah*, p. 415].
46 Daumas to the Ministry of War, FR ANOM GGA1E219, 03-02-1848.
47 ʿAbd al-Qādir to Louis Philippe, FR ANOM GGA1E219, 03-02-1848.
48 E.g. Bouyerdene, 2008, p. 99.

ous status to be resolved as soon as possible.[49] They repeatedly express concern over facilitating the Arabs' 'dwelling, their customs, and their religion'[50] in keeping with 'their habits and customs'.[51] In spite of some suggestion of distrust for Boissonet,[52] assigned to him at Amboise, ʿAbd al-Qādir's relationship with his handlers Desgranges, l'Heureux, and Daumas seems to have been quite cordial. ʿAbd al-Qādir's friendship with Daumas even resulted in his contributing to the latter's book on horses and horsemanship.[53]

It is also clear that ʿAbd al-Qādir benefitted from the support and sympathy of notable French figures further beyond the confines of the chateaux which contained him. He would renew his acquaintance with the former Bishop of Algiers, now Monseigneur, Dupuch – long famous for his commitment to social works,[54] whom de Tocqueville had described as 'having something of the saint and the Gascon about him'.[55] Dupuch, who had facilitated prisoner exchanges with and sent clerical emissaries to ʿAbd al-Qādir in Algeria,[56] became one of the most vocal French advocates for his release. In 1849 he published a text (dedicated to Louis Napoleon, then President of the Republic) devoted entirely to praising ʿAbd al-Qādir's virtues and demanding an end to his imprisonment.[57] Like Daumas, who had been assigned to the French consulate in Mascara, Dupuch could also speak to him of Algeria. Experience in North Africa was common among his visitors, but as a *cause célèbre* he found support from multitudes unconnected to the lands of his birth.

So accustomed had ʿAbd al-Qādir apparently become to being treated as a great dignitary, in fact, that by the end of his time in France he would complain at the insufficient warmth of his reception by the people of Marseilles.[58] It would

49 E.g. Daumas to L'Heureux, FR ANOM GGA1E219, 25-01-1848; Daumas to the Ministry of War, FR ANOM GGA1E219, 25-01-1848; L'Heureux to the Ministry of War, FR ANOM GGA1E219, 29-03-1848; Daumas to the Ministry of War, FR ANOM GGA1E219, 29-03-1848; L'Heureux to the Ministry of War, FR ANOM GGA1E219, 22-04-1848…

50 L'Heureux to the Ministry of War, FR ANOM GGA1E219, 06-02-1848.

51 Daumas to the Ministry of War, FR ANOM GGA1E219, 29-03-1848.

52 E.g. ʿAbd al-Qādir's deliberate circumvention of Boissonet: De Nollentz to the Foreign Ministry, Correspondance Politique des Consuls/Turquie/Brousse/1, 20-12-1852.

53 *Les Chevaux du Sahara et les mœurs du désert*, published in 1858.

54 Julien, 1964, p. 160.

55 Tocqueville, 2001, p. 43. Gascon, in this context, refers both to Dupuch's family origins and a term for braggart.

56 Lacrouts to the State Department, A2 Cab. 14/8, 21-06-1841; Chasteau to the Ministry of Foreign Affairs, Correspondance Politique/Maroc/14, 06-09-1845.

57 Dupuch, 1849, *passim*.

58 De Nollentz to the Foreign Ministry, Correspondance Politique des Consuls/Turquie/Brousse/1, 20-12-1852.

be the more august of his sympathisers, however, who would play the largest role in securing his release. The captive ʿAbd al-Qādir was visited by 'persons of high office, and wielders of authority, and leaders of war, competing with one another to demonstrate their respect for and exaltation of the dynamic amīr',[59] his son proudly recalls. ʿAbd al-Qādir's greatest supporters were drawn from the same ranks as those who had most ardently opposed him.

Many British and French aristocrats and literary figures worked to secure his liberation. In addition to Monseigneur Dupuch, the Count D'Orsay, the Marquess of (later Lord) Londonderry, the Countess Barbotan, Lord Brougham,[60] the Duke of Wellington,[61] Viscount Maidstone,[62] Alexandre Dumas,[63] William Makepeace Thackeray,[64] and Victor Hugo,[65] among others, voiced sympathy for him. As well as pressuring Louis Napoleon and the press with a letter-writing campaign, Londonderry, D'Orsay, and Barbotan in particular hatched a plot to release copies of Lamoricière and d'Aumale's correspondence. This contained the promises made to ʿAbd al-Qādir and his brothers on their respective 'surrenders',[66] and its potential release was intended to cause a scandal by revealing the perfidy of the French authorities. France's honour, the security of its new colony, and the changing political landscape thus all weighed in Louis Napoleon's balance – a balance decidedly shifted by his successful *coup d'état* of 1851, and transition from being France's first President to being its last Emperor.

In his private correspondence, Louis Napoleon consistently claimed to seek ʿAbd al-Qādir's liberation (without wanting to endanger the peace of Algeria); none would be happier than he to free him, he would claim.[67] This private admission is made dramatically public when in 1852 the French press reports Louis Napoleon's declaration that ʿAbd al-Qādir must be liberated 'as the honour of France is at stake'[68] – a phrase he had earlier put privately in writing to Londonderry.[69] It would not be until the end of 1852, however, that ʿAbd al-Qādir was permitted to

59 *Tuḥfah*, p. 523.
60 D'Orsay to Londonderry, D/Lo/C 74, 26-05-1851 and 02-07-1851.
61 D'Orsay to Londonderry, D/Lo/C 74, 02-07-1851 and 05-10-1851.
62 Maidstone published *Abd-El-Kader: a poem in six cantos* in 1851; Count D'Orsay planned to have an orientalist translate it into Arabic for the benefit of ʿAbd al-Qādir [D'Orsay to Londonderry, D/Lo/C 74, 11-06-1851.
63 D'Orsay to Londonderry, D/Lo/C 74, 08-10-1851.
64 Discussed in Abdel-Jaouad, 1999, p. 196.
65 D'Orsay to Londonderry, D/Lo/C 74, 26-05-1851; Julien 1964, p. 258 – 9.
66 Barbotan to Londonderry, D/Lo/C 137, 24-04-1851.
67 Louis Napoleon to Londonderry, D/Lo/C 458, 29-03-1851.
68 *La Presse*, 13-10-1851; D'Orsay to Londonderry, D/Lo/C 74, 14-10-1851.
69 Louis Napoleon to Londonderry, D/Lo/C 458, 13-09-1851.

correspond freely with these supporters – and even then he was expressly forbidden from taking up the invitation to attend the funeral of Wellington.[70] ʿAbd al-Qādir would ultimately express his gratitude, however, for their 'statesmanship with the pointedness of a cavalier's rapier',[71] sending them his customary equine gifts, including a black steed for 'his dear friend'[72] Londonderry.

While the general circumstances of his release, such as Louis Napoleon's consolidation of power and aristocratic campaigns on ʿAbd al-Qādir's behalf, have been remarked upon, the circumstances of his release do demand further attention. His notoriety ensured that whatever decision was reached about him could not help but be a significant event. Adroitly managing the situation, Louis Napoleon's government transformed an embarrassing problem into a grand piece of political theatre.

3.3 Release

Louis Napoleon concluded his triumphal march around France in late 1852 with what the French press described as an act of 'national generosity': his declaration that ʿAbd al-Qādir would be freed.[73] Though this was presented as a freely-made decision concluded in light of ʿAbd al-Qādir's 'long imprisonment, resignation, and often expressed submission to the will of France',[74] Louis Napoleon's public and private assertions that 'the honour of France is at stake' seem to have been the deciding factor. In liberating ʿAbd al-Qādir, Louis Napoleon succeeded in transforming an internationally visible blemish on France's honour into a mark of pride for his new government – scoring a double public relations coup. A gratified ʿAbd al-Qādir is reported in the French newspapers as declaring to the magnanimous Prince-President that 'your [Christian] religion just as ours enjoins submission to Providence. If France is mistress of Algeria, it is what God has willed, and France will never renounce her conquest.'[75] In one dramatic gesture, Louis Napoleon positioned himself domestically as morally superior to his predecessors whose wavering and treachery had first imprisoned ʿAbd al-Qādir and then failed to release him, and internationally as the rightful ruler of France's Algerian possessions – apparently recognised even by their former amīr.

70 Minister of War to Commanding Officer at Tours, FR ANOM GGA1E234, 16-11-1852.
71 ʿAbd al-Qādir to D'Orsay, in D'Orsay to Londonderry, D/Lo/C 74, 06-09-1851.
72 ʿAbd al-Qādir to Londonderry, D/Lo/C 137, 13-07-1853.
73 Extract from *Le Mubacher*, FR ANOM GGA1E235, 01-11-1852.
74 *Ibid.*
75 *Ibid.*

ʿAbd al-Qādir would travel to Paris to offer praise and gratitude to the king at the centre of French power. His initial intention had been to deliver a speech of thanks. He was convinced by the French, however, to deliver his address in the form of a signed letter (including some alterations),[76] which would immediately be circulated for the purposes of propaganda – particularly in French Algeria.[77] He was shown a print reproduction of the letter while visiting the Parisian presses: the public character of his private thanks for Louis Napoleon must have been quite apparent to him.

ʿAbd al-Qādir's letter of thanks was delivered with the words 'I owe you the liberty that others promised me, but which you yourself did not promise me.'[78] 'When God wished me to make war on the French I came out guns blazing to the fullest, and when he wished me to cease the combat I withdrew,' ʿAbd al-Qādir writes.

> 'My religion and my noble origin enjoin me to keep faith and reject all fraud. I am a Sherif... I am witness to the grandeur of your Empire, the strength of its troops, the immensity of the wealth of France, the justice of its leaders and the rightness of their actions. One cannot imagine any who might defeat or oppose your will, save all-powerful God.'[79]

Throughout his visit to the capital, ʿAbd al-Qādir took exaggerated pains to present himself as having been pacified. His dearest hope of liberation now seemed palpably close at hand, and he would do nothing to endanger it. He even went so far, while visiting the royal stud, as to feign a diplomatic distaste for horses (which remained his passion throughout his life, reflected in his contribution to Daumas' later writing,[80] and were invariably his choicest gifts to friends and allies, in keeping with centuries-old conventions) on the spurious grounds that 'horses are a symbol of war, and he a man of peace.'[81] It is unclear if he intended this exaggerated obsequiousness as ironic, but other comments of the time were more unmistakably barbed. Remarking on the changes in government

---

76 Ministry of War to the Governor-General of Algeria, FR ANOM GGA1E235, 12-11-1852; it is not recorded which alterations were made to the text.

77 A despatch from the Ministry of War to the Bureau of Arab Affaires (FR ANOM GGA1E235, 06-11-1852) recommends this 'completely spontaneous' letter be published immediately in *Le Mubacher* and the *Moniteur Universel*, which it duly was.

78 Extract from *Le Mubacher*, FR ANOM GGA1E235, 15-11-1852.

79 Extract from *Le Mubacher*, FR ANOM GGA1E235, 01-12-1852.

80 Daumas, 1858.

81 Extract from *Le Mubacher*, FR ANOM GGA1E235, 15-11-1852.

during his captivity he observed that 'We have had the same constitution from the days of Muḥammad; but then we are barbarians.'[82]

On returning to Amboise, ʿAbd al-Qādir and several of his male companions would provide additional support to the new regime through their much-publicised casting of votes 'nominating the Sultan'[83] as part of the national plebiscite on Empire. It does not seem entirely appropriate to view this gesture as a vote against the Republic and in favour of Empire, though it was effectively both. Rather, ʿAbd al-Qādir and his men must be understood as thanking Louis Napoleon personally – nominating him as Sultan, as they put it. This was not the democratic vote of a republican citizen, but a diplomatic gesture of gratitude for a greatly beneficent act; it should be understood in terms of patronage, not political philosophy. There is ample reason to doubt ʿAbd al-Qādir's interest in or understanding of French constitutional politics, but none to doubt his affection for his liberator. ʿAbd al-Qādir would, in fact, maintain a high personal regard for Louis Napoleon until the moment he would send his widow condolences from Damascus.[84]

> 'We regard ourselves today as French through the friendship and affection shown and the good treatment done to us... His Imperial Highness the Sultan [Louis Napoleon], most just of the just, most generous of the generous, has counted us as among his children and his soldiers, deigning to give me a sabre with his own Imperial hands',[85]

ʿAbd al-Qādir reportedly announced in casting his vote. Though he had repeatedly declared himself the child or brother of his French captors from the very first days of his imprisonment,[86] his emollient declarations had gained a new credibility now that they reciprocated the beneficence to justify them. He sang much the same song he had for the past four years, but where once his words fell on deaf ears they now found rapt attention. With the changed political context of ʿAbd al-Qādir's liberation, a rhetoric aimed at allaying fears was transformed into a rousing endorsement of French Imperial power... and with it, of the 'Road to Damascus' narrative of ʿAbd al-Qādir's conversion.

82 *New York Daily Times*, 15-01-53, p. 6; Abdel-Jaouad, 2008, p. 83.
83 Extract from *Le Mubacher*, FR ANOM GGA1E235, 01-12-1852.
84 Robin to the Ministry of Foreign Affairs, Damas/Consulat/65, 01-02-1873.
85 *Ibid.*
86 E.g. in his letters to 'his father' Louis-Phillipe and 'brother' Lamoricière, FR ANOM GGA1E219, 21-01-1848 and17-03-1848.

3.4 A 'Road to Damascus' Moment?

It is difficult to imagine how ʿAbd al-Qādir's liberation could have been presented by the French establishment of its time other than as a moral triumph over a once-feared enemy. It is similarly understandable that the dramatic change in his overt relationship with France – the end of his war against them – would incline many to infer a covert change within ʿAbd al-Qādir himself. A narrative of personal transformation from opposition to endorsement of France seemed as psychologically attractive as it was undoubtedly politically convenient. The idea of ʿAbd al-Qādir experiencing a French epiphany on his road from Mascara to Damascus has remained a recurring theme in his western biographies ever since.

The fact that this narrative remains so attractive in spite of the dearth of supporting evidence bears discussion; even when most full of praise for France, ʿAbd al-Qādir's dearest wish remained to leave it for Muslim lands. So also does the changing characterisation of the 'conversion' itself. His earliest and latest biographers agree that his perspective was revolutionised during those years of imprisonment, yet offer quite different accounts of this putative change, its motive force, and its ultimate significance.

To what was ʿAbd al-Qādir thought to have been converted, and by whom? His French contemporaries had little doubt: ʿAbd al-Qādir was the beneficiary of what would come to be known as the universal French *mission civilisatrice.* 'He was touted as an example of an Arab who had become civilised as a result of exposure to Europe, and his service to France represented Algeria's recognition of French dominance.'[87] When noting the Algerian ʿAbd al-Qādir's belief that *jihād* is a religious obligation, his first French biographer is quick to note that he 'has since demonstrated how much he has rejected such intolerant ideas.'[88] In point of fact, ʿAbd al-Qādir maintained a traditionally conventional view of the obligation to *jihād* until his death;[89] what is important here is Bellemare's conception of its significance to ʿAbd al-Qādir and his conversion. Bellemare's biography of ʿAbd al-Qādir does not concern itself with the rich history of Islamic thought; well furnished with archival reports and personal interviews, his focus is more material than conceptual. *Jihād*, in the context of Bellemare's day as so often today, stood for him for fanaticism and havoc rather than an elaborated

87 Achrati, 2007, p. 146.
88 Bellemare, 1863, p. 248.
89 E.g. *Mawāqif*, vol. 1, pp. 155–156; 'there is no escaping from [*lā budda min*] *jihād* and righteous intent, that is, waging *jihād* and having purpose, joining together the witnessing of the Truth and the implementation of the legal rules, the fighting of the enemies of Islam until they pay the *jizyah* and become subordinated, and the illicit is changed into the licit.'

ethico-legal category. It was the former which ʿAbd al-Qādir was presumed to have initially adhered to and later abandoned – not the latter, as the Algerian himself would have seen it throughout his own life. His conversion to Francophilia was primarily depicted as a flight from the fanaticism of his fellows towards the civilised comportment of France.[90] ʿAbd al-Qādir had been, one might add in the terms of his own *Risālah on Hijrah*, a hypocrite.[91]

While (over-)[92]stressing the spontaneity of his avowals of gratitude to France in general and Louis Napoleon in particular, and insisting that he 'required no political motives, but only religious ones,'[93] Bellemare's account of ʿAbd al-Qādir's change is essentially secular. There is no suggestion that his religious makeup was changed by his imprisonment or his conversion from foe to friend of France. No doctrines are embraced, and none rejected; no metaphysics is overturned, no ethics revolutionised. Quite the contrary: Bellemare makes a point of ʿAbd al-Qādir's steadfastness in his religious position, even when describing his courteous attitude to Christians. A priest, ʿAbd al-Qādir is reported as saying, is a

> 'man who believes in God, who is exactly obedient to the precept of a divine revelation, the only fault of which is being previous to his own. He complains at [the priest's] error, no doubt...[but] he is the marabout of another religion: he honours his conviction.'[94]

When informed of the intention of a young *curé* to try to convert him to Catholicism, ʿAbd al-Qādir gamely replies that 'it would be a triumph for me to convert a Christian marabout to my religion.'[95] Monseigneur Dupuch echoes that ʿAbd al-Qādir's religious conviction in France was 'as sincere as it was profound and unalterable',[96] and of the same high character as it had been in Algeria.[97] What was most important about his change of heart to his European contemporaries was his policy towards others, particularly the French, not the private affairs of his

90 Bellemare's closing lines [1863, p. 455] on ʿAbd al-Qādir record that 'though he aroused fanaticism, he was free of it himself.' 'Though not a fanatic himself,' writes Churchill [1867, p. 31], 'Abdel Kader well knew the latent fires of fanaticism which slumber in every Muslim breast.'
91 *Tuḥfah*, p. 416 – ʿAbd al-Qādir refers to those 'Mudejar' Muslims who remained under Christian rule in Spain as hypocrites.
92 Bellemare [1863, p. 392] makes a point of the supposedly spontaneous character of a highly stage-managed event – ʿAbd al-Qādir's delivery of a letter of thanks to the Prince-President.
93 Bellemare, 1863, p. 453.
94 Bellemare, 1863, p. 452.
95 Bellemare, 1863, p. 453.
96 Dupuch, 1849, p. 16.
97 Dupuch, 1849, p. 17.

heart. Public reason, not private conviction, is seen as the key to his joining of the ranks of the civilised.

'Abd al-Qādir's 20th-century biographers, however, have retained the conversion narrative while casting it in a new and more private light. Far be it from these scholars to endorse the discredited colonial project; other motivations are at play, even if the narrative structure persists. Increasing interest in Islamic thought, patterns of cross-fertilisation across the Mediterranean, and the availability of 'Abd al-Qādir's spiritual writings in French and English translation, on the other hand, have all played their part in shifting attention to his personal experience. Less Eurocentric, but still focused on contact with Europe as central to 'Abd al-Qādir's biography,[98] these later approaches hinge on his status as a Sufi. Sufism, not discussed in any depth by 'Abd al-Qādir's 19th-century biographers, increasingly takes centre stage in the play of his 'Road to Damascus' conversion. In the work of many modern writers, it is not Civilisation which enlightens the captive, so much as Mysticism – though both are presumed to be essentially Europhile. For some, '[t]he captivity of 'Abd al-Qādir in France has an incontestable esoteric significance. It is the corner-stone of the geo-spiritual strategy of east-west relations in Modernity.'[99]

The narrative arc remains otherwise unchanged: 'Abd al-Qādir's warlike fervour is transfigured on the terraces of Amboise and the halls of Versailles to pacific amity through his adoption of a cosmopolitan ethic valuing tolerance, forbearance, and forgiveness. Lightning strikes, and sectarian Saul of Tarsus becomes universalist St Paul. The distinction between 19th- and 20th-century narratives is that such an ethic is more explicitly attributed to certain values of France in the first instance, and of Islamic civilisation in the second. 'Abd al-Qādir does not find civilisation so much as he finds enlightenment – though both lead him to love France.

This enlightenment, it will be seen, has increasingly been described in terms of Sufism. Sufism is not a homogeneous tradition, however, and has given rise to numerous internal disputes. Characterising 'Abd al-Qādir's particular form of Sufi Islam and its 20th-century western receptions and re-imaginings will there-

98 It should be noted that the concerns of 'historians of eighteenth and nineteenth century Islam' have been broadly criticised for having 'tended to be framed with an "accommodationist/rejectionist" conceptual model that characterises movements for change in modern Islam as either being "accommodationist" towards the impact of the West.... or rejectionist' [O'Fahey, 1990, p. 5].

99 Djeradi in Geoffroy et al., 2010, p. 226.

fore require engagement with his *Kitāb al-Mawāqif*, compiled in Damascus.[100] It is excerpts from his writing during his years in Damascus which biographers typically adduce as textual evidence of his 'new' position, adopted during or after his time in France. Similarly, ʿAbd al-Qādir's actions during the July of 1860 have from the earliest biographies been offered as the practical evidence of his 'new' attitude.[101] Those events, too, will be discussed in the coming chapters. Suffice it at this point to remark only that both forms of evidence of French 'conversion' rely for the most part on ex-post-facto inferences dependant on narrative 'backshadowing'[102] and interpretations which cannot easily be sustained in light of all the available evidence.

Some historians have argued for the emergence in France of ʿAbd al-Qādir's metaphysical Sufism by 'negative' means. That is, simply by denying the credibility of an earlier, Algerian, ʿAbd al-Qādir having a genuine spiritual dimension. His and others' earlier and later claims to the contrary were, according to this school of thought, 'merely an attempt to increase his prestige'.[103] Such remarks have already been argued to be over-stated, founded on false dichotomies, and out of keeping with the rich history of spirituality among (Muslim and non-Muslim) political leaders. In few biographies is ʿAbd al-Qādir's change of heart itself treated as anything other than axiomatic, however: few attempts have been made to explicitly analyse and evidence what has been taken for granted as an obvious given. Among ʿAbd al-Qādir's recent biographers, however, Itzchak Weismann distinguishes himself in engaging directly with the crucial 'Road to Damascus' narrative at the heart of most depictions of his life.

Weismann provides the most explicit and appealing explanation for ʿAbd al-Qādir's putative French transformation. While it is far from alone in presenting him as committed by his experience of France to 'Ibn al-ʿArabī's Sufi philosophy as a way to prepare Muslims intellectually to meet the challenges of European civilization,'[104] it stands out in its psychological vividness:

> 'The decisive period in the spiritual development of Amir ʿAbd al-Qādir al-Jazāʾirī was deferred, however, until after his surrender to the French in 1847... In the wake of the 1848 [French] revolution ʿAbd al-Qādir's situation deteriorated, as his large entourage was separated from him and he was allowed almost no contact with the outside world. In this pe-

100 This will become the concern of later chapters, as this book follows the chronological progression of ʿAbd al-Qādir's life.

101 As, for instance, in Bellemare's reference to ʿAbd al-Qādir's freedom from fanaticism, above [Bellemare, 1863, p. 455].

102 This term is borrowed from Michael André Bernstein.

103 Danziger, 1977, p. 181. See also, for instance, Achrati, 2007, p. 142.

104 Heck (ed.), 2007, p. 3.

> riod of disillusionment and despair he went through an acute spiritual crisis, which led him to the teaching of Ibn al-ʿArabī [and] the new attitude that ʿAbd al-Qādir adopted toward western civilisation in consequence... To Louis Napoleon he promised that, "Now I am among those who use the pen, not those who use the sword."'[105]

This characterisation of the 'psychological mechanism which led ʿAbd al-Qādir to adopt the theosophy of Ibn al-ʿArabī...[as] consolation for the crisis he underwent during his captivity'[106] is unsatisfying for a number of reasons, however.

Firstly, it exaggerates ʿAbd al-Qādir's isolation. Solitary confinement is a form of torture that often results in psychological breaks, but ʿAbd al-Qādir was constantly surrounded (even when he voluntarily withdrew himself in seclusion) by a retinue of many dozen friends and family who relied upon him as a father, teacher and leader. He was also in (however censored and interrupted) correspondence with significant public figures throughout Europe, as has been shown, interviewing many of them face to face. It is also very unclear that he ever gave up on his dream of leaving France and re-uniting with his compatriots – as he would spend the subsequent years doing. While ʿAbd al-Qādir's contact with the broader French population certainly waxed and waned, it is unclear to what extent he either welcomed its increase or regretted its diminution.

Secondly, on a psychological level, it assumes not only that ʿAbd al-Qādir did in fact experience a psycho-spiritual nadir on exposure to Europe, but that the Sufism of Ibn al-ʿArabī is a natural consolation for such a crisis. While we have seen that he warned of the possibility of suicides in his group[107] (though these would not in fact take place), both the earliest biographies and the archival reports on his imprisonment are consistent in their depiction of his own comportment. ʿAbd al-Qādir is seen time and again as giving an impression of serenity and resignation to the will of God – the virtues he commended to his followers on leaving North Africa[108] and on arrival in France,[109] and which are conventionally understood by Sufis as the virtue of *tawakkul*. Churchill[110] quotes Dupuch[111] on ʿAbd al-Qādir: '...you will find him mild, simple, affectionate, modest, resigned, never complaining; excusing his enemies...', while Bellemare recalls his 'gentle resignation'.[112] ʿAbd al-Qādir's own son and biographer omits

---

105 Weismann, 2001a, p. 150.
106 Weismann, 2001a, p. 183.
107 E.g. Daumas to the Ministry of War, FR ANOM GGA1E219, 29-03-1848.
108 ʿAbd al-Qādir to various, FR ANOM GGA1E217, 08-01-1848.
109 L'Heureux to the Ministry of War, FR ANOM GGA1E219, 14-01-1848.
110 Churchill, 1867, p. 280.
111 Dupuch, 1849, p. 16.
112 Bellemare, 1863, p. 377.

to mention any long night of the soul endured by his father, recalling instead his dignity and the esteem of his captors for the 'dynamic amīr'.[113] It is certainly imaginable that ʿAbd al-Qādir, given his responsibilities to his followers, concealed some form of psychological collapse from them. Whether for this reason or because it simply never happened, it is to European sources that we must look in search of evidence of a life-defining change.[114]

Assuming that he successfully kept such a crisis secret, further questions of plausibility arise. Why now? What is it about the situation which allows us to infer the existence of this putative breakdown? The obvious stress and powerlessness of the situation suggest themselves. Yet the by-now middle-aged ʿAbd al-Qādir was no stranger to hardship, to put it mildly. His predilection for asceticism is unchallenged even by historians sceptical of his religious motives, as we have seen. He had as a boy already been the subject of extended house arrest in the last days of the hostile and suspicious Ottoman regime in Algeria.[115] More harrowingly, he had waged a protracted and bloody guerrilla war against an overpowering enemy who practised collective punishment and scorched-earth tactics, leaving tens of thousands dead – friends and family among them. It is unlikely that he felt no responsibility for those many deaths, nor suffered them less keenly than that of his infantry officer who accidentally choked to death in his sleep at Toulon. ʿAbd al-Qādir and his shrinking caravan-headquarters had spent years evading French and ultimately Moroccan armies, while suffering increasingly vitriolic physical and propaganda attacks from people they had once counted as brothers.[116] He had buried children[117] and brushed with his own death.[118] No objective metric of suffering is available to us, but it is far from self-evident that ʿAbd al-Qādir's peaceful captivity with his family and entourage at castles like Amboise, a Royal Chateau overlooking the Loire valley, famed as the birthplace of the French formal garden and site of the tomb of Leonardo da Vinci, necessarily represented an intolerable nadir in his experience.

113 *Tuḥfah*, p. 523.

114 A partial exception must be made in the case of a third-hand anecdote published by Jawād al-Murābiṭ some decades after ʿAbd al-Qādir's death, in which he suggests that Amboise saw a new level of spiritual vision (*ufuq rūḥānī*) for ʿAbd al-Qādir [Al-Murābiṭ, 1966, p. 18.].

115 Churchill, 1867, pp. 8–9, Danziger, 1977, p. 57.

116 This propaganda campaign has best been described by Bennison in her works drawn on by this study.

117 Bugeaud to the Ministry of War, FR ANOM GGA1E113, 30-10-1837; Daumas to Oran Command, FR ANOM GGA1E116, January 1839.

118 Most famously when the horse he was riding was killed under him during battle [Chasteau to the Ministry of Foreign Affairs, Correspondance Politique/Maroc/16, 12-01-1846].

As regards the interpretation of Ibn al-ʿArabī's Sufi Islam attributed to him – again, coming chapters will bring deeper engagement with this complex question through examining of excerpts from his *Kitāb al-Mawāqif.* Suffice it to say at this point that although many people have found the writing of Ibn al-ʿArabī an enormous comfort and source of guiding insight toward a more tolerant, pluralistic, and peaceful world, such an experience is not inevitable. Not all who read Ibn al-ʿArabī are comforted by him, nor are all those who are comforted readers of Ibn al-ʿArabī. Ibn al-ʿArabī did not advocate pacifism, nor are all of those who have followed him pacifists. Still less are all who honour him favourably disposed towards 'western civilisation', though Weismann, like many other contemporary writers, implies this to be a logical 'consequence'[119] of a turn towards the Andalusian master (Ayatollah Ruhollah Khomeini, scholar of Mullah Sadra and Ibn al-ʿArabī while also being the hammer of 'westoxification', is a dramatic counter-example, were one needed – and this even after his own years on French soil). Ibn al-ʿArabī himself, it is probably safe to assume, wrote what he did in order to express the truth of his experiences and the majesty of God, not to offer a soothing palliative to distraught feelings, wounded pride, or to reconcile Islam with an as-yet unknowable European modernity. In spite of its initial attractiveness, therefore, there is nothing conceptually necessary about the causal chain with which Weismann presents us. Neither the push factor of ʿAbd al-Qādir's crisis, nor the pull of his revolutionised attitude to western civilisation (assuming both are convincing) demand a new departure towards Ibn al-ʿArabī as a mediating factor. Is there, then, less speculative evidence for ʿAbd al-Qādir's purported change of heart?

That his writing in captivity did evince familiarity with the characteristic language of Ibn al-ʿArabī has already been established by several authors.[120] This may be adduced as documentary evidence of the transformation which Weismann describes – a sign of his adoption of Ibn al-ʿArabī and hence proof of his spiritual transformation. It must however be noted that there is no evidence that ʿAbd al-Qādir had any of Ibn al-ʿArabī's texts with him in captivity. As such, this fact is more reasonably taken as indicating that his knowledge of the famed Murcian mystic predated his imprisonment. That is, he had already taken an interest in him while studying and ruling in Algeria. Ibn ʿArabī was not held in the same suspicion in ʿAbd al-Qādir's days as would become the case in the 20th century – still less in the Qādirī and Naqshbandī Sufi societies to which he had been connected since before his rise to political power in Algeria. That he might have adopted a

119 Weismann, 2001a, p. 150.
120 Chodkiewicz, 1995, pp. 6, 185; Shinar, 1965, p. 160.

new emotional attitude towards ideas and devotions in which he was already practiced is perfectly possible, of course, but must remain speculative.

It is certainly the case that ʿAbd al-Qādir would devote more of his time in later life to teaching in Sufi milieus – very much including the texts of Ibn al-ʿArabī. It is true that his teaching career flowered in his later life, as is conventionally considered seemly among Sufis: a Sufi instructor is after all known as a *shaykh*, a word explicitly denoting an *older man*. It is not true, however, that this represents any break from his original background and upbringing – even barring Roches' famous accounts[121] of ʿAbd al-Qādir's mystical transports during the siege of ʿAin Māḍī. Educated in a Sufi *zāwiyah*, the favoured son of a prominent Sufi Shaykh, already inducted into several Sufi *ṭuruq*, involved in inter-*ṭarīqah* rivalry, ʿAbd al-Qādir had already during his Algerian rule studied Sufi texts and used Sufi signs – from references to the *ṭarīqah muḥammadiyyah*[122] in the naming of his state symbols,[123] to self-presentation as a marabout elevating other marabouts to power.[124] It is perfectly reasonable to connect his years of teaching Sufism in his later life with this early upbringing and education in an expressly Sufi environment. Shinar's observation that ʿAbd al-Qādir's career as a teacher of Sufism 'did not constitute a break of continuity, but rather the ripening of seeds'[125] seems the natural conclusion to draw from this evidence, if any particular development need be inferred. A counterfactual ʿAbd al-Qādir living out his days at his family *zāwiyah* in a late-Ottoman North Africa never invaded by France would not astonish were he to evince interest in 'the Greatest Master' Ibn al-ʿArabī. Nor, moreover, would anyone feel obliged to speculate over what psychological crisis might have driven him to such an interest.

The narrative of dramatic conversion to (Ibn al-ʿArabī's) Sufism as a result of exposure to Europe, conversely, does not seem to arise from a need to make sense of ʿAbd al-Qādir's life story. It is quite comprehensible without the imputation of such an event. Rather, the impetus comes from an imperative to situate his relationship with the west as central to his spiritual character and teaching. It is in this respect directly relatable to the special status of ʿAbd al-Qādir as an inheritor of the mantle of Ibn al-ʿArabī, in that both figures have taken on dramatically ecumenical roles in the 20th and 21st century west. Far from the imperial-

121 Roches, 1904, pp. 140 – 141.

122 See Chapter Five, as well as the discussion in O'Fahey [1990] on the putative connections between this language and the controversial category of 'Neo-Sufism' advanced by Fazlur Rahman and others.

123 *Tuḥfah*, pp. 199, 201; Martin, 1976, p. 59; Shinar, 1965, pp. 146 – 7.

124 E.g. Shinar, 1965, p. 173.

125 Shinar, 1965, p. 160.

ism of ʿAbd al-Qādir's earliest biographies, this more benign form of Eurocentrism will be discussed in greater depth during Chapter Five's exploration of his *Kitāb al-Mawāqif*'s reception in the west. The current chapter, meanwhile, remains focused on ʿAbd al-Qādir's years in French captivity.

3.5 Continuity

How can ʿAbd al-Qādir's captivity be viewed, then, if we reject the gamut of 'Road to Damascus' narratives which have been developed around it? While this study argues for the significance of continuity as opposed to rupture and change, one need not caricature those years as static, suspended animation. An alternative view might see his attitude affected less by crisis and conversion than by a growing respect for the likes of Daumas and Louis Napoleon, ultimately crystallised into personal friendships.

ʿAbd al-Qādir was certainly impressed with certain aspects of French culture. He already respected French technical sophistication. In Algeria he had hired Europeans to run his (in the event rather abortive) factories and drill his troops, and he would continue to hire European specialists and support technological development in Anatolia and the Levant. It certainly seems to be the case that he was newly impressed by French piety, however. There are numerous accounts of his seeking out in particular the company of clerics and showing an interest in the architecture of religion.[126] 'The temple where the Deity was worshiped was invariably the first place to which he directed his steps,' reports an approving Churchill in suggestively idiosyncratic terms.[127]

Such accounts must be weighed, however, against the low regard ʿAbd al-Qādir seemed to have held for French piety while in North Africa.[128] His had been a moral horror shared also by Christian visitors to the fledgling colony, who were appalled by the lack of religious scruples among the colonists.[129] The conquering French

126 Clayton, 1975, p. 265.

127 Churchill, 1867, p. 296. The unusual phrasing of this sentence ('temple' rather than Church; 'the Deity' as opposed to God) suggests the influence of the ('post-Christian') monotheistic Deism popular among certain educated circles of Europeans at the time – presaging ʿAbd al-Qādir's brief contact with (often Deistic) Freemasonry in the 1860s and his 20th century adoption by European esotericism [discussed in this book's chapter on the *Kitāb al-Mawāqif*].

128 E.g. the accounts of ʿAbd al-Qādir's speeches included by Roches' report to the Ministry of Foreign Affairs [Correspondance Politique/Maroc/15; 13-11-1845], in which he accuses the French of suppressing religion, putting mosques to profane use, buying the virtue of women, and abrogating rights to justice.

129 Julien, 1864, p. 159.

failed to produce any Christian religious buildings until almost a decade after the French invasion, in fact: in 1839.[130] The French furthermore surprised their Muslim counterparts by failing to include clerics at negotiations,[131] honour their treaties,[132] or respect conventions of warfare.[133] What is more, the stark demographic imbalance among the first waves of colonists (about 2:1 male to female, reaching almost 3:1 in Algiers itself),[134] combined with their general unwillingness or inability to take local wives, led to an a dramatic increase in prostitution – a fact which had scandalised ʿAbd al-Qādir and his compatriots.[135]

The *Risālah on Hijrah* he authored, discussed above, contains a great deal of evidence about his perception of the 'Algerian' French as religiously retrograde and lapsed Christians, not just *naṣārah* but *kuffār* and 'people of perdition'. In France he certainly seems to have modified his views on this point.

> 'On entering the church of la Madeleine, [ʿAbd al-Qādir] said to the priest who accompanied him, "When I first began my struggle with the French I thought they were a people without religion. I found out my mistake. At all events, such churches as these would soon convince me of my error."'[136]

There is scant evidence to suggest that he revised his view of the status of Christianity as a revelation. Rather, he appears to have re-appraised his view of the French people's relationship with that revelation.

This growing respect for French piety did not translate into any deep interest in French culture in general, however. This is evidenced by the fact that ʿAbd al-Qādir did not make the relatively modest initial effort of learning French during his years in France. Without exception, all of his verbal and written communications with French speakers both in France and during his Damascene decades,

130 Julien, 1864, p. 160.
131 Clayton, 1975, p. 67.
132 ʿAbd al-Qādir's constant complaint to other powers during his Algerian career: ʿAbd al-Qādir to 'The English King', FO 52/40, 02-09-1835; Lieb to the State Department, A2 Cab. 38/8, 30-04-1836; ʿAbd al-Qādir to Aberdeen, FO 3/44, 10-03-1842.
133 The 'scorched earth' policies refered to earlier in this book, such as the infamous Dahra massacre.
134 Julien, 1964, p. 158.
135 E.g. Daumas' interrogation on this subject by the ʿAbd al-Qādir's Qā'id in Mascara: FR ANOM GGA1E116, 23 – 06 – 1839; ʿAbd al-Qādir's preaching against the French colonists 'buying the virtue of women', Correspondance Politique/Maroc/15, 03-11-1845.
136 Churchill, 1867, p. 295.

many of which are drawn upon throughout this book, were carried out in Arabic and through translators.[137] It is clear from his many intellectual achievements that acquiring the language of his 'adoptive nation' would hardly have been beyond him. One might draw a contrast with Arab Muslims of the period who did evince such interests. The Egyptian Rifāʿah Al-Ṭahṭāwī, for instance, had spent a comparable duration in France a decade earlier. While there, he

> 'acquired a precise knowledge of the French language and the problems of translating it into Arabic. He read books on ancient history, Greek philosophy and mythology... a life of Napoleon, some French poetry, including Racine, Lord Chesterfield's letters to his son; and most important, something of the French thought of the eighteenth century – Voltaire, Condillac, Rousseau's *Social Contract*, and the main works of Montesquieu.'[138]

None of this could be said of ʿAbd al-Qādir, and there is little evidence that this period represented a 'European turn' in his thought in this respect.

The case can safely be made that ʿAbd al-Qādir's impression of French civilisation was improved by his time in France – especially once he had been released and widely fêted. It is not clear that this improvement, however, was sufficient to bring about either devoted Francophilia or a 'disillusionment and despair... an acute spiritual crisis'[139] demanding a new spiritual departure. One may also safely assume that ʿAbd al-Qādir's gratitude to Louis Napoleon for undoing the treachery of Louis Philippe was quite genuine. The Ottoman Sultan, on meeting him, would later remark that he had 'never heard a man speak so ill of one man and so well of another as Abd el-Kader had spoken of Louis Phillippe and Louis Napoleon'.[140] We have already seen ʿAbd al-Qādir praise Louis Napoleon for fulfilling French promises 'he himself had not made': he viewed the rulers of France as separate individuals, not fungible representatives of a corporate polity.[141]

Finally, there is no reason to doubt that he felt bound by the promises he made during his captivity and release; the terms of the oaths publicly taken by ʿAbd al-Qādir and his companions (such as those quoted above) were absolutely solemn. No more solemn are easily imaginable, in fact. In spite of protests

---

137 Blunt [1947, p.279] does assert that by the end of his life, ʿAbd al-Qādir eventually learned to 'speak French passably...[but] still preferred to make use of an interpreter'. Evidence of this unconvincing assertion is lacking, however.

138 Hourani, 2008, p. 69.

139 Weismann, 2001a, p. 150.

140 Rose to the Foreign Office, FO 195/385 and FO 78/928, 11 – 01 – 1853.

141 In this, as in so much else, ʿAbd al-Qādir's attitude is a decidedly not a Modern one.

at the time of his release, especially from French colonists in Algeria who feared his return[142] (with lingering suspicion long after), there is no evidence that he would ever be unfaithful to those promises. The generous pension which would be paid to him in perpetuity by France, along with the political benefit he would derive from balancing French and Ottoman powers against one another to his own advantage, would in any event have provided ample inducement to keeping faith for a less scrupulous man in ʿAbd al-Qādir's position.

Returned from Paris, his release secured and prosperity guaranteed, ʿAbd al-Qādir had only to prepare his followers for their long-delayed voyage east. By this time, negotiations had already been underway between France and the Ottoman Empire regarding where he would be sent. For its part, the British government also pressed the Ottomans to accept ʿAbd al-Qādir – albeit as a favour to France and abjuring all responsibility for any intrigues in which he might once more involve himself.[143]

Before 1852 was out, the Ottoman Minister of Foreign Affairs had confirmed that ʿAbd al-Qādir would live at Bursa, accepted as a gesture of amity towards France, with whom the Ottoman Sublime Porte shared concerns over ʿAbd al-Qādir's potential for mischief.[144] ʿAbd al-Qādir himself was soon appraised of the fact that the Porte had purchased a 'very large' domicile for him in Bursa, to which a French steam frigate would transport him and his companions, and where he would be re-united with old friends including his former representative (*wakīl*) among the French in Algeria, Hadj el-Habeb al-Maher.[145] There he would also receive his stipend from the French government, which would be managed by an agent of France, initially Boissonet. After ʿAbd al-Qādir protested at this,[146] it was accepted that he would be paid directly, with Boissonet instructed to depart Bursa as promptly as possible after their arrival.[147]

All these arrangements in place, ʿAbd al-Qādir and his companions would set out from Marseilles at the close of the year, visiting the active Mount Etna

---

142 E.g. Bône Chamber of Commerce to the Ministry of War, FR ANOM GGA1E235, 21-08-1852; Algiers Chamber of Commerce to the Ministry of War, FR ANOM GGA1E235, 31-08-1852, 01-09-1852.

143 Malmesbury to Cowley, FO 146.445, 25-10-1852.

144 Fuad Effendi to de la Valette, Correspondance Politique/Turquie/310, 07-11-1852.

145 De Lhuys to ʿAbd al-Qādir, Correspondance Politique des Consuls/Turquie/Brousse/1, 11-12-1852.

146 ʿAbd al-Qādir to de Lhuys, Correspondance Politique des Consuls/Turquie/Brousse/1, 12-12-1852.

147 De Lhuys to ʿAbd al-Qādir, Correspondance Politique des Consuls/Turquie/Brousse/1, 16-12-1852.

and a Sicilian Benedictine monastery as honoured guests *en route*.[148] Finally returned to the Muslim world at Istanbul, ʿAbd al-Qādir and his companions were free at last – but their story far from over.

148 Boissonet to de Lhuys, Correspondance Politique des Consuls/Turquie/Brousse/1, 28-12-1852.

4.0 Chapter Four – From Istanbul to Damascus, 1853–1864

We shall now follow ʿAbd al-Qādir from the moment of his setting foot on Muslim soil until his return from his final pilgrimage to Mecca. This will span the years between 1853 and 1864, describing his reception in Istanbul, his establishing of an Algerian colony in Bursa, his pilgrimage to Jerusalem, and his settling in Damascus. It will be necessary to discuss his most famous written work of the period as well as his most celebrated martial exploit: the *Dhikrā al-ʿĀqil* and his heroic defence of Damascus' Christians at the head of a North African emigrant militia. In the process, we shall engage with the manner in which these have been represented in the secondary literature as evidence for the 'conversion experience' ʿAbd al-Qādir is presumed to have undergone while captive in France. The result will be an account of his first decade after his release by Napoleon III, one that obviates the need for the narratives of conversion and permits us to see his life and its many stages in terms of continuity rather than disjuncture.

4.1 An Algerian Island off the Sea of Marmara

ʿAbd al-Qādir and his entourage arrived in Istanbul on the 7th of January, 1853. The Ottoman capital fêted him as a 'Champion of Islam' – a cause to which he demonstrated his devotion by repeated visits to the mosque on the day of his arrival.[1] He had finally achieved the goal he had demanded, from his *Risālah on Hijrah* to his departure from North Africa to his prison letters to the King of France: he had finally been permitted to migrate from Christian lands and return to the bosom of a Muslim community. The community, in turn, welcomed him. Before departing for his allotted home of Bursa, he was received by the most senior figures in the Empire – including the Foreign Minister, the Shaykh al-Islam, the Grand Vizier, and the Ottoman Sultan himself.[2] In spite of French protestations, ʿAbd al-Qādir was presented to the Sultan by the Grand Vizier, to the exclusion of the nonplussed French diplomatic staff.[3] From the moment of his disembarkation, ʿAbd al-Qādir found himself embroiled in Ottoman reservations about French claims to the former

1 Rose to the Foreign Office, FO 195/385 and FO 78/928, 11-01-1853.
2 Boissonet to the Ministry of Foreign Affairs, Correspondance Politique des Consuls/Turquie/Brousse/1, 15-01-1853; De la Valette to the Ministry of Foreign Affairs, Correspondance Politique/Turquie/311, 15-01-1853.
3 Rose to the Foreign Office, FO 195/385 and FO 78/928, 08-01-1853.

DOI 10.1515/9783110499513-006

Beylik of Algiers – and hence about his own ambiguous national status.[4] Both the French and the Ottoman authorities wished to claim ʿAbd al-Qādir as their own subject – both to retain a symbol of their respective claims to territory and so as to control him. This issue, which had been raised by the Moroccan court for opposite reasons a decade earlier,[5] would persist until ʿAbd al-Qādir's death and beyond. (Only in the 20th century would the Ottomans relinquish their claim on 'Ottoman North Africa'[6].) While it sometimes made his position precarious, he would soon turn this to his benefit, carving out a niche for himself beyond the complete control of either party.

Given the narratives of conversion discussed in the previous chapter, can we question the Porte's concerns over ʿAbd al-Qādir's affiliation? Had not ʿAbd al-Qādir declared during the plebiscite on Empire that he was French on that day – and perhaps afterwards? The British Ambassador to Constantinople, present at ʿAbd al-Qādir's arrival, presents a more ambiguous picture of the *amīr*'s stance. ʿAbd al-Qādir's embrace of Napoleon III, as he himself had said and as we have already noted, distinguished the latter for having 'fulfilled promises that others had made, but he had not;' it was to Napoleon III's magnanimity that ʿAbd al-Qādir felt obliged, less than that of a corporate entity called 'France'. ʿAbd al-Qādir distinguished clearly between the persons of the current and previous French leaders on the one hand and of the French in general on the other. He boasted to the Ottoman Sultan's chamberlain of having 'killed 100,000 Frenchmen', while – as the previous chapter has mentioned – '[t]he Sultan said he had never heard a man speak so ill of one man and so well of another as Abd el-Kader had spoken of Louis Phillipe and Louis Napoleon.'[7] The British Ambassador describes ʿAbd al-Qādir as appearing very grateful to Napoleon III, yet still inclined to 'assert Musulman supremacy over the French'.[8]

There was no suspicion that ʿAbd al-Qādir had either the immediate means or the intention to assert such supremacy by force, and his passage to his new home at Bursa was duly expedited. Once settled, he became a magnet for North African émigrés, particularly those who had followed him in the past. He was even permitted a correspondence with followers in Algeria, albeit (unsurprisingly) subject to French surveillance.[9] Though highly respected by the Turk-

4 Rose to the Foreign Office, FO 195/385 and FO 78/928, 11-01-1853.
5 Bendris to Drummond Hay, Correspondance Politique/Maroc/11, 20-07-1844; see Chapter One.
6 Julien, 1964, p. 1.
7 *Ibid.*
8 *Ibid.*
9 De Lhuys to Nollentz, Correspondance Politique des Consuls/Turquie/Brousse/1, 02-03-1853.

ish population of Bursa, ʿAbd al-Qādir avoided contact with them;[10] he immediately became the undisputed head of what amounted to an Algerian colony. He found himself once again ruling over an Algerian population – not by the coast of the Mediterranean, but by that of the Sea of Marmara.

The Arab community rapidly growing[11] around ʿAbd al-Qādir was largely dependent upon him, and revered him as their patron.[12] He soon began the project of acquiring farmland outside of the city so as to provide gainful occupation for his followers.[13] Just as he had enlisted Europeans to introduce modern technical innovations during his rule in Algeria, so too did he hire several Polish farmers to assist in the running of his agricultural enterprise at Bursa, using novel European methods.[14] For his own part, and when not overseeing his farmlands, ʿAbd al-Qādir occupied himself with his perennial interests of religion and warfare.

As well as providing religious instruction to his family and followers[15] as he had done in Algeria and in France, ʿAbd al-Qādir continued his long-standing practice of study and patronage of scholarship. As he had done in Algeria, so once more he set his agents to collecting manuscripts.[16] While he had failed in his youthful project of building a library at Tagdempt, he would contribute to the world of letters during the following years by assembling an edition of Ibn al-ʿArabī's monumental *Futūḥāt Makkiyyah* – of which he has been described as 'the first modern editor'.[17] He would also begin composing, at the request of the French Asiatic Society, a prose text entitled *Dhikrā al-ʿĀqil wa Tanbīh al-Ghāfil,* which he would have translated into French in Damascus. Its contents and reception will be discussed below, as will its part in the narratives of conversion which have developed around ʿAbd al-Qādir.

10 Rousseau to the Ministry of Foreign Affairs, Correspondance Politique des Consuls/Turquie/Brousse/1, 04-05-1853.

11 Rousseau to the Ministry of Foreign Affairs, Correspondance Politique des Consuls/Turquie/Brousse/1, 23-10-1853.

12 Rousseau to the Ministry of Foreign Affairs, Correspondance Politique des Consuls/Turquie/Brousse/1, 20-05-1854.

13 Rousseau to the Ministry of Foreign Affairs, Correspondance Politique des Consuls/Turquie/Brousse/1, 13-11-1853.

14 Rousseau to the Ministry of Foreign Affairs, Correspondance Politique des Consuls/Turquie/Brousse/1, 14-12-1853.

15 Rousseau to the Ministry of Foreign Affairs, Correspondance Politique des Consuls/Turquie/Brousse/1, 04-05-1853.

16 Rousseau to the Ministry of Foreign Affairs, Correspondance Politique des Consuls/Turquie/Brousse/1, 04-05-1853.

17 Étienne, 2003, p. 269.

As for ʿAbd al-Qādir's martial interests, rumours that he would be given a senior command within the Ottoman military proved false[18] – though perhaps his anti-Ottomanism might have prevented him from taking up such an offer even had it been made. Nevertheless, he maintained a keen interest in military affairs: his French handler in Bursa recounts that ʿAbd al-Qādir would often press him for news on the Crimean War,[19] enjoying mapping out Allied and Russian strategic positions and discussing military tactics.[20] The exaggeratedly pacific stance which had in Paris led ʿAbd al-Qādir to diplomatically feign aversion even to horses on the grounds of their martial symbolism,[21] had been abandoned. His duty of care towards his numerous followers, however, had not.

Beyond supplying financial, technical, and moral support for his community, ʿAbd al-Qādir also leveraged his value to France against both French and Ottoman claims against himself and his people. He thereby acquired the influence to intercede against other local influences, beginning to eke out for himself an ambiguously independent political space. He sent numerous letters to the French government to enlist their help when his own influence with the Ottomans proved insufficient, or in support of Arabs accused by French authorities[22] – a pattern which would continue until his death.[23] This strategy was as evident to the French as it was to the Ottomans, but ʿAbd al-Qādir never pushed his luck to breaking point – in spite of a brief falling-out with his French handler in Bursa[24] – the first in a series of quarrels between the amīr and French representatives. His habit of demanding free passage at French expense for his followers from North Africa (even complaining at the suggestion that this be below decks rather than in cabins)[25] did cause consternation in both Ministries both

18 Rousseau to the Ministry of Foreign Affairs, Correspondance Politique des Consuls/Turquie/Brousse/1, 26-07-1854.

19 Rousseau to the Ministry of Foreign Affairs, Correspondance Politique des Consuls/Turquie/Brousse/1, 24-02-1855.

20 Rousseau to the Ministry of Foreign Affairs, Correspondance Politique des Consuls/Turquie/Brousse/1, 26-07-1854.

21 Extract from *Le Mubacher*, FR ANOM GGA1E235, 15-11-1852.

22 E.g. ʿAbd al-Qādir to Napoleon III, Correspondance Politique des Consuls/Turquie/Brousse/1, 30-05-1853; ʿAbd al-Qādir to de Lhuys, Correspondance Politique des Consuls/Turquie/Brousse/1, 30-05-1853.

23 E.g. ʿAbd al-Qādir's intercession with French representatives to the Porte, two years before his death, on behalf of Hauache Bey – enclosed with Flesch's despatch to the French Constantinople Embassy, Damas/Consulat/35, 21-05-1881.

24 De Lhuys to Rousseau, Correspondance Politique des Consuls/Turquie/Brousse/1, 08-06-1853; Rousseau to de Lhuys, Correspondance Politique des Consuls/Turquie/Brousse/1, 28-06-1853.

25 ʿAbd al-Qādir to de Lhuys, Correspondance Politique des Consuls/Turquie/Brousse/1, 14-06-1853.

of Foreign Affairs and of War, however.[26] Concerns were also voiced over the rapid growth of ʿAbd al-Qādir's Algerian colony in Turkey, especially with regard to the suspicions it seemed likely to arouse in the Ottoman government.[27]

The diplomatic awkwardness of locating a sizeable Algerian colony (let alone one enjoying French patronage) so near to Istanbul in fact dissipated in the event. By early 1855 the Algerian community had begun to diminish in size, with people driven away by the relative cold and damp of the winter in comparison to their North African homelands.[28] March saw the arrival of a series of destructive earthquakes, which would ultimately leave Bursa ruined and largely deserted.[29] By April, ʿAbd al-Qādir and his community had fled to his country estates, where most lived in tents. Under the circumstances, it was relatively easy for him to acquire French acquiescence with his move away from Bursa, in spite of understandable French qualms over his living in majority-Arab territories. [It has recently been suggested in the secondary literature that fear of a Russian invasion might have motivated ʿAbd al-Qādir's move.[30] This seems unlikely, especially given how assiduously he kept himself informed as to the progress of the Crimean War, which had by this point turned against Russia.] A brief return to Paris via Istanbul[31] to plead his case before Napoleon III (whose coronation ʿAbd al-Qādir had not been invited to attend)[32] proved sufficient to that end – as well as occasioning his celebrated visit to the Great Exposition.[33] By the end of the year, he was welcomed to his new home in Damascus.

26 E. g. Ministry of Foreign Affairs to Rousseau, Correspondance Politique des Consuls/Turquie/1, 06-08-1853 and Ministry of War to Ministry of Foreign Affairs, Correspondance Politique des Consuls/Turquie/Brousse/1, 20-08-1853.

27 Ministry of War to Ministry of Foreign Affairs, Correspondance Politique des Consuls/Turquie/Brousse/1, 18-11-1853.

28 Rousseau to the Ministry of Foreign Affairs, Correspondance Politique des Consuls/Turquie/Brousse/1, 24-02-1855.

29 Rousseau to the Ministry of Foreign Affairs, Correspondance Politique des Consuls/Turquie/Brousse/1, 20-03-1855; 15-04-1855; 18-04-1855; 22-04-1855.

30 Penot, 2008, p. 40.

31 Ministry of War to the Ministry of Foreign Affairs, Correspondance Politique des Consuls/Turquie/Brousse/1, 31-08-1855.

32 Rousseau to the Ministry of Foreign Affairs, Correspondance Politique des Consuls/Turquie/Brousse/1, 01-06-1853.

33 E.g. Étienne, 2003, p. 260.

4.2 A Reminder to the Reasonable and an Admonishment to the Negligent

Before continuing with our account of ʿAbd al-Qādir's Levantine years, some attention must be addressed to his writings of the time. As mentioned above, the period at hand saw ʿAbd al-Qādir compose the text known as the *Dhikrā al-ʿĀqil wa Tanbīh al-Ghāfil*, partly building upon his earlier, polemical *Miqrāḍ al-Ḥādd*, composed in France. He would later have the newer text translated into French by 'a Christian consular translator from a noble family in Damascus, who excelled to a greater degree in his French than in his Arabic,'[34] and sent to France at the behest of the Asiatic Society. An essay on the absolute necessity of the divine revelation, ʿAbd al-Qādir himself describes it as 'an urging to contemplation and a condemnation of unthinking emulation'.[35] The treatise's central theme is the necessary dependence of the intellect, in spite of its great virtues, on divine guidance through revelation. The translated text was sent to the French academy in what appears to have been a gently proselytising spirit, chiding his academic audience lest they succumb to intellectual arrogance. Its contents and reception will be discussed here – both because of the insights it offers into ʿAbd al-Qādir's mind, and also because it has come to be represented as evidence for the narratives of conversion whose applicability to ʿAbd al-Qādir's life we have been putting into doubt.

The main text of the *Dhikrā* itself opens with an elaboration on an (unattributed) maxim taken from one of Abū Ḥāmid al-Ghazālī's major works: know people by way of the truth, rather than truth by way of people.[36]

> 'Know this: it is incumbent on the reasonable person (*al-ʿāqil*) that he consider each utterance [on its own terms], rather than analysing the one who makes the statement. If the utterance is true [in itself], then accept it, regardless if its speaker was well-known as truthful or as given to falsehood. Indeed, gold may be brought forth from dust, the narcissus from a bulb, anti-venom from serpents, roses from the thorns. Thus the reasonable person knows people by means of the truth, not the truth by means of people. The word of wisdom is the goal of the reasonable person's search, which he takes from everyone with whom he finds it, irrespective of whether that [other] person be contemptible or exalted. [Even] the least [in degree of stature] among the reasonable is distinguished from the general population by a number of factors, among which is the fact that he does not detest honey if he finds it in the cupping glass of the cupper.[37] He knows that blood is unclean not because of its setting, but

34 The words of Dr. Ḥaqqī, editor of the 1966 Damascus edition [*Dhikrā*, p. 9].

35 *Dhikrā*, p. 30.

36 Al-Ghazālī, 1981, p. 114.

37 A reference to an antiquated medical practice (advocated by the Prophet, according to al-Bukhārī), involving the blistering of the patient's skin by means of heated 'cups'.

> due to its own intrinsic nature [*bi-dhātihi*]. If honey is free of this [unclean] characteristic then this property is not transferred to it through its being placed in the conventional locus of unclean blood. One is not, therefore, obliged to flee from it. [The contrary] is a vain delusion, prevalent among the majority of the people. It is the association of speech with its speaker, accepting it on the basis of [the people's] high regard for him, even if the utterance were false [*bāṭil*]. [Similarly,] if they associate the speech with one of whom they think badly, they reject it – even if the utterance were true [*ḥaqqan*]. Always they know the truth by means of men, not men by means of truth.'[38]

This opening gambit is more subtle a piece of inter-cultural rhetoric than it might immediately appear. As well as echoing one of the most famous and respected writers of the Islamic tradition, al-Ghazālī, the text can easily be read as an urging to his eventual (non-Muslim) French audience that they not reject his ideas out of hand on the basis of their Islamic character or on grounds of hostility to himself.

With respect to what one might call the philosophical content of the *Dhikrā*, another opening passage requires reproduction here. It pertains not only to the identity of the piece's subject (*al-ʿāqil*, loosely speaking 'the rational or mentally competent person'), but also his distinguishing characteristics (*ʿaql* and *ʿilm*, loosely speaking 'intellect and knowledge' – the latter proceeding from the former 'like the fruit from the tree'):[39]

> 'The person of knowledge is one with a facility for distinguishing among utterances between truthfulness [*ṣidq*] and falsehood [*kidhb*], among doctrines between the true and the false [*bayna al-ḥaqq wa al-bāṭil fī al-ʿitiqādāt*] and among actions between the beautiful and the ugly [idiomatically 'virtuous and vicious'; *al-jamīl wa al-qabīḥ fī al-afʿāl*]. He is not confounded by doubts as to [the difference between] true and false, lies and honesty, beauty and ugliness.'[40]

What ʿAbd al-Qādir is discussing when he speaks of reason or reasonableness in this text is essentially the facility for discernment [*idrāk al-farq*] – between different things, states, and courses of action. It is because of such usages that the term *ʿāqil* is in Islamic law the standard word for 'a suitable witness',[41] accountable for their deeds[42] and aware of the difference between right and wrong. We see in the passage quoted above that this faculty includes inter-personal and aesthetic as well as logical and ethical spheres. It is further divided between universal 'necessities' (*ḍarūriyyāt*) and specific knowledge informed by experi-

38 *Dhikrā*, pp. 33 – 34.
39 *Dhikrā*, p. 49.
40 *Dhikrā*, pp. 34.
41 Cornell, 1998, p. 78.
42 Stelzer in Winter (ed.), 2008, p. 171.

ence.[43] He compares the former to the knowledge of a would-be writer who knows the letters of script, but not how to arrange them meaningfully.[44] As in the *Miqrāḍ*, knowledge informed by experience is throughout the text given preference over pure abstraction – indeed the term *ʿāqil* is at one point said to be truly appropriate only for possessors of experience-based knowledge[45] – as much a Sufi *topos* as an empiricist assertion.

This facility of mind, conceived on whichever level, is throughout the text treated as absolutely necessary to human success and fulfilment. In fact, this discerning consciousness, related to a tendency to make decisions on the basis of one sort of 'evidence' or another (*bil-dalīl*),[46] is asserted to be the generic distinguishing characteristic of humanity.[47] This is not to say that such reasonableness[48] is sufficient unto itself, however. On the contrary, ʿAbd al-Qādir presents this facility as essentially limited, contingent, prone to error, and ultimately inadequate to the task of gaining a sure footing in the eternal verities. *ʿAql*, while perhaps a necessary condition for the good human life, is throughout this text rejected outright as a sufficient one.

The solution, according to ʿAbd al-Qādir in another echo of al-Ghazālī tinged with Sufi symbolism, is divine intervention – through illumination and legislative revelation:

> 'Just as the seeing eye is incapable of perceiving things unless lights shine upon them as does the Sun, thus is the reasoning mind incapable of flawlessly perceiving the realities [*idrāk al-ḥaqā'iq dūna khaṭa'*] unless there shine upon it the lights of that success and guidance granted it by God the Most High [*anwār al-tawfīq wa al-hidāyah min allah taʿālā*].'[49]

43 E.g., *Dhikrā*, p. 51.
44 *Ibid.*
45 *Dhikrā*, p. 50.
46 *Dhikrā*, p. 34. The 'ambiguous' Arabic term can be employed both for evidence of an experimental and of an argumentative sort [van den Bergh, *EI2*, entry on *dalīl*].
47 *Dhikrā*, pp. 39–40, 41: this facility is described as man's 'characteristic' (*khāṣiyyat al-insān*) which 'distinguishes him from the other existent things'... it is 'the completion of man' (*kamāl al-insān*), which all people 'intrinsically love'.
48 The term 'reasonableness' is included here as an alternative translation to 'rational', as the Arabic term in this context overlaps with understandings of each in certain English-language discussions of this distinction (such as that of Stephen Toulmin [2001, *passim*], who distinguishes 'reasonableness' as reason contextualised by lived experience in a manner relatable to ʿAbd al-Qādir's typology's forms of reason informed by experience). This translation has also been used by writers on Islamic ethics (e.g. Stelzer in Winter ed., 2008, p. 171).
49 *Dhikrā*, p. 38.

ʿAbd al-Qādir states clearly and repeatedly that there are forms of knowledge and its objects beyond those graspable by the mind alone. These, among human beings, are reached only by the Prophets, thereby necessitating others' cleaving to the revelations the Prophets bring:

> 'The minds of the Prophets [*ʿuqūl al-anbiyā'*] are unlike the minds of the rest of the people [*laysat ka-ʿuqūl sā'ir al-nās*]...The sciences [*al-ʿulūm*] do not reach or lead to the realities of things except through trusting in the Prophets and following them... this is to say that the sciences of the Prophets are greater than those of the mind [*al-ʿaql*]... And beyond the mind is another degree [*ṭawrun*] and another matter [*amrun*], from which the mind is separated and which it cannot reach on its own – but rather only through something else, [just] as the sensoria are isolated from the objects of the mind.'[50]

ʿAbd al-Qādir then posits an additional organising principle (or principles) prior to that of *ʿaql*. *ʿAql* is described as only one of four human 'powers' (*quwwāt*), the judicious balance (*ʿitidāl*) between which results in a complete or perfect person (*insān kāmil*).[51] The *quwwah ʿaqliyyah* is itself furthermore governed by a golden mean of moderation. Immoderately too much or too little *ʿaql* (*ifrāṭ* or *tafrīṭ*) will result in blameworthy (*madhmūmah*) characteristics: 'deceit, spite, swindling, slyness and fraud' in the first instance, and 'simple-mindedness, imbecility, confusion, stupidity, and madness' in the second.[52] Inasmuch as all of this is the case, one must assume that these 'judicious balances' are the embodiment or result of principle(s) other than *ʿaql* itself. Such principle(s) are not determined by *ʿaql*, but rather *ʿaql* is subject to them; the fact that there can be a notion of 'too much *ʿaql*' rules it out as self-sufficient regulating principle. *ʿAql* itself is clearly not in itself the ultimate organising force for ʿAbd al-Qādir. Divine decree and guidance provide play that role.

The *Dhikrā*, then, represents both an exhortation to the cultivation of discernment, and a pious reiteration of the need for divine revelation. It is this view which explains the work's title: '*a reminder to the reasonable and an admonishment to the negligent*'. The 'admonishment to the negligent' is clear: the human faculty of discernment requires effort and attention, according to ʿAbd al-Qādir, and must not be neglected in favour of complacent imitation of those around one. The 'reminder', on the other hand, is not aimed at 'the negligent' such that he might become reasonable, but at the 'reasonable man' himself. This reminder is intended to underline the indispensability of divine revelation

---

50 *Dhikrā*, pp. 52, 82–3.
51 *Dhikrā*, p. 57.
52 *Dhikrā*, p. 57–8.

as that which alone makes reasonableness a reasonable proposition. That such revelation is embodied in the Islamic Shariah does not come into question for ʿAbd al-Qādir.[53] After all, Ibn al-ʿArabī's characteristic 'mystical etymology' (in which ʿAbd al-Qādir generally follows him: see Chapter Five) of the term *ʿāqil* defines it through its root *ʿayn-qāf-lām* (usually to *bind, tie*, or *tether*), as 'the one who binds himself to God... to His Command and His prohibition'.[54] However, it is not primarily as a pietistic or moralising text that the *Dhikrā* has recently been represented, as we shall see below, but as something quite different – something more decidedly modern, and something explicitly implicated in the 'Road to Damascus' narratives of conversion developed around him.

Before continuing to a discussion of the *Dhikrā*'s deployment in the service of such narratives in the secondary literature, a final explication is necessary. This relates to the abovementioned characterisation of the *Dhikrā* as 'an urging to contemplation and a condemnation of unthinking emulation'.[55] The late 19th and 20th centuries have seen momentous new movements arise in Islamic thought, many of which question a great deal of traditional thinking. There exists a danger of anachronistically reading ʿAbd al-Qādir's criticism of imitation [*taqlīd*] as a call for free-thought such as those which more modern Muslims have made. It is nothing of the sort.

ʿAbd al-Qādir is not proclaiming a Kantian *sapere aude.*[56] *Taqlīd*, though translatable in unpalatable terms as 'imitation', is a more neutral term in the history of Islamic thought, perhaps better rendered in English as 'respect for (arguments from) authority'. Certain forms of *taqlīd* are traditionally seen as defensible and even necessary, and ʿAbd al-Qādir seems to take this for granted throughout his work. As a follower and teacher of the Mālikī *madhhab*, moreover, as Commins rightly points out,[57] ʿAbd al-Qādir himself cannot be considered to be calling for absolutely free individual *ijtihād* or theological judgement, as some 20th-century Muslim thinkers were later to do.[58]

---

53 The orthodoxy of ʿAbd al-Qādir's view of the relationship between Islam and the other 'Abrahamic' monotheisms is accepted by Commins [1988, p. 124], though as will be seen it has not been recognised by all other writers. This matter will recur during the coming discussion of ʿAbd al-Qādir's *Kitāb al-Mawāqif* in Chapter Five.

54 Stelzer, in Winter (ed.), 2008, p. 172.

55 *Dhikrā*, p. 30.

56 The Enlightenment epigram *par excellence:* 'Dare to be wise' by thinking for oneself in the face of traditional authority, from Kant's [1874] essay *What is Enlightenment?*

57 Commins, 1988, p. 123.

58 'The term [*taqlīd*] has been widely adopted into Orientalist discourse where it is almost invariably translated as "blind submission". The same is broadly true of modernist Islamic discourse. The absence of any positive assessment of this term in modern commentary tends to produce a negative

The existence of the *madhdhāhib* is itself related to the question of *taqlīd*; *madhdhāhib* evolved partly as systematic sources for emulation in the more technical questions – contingent on more fundamental matters which were not to be emulated; *furūʿ* as opposed to *uṣūl*, in a typical distinction – 'juristic' rather than 'creedal' matters. Nowhere does ʿAbd al-Qādir reject his *madhhab*, and we have already seen his respect for the Mālikī, and to a lesser extent Shāfiʿī, *madhhab* in his *Risālah on Hijrah*. He would continue his connection with Mālikī jurisprudence until his death, giving classes in Damascus[59] as he had at Amboise.[60] His position, then, seems closer to that of the likes of authorities such as al-Shāfiʿī who forbade *taqlīd* only to those capable of reaching the correct conclusions on their own[61] than to the 20th-century Muslims who reject accepting traditional authority in general.[62]

That this more moderate position is the one argued for by ʿAbd al-Qādir is made clear in the *Dhikrā* when he specifies precisely which kind of *taqlīd* he opposes: 'absolute imitativeness to the exclusion of reason' [*al-taqlīd al-maḥḍ maʿ ʿazl al-ʿaql*][63] – a quite conventional admonition also to be found in his earlier *Risālah on Hijrah.*[64] Rather, ʿAbd al-Qādir's criticism of *taqlīd* is both a call for Muslims to exert themselves more fully in understanding their religion, and a gentle chiding of his Christian audience for their continued adherence to their parents' religion in spite of its flaws and supersession. [65]

The historical context of the *Dhikrā*'s writing is certainly remarkable: an invitation from the French academy to a Muslim writer, let alone one famous for his fifteen-year struggle against France. Its content, however, is far less novel; ʿAbd al-Qādir's arguments in the *Dhikrā* are uncomplicated and uncontroversial.

view of more than 1,000 years of Islamic history... Since the late 19th century, many western scholars and modernist Muslims have characterised the earlier Islamic tradition as dominated by *taḳlīd*, meaning blind imitation. This reflects lack of sympathy and understanding on the part of the western scholars; on the part of Muslims, it reflects a desire for radical reform, usually associated with a return to the time before *taḳlīd* became established. The motive here is technically fundamentalist, though associated indifferently with liberal or conservative views... Neither in theory nor in practice, in spite of the intimations of Orientalists and modernising Muslims, can it be recognised as essentially a principle of stasis...' – Calder, *Encyclopaedia of Islam 2*, entry on *taḳlīd*.

59 Goldziher, 1981, p. 242.

60 *Tuḥfah*, pp. 529–530.

61 Thereby permitting it to those who are (for whatever reason) incapable.

62 See Calder, *ibid.*

63 Al-Jaz'āirī, 1966, p. 83. Emphasis added.

64 '[The Prophet's] saying that they would follow the [bad] examples of those before, span for span and cubit for cubit – this up to the point that, had those entered the burrow of a lizard, so must they [also] enter it... Bukhārī, in his *Ṣaḥīḥ* [Book 56, number 662], relates this' *Tuḥfah*, p. 412.

65 *Dhikrā*, p. 36. For a discussion of *taḥrīf*, see for instance Tarakci and Sayar, 2005, pp. 227–245.

Nevertheless, its remarkable historical setting has led to it being held up as a new intellectual departure. It is this development which will now be discussed.

4.3 The *Dhikrā* and a European Conversion

Some disagreement exists in the secondary literature as to the nature of the *Dhikrā*'s genesis and significance. Where Commins and Weismann present the *Dhikrā* as 'directed primarily to Muslims,'[66] Michel Chodkiewicz seems convinced that ʿAbd al-Qādir's original target audience were the non-Muslim Frenchmen 'whose ability to understand the traditional teachings of Islam the Amir had good reason not to overestimate,'[67] dismissing it as 'lacking originality'.[68] Weismann, following Chodkiewicz, characterises this and the later *Kitāb al-Mawāqif* as of 'two entirely different types'[69] – adding also that the *Dhikrā* is particularly distinguished by its 'rationalist character'.[70] Commins, too, remarks on its drawing on the 'rationalistic tradition of classical Islamic philosophy'.[71]

A putative rationalism plays a major role in narratives describing ʿAbd al-Qādir's supposed 'conversion' to a new view of the world on exposure to 'rational' French civilisation. The work of Weismann in particular attempts to systematically present this characteristic as evidence for ʿAbd al-Qādir's new departure after his imprisonment by France – which we have already seen (in Chapter Three) to be the psychological crux of his and other biographies of the *amīr*. ʿAbd al-Qādir, it is claimed, 'integrat[ed] his profound religious faith with the rationalist mode of thinking underlying the achievements of the west.'[72] He is presented as 'modernis[ing] Akbarī thought... [through] his redefinition of the relationship between mysticism and rationalism in Islam.'[73] He has been described as offering a 'rationalistic and humanistic understanding of the Akbari teaching, which was ultimately reflected in the readiness of the incipient bourgeoisie in the cities to be integrated into the emerging new world order under European hegemony.'[74] He

66 Weisman, 2001a, 159.

67 Chodkiewicz, 1995, p. 187.

68 Chodkiewicz, 1995, p. 187; this criticism is not repeated when he compares ʿAbd al-Qādir closely to Ibn al-ʿArabī, whose ideas that author holds in higher esteem.

69 Weismann, 2001, p. 154.

70 *Ibid.*

71 Commins, 1988, p. 123.

72 Weismann, 2001a, p. 157.

73 Weismann, 2001a, p. 154.

74 Weismann, 2001b, pp. 66, 70, 71.

is shown as introducing from Europe the 'major bas[es] of modernity',[75] while 'adapt[ing] the Sharīʿa... by an essentially rationalist reinterpretation of the Islamic sources or by directly borrowing from the west.'[76]

This interpretation, however, does not seem to be supported by the evidence, resulting less from the given facts than from the artificial 'Road to Damascus' narrative structure which has been imposed upon ʿAbd al-Qādir's biography. It should be stressed at the outset that ʿAbd al-Qādir's text does not explicitly engage with any thinkers, rationalist or otherwise, from the European Enlightenment nor the 19th-century France of his day. We can search in vain for direct quotations from modern western philosophers in this or any of ʿAbd al-Qādir's other writings. This significant absence is explicable by the suggestion that ʿAbd al-Qādir never read them – indeed, he could not have done so, lacking knowledge of European languages.

Rather than adducing direct evidence, the assertion that the *Dhikrā* illustrates a post-imprisonment European turn in ʿAbd al-Qādir's thought entails a more circumstantial argument. It relies on discerning in the amīr's writing from this point onwards a specifically modern and European rationalist quality in spite of its failure to engage explicitly with the debates that make that term conventionally meaningful. Moreover, this argument must necessarily be made *malgré lui*; as ʿAbd al-Qādir himself does not explicitly avow this novel quality, it must be imputed to him. *Pace* Weismann, however, this study supports the views of Chodkiewicz and Commins that this particular text [later writings are addressed in Chapter Five] is not intellectually innovative within its Islamic context. It adds, moreover, that it is also not usefully described as rationalist.

'[D]isputes about the nature of rationality... are apparently as manifold and as intractable as disputes about justice,' notes Alasdair MacIntyre.[77] 'Rationalism', meanwhile, has acquired numerous differing applications in a variety of fields and periods, from the precise to the vague and impressionistic – not least in topics touched by what Edward Said has termed 'Orientalist' discourses. Orientalists of the sort criticised by Said use it simply to indicate some kind of similarity to (normatively 'rational') European standards. Still less tangible usages are possible; one might even go so far as to speak of the geometric 'rationalist aesthetic'[78] of French formal gardens such as those which were first planted at ʿAbd al-Qādir's final prison, the Chateau d'Amboise. This, at least, might fall

---

75 Weismann, 2001b, pp. 66.
76 Weismann, 2001a, p. 7.
77 MacIntyre, 2004, p. 2.
78 E.g. Toulmin, 2001, p. 38.

within ʿAbd al-Qādir's experience. It has already been made clear, however, that something both more significant and more endemic to European modernity is intended by writers such as Weismann who see ʿAbd al-Qādir's later thought as transformed by modern European ideas. He did not 'adapt the Shariah'[79] and 'modernise Akbarī thought'[80] on the basis of a preference for rectilinear planting patterns, nor is he likely to have seen them as 'the bas[es] of modernity',[81] 'underlying the achievements of the west'.[82]

It is in terms of the history of European philosophy that we find a more plausible candidate for the 'European rationalism' imputed by Weismann to ʿAbd al-Qādir. Typically used in opposition to the term 'empiricism',[83] it attempts to describe certain Enlightenment debates as to the ultimate source of reliable knowledge (too subtle and wide-ranging for the current context to permit more than this very rough outline). These were specialised discussions predicated on such notions as that of the disembodied mind (*res cogitans*) and mindless matter (*res extensa*),[84] and a binary opposition between knowledge arising independent from (*a priori*) or dependent upon experience (*a posteriori*) in the world. Where the archetypical empiricist (whom historical individuals tended not to embody) is considered to give absolute priority to physical investigation of the material world on the basis of a *tabula rasa* intellect,[85] the perfect rationalist saw abstract, pre-experiental, *a priori* thought as the preeminent path to Truth. This debate was increasingly closed in the 19th and 20th centuries by numerous philosophical and scientific developments.[86] Were one to attempt to relate ʿAbd al-Qādir's *Dhikrā* to this form of rationalism, even notwithstanding his failure to

---

79 Weismann, 2001a, p. 7.

80 Weismann, 2001a, p. 154.

81 Weismann, 2001b, pp. 66.

82 Weismann, 2001a, p. 157.

83 These positions are sometimes (also not un-problematically) referred to as 'Continental Rationalism' and 'British Empiricism'.

84 These terms are famously used in by *ur*-rationalist René Descartes in his seminal 17th-century *Meditations on First Philosophy.*

85 The classic argument to this effect is found in John Locke's *An Essay Concerning Human Understanding.*

86 By, among many others, Kant's 1781 *Critique of Pure Reason*; Kierkegaard's 1844 *Philosophical Fragments*' psychologising of the Cartesian *cogito*; Pierce and James' 20th-century Pragmatism; the analytic work of Willard Van Orman Quine (particularly his "Two Dogmas of Empiricism" which attacks *a priori/posteriori* distinctions [Quine, 1980, pp. 20–46]); or the writing of Martin Heidegger (for instance on the 'pre-ontological' status of the world in which a given *Dasein* takes part). Critiques of such views have moreover not been limited to departments of philosophy. For discussions of this question from the perspective of cognitive science, for instance, see Lakoff and Johnson, 1999.

take part in the formal discourses involved, one would not find an easy fit.[87] Indeed, one might more easily paint him as opposed to rationalism.

We have seen in this study's earlier discussions of the *Miqrāḍ* and *Dhikrā* that 'Abd al-Qādir privileged knowledge informed by experience in the world over purely abstract ideas – in direct contradistinction to a rationalist's *a priori* idealism. Furthermore, we have seen 'Abd al-Qādir both explicitly and implicitly reject his closest analogue to Enlightenment 'reason' (*'aql*, variously rendered as 'reason', 'reasonableness', 'mental competence', and 'discernment' throughout this chapter) as ultimate guide or path to perfection. His very acceptance of the indispensible reality of the 'inimitable' Divine Revelation is itself a stance which has in other contexts been argued to automatically preclude its proponent's description as 'rationalist'.[88]

Conversely, it has been argued that 'rationality turns to rationalism when reason is prior to revelation.'[89] In terms of the European history of religion, specifically what Weismann has called 'the essentially rationalist interpretation of the Islamic sources',[90] we see a special application of 'rationalism' to the Judaeo-Christian sources. This development is often attributed to Baruch Spinoza's 17th-century *Tractatus Theologico-Politicus*, with salient 18th- and 19th-century contributions by the likes of Reimarus and Ernest Renan (whose *Life of Jesus* was published in 1863 to great controversy and acclaim). Treating scripture as historical texts with human authors, explaining miracles as natural events, rejecting allegory and mystery in favour of literal interpretation and natural reason, this rationalist tradition in biblical hermeneutics is not obviously in evidence in 'Abd al-Qādir's *Dhikrā*... Still less so in his subsequent *Kitāb al-Mawāqif:* a mystical, allegorical, and overtly metaphysical text. There is no evidence to suggest that 'Abd al-Qādir would have found the idea that the Qur'ān is a human artifact rather than divine revelation anything other than scandalous or absurd.

---

87 One might perhaps draw some limited comparisons between individual positions taken by individual rationalists and those taken by 'Abd al-Qādir – such as the fact that both he and Leibniz happen to present man as some sort of microcosm. Conversely, one might point out that he and the critic of rationalism Johann Gottfried Herder (like Ibn Khaldūn!) relate geography and climate to human character. It is far from evident in either case that such vague parallels are the result of 'Abd al-Qādir adopting modern European ideas, however. One might more successfully argue that 'Abd al-Qādir is, directly or indirectly, influenced by dubiously 'European' writers of antiquity and the classical, such as Plato and Aristotle, or Porphyry and Plotinus. This seems, however, an entirely different sort of argument from that brought by Weismann, and would not justify his psychological account.

88 Abrahamov, 1998, p.x.

89 Abrahamov, in Winter *et al.*, 2008, p. 246.

90 Weismann, 2001a, p. 7.

Yet another, still broader understanding of rationalism might be in question, however. This is one which falls somewhere between the philosophically precise and the impressionistic. It is this understanding which is best suggested by Weismann's attributing of 'the achievements of the west' to a 'rationalistic mode of thinking'.[91] This is the sense of rationalism evoked by the popular image of the *savant*, the natural philosopher or scientist of the time, whose technological innovations did so much to cement Europe's pre-eminence on the world stage. Certainly, great advances were being made in the natural sciences in France during ʿAbd al-Qādir's lifetime and immediately prior. These include the introduction of the metric system in 1795, developments in mathematics,[92] physics,[93] chemistry,[94] astronomy,[95] mechanics,[96] medicine,[97] biology,[98] or the opening of the École Polytechnique in 1794.

If one were to attempt to generalise from these developments to a stereotypical image of a 'rationalist mode of thinking', one might characterise it in terms of its abandoning of metaphysical speculation in favour of 'useful knowledge'; its argument on the basis of empirical evidence, inductive inference, deduction, theory construction and falsification; its methodological affinity for classification, collection, cataloguing; and its favouring of materialistic and mechanistic explanations through the language of mathematics. None of these characteristics, however, are strikingly in evidence in ʿAbd al-Qādir's case. It is difficult to see him adopting such a 'mode of thinking' except insofar as he was a technophile – perhaps a necessary, but hardly a sufficient conditon for inclusion among such scientific 'rationalists'. Moreover, we have already seen him to seek out (European) technological innovations many years prior to his time in France [see Chapter One].

The assumption that ʿAbd al-Qādir's mere presence on the same continent as rationalist thinkers must have granted him a significant appreciation of their ideas implies a questionable historicism. However salient the rationalist *philosophes* or scientific *savants* may be to our own impressions of the century leading up to ʿAbd al-Qādir's time in France, their ideas were neither universally understood, nor universally accepted, nor everywhere transparently in evidence. One cannot reliably assume that the (generally Catholic and Monarchist) clerics, mili-

91 Weismann, 2001a, p. 157.
92 E.g. Legendre, Lagrange, Monge, Carnot, Fourier, Galois, Cauchy.
93 E.g. Galvani, Prevost, Fresnel, Ampere.
94 E.g. Lavoisier, Leblanc, Proust, Berthollet, Clement and Desormes, Dulong-Petit.
95 E.g. Laplace, Delambre, Messier.
96 Such as the development of steam engines, mining, road- and bridge building, canals etc.
97 E.g. Pinel, Desault, Bichat.
98 E.g. Lamarck, Cuvier, the early effects of Darwin

tary officers, and aristocrats who were ʿAbd al-Qādir's points of contact with French culture would have shared such views, let alone expounded them to him in adequate depth through translators. In none of his works does ʿAbd al-Qādir quote rationalist philosophers, nor natural scientists, nor does he substantively re-articulate their views in his own terms. His style betrays none of the preoccupation with mathematics and geometry which characterise the work of the thinkers such as Descartes or Spinoza, let alone those practising natural science. Rather, the traditional Islamic sciences of textual interpretation, Qur'ānic reference, and conventional poetic imagery of sky, animals, and polished mirrors[99] predominate from his earliest to his lattermost writings. In this respect, one may again juxtapose ʿAbd al-Qādir with his Arab Muslim contemporaries who *did* read European writers and who were clearly influenced by them in the content and structure of their writing – such as Rifāʿah Al-Ṭahṭāwī.[100]

All of these factors speak against ʿAbd al-Qādir's thought being described as 'rationalist' in any but the very broadest, least informative, and least specifically European or modern of senses.[101] That is, as exhibiting some degree of concern for consistency and structure in a reality which includes ideas of some description and which takes technical questions seriously. The *Dhikrā* is certainly a more directly and less poetically written work than the *Kitāb al-Mawāqif*, for instance, and still less a *dīwān* of pure verse. It is also true that it presents the mental faculties (*ʿaql*) as among mankind's distinguishing characteristics, marking us off from animal species. Finally, it argues for the great importance of the mind's cultivation, albeit never for its supremacy nor for its self-sufficiency. If such very broad and imprecise criteria were sufficient to establish 'rationalism', however, we must fill the world with 'rationalists' at countless historical periods and geographical locales. Such broad and imprecise criteria, moreover, render at best meaningless and at worst chauvinistic the category's arrogation as a European (Enlightenment) preserve. The term, so broadly understood, unavoidably loses its special relevance to the European period contemporary to which ʿAbd al-

99 See, for instance, *Dhikrā*, p. 37. The later *Kitāb al-Mawāqif* does include a novel twist on these time-worn metaphors through its inclusion of the recently-invented photographic camera, however: 'Lustrous bodies are among the greatest symbols for the divine self-manifestations. This is particularly the case with the mirror, and includes the light-based device of our own time, the photograph' [*Kitāb al-Mawāqif*, vol. 2, p. 248].

100 E.g. Hourani, 2008, p. 69.

101 It should be noted that Weismann's study, when not making the case for ʿAbd al-Qādir's adoption of European ideas, uses 'rationalism' to characterise (*inter alia*) both the Mameluk and Ottoman empires, 20th-century Islamic reformers in general, European Modernism, 'western civilisation' in general, the Muʿatazilites, the Falāsifa, both Aristotle and Plato, and Abū Ḥāmid al-Ghazālī [Weismann, 2001a, pp. 2–3, 5, 7, 154–155, 165, 265, 156, 157].

Qādir lived, and hence also to Weismann's attempted illustration of 'the western rationalism ['Abd al-Qādir] now advocated'.[102]

'Rationalism', if understood loosely as a respect for reason and a concern for its cultivation, or indeed an interest in technical matters,[103] has never been exclusively endemic to Europe. As Josef Van Ess reminds us,

> 'for Muslims, reason, *ʿaql*, has always been the chief faculty granted human beings by God. Of course, this was not the independent reason characteristic of the Enlightenment period, but rather an intelligence subject to the will of God.'[104]

On the evidence of ʿAbd al-Qādir's writing in general, and that of those sections of the *Dhikrā al-ʿĀqil* quoted here, it is evidently this mainstream Islamic sense of reason (*ʿaql*) which ʿAbd al-Qādir advocated, rather than an intellectual appropriation from the European Enlightenment. If one were to insist on European comparisons, in fact, one might conclude that the *Dhikrā al-ʿĀqil* is closer to St. Thomas Aquinas' 13th-century *Summa Theologica*[105] than it is to such modern European developments.

All of this reflects directly upon the narratives of conversion projected onto ʿAbd al-Qādir's life. If the view that his philosophical 'rationalism' is 'borrowed from Europe' is unjustified, as we have argued, then the case for a psycho-spiritual transformation evidenced by such a process is also called into question. Nevertheless, the *Dhikrā* has also been employed as evidence for a 'converted' ʿAbd al-Qādir not only through the philosophical mischaracterisation of its generic 'rationalist' quality, but also through the employment of one specific passage among its contents. That employment, too, has been misleading.

---

102 Weismann, 2001a, p. 309.

103 Weismann also conflates rationalism and science as 'scientific-rationalistic' [e.g. 2001b, p. 57] in the course of his arguments – though this conflicts both with the fact that ʿAbd al-Qādir's interest in technological developments have been shown in Chapter One to predate his imprisonment in France, and with the fact that the historical development of the modern scientific method was just as often carried forward by empiricist opponents of philosophical rationalism – as much Francis Bacon as René Descartes, so to speak.

104 Van Ess, 2006, pp.153–4.

105 The First Article, First Part of the *Summa*, for instance, argues that 'it was necessary for man's salvation that there should be a knowledge revealed by God, besides philosophical science built up by human reason. Firstly, indeed, because man is directed to God, as to an end that surpasses the grasp of his reason: *The eye hath not seen, O God, besides Thee, what things Thou hast prepared for them that wait for Thee* (Isaiah 64:4). But the end must first be known by men who are to direct their thoughts and actions to the end...'

One particular excerpt from the *Dhikrā* has been widely used to demonstrate ʿAbd al-Qādir's supposed conversion from fervent Muslim zealot to reasonable religious pluralist following his exposure to enlightened French civilisation. The passage in question, quoted as evidence of his new-found pluralism by Étienne, Clayton, Bouyerdene, Azan, and Weismann (among numerous others), reads as follows:

> 'Religion is one by the consensus of the Prophets... If the Muslims and the Christians were listening to me their differences would be removed and they would become inwardly and outwardly brothers. But if they do not listen to me... only the Messiah will remove their differences when he comes... and even he will not succeed in bringing about accord, though he will be able to resurrect the dead and heal the blind and the leper, but with the sword.'[106]

This passage might be understood to suggest that ʿAbd al-Qādir is denying the reality of distinctions between Christians and Muslims, or between Christianity and Islam. This is certainly how it is presented in the secondary literature. '[A] central theme that ʿAbd al-Qādir al-Jazā'irī sought to convey... was that there is a fundamental harmony between Islam and western-Christian civilisation.'[107] The former 'opponent' of 'western civilisation' is transformed into a cosmopolitan 'bridge between cultures'.[108] It might even be seen as a total relegation of religion to a private sphere of purely personal conviction, as its most recent French editor does in his (unjustified) assertion that '[w]ell before the separation of Church and State in France, Abd el-Kader advocated the return of religion to the private space.'[109] All such views would contrast starkly with the more exclusivist impression we have discussed in his *Risālah on Hijrah*, and help justify a dichotomous reading of ʿAbd al-Qādir's life. It would constitute textual evidence for his conversion from conservative Islamic supremacism to a very modern pluralist, relativist, or even secular position.

Such readings are tendentious, however. It is clear that ʿAbd al-Qādir expressed the sentiment quoted above to the French Asiatic Society in a spirit of dialogue and openness. The widespread presumption that this spirit was informed by a newfound pluralism, rather than a long-held, conventional, and conservative Muslim attitude towards previous Abrahamic revelations, however, remains unjustified. That religion is one (and Islamic) by consensus of the prophets is the mainstream Muslim view of the roles of the prophets. It certainly

---

106 *Dhikrā*, p. 107. Quoted in Weismann, 2001a, p. 160; Étienne, 2008, pp. 94 – 95; Clayton, 1975, pp. 274, 295; Azan, 1925, p. 284; Bouyerdene, 2008, p. 211.
107 Weismann, 2001a, p. 160.
108 Kiser, 2008, p. ix.
109 Sfeir, 2011, p.9.

need not imply either thoroughgoing religious pluralism or the abnegation of Islam's finality or superiority. Rather, it is traditionally understood as being proof of it – as ʿAbd al-Qādir himself maintains in his later writing [see Chapter Five]. Speaking in the plural of prophets while intending a single and Islamic revelation is a convention established in the text of the Qur'ān which we have already seen reflected in ʿAbd al-Qādir's *Risālah on Hijrah*, wherein he speaks of pious believers at the time of Moses 'holding fast to the bonds of Islam [that is, not 'the bonds of *Judaism*']'.[110] There is no reason to presume that the eventual 'brothers' accord in the passage above is intended as anything other than Islam as it has historically been understood by Muslims. Nor, even if the 'brothers' were to be seen as representing different faiths, is there any reason to presume that their relation will be one of equals. ʿAbd al-Qādir, his father's favoured son, was after all the product of a patriarchal society.

The religious pluralist reading also ignores this text's eschatological character: its reference to the Messiah bringing accord 'by the sword'. The well-known Prophetic narration to which ʿAbd al-Qādir is referring in this passage also assumes Islam to comprise mankind's final accord. It is a commonplace of Muslim eschatology that the victorious Messiah will return to Earth (purportedly via the 'Jesus Minaret' or *madhanat ʿĪssā* on the eastern corner of the Umayyad Mosque in Damascus at which ʿAbd al-Qādir often prayed and gave lessons) so as to do battle with the misleading 'anti-Christ' *dajjāl* and kill or convert the remaining unbelievers to Islam. The *Ṣaḥīḥ* of al-Bukhārī, which ʿAbd al-Qādir is said to have memorised,[111] contains the following *ḥadīth*, to which he seems to allude: 'By Him in whose hands my soul rests, Jesus, the Son of Mary, is to descend amongst you as a just ruler. He will break the cross, kill the pig, abolish *jizyah* [the tax paid by non-Muslim minorities] and wealth will increase…'[112] ʿAbd al-Qādir's reference to 'the sword' can only refer to the expected Messiah's apocalyptic purification of the world for Islam through his destruction of swine and crucifixes – symbols of the heretical innovations to God's eternal religion introduced by pre-Qur'ānic monotheists [*taḥrīf*]. The abolition of the *jizyah* similarly represents the end of the by-then defunct *dhimmī* system of protection and tolerance (which ʿAbd al-Qādir supported in Algeria and Damascus) for the by-then converted non-Muslims. ʿAbd al-Qādir can only be seen as making a thoroughgoing pluralist point in this passage if we ignore both the text's context and its symbolic content, and project a pluralist intention onto the text from the outset.

110 *Tuḥfah*, p. 412.
111 Abun-Nasr, 2007, p. 203; Al-Bayṭār, 1963, p. 887.
112 *Ṣaḥīḥ* of al-Bukhārī, Volume 3, Book 34, Number 425.

Again, none of this is to suggest that the *Dhikrā*, nor its author, is anti-Christian. This was far from the case. In the text, ʿAbd al-Qādir recognises that the continued existence of Christian kingdoms is ordained by God to continue until the end of time – also a corollary of *ḥadīths* such as that quoted above, and of his own reference to Islamic eschatology. Its opening echo of al-Ghazālī demands openness to the possibility of benefiting from the ideas of any person, even those to whom one might feel opposed – a theme which would recur in his *Kitāb al-Mawāqif*.[113] These are already sufficient admissions as to allow for Islamo-Christian co-existence and co-operation in the world. One need not demand that ʿAbd al-Qādir also abandon or relativise his faith in the Qur'ānic revelation to adapt to this fact. It is also an admission conceivable by and accessible to any Muslim, not only to elite Sufis who have lived in Europe, and – unlike accounts of his 'conversion' by French ideas – does not rely upon any specifically European genius, be it Christian or secular.

What cannot reasonably be sustained is to inflate ʿAbd al-Qādir's attempts at inter-religious dialogue into the endorsement of a less Islamocentric perspective than that for which he spilled so much ink and so much blood throughout his life. This inflation is characteristically associated with perceiving ʿAbd al-Qādir's life as marked by a critical discontinuity. The seductive 'Road to Damascus' narrative distorts his ideas and intentions as he himself expressed them: reason enough, perhaps, for future readers to be wary of it. In justifying itself it does not misrepresent only the context of his writing, however, but also his actions. Where the *Dhikrā* has been misguidedly advanced as physical evidence for ʿAbd al-Qādir's conversion by France, so too has one of the most heroic actions of his life: his part in the sectarian violence of Damascus in 1860. This episode will be discussed below, as soon as the intervening events have been described.

4.4 Arrival in Damascus, 1855

In spite of the French consul's suggestions that they arrive together, ʿAbd al-Qādir rode into Damascus without him.[114] While he would continue to reap the benefits of his association with France, his arrival in Damascus, like that in Istanbul, and his subsequent visits to Jerusalem, Egypt, and the Hejaz, would be as a man free of French control – an issue which was soon to cause

113 E.g. 'God will place some truths upon the tongues of people who are unworthy to speak them such that they might be known by those who are worthy.' – *Mawāqif*, p. 768.
114 Outrey to Thouvenal, Constantinople, *Damas/Consulat/9*, 10-12-1855.

some diplomatic embarrassment. ʿAbd al-Qādir's 'character as Shaykh and Sherif' led to his being welcomed by a host of Damascene dignitaries, including 'all' of the city's religious leaders, 'most' of its officials, and 'a large number' of other local notables.[115] His imperious stance toward the Ottoman authorities, including demanding the handing over of a series of large government properties, soon led to friction, however. His demanding and rejecting as inadequate a series of great houses formerly occupied by Pashas, for instance, was described by Mahmoud Pasha as 'a humiliation to which he refuses to submit'.[116] From the perspective of the Ottoman rulers of the city, ʿAbd al-Qādir was an upstart, an unwelcome guest whom they tolerated only grudgingly. While he was offered no official position in the city or province's government, he did not shrink from involving himself in local politics by less direct avenues.

Aside from occasional efforts at influencing nominations for official posts,[117] this influence was most markedly exerted through another traditional metier of the Sufi Shaykh: council and mediation – the role which had prepared both himself and his father for power in Algeria.[118] Besides negotiating local disputes by virtue of his respected status,[119] his influence was only augmented by his ambiguous nationality. He developed the gaining of exemptions from Ottoman taxes for putatively 'Algerian' inhabitants of the area into something of an industry. In point of fact, he used such exemptions as a form of patronage for his followers, and they thereby became less beholden to other authorities and more loyal to him. In the process, he played the French and Ottoman authorities off against each other, and both would from time to time attempt to check his manoeuvring.

1861, for instance, saw an abortive Ottoman push to subject the North-African community following ʿAbd al-Qādir to taxation, which included several arrests.[120] This practice has been noted by Étienne, who downplays the degree to which it also reflected ʿAbd al-Qādir's abuse of French trust.[121] The French authorities, for their part, had also grown increasingly exasperated with ʿAbd al-Qādir's habit of fraudulently including non-Algerian Muslims under the register for exemptions.[122] We have already explored the conceptions of community and sover-

115 *Ibid.*

116 Moore to Redcliffe, *FO 195/519*, 07-07-1856.

117 *Ibid.*

118 Seraulky, 1990, pp. 53–55.

119 E.g. Local *ʿulemā*' approaching ʿAbd al-Qādir to mediate between Greek agents and local Damascenes, Outrey to the Ministry of Foreign Affairs, *Damas/Consulat/12*, 12-01-1857.

120 Hecquard to the Ministry of Foreign Affairs, *Damas/Consulat/37*, 04-11-1861.

121 Étienne, 2003, pp. 267, 414.

122 Hecquard to the Ministry of Foreign Affairs, *Damas/Consulat/37*, 28-06-1861.

eignty understood by ʿAbd al-Qādir, and their distinctness from European (Romantic) nationalism. It seems unlikely that he felt himself to be evangelising Damascene Tunisians and Moroccans into French citizenship. Rather, by registering his followers as subjects of France, he prevented the Ottoman authorities from making demands on them, while making them still more dependant not so much on France as on himself. He was making the very most of his anomalous position to benefit both himself and the growing community of which he was the undisputed head. ʿAbd al-Qādir's French and Ottoman[123] pensions, and his growing trade investments supplied him with an even more direct forms of financial patronage. These covered, not least, involvement with the Hauran grain trade,[124] the Hejaz Railway,[125] and nascent Suez Canal projects – the latter of which led to Ferdinand de Lesseps attempting to purchase ʿAbd al-Qādir an estate nearby,[126] much to the alarm of the Egyptian authorities, who forbade it in the strongest terms.[127]

ʿAbd al-Qādir was a wealthy and highly visible figure who donated both to charity and to the support of scholars and the wider North African community in the area. He organised private classes on *ḥadīth*, Mālikī law, and Sufism, as well as teaching publicly at the renowned Umayyad mosque in the ancient heart of the old city. The presence of the North African community, which he continued to attract to him as he had in Bursa, led to the re-establishment of the office of Mālikī Muftī in the city – a station filled by a friend and alleged co-conspirator of ʿAbd al-Qādir's.[128]

Meanwhile, his considerable income permitted him to support the refurbishment of the *Dār al-Ḥadīth al-Ashrafiyyah*, an erstwhile centre of the study of narrations of the Prophet Muḥammad. Evincing his scrupulous concern for upholding the Shariah, including the obligations it imposes towards non-Muslim subject populations (*ahl al-dhimmah*), he negotiated a financial settlement for the Christian wine-seller whose adjoining storage of the illicit drug had scandalised other Muslims.[129] In this, he echoed a Damascene tradition in which the caliph ʿUmar is said to have destroyed a mosque because 'his governor had forcibly expropriated the house of a Jew in order to build the mosque in its place.'[130] Hav-

123 Outlined by Thouvenal to Outrey [Damas/Consulat/66, 27-08-1857].
124 Schatkowski Schilcher, 1981, pp. 159 – 179.
125 Schatkowski Schilcher, 1981, p. 174.
126 Hecquard to the Ministry of Foreign Affairs, *Damas/Consulat/24*, 21-01-1865. It seems likely that ʿAbd al-Qādir's contact with De Lesseps was encouraged through his brother Edmond De Lesseps, French consul in Beirut.
127 Discussed by Étienne, 2003, pp. 388 – 9 and 393 – 4.
128 King, 1997, p. 71.
129 Weismann, 2001a, pp. 202 – 3.
130 Goldziher, 1981, p. 36.

ing restored the *Dār al-Ḥadīth* while doing justice by all concerned, ʿAbd al-Qādir gave its inaugural lecture on *ḥadīth.*[131]

In these respects, he contributed to the life of the city in a lasting institutional respect, while his personal connections with figures such as ʿAbd al-Razzāq al-Bayṭār and Tāhir al-Jazāʾirī would lead to his influence being felt by the next generation of Islamic thinkers.[132] His private lessons on a Sufi exegesis of the Qurʾān, recorded at his students' behest, would in turn comprise his greatest literary legacy: the *Kitāb al-Mawāqif* whose contents and reception will be discussed in Chapter Five. Its material is heavily influenced by the works of Muḥyī al-Dīn Ibn al-ʿArabī, and there is even some suggestion in the archival sources that ʿAbd al Qādir 'pretended to be the descendant of Sheikh Muheddeen, a famous Mussulman Saint... whose mausoleum is here [in Damascus]';[133] certainly his new proximity to the final resting place of his 'Great Master' will have pleased him greatly.

If the move to Damascus provided ʿAbd al-Qādir with greater opportunities for economic investment, patronage, and cultural engagement, it also offered the chance to spread his wings in a more physical sense. Differences of opinion soon emerged between him and the French authorities as to his status as a free man, particularly his right to travel and concomitant French fears of 'abandoning the control we have over him'.[134] The French authorities insisted, in spite of his claims that he had been completely liberated by Napoleon III,[135] that the 'principle must be maintained' that ʿAbd al-Qādir was obliged to seek French permission before traveling.[136]

Though he was permitted his pilgrimage to Jerusalem in 1856, he used the opportunity to make a point against the French diplomatic corps. While in Jerusalem, ʿAbd al-Qādir refused to visit the French consul as he was expected to do, causing considerable embarrassment and consternation. He was felt throughout the episode to have 'displayed tendencies suggesting he owes nothing to the French authorities'.[137] What is more, this omission on ʿAbd al-Qādir's part was sufficiently significant to have been noted also by the diplomats of other coun-

---

131 Al-Bayṭār, 1963, p. 897.

132 Weismann and Commins have contributed excellent studies of his students as they relate to him, in their works drawn on by this book. ʿAbd al-Qādir's children would also play prominent roles, with his grandson, Saʿīd al-Jazāʾirī, briefly taking power in the aftermath of the Ottoman withdrawal in late September 1918.

133 Wood to the Foreign Office, *FO 78/1118*, 08-12-1855.

134 Outrey to Thouvenal, *Damas/Consulat/9*, 19-03-1856.

135 *Ibid.*

136 Outrey to Walewski, *Damas/Cosulat/12*, 14-03-1856.

137 Outrey to the Ministry of Foreign Affairs, *Damas/Consulat/12*, 10-10-1856.

tries, including Britain.[138] In addition to noting his slight of the French consul, the British representative in Jerusalem complained of ʿAbd al-Qādir's impolitic mention of British arms supplies while recounting his battles against France to the Pasha in the presence of a French dragoman.[139] In Jerusalem as in Istanbul, ʿAbd al-Qādir boasted of his battles in North Africa – his role as *mujāhid* for which so many Levantines also admired him – without the shame one might imagine in a person supposedly converted to deep loyalty to Christian France...

This entire episode, like other quarrels between ʿAbd al-Qādir and French authorities described above, has gone unrecorded in the secondary literature. Though his pilgrimage has occasionally been noted by French historians, these events have been tactfully elided.[140] Those texts, in keeping with their respective 'Road to Damascus' narratives, have invariably presented ʿAbd al-Qādir's relations with French representatives as more cordial and less conflictual than in fact they were. This phenomenon will be evidenced again later in the present chapter.

Throughout his pilgrimage to Jerusalem, ʿAbd al-Qadir was

> 'held in high reverence by the Moslems as a Confessor of their Faith, they addressed him by the title of Moulai, or my Lord... It is not to be supposed that Abd el-Kader is less of a Moslem devotee for the imprisonment which he endured in France: it may be that he has yet a career before him.'[141]

Such suspicion of his power and plans was not an isolated incident. British diplomatic staff repeatedly expressed anxiety over ʿAbd al-Qādir's influence and intentions, and on

> 'the impolicy of allowing Abd el-Kader to live at Damascus. While on the one hand he affects a life of seclusion and sanctity, on the other he betrays... a desire to increase his influence and consideration with the Mahometans in this country.'[142]

Western fears as to how he might choose to focus the considerable 'hard power' potential his great notoriety, wealth, and ambiguous national status granted him were soon to be considerably diminished, however. While suspicions would persist in diplomatic circles, ʿAbd al-Qādir's popular image in the western world would soon be transformed once again. As sectarian violence spread through

138 Finn to Clarendon, *FO 78/1217*, 25-09-1856.
139 *Ibid.*; Finn was concerned, of course, about the potential embarrassment of Britain – not the French interpreter's possible discomfort at being reminded of ʿAbd al-Qādir's combat against France.
140 E.g. Étienne, 2003, p. 266 – 7.
141 Finn to Clarendon, *FO 78/1217*, 25-09-1856.
142 Moore to Redcliffe, *FO 195/519*, 07-07-1856.

Lebanon and Syria towards Damascus, he would soon find himself the hero of the hour from Athens to Washington. His comportment during the summer of 1860 would soon establish itself in his western myth as the active fruition of his 'conversion' from Algerian warlord to devoted servant of France, from Muslim 'fanatic' to pluralist champion of Christianity.

4.5 Riot, Rescue, and Representation

The summer of 1860 would see the city of Damascus plunged into chaos, the likes of which ʿAbd al-Qādir had not experienced since leaving North Africa. Violence had already been festering in the wider Levant, and had drawn the attention of the major regional powers.

> 'The events in Damascus took place in the immediate aftermath of sectarian violence in Mount Lebanon and were the culmination of a series of attacks on Christians across Greater Syria (*bilād al-shām*) – Aleppo in 1850, Nablus in 1856, and tensions in other towns that did not lead to bloodshed.'[143]

Numerous causes in addition to the obvious sectarian element[144] have been adduced – including resentment at the recent Tanzimat reforms[145] and the relative success of Christians during an economic downturn[146] – yet the consequences were clear. A series of urgently-worded letters protesting the growing violence had already been jointly sent to local leaders by Britain, France, Russia, Prussia, and Austria.[147] For his part, ʿAbd al-Qādir also attempted to calm sectarian strife by words and persuasion – though this would ultimately prove to be insufficient.

By June, the likelihood of major disturbances troubling Damascus had reached such a level that he approached the French consulate with an offer of protection in exchange for arms and supplies for approximately a thousand of his Algerian supporters. Lanusse, the acting consul, was initially reluctant to acquiesce but soon decided on the necessity of this step, so long as it could be kept secret.[148] By this time, Lanusse records that ʿAbd al-Qādir had already managed

---

143 Rogan, 2004, p. 493.

144 See for instance, Makdisi, 2000, pp. 145–148. Makdisi correctly notes, of course, that 'there has never been a pure sectarianism' [*op.cit.*, p. 165].

145 E.g. Ma'oz, 1969, *passim.*

146 E.g. Masters, 1990, p. 4.

147 The Five Powers to various, *PA XIII Botschaft Konstantinopel/Karton 32*, 21-06-1860; 25-06-1860; 27-06-1860; 01-08-1860.

148 Lanusse to the Ministry of Foreign Affairs, *Damas/Consulat/12*, 19-06-1860.

to avert no fewer than two earlier outbreaks of sectarian violence through his intercessions with local notables and religious scholars.[149] While refraining from opposing Lanusse's decision, the ambassador to Constantinople expressed French official trepidation at arming ʿAbd al-Qādir and the Algerians: – who had left Algeria 'as least so much because of their hatred for France as due to their devotion to ʿAbd al-Qādir'.[150]

By the second week of July tensions had erupted into several days of carnage, described by the British consul as 'the most frightful calamity it was ever my lot to witness'.[151] A wave of sectarian violence broke on the largely Christian district of Bāb Tūmā in the North-East of Damascus' Old City.[152] Beginning with the drawing of crucifixes on public pavements, on which passers-by were to walk by way of insult, antipathy escalated to full-scale violence. Embassies were attacked, houses burned, 'many hundred'[153] killed, and women 'publicly violated... the most savage barbarism... the description of which would demand volumes'.[154] ʿAbd al-Qādir and his many armed followers, however, acted swiftly to gather the city's Christians at defensible locations – chiefly his own palatial home,[155] which was attacked by the rioters 'four or five times',[156] and the Citadel.[157] His militia's fortitude proved sufficient to hold off the murderous rioters and thereby save the lives of many thousands of innocent people.

While all of the western consuls unite in their praise for ʿAbd al-Qādir's actions, several also cast pointed aspersions upon the inaction and potential complicity of the Ottoman authorities. 'Grave suspicions rest on the conduct of the Pasha... It is notorious that for some days the Algerians of His Highness the Emir Abd al-Kader saved from the ruins several hundreds before the Pasha thought of doing so.'[158] While ʿAbd al-Qādir's men rescued 'over 13,000' innocents, this 'most savage barbarism... was not the result of an explosion of fanaticism, but rather of an organised plot, long-planned in Lebanon and all of

149 Lanusse to the Ministry of Foreign Affairs, *Damas/Consulat/12*, 02-07-1860.
150 Lavalette to the Ministry of Foreign Affairs, *Constanintople/Ambassade/C/247*, 11-07-1860.
151 Brant to the Foreign Office, *FO 78/1520*, 16-07-1860.
152 It is worth remarking how concentrated the violence seems to have been upon this district, in spite of significant Chrisitan populations in the ajoining Bāb Sharqī and the Meidān, for instance. Speculation as to the reasons for this are beyond the scope of the present discussion, however.
153 Johnson to the State Department, A2 Cab. 40/9, 14-07-1860.
154 Outrey to Lavalette, *Damas/Consulat/10*, 28-07-1860.
155 Johnson to the State Department, A2 Cab. 40/9, 21-07-1860.
156 Outrey to Lavalette, *Damas/Consulat/10*, 28-07-1860.
157 Lanusse to the Ministry of Foreign Affairs, *Damas/Consulat/12*, 17-06-1860.
158 Brant to the Foreign Office, *FO 78/1520*, 16-07-1860.

Syria.'[159] Testimony delivered to the British by a 'Turkish Muslim officer'[160] who had been part of efforts to protect about two hundred Christians in the customs house is still more pointed. This 'sedition' is placed squarely at the feet of the irregular militia, as well as the failure of the city's notables other than 'Abd al-Qādir to respond with sufficient alacrity.

The United States' consular agent makes clear that 'Abd al-Qādir shared such suspicions of the local notables, sending eight armed Algerians to the house of Mustapha Bey to recue the agent from a man they all suspected of involvement in the violence.[161] A letter sent by 'Abd al-Qādir after the riots praises certain unnamed Muslim notables for their efforts in protecting the embattled Christians, while placing blame squarely on the shoulders of the Ottoman establishment: 'Damascus has a governor, but it is the same thing as if it had none.'[162]

In spite of such condemnation, however, and notwithstanding his 'very pronounced antipathy toward the Turks',[163] 'Abd al-Qādir appears to have taken pains to recognise the established power structure of Ottoman Damascus, making no effort to overturn it. The British consul records that 'Abd al-Qādir voluntarily submitted to the authorities even to the extent of hampering his own movements, in a manner illustrative of the distrust and inefficacy which hamstrung the Ottoman response.

> 'Had the Mushir authorised His Highness ['Abd al-Qādir], when at the head of his men, to fire on the mob, in all probability the calamity might have been averted. His Highness told me in answer to my question that three times he ineffectually asked permission to use his arms, once he obtained it verbally from the Mushir but on reaching his house, it was withdrawn by a written note. Whether the outbreak would have been checked by His Highness had be been fully trusted, will of course remain a matter of opinion, but it is a patent fact that thousands owe their lives to his liberality, energy and presence of mind.'[164]

While the Ottoman authorities had undoubtedly been slow to move against the rioters, when a response came it was often a deadly one. Centralising power to himself, Fuad Pasha began rounding up the ringleaders of the insurrection even as 'Abd al-Qādir's men remained on the streets.[165] To the irritation of the local elite, 'Abd al-Qādir was the only notable initially granted an audience

159 Outrey to Lavalette, *Damas/Consulat/10*, 28-07-1860.
160 Unnamed, *FO 226/131*,——1960.
161 Meshaka to Johnson, *A2 Cab. 40/9*, 25-10-1860.
162 "The Damascus Massacres, letter from Abd-el-Kader", *New York Times*, 20-08-1860.
163 Outrey to the Ministry of Foreign Affairs, *Damas/Consulat/12*, 10-10-1856.
164 Brant to the Foreign Office, *FO 78/1520*, 24-07-1860.
165 Outrey to Lavalette, *Damas/Consulat/10*, 22-08-1860.

with the Pasha, who called for ʿAbd al-Qādir's militia to operate temporarily alongside Ottoman troops 'so as to inspire confidence among the Christians'.[166] These were subsequently ordered to disarm, though many refused to do so,[167] and ʿAbd al-Qādir made it 'very evident [that] he considers it as a most ungracious acknowledgement of the service he and his men rendered.'[168] This would not lead to conflict, however; the Ottoman authorities were more concerned with being seen to punish the rioters. Before a month had passed, 'one thousand and three arrests [had] been made and forty five [had] been condemned to death of those who were implicated in the massacre.'[169] 'Ottomans and Europeans... applauded the brutality of Fuad Pasha'[170] in punishing the criminal rioters. 'The Ottoman officials... paid compensation to the Christian survivors, and had more or less completed the reconstruction of the destroyed Christian quarters of Bāb Tūmā and [adjoining] Bāb Sharqī in the course of the 1860s.'[171] Meanwhile, the Porte showered praise on ʿAbd al-Qādir, who received a very flattering letter from the Grand Vizier along with the news that he would be the recipient of the Grand Order of the Medjidiye – with Lanusse recognised for his support of ʿAbd al-Qādir with the Order of the Medjidiye, 4th Class.[172]

The Christian Powers similarly wasted no time in recognising the heroism of ʿAbd al-Qādir and his supporters. On the 21st of October, he was awarded the Grand Cordon of the Legion of Honour, in 'perfect appreciation of his moral valour',[173] with money and lesser honours distributed among his partisans. The King of Sardinia awarded him with the Grand Cordon of Saints Martin and Lazarus,[174] Greece with the Grand Cross of the Order of St Saviour,[175] Britain with a carbine presented on behalf of Queen Victoria,[176] and the United States with a pair of silver mounted Colts pistols in an ornamented case bearing the inscription 'From the President of the United States of America to his Excellency Said Abd el-Kader, 1860'.[177] Archival evidence makes clear that ʿAbd al-Qādir took an understandable pride in these well-deserved honours, to the point of express-

---

166 Outrey to Lavalette, *Damas/Consulat/10*, 01-08-1860.
167 Churchill, 1867, p. 319.
168 Wrench to the Foreign Office, *FO 78/1520*, 29-11-1860.
169 Johnson to the State Department, *A2 Cab. 40/9*, 18-08-1860.
170 Makdisi, 2000, p. 146.
171 Rogan, 2004, p. 509.
172 Lavalette to the Ministry of Foreign Affairs, *Constantinople/Ambassade/C/247*, 28-08-1860.
173 Outrey to the Ministry of Foreign Affairs, *Damas/Consulat/11*, 22-10-1860.
174 Outrey to Lavalette, *Damas/Consulat/11*, 01-10-1860.
175 Wrench to the Foreign Office, *FO 78/1520*, 28-11-1860.
176 Brant to the Foreign Office, FO 78/1520, 20-11-1860.
177 Johnson to the State Department, A2 Cab. 40/9, 21-09-1860.

ing disappointment when it initially appeared that Britain would not send gifts as other states had done.[178] Nevertheless, he himself insisted that he did not act in the hope of receiving rewards. Rather, it was 'as a man of action',[179] as he described himself to the French Consul some months later, that he had felt compelled to combat the disorder and iniquity of the rioters.

'Abd al-Qādir's own comments on his comportment, in the various letters and interviews which followed, were quite consistent. The rioters were committing vile and criminal injustice against the innocent and against the Islamic law, which he, as an authoritative figure and a 'man of action' felt compelled to put down. He had 'only done his duty',[180] he repeatedly wrote, in 'protecting the *dhimmis* [non-Muslim minorities within an Islamic community] against those who would harm them...[motivated by] nothing other than obedience to our sacred law and the principles of humanity – in truth, our law encompasses all qualities and all virtues as a necklace embraces a neck.'[181]

The Christians of the city, like the vintner he had civilly bought out during his refurbishment of the *Dār al-Ḥadīth*, were entitled to the protection and respect from the Muslim majority that their *dhimmī* status afforded them (ongoing Ottoman legal reforms notwithstanding). More broadly, 'Abd al-Qādir had already involved himself in local sectarian politics (involving Maghrebis, Kurds, Arabs, Druze, Greeks and others) so as to avert conflicts, and would do so again – whether or not French interests were involved.[182] His engagement fitted a clear pattern, long practised by his maraboutic family, of mediations and interventions to keep the peace.

Such were the lights in which his co-religionists saw his actions at the time, as archival evidence substantiates. In spite of lingering suspicions about the true motivations of the Ottoman authorities, subsequent years saw the view that 'Abd al-Qādir had performed 'the greatest service to Islam' become quite unanimous among local Muslims, from Bedouins to 'the most influential religious scholars'.[183] This view is further reflected in the support he would find among the Damascene *'ulemā* some years later, as they worked together to diffuse ethnic

---

178 Foreign Office to Brant, FO 78/1520, 31-10-1860.

179 Outrey to the Ministry of Foreign Affairs, *Damas/Consulat/13*, 17-04-1861.

180 Quoted in *The Times*, Thursday, Nov 13, 1873, pg. 5.

181 'Abd al-Qādir to Shamyl [Imām Shāmil], quoted in Étienne, 2003, p. 321.

182 E.g. Outrey to the Ministry of Foreign Affairs, *Damas/Consulat/12*, 12-01-1857; Lanusse to the Ministry of Foreign Affairs, Damas/Consulat/12, 02-07-1860; Bertrand to Consulate General, Beirut, *Damas/Consulat/27*, 23-03-1867; report to the Ministry of Foreign Affairs, *Damas/Consulat/26*, 10-07-1868.

183 Hecquard to the Ministry of Foreign Affairs, *Damas/Consulat/15*, 20-10-1862.

tensions which threatened violence once more – many using Friday Sermons to preach co-existence with Christians while he toured 'all the religious establishments'.[184] The mainstream resonance of 'Abd al-Qādir's principled position has been consistently downplayed by European scholars who emphasise his unique 'Greatness' and distinctness from his co-religionists.[185] Yet it did indeed have such a resonance – both through its essential humanity and through the traditions of mainstream Islamic ethics, even as these were being transformed by Ottoman legal reforms.

In exchange for submission to the Muslim majority, the non-Muslim *dhimmī* population is traditionally entitled to a degree of self-governance and to the protection of the Muslim majority. The concomitant right of the *ahl al-dhimmah* to freedom from persecution by the Muslim majority, while sometimes insufficiently observed, is an Islamic legal principle of extremely long standing.[186] While 'Abd al-Qādir suspected the nascent Ottoman model of European-style equal citizenship,[187] he had grown up with the *dhimmī* model, practised it in his state,[188] and refers to it repeatedly in his writings – from his early *Risālah on Hijrah* to his posthumous *Kitāb al-Mawāqif.* In his letters of the time, he distinguishes between 'Muslims' who protected the innocent, and the Ottoman governors who reneged on their duties.[189] In the words of his student al-Bayṭār, 'Abd al-Qādir had acted according to the Islamic injunction of commanding the right and forbidding the wrong, *al-amru bil-ma'rūf wa al-naḥyī 'an al-munkar.*[190] His actions will certainly have been seen as such by many of his Muslim contemporaries. This will not have struck them as ethico-legally parochial, but rather a natural expression of Islamic norms they understood to be *ipso facto* universal.

Yet this account of 'Abd al-Qādir's motivations, so utterly in keeping with the circumstances which originally raised him to power in Algeria as a leader pledged to impose the order of Shariah on the anarchy of civil strife, remains strikingly absent in western literature. This fact would be telling enough in itself, were it not for the alternative motivations which are to be found in its place in

184 Bertrand to the Ministry of Foreign Affairs, *Damas/Consulat/27,* 23-03-1867.

185 Julien [1964, p. 208–209], for instance, describes them en bloc as quite unable to understand 'Abd al-Qādir's motivation, and as reproaching him for acting on it.

186 E.g. Goldziher, 1981, pp. 34–36.

187 Bouyerdene, 2008, p.123.

188 Scott, 2010, p. 5.

189 'Abd al-Qādir to the management of the Krey Silkworks, *The New York Times*, August 20, 1860.

190 Al-Bayṭār [1963, p. 897] describes 'Abd al-Qādir simply as 'exerting himself for the sake of what is known to be moral (*al-ma'rūf*)', while describing the rioters as 'bestial villains (*al-ashqiyā' al-mutawaḥḥishīn*)'.

western biographies of ʿAbd al-Qādir. Not only do these fail to recognise this biographical continuity, but they impose an artificial discontinuity. Western accounts have almost unanimously seized upon the Damascus Riots of 1860 as proof of ʿAbd al-Qādir's new departure. Rather than upholding order, enforcing the Shariah, saving innocents, or protecting *dhimmīs* (a category at least one of ʿAbd al-Qādir's western biographers has described as 'humiliating'),[191] he has been presented as siding with symbolic proxies for Europe.

Rather than being interpreted in terms of the Islamic law and morality to which ʿAbd al-Qādir devoted his life as a leader and as a teacher, therefore, his deeds were represented as a favour to France, and an endorsement of French ambitions in the Muslim world.[192] No evidence of ʿAbd al-Qādir stating that this was his intention has yet been adduced, nor even deemed necessary. So, this decidedly Eurocentric interpretation has survived to this day; the *Encyclopaedia of Islam* still records ʿAbd al-Qādir's defence of the Damascene innocent as a proof of loyalty to France.[193] Some writers have been more specific, presenting ʿAbd al-Qādir as acting for the sake of some subset of the French, such as Napoleon III himself[194] or Catholic nuns:[195] these accounts have at least some basis in that his avowed respect for the person of Napoleon III and the vocation of Christian clerics has already been established. More recent western accounts of ʿAbd al-Qādir's part in the Riots have widened this Eurocentric interpretation, however. Rather than defending French Christians – the minority of those whom he saved, most of whom were naturally Christian *Arabs* (predominantly of Eastern denominations uncommon in Europe) – his deeds have been re-purposed as proof of his conversion not only to Francophilia, but to a pro-western religious pluralism. He is seen as having struck a blow for all Christians, everywhere, and moreover for their equality with Muslims.[196] This new interpretation has some roots in the old, of course. In its contemporary France, 'sectarian violence was deemed primordial behaviour that emanated from what Napoleon III described to his troops (about to embark for Syria) as "the fanaticism of a previous

---

191 E.g. Danziger, 1977, p. 202.

192 "Abd al-Qadir became emblematic of French success… his service to France represented Algeria's recognition of French dominance' [Achrati, 2007, p. 146].

193 De Cossé-Brissac, *EI2* entry on *ʿAbd al- Ḳādir b. Muḥyi al-Dīn al-Ḥasanī:* 'It was [in Damascus] that he proved in a very special way the sincerity of his loyalty, by delivering the French consul and saving several thousand persons when the Druses tried to massacre the Christian population.'

194 E.g. Bellemare, 1863, pp. 386, 439, 450.

195 E.g. Bellemare, 1863, pp. 398, 441.

196 E.g. Gai Eaton, 1985, p. 38; Chodkiewicz, 1995, pp. 19–20.

century"', this interpretation playing its part in 'how a knowledge of sectarianism as antimodern was [then being] produced'.[197]

These Eurocentric accounts of ʿAbd al-Qādir's motives can hardly be sustained for a number of reasons. They cannot draw on primary evidence of ʿAbd al-Qādir's own accounts; nowhere does the *amīr* say that he acted for the sake of France, or Christianity, or religious pluralism in the cause of Islamic rapprochement with the west. Again unlike the account presented here, they require a new psychology of ʿAbd al-Qādir and a 'Road to Damascus' conversion to explain it, for which evidence is wanting; they are discontinuous with what we know about his previous four decades of life. Finally, they depend on the psychology of one individual alone – ʿAbd al-Qādir himself. But in fact he did not act alone, but in tandem with many hundreds of other North African, Syrian, and Turkish Muslims, not all of whom could have been motivated by blind obedience to ʿAbd al-Qādir or devotion to French interests. Conversely, the explanation offered here would have seemed as natural to them as to him, as it draws on broad social mores and explicit ethical traditions rather than a private and mysterious personal experience to which others had no access.

The distorting influence of the 'Great Man' theory of history, which earlier exaggerated ʿAbd al-Qādir's 'otherness' from his fellows in Algeria, should not be embraced in this instance, either. Nor should recognising ʿAbd al-Qādir's undoubted heroism require us to discard that of all those others who behaved just as nobly as he did. The former Janissary Muḥammad Chaouche was made to wait two decades before his defence of Christian innocents during the 1860 Riots was officially recognised,[198] for instance – how many others are waiting still?

This is not to say that the moral and Shariah-minded explanation argued for here, and endorsed by ʿAbd al-Qādir's co-religionists in the event, excludes all other possible contributory motivations. While ʿAbd al-Qādir's defence of the innocent from the murderous rioters was certainly magnanimous, it is not the intention here to beatify him. The political and financial benefit which ʿAbd al-Qādir accrued from the west, and France in particular, might certainly be adduced as a contributory political motivation – albeit in spite of his own explicit claims that he did not act in the hope of reward. [199] Such speculation is justifiable even given that his success was not assured, and that his French stipend was in no way dependant on his providing such services, which we have seen

197 Makdisi, 2000, pp. 146, 147.

198 Flesch to Constantinople Embassy, *Damas/Consulat/35*, 08-05-1881.

199 Outrey to the Ministry of Foreign Affairs, Damas/Consulat/13, 17-04-1861.

were not endorsed by acting-consul Lanusse's superiors, and by Lanusse himself only *in extremis*.

While in principle protecting French interests may have contributed to his decision, it must be noted that the contrary is also perfectly plausible. On this converse view, ʿAbd al-Qādir's defence of the Christians of Damascus might just as easily have been aimed at averting the growing threat of European military retaliation against his coreligionists, a French expansion into the Levant, and a repetition of his experiences in Algeria. It must be remembered that the protection of Christian minorities was during the 19th century a primary pretext for the penetration of the region by European powers. This latter interpretation, though absent in western biographies, is favoured by many in present-day Damascus.[200] It too is supposition, however.

What is clear is that ʿAbd al-Qādir found himself, after the dust of the riots had settled, in a more prominent position than he had enjoyed since surrendering to Lamoricière and d'Aumale on the plains of North Africa. As once his father had brought him in his youth on a lengthy pilgrimage comprising the Ḥajj and Sufi devotions, so the aging ʿAbd al-Qādir would repeat the process. Where before he had followed his visit to Mecca by taking the Naqshbandī *ṭarīqah* under Shaykh Khaled, so now he followed his visit to the *Kaʿabah* with Shādhilī devotions under Shaykh Muḥammad al-Fāsī. Both journeys, as a young man and in middle age, will have been spiritually significant to him, as all pilgrimages are to all pilgrims – but one cannot but surmise a personal element of remembrance of his father. Whether consciously or not, moreover, ʿAbd al-Qādir's final Ḥajj also reproduced his father's more worldly considerations.

Where Muḥyī al-Dīn had brought his son on the pilgrimage route east in part so as to evade the hostility of the Algerian Ottomans, so also did ʿAbd al-Qādir bin Muḥyī al-Dīn's journey take him away from the resentments of the Ottoman establishment in Syria.[201] Where Muḥyī al-Dīn's pilgrimage, replete with visions and prophecies, enhanced his religious kudos and cemented his political preeminence, so also would ʿAbd al-Qādir's pilgrimage redound to his credit, a testament to his piety, power, and divine favour. His followers duly commemorated the event in poetic formulae,[202] a hagiographic tradition continued even in some

---

200 Reiterated, for instance, in a recent report in *al-Quds* on the renovation of ʿAbd al-Qādir's palace in Damascus [*Al-quds al-ʿarabī*, 7th of November, 1428 *hijrī*, p. 12]. A similar view is taken by Badīʿah al-Ḥasanī Al-Jazāʾirī [2000, p. 228].

201 Suggested, for instance, by John King [1997, p. 69].

202 Al-Bayṭār, 1963, p. 898: 'One day [ʿAbd al-Qādir] took the Shādhilī *ṭarīqah* from the Knower of God Shaykh Muḥāmmad al-Fāsī, and he secluded himself for a time in the cave of Ḥirāʾ and he reached that which he sought and acquired that which he desired and the treasury of secrets

modern biographies' mystically vague references to his 'attainment of the goal',[203] 'probably experiencing an initiatic death'[204] while secluded in devotions at the cave in which Muḥammad received the Qur'ān. ʿAbd al-Qādir, for his part, composed a short poem for al-Fāsī before taking his leave[205] – he has left no more evidence of a spiritual turning point in his life here than elsewhere.

When ʿAbd al-Qādir returned at last to Damascus, on the 23rd of June 1864, the solidification of his status as a major figure on the Levantine scene was made dramatically manifest. After disembarking at Beirut, his opulent carriage – drawn by four horses – was accompanied by a retinue of riders which would swell and swell as his short journey progressed. While it included two officers and fifty cavaliers despatched by the Ottoman authorities as a mark of respect, the vast bulk of his victorious caravan was made up of his own adoring followers. By the time he entered Damascus, he was accompanied by over a thousand horsemen,[206] and spent the subsequent days receiving visits from all of the most significant notables of the city – including both the principal Ottoman authorities and the representatives of the western Great Powers.[207]

In spite of his considerable political profile and economic clout, however, his final decades are now chiefly remembered for the lessons on Sufism which he gave to a small circle of students. Transcripts of these lessons would be published after his death as the *Kitāb al-Mawāqif.* Its contents, and its role in the perpetuation of 'Road to Damascus' narratives surrounding ʿAbd al-Qādir, will be discussed in the next chapter.

---

was opened to him and the symbols of the veil were lifted from him and lightning flashed for him and conceptions flowered forth from pure waters.'

203 Weismann, 2001a, p. 162.

204 Bouyerdene, 2008, p. 187.

205 Al-Bayṭār, 1963, p. 898.

206 Hecquard to the Ministry of Foreign Affairs, Damas/Consulat/18, 19, and 23; 01-07-1864.

207 *Ibid.*

5.0 Chapter Five – *Sīrah Ṣūfiyyah:* Sufism, Suspicion, and the *Kitāb al-Mawāqif*; 1864–1883

'God the Most High said: "And He is with ye wherever ye are."[1]

Linguistically,[2] 'with-ness'[3] denotes the merging one thing with another, and it means companionship [*ṣuḥbah*]. That is to say, therefore: He – the Most High – is with ye, in whichever of your states ye might find yourselves, existent or non-existent [*mawjūdīn aw ma'dūmīn*], for He is your Being.... Or, He is with ye wherever ye are in terms of [your] conformity or rebellion [to and against His Law], for ye are under the ineluctable power of His Divine Names, the Guide [*al-Hādī*] and the Misleader [*al-Muḍill*]... He – the Most High – is with us, but we are not with Him [*hūwa – ta'ālā – ma'nā wa lasnā ma'uhu*]...'

-'Abd al-Qādir al-Jazā'irī[4]

A brief historical overview of 'Abd al-Qādir's final years in Damascus will now set the frame for an analysis of his final written work and its reception in the western literature. This chapter's approach to 'Abd al-Qādir will be developed through engaging with both the original Arabic text and the pre-eminent existing translation and treatments of 'Abd al-Qādir's theology. This is intended to contribute to our attempt to offer a 're-evaluation of ['Abd al-Qādir's] life [which] integrates the various facets and stages of his career',[5] free of dependence on 'Road

---

1 Qur'ān 57:4

2 *Lughatan* – This usage, as well as the initial quotation, are very reminiscent of standard *mufassir* (exegete) style, suggesting from the outset that 'Abd al-Qādir wishes his ideas to be understood as relating to and based in the Qur'ān.

3 *Ma'īya* – the Arabic term, literally 'with-ness', can conventionally be given a range of translations, from accompaniment and escorting to concurrence and synchronicity, and thus has a potentially wider meaning and significance than these English equivalents.

4 *Mawāqif*, pp. 761–764.

5 In this case called for by Commins, 1988, p. 131

DOI 10.1515/9783110499513-007

to Damascus' narrative impositions. It will become clear that a degree of systematic bias remains apparent in the major presentations of his thought. This bias has been a major element in the dichotomous approach to ʿAbd al-Qādir that is founded on narratives of dramatic conversion. Its presence will be explored through comparisons with the primary sources, and finally related to its historical origins in modern European cultural and religious history.

After his triumphant return to Damascus in 1864, ʿAbd al-Qādir would discover that during his absence a plot had been hatched by a group centred on Hassan Bey (a.k.a. Colonel O'Reilly) to expel the Turks from Syria and install ʿAbd al-Qādir as the new ruler.[6] Though the plan, described as 'stupid'[7] by the British consul, came to nothing, it was indicative of ʿAbd al-Qādir's raised political profile after the events of 1860. O'Reilly's plot, while misguided, was not delusional. While ʿAbd al-Qādir would make no efforts towards overthrowing the Ottomans, he would indeed in the 1870s become involved in a plot, including ʿĀdil al-Ṣulḥ and the Muftī Hassan Taqī-al-Dīn al-Ḥusnī, to assume power in the event that Ottoman rule should collapse.[8] While the 1860s arguably represented the acme of ʿAbd al-Qādir's status in the Levant, he remained a pre-eminent figure until the end of his life.

His status is illustrated by the fact that by 1881, less than two years before his death and in spite of his ailing health, ʿAbd al-Qādir was still considered among 'the three great leaders of the Arab party'[9] in the region. Less than a year before his death, his presence in Damascus, especially given his relative autonomy and patronage from France, assured his still being seen as 'a permanent danger'[10] by the Ottoman authorities. The political establishment, as a consequence, kept him at arm's length – as did the Viceroy of Egypt, who was so horrified by the prospect of Ferdinand de Lesseps offering ʿAbd al-Qādir a farm near Suez as to threaten reprisals against the Suez Canal Company.[11] In spite of ʿAbd al-Qādir's enormous notoriety, considerable wealth, and political influence, both over the region's North African immigrants and as a mediator between local and international powers, his formal power was reined in whenever possible. Over a

---

6 E.g. De Lhuys (Ministy of Foreign Affairs) to Hecquard, *Damas/Consulat/22*, 25-09-1862; Hecquard to de Lhuys, *Damas/Consulat/69*, 16-10-1863.

7 Rogers to the French Consulate, *Damas/Consulat/66*, 16-10-1862.

8 King, 1997, p. 71. This agreement was allegedly reached in 1877, and concerned a prospect which was by that time quite plausible – the Ottoman Empire was by this time very much the 'Sick Man of Europe'.

9 Flesch to the Ministry of Foreign Affairs, Damas/Consulat/33 and 35, 17-05-1881.

10 Portalis to the Ministry of Foreign Affairs, Damas/Consulat/14, 30-05-1882.

11 Étienne, 2003, pp. 388–9 and 393–4.

decade subsequent to the 1860 Riots, Richard Burton illustrated the continued hostility of the Ottoman establishment toward ʿAbd al-Qādir. Reporting on disturbances surrounding the handling of a convert for apostasy at the Ummayad Mosque, he remarked that

> 'it is generally believed that an effort will be made to blame Abd el-Kader... he is hated by the local authorities because his strong influence among his coreligionists is some check to the general maladministration of the province.'[12]

Western powers, too, continued to harbour concerns as to ʿAbd al-Qādir's political potential. In 1867, for instance, the Russian consul became convinced that he was plotting with Rashid Pasha and Druze leaders to attack the Christians of Damascus – to the point of making a complaint against him to the Ottoman authorities.[13] Again, such suspicions did not disappear with ʿAbd al-Qādir's advancing years and failing physical health. The degree to which this was the case is illustrated by an interview in 1880 between the British ambassador to Istanbul and 'Abdulrahman Husni Bey', an employee of the Porte claiming to be a nephew of ʿAbd al-Qādir.[14] This informant describes ʿAbd al-Qādir's very extensive influence and patronage while accusing him of fomenting revolution against the Ottomans in 1869, and of being party to anti-British plots on the part of the French – all of which the ambassador reports as unsubstantiated but definitely credible. It is also interesting to note with regard to that interchange, that Abdulrahman Husni Bey describes him as 'quite favourable to France *in spite of all that might be said by himself and others to the contrary*', referring repeatedly to ʿAbd al-Qādir's 'simulated *hostility to France*'.[15] The credibility of such assertions, which were likely to have been motivated by Ottoman attempts at sowing discord between regional competitors, seems less striking than the fact that the British ambassador found them so convincing. The modern impression of the Damascene ʿAbd al-Qādir as a Francophile religious recluse was very evidently not shared by the European, Egyptian, or Ottoman government agents of his day.

As for what we know with certainty about ʿAbd al-Qādir's relationship with France during these years, we can say relatively little. He continued to draw his generous monthly stipend,[16] leveraging French influence to aid his followers and

---

12 Burton to Eliot, FO 195/976, 12-07-1871.

13 Bertrand to the Consulate General in Beirut, *Damas/Consulat/27*, 21-03-1867.

14 Sandison to Salisbury, FO 78/3081, 24-01-1880 (enclosing memorandum dated 22-02-1880).

15 *Ibid.* Emphasis added.

16 This continued until his death: e.g. Portalis to the Ministry of Foreign Affairs, *Damas/Consulat/34*, 04-10-1882; 31-10-1882; 20-12-1882; 20-12-1882; 03-01-1883; 03-03-1883; 02-04-1883; 02-05-1883.

allies,[17] and from time to time sending a letter of good will[18] or attending a handful of formal occasions[19]- though he displayed greater enthusiasm to meet the wife of his benefactor Napoleon III on her visit to Egypt in 1869. On the whole, he derived considerable benefit from his connection with France, but offered very little in return – save a single monetary donation to the victims of the Franco-Prussian War offered in gratitude for the eventual pardon of the efforts by his brilliant but disobedient son Muḥyī al-Dīn[20] to liberate Algeria. It is notable that that donation coincided with this pardon, yet post-dated the end of the War by some two years: the implication is obvious. ʿAbd al-Qādir's aim may also have been to secure the continuation of his own stipends and patronage after the fall of Napoleon III's Second Empire at the hands of newly-united Germany, moreover.

ʿAbd al-Qādir's only significant act in support of French interests during these decades was in fact a negative one: he consistently abstained from breaking his solemn vow not to interfere with the affairs of France in the Maghreb, in spite of efforts to enlist him by North African rebels.[21] It was in the course of his attempts at securing clemency for his son Muḥyī al-Dīn that a letter, supposedly written by ʿAbd al-Qādir, was circulated in Algeria, recognising the legitimacy of French rule. It is probably the clearest evidence that has been produced of his verbal support for France. Yet even this gesture's authenticity has been questioned,[22] and for good reason: its phrasing is quite uncharacteristic and suggestive of French authorship, referring for instance to Muḥammad and the Qur'ān as '*your* Prophet and *your* Book'.[23] It is far from clear that he should be understood

---

17 E.g. Ministry of Foreign Affairs to Hecquard, *Damas/Consulat/22 and 69*, 24-09-1864; Hecquard to the Ministry of Foreign Affairs, *Damas/Consulat/24*, 20-12-1864; Hecquard to the Ministry of Foreign Affairs, *Damas/Consulat/27*, 02-01-1865; Hecquard to the Ministry of Foreign Affairs, *Damas/Consulat/24*, 01-02-1866; ʿAbd al-Qādir to the Consulate General, Beirut, *Damas/Consulat/28*, 19-06-1869; Ministry of Foreign Affairs to Roustan, *Damas/Consulat/69*, 04-10-1869; Flesch to the French embassy in Constantinople, *Damas/Consulat/35*, 21-05-1881 .

18 E.g. ʿAbd al-Qādir to the Emperor, Empress, and Foreign Minister of France, *Damas/Consulat/26*, 30-x-1867.

19 E.g. Bertrand to the Ministry of Foreign Affairs, *Damas/Consulat/65*, 22-05-1871; Flesch to the Ministry of Foreign Affairs, *Damas/Consulat/33*, 16-12-1880; Flesch to the French embassy in Constantinople, *Damas/Consulat/33 and 35*, 17-05-1881; Flesch to the Ministry of Foreign Affairs, *Damas/Consulat/33*, 15-07-1881.

20 Robin to the Ministry of Foreign Affairs, *Damas/Consulat/65*, 25-01-1873.

21 E.g. Flesch to Constantinople, *Damas/Consulat/33*, 24-03-1881; Portalis to the French embassy in Constantinople, *Damas/Consulat/35*, 02-07-1882.

22 E.g. Étienne, 2003 p. 414.

23 Bertrand to the Ministry of Foreign Affairs, *Damas/Consulat/65*, 22-04-1871. Emphasis added.

at this time as endorsing French rule over Algerian Muslims, and once again credible evidence exists to the contrary.

ʿAbd al-Qādir's honour-bound refusal to become personally involved in North African politics did not preclude his resenting the French conquest. An American diplomat offers the following impression of late 1860's ʿAbd al-Qādir, conflicting dramatically with that found in the standard French narrative of cheerful submission to the colonial project:

> 'Though it does not appear to be [ʿAbd al-Qādir's] intention to resume the war for the independence of his country he has not lost interest in it, for he once remarked that he would have been pleased if Mr [U.S. Secretary of State William H.] Seward had written a note to the French government in regard to their occupation of Algeria, similar to that relative to their seizure of Mexico [in 1864], apparently having no doubt that the effect would be a like abandonment [in 1867] of their conquest.'[24]

Whatever his hopes, neither a collapse of Ottoman rule in Syria, nor of French rule in North Africa would come to pass during ʿAbd al-Qādir's lifetime. By the early 1880s, his health failing, he knew he was not long for this world. When in late 1882 he sent his son al-Hāshimī to Istanbul to consult medical doctors,[25] he would begin making arrangements to financially support him on his return in the Spring of 1883:[26] ʿAbd al-Qādir could not count on being alive to see him in person. By the summer, ʿAbd al-Qādir would be dead,[27] his body buried with that of Muḥyī al-Dīn ibn al-ʿArabī. His family refused the French consul's offer to defray the costs of the burial, insisting instead on paying all expenses themselves.[28] His descendants, ever proud of his memory, remain in the city to this day – even if ʿAbd al-Qādir's remains have long since been repatriated to Algiers.[29]

It is not so much for all of this that the final years of ʿAbd al-Qādir's life are remembered, however, so much as for their literary production. Throughout his time in Damascus, as in Anatolia, France, and Algeria before, ʿAbd al-Qādir gave lessons and lectures to those who would listen. These focused on Islamic sciences, on Mālikite jurisprudence[30] and Sufism. ʿAbd al-Qādir's 'magnum opus', the

24 Johnson to the Department of State, A2 Cab. 40/9, 31-12-1869.
25 Portalis to the French Embassy in Constantinople (enclosing letter from ʿAbd al-Qādir to same), *Damas/Consulat/35*, 12-10-1882.
26 Portalis to the Ministry of Foreign Affairs, *Damas/Consulat/34*, 05-02-1883.
27 Portalis to the Ministry of Foreign Affairs, *Damas/Consulat/14*, 03-05-1883.
28 Portalis to the Ministry of Foreign Affairs, *Damas/Consulat/34*, 03-07-1883.
29 This occurred in 1968.
30 Goldziher, 1981, p. 242.

voluminous *Kitāb al-Mawāqif fī al-Taṣawwuf wa al-Wa'ẓ wa al-Irshād*,[31] was a product of his role as a teacher of Sufi thought. Published posthumously, it comprises a large collection of un-ordered 'lecture notes' transcribed during lessons he gave. The recording of these hundreds of talks was carried out at the behest of Moḥammad al-Khānī, once connected to Shaykh Khāled al-Naqshbandī, whom a young 'Abd al-Qādir had met during his pilgrimages from Algeria with his father, as well as 'Abd al-Razzāq al-Bayṭār and Muḥammad al-Ṭanṭawī.[32] It is only thanks to the insistence of these pupils that we have any substantial insight into 'Abd al-Qādir's personal understanding of Sufism. We have seen since Chapter One that he was raised as a Sufi, considered a marabout, and was unsurprisingly conversant with such influential figures as 'Abd al-Qādir al-Jīlānī,[33] al-Ghazālī,[34] and Ibn al-'Arabī[35] since his youth – but only after his death would the details of his views become accessible to those outside his closest circles.

Less a monograph than a series of lectures on Sufi exegesis, each chapter of the *Kitāb al-Mawāqif* typically begins with a quotation from the Qur'ān, which is then expanded upon and interpreted. It is vital to note at the outset that 'Abd al-Qādir and his students will have understood the lessons which comprise the *Kitāb al-Mawāqif* not primarily as an exposition of his ideas, nor even those of the Sufi authorities he quotes – but as reading the Qur'ān. The Qur'ānic text is the touchstone and ultimate authority in the *Kitāb al-Mawāqif*, as it is for 'Abd al-Qādir's practice of Islam. Quoting 'Abdallah ibn 'Abbās and Abū Madyan, 'Abd al-Qādir reminds his students that 'not a bird stirred its wing in the sky but we find it in God's book,' while 'the *murīd* [seeker] is no *murīd* until he has found all that he seeks within the Qur'ān'.[36] It bears constant repetition that in all of these respects, 'Abd al-Qādir espoused views as typical of the mainstreams of the discourses he uses as was the case in his more jurisprudential writing.

---

31 The text is sometimes given an alternative subtitle, but is invariably known as the *Kitāb al-Mawāqif*, given 'Abd al-Qādir's repeated reference throughout the text to 'these *Mawāqif*'.

32 Chodkiewicz, 1995, p. 17.

33 Al-Jīlānī is the eponymous founder of 'Abd al-Qādir's family Sufi brotherhood, the *ṭarīqah qādiriyyah*.

34 Al-Ghazālī is quoted in his *Risālah on Hijrah*, for instance, and extensively paraphrased in his *Dhikrā al-'Āqil* (see Chapters Two and Three).

35 Textual evidence of 'Abd al-Qādir employing Ibn al-'Arabī's characteristic lexicon (evident throughout the *Kitāb al-Mawāqif*) has been identified at least as early as his imprisonment in France [e.g. Chodkiewicz, 1995, pp. 6, 185; Shinar, 1965, p. 160), at which time he had no texts of Ibn al-'Arabī with him: his conversance with such ideas must logically predate his imprisonment.

36 *Mawāqif*, p. 1277 – Ibn 'Abbās and Abū Madyan, respectively.

The interpretations given are less frequently those of the conventional *mufassir* [exegete], though these are also mentioned and always accepted as legitimate – and though some Sufis have written texts of extremely conventional *tafsīr.* Rather, the readings taken by ʿAbd al-Qādir here have a more specialist or esoteric character (in the strict sense of requiring an education and experience not shared by the wider population – specifically in Sufi exegeses).[37] It is for this reason that the text has frequently been described as primarily concerned with that specialised school of Sufi hermeneutics identified by the term '*waḥdat al-wujūd*',[38] a 'commentary on Ibn al-ʿArabī'[39] – as, in a certain sense, it is. It is conspicuously faithful in form and in content to a centuries-long established family of traditions within Sufism – one focused heavily on the prodigious writings of Ibn al-ʿArabī. This is not to say that he will have felt Ibn al-ʿArabī (or Qūnawī, whose reception of Ibn al-ʿArabī is also evident in the *Mawāqif*, or whosoever) to have created such ideas – but simply to have uncovered or explained truths which were eternally present in the scriptural text. This attitude is of course typical of the sincere exegete, and ʿAbd al-Qādir presents his interpretations as anything but religious innovation [*bidʿah*], a heresy in Islam.[40]

Even when ʿAbd al-Qādir vividly recounts his own mystical transports – some of the most salient departures from the more conventional approach of the traditional *mufassir* – these are invariably[41] mediated through the text of the Qur'ān. More than mediated, in fact: ʿAbd al-Qādir's accounts of his mystical experiences as he describes them are largely constituted by the Qur'ānic text itself. One verse or another will explode into his consciousness, as though sent to

---

37 See, for instance, Alexander Knysh's entry on 'Ṣūfism and the Qur'ān' in the *Encyclopaedia of the Qur'ān.*

38 ʿAbd al-Qādir does occasionally use this term, roughly translatable as 'the One-ness of Being' (though Ibn al-ʿArabī himself did not use the phrase, but only his followers after al-Qunāwī) – e.g. *Mawāqif*, p. 33. It is a notoriously problematic label, not least because it might be read as endorsing a pantheistic position (*ittiḥād*) which Sufis of this tradition frequently reject as heretical (and which is famously one of Ibn Taymiyya's main charges against Ibn al-ʿArabī). Ibn Taymiyya's charges of innovation rested squarely on a reading of Ibn ʿArabī that 'consistently identifies God's existence with that of his creatures' – Knysh, 1999, p. 100.

39 Kiser, 2008, p. 288.

40 *Mawāqif*, p. 26 denies that the Sufis bring anything new to the religion – though they may uncover understandings of it hitherto unknown in the community.

41 E. g. Even what appear as rare exceptions to this rule – such as when ʿAbd al-Qādir recounts a vision of the Prophet, who says to ʿAbd al-Qādir 'you are my child, and accepted by me' [*Mawāqif* p. 170], Qur'ānic verses are soon employed as glosses and justifications.

fill the space created within him by his 'remembrance' (*dhikr*) of God.[42] He does not present himself as receiving insights which he then applies to the text, but rather fragments of the texts are themselves imbued with insight.

Such experiences are reflected in the fragmented structure of the text, and will have contributed to it as much as the exigencies of day-to-day teaching. Again, the *Kitāb al-Mawāqif* is not a single continuous text, but a collection of related discussions of various verses, sayings, and spiritual stations – with a great deal of repetition. This piecemeal method of exposition occasions some difficulties for attempts to summarise or systematise ʿAbd al-Qādir's teachings, or condense the voluminous *Kitāb al-Mawāqif* into a more easily digestible form. Though his teachings in the *Kitāb al-Mawāqif* do evince definite themes and consistent conceptual structures, he does not argue in the fashion of a rationalist philosopher, by systematically layering inferences on specific premises. Nothing could be further from the geometric order of Spinoza's *Ethics* or Leibniz's *Monadology* than the *Mawāqif*'s magnificent jumble of discussions. As such, every systematisation of ʿAbd al-Qādir's teaching runs the risk of falsifying his project by presenting him as propounding an *a priori* metaphysical scheme anterior to his reading of the Qur'ān: the reverse of the situation as he himself portrays it. What is more, any exclusive focus on texts – while necessary and illuminating – neglects the element of *praxis* which is very arguably more central to the Sufi path than exposition alone; a practising Sufi need not teach Sufism, but a Sufi teacher must surely practise it. Nevertheless, certain themes can be found constantly repeated throughout the teachings, and the sense of a coherent metaphysical structure is difficult to ignore, even if it is not expressed as it might have been by most European philosophers.

Therefore, some attempt must be made here to give an account of the *Kitāb al-Mawāqif*'s contents. This course is followed here both because it throws light on the inner dimension of the religious practice which played so dominant a role throughout ʿAbd al-Qādir's life, and because a textual basis will be required in order to refute some of the mischaracterisations of his Sufi thought common in the secondary literature. These mischaracterisations, which will be explored further below, have played a crucial role in the construction and apparent vindication of 'Road to Damascus' narratives of ʿAbd al-Qādir's life.

---

42 E.g. *Mawāqif*, pp. 158–164 recounts a sequence of trance-visions, with ʿAbd al-Qādir alternating between absorbed *dhikr* and 'returning to his senses', each time focussing on a single phrase from the Qur'ān.

5.1 Major Themes in the *Kitāb al-Mawāqif*

While the lessons which make up the *Kitāb al-Mawāqif*'s chapters are not obviously ordered, and contain a great deal of repetition, it is surely significant that the first chapter opens as it does. The first words of the *Kitāb al-Mawāqif* are the Qur'ānic verse '*Ye have indeed in the Messenger of Allah a beautiful pattern (of conduct)* [*uswah ḥasanah*]'.[43] The various roles of Muḥammad – as prophet, as exemplar, as archetype, as cosmic principle – form a constant *Leitmotif* throughout the text. Using a lexicon inherited from the Andalusian 'Greatest Shaykh' (as 'Abd al-Qādir, like many others, reverentially refers to him)[44] Muḥyī al-Dīn Ibn al-'Arabī, 'Abd al-Qādir presents Muḥammad and his followers as God's creatures with the greatest capacity to receive and reflect God's divine nature through the Qur'ānic revelation:

> 'Not all knowledge befits all people, nor do all people befit all knowledge, but for each knowledge there is a people (*ahl*) who are prepared to receive it (*lahum isti'dād li-qubūlihi*)...
>
> Everyone who speaks the language of a given prophet is the inheritor (*wārith*) of that prophet, for [that prophet] is the master of that language. [But] one who speaks through the Qur'ān is the inheritor of all the prophets, which is to say he is Muḥammadan (*muḥammadī*), because the Qur'ān encompasses all languages (*mutaḍammin li-jamī' al-lughāt*) just as Muḥammad's station (peace be upon him) encompasses all stations (*mutaḍammin li-jamī' al-maqāmāt*).'[45]

The finality and universality of the Qur'ānic revelation is reflected in the *Kitāb al-Mawāqif* through a concomitant universalising of the Prophet Muḥammad into a cosmic metaphysical criterion. If the Qur'ān epitomises truth as transmitted from God to man, so the Prophet who received and first recited it must epitomise the human locus of truth. The *imitatio Muḥammadi* merges with a mystical ontology to give rise, drawing on the lexicon of Ibn al-'Arabī, to an ahistorical Muḥammadan Reality (*ḥaqīqah muḥammadiyyah*).[46] Muḥammad is not only a historical model of human excellence for 'Abd al-Qādir, he is the final cause of and ultimate *telos* towards which all human excellence by definition inclines:

---

43 Qur'ān 33:21; *Mawāqif*, p. 27.

44 The Kitāb al-Mawāqif is deeply endebted to the Andalusian 'Seal of Sainthood', as scholar of Ibn al-'Arabī Michel Chodkiewicz [1995, p. 14] has rightly pointed out. This is true both in its lexicon – employing characteristic concepts such as *tajallī*, *isti'dād*, *fayḍ*, *a'yān thābita* – and the positions its takes – for instance in relation to the fate of Pharoah and the nature of eternity. Ibn al-'Arabī is far from being the only authority quoted of course, and not the only one given honourifics: e.g. '*al-'ārif al-kabīr*' al-Shādhilī [*Mawāqif*, p. 326].

45 Mawāqif, p. 159.

46 For a discussion of this term in Ibn al-'Arabī's writing, see al-Ḥakīm, 1981, pp. 347–352.

> 'Every spirit comes from the universal Muḥammadan spirit, albeit in imperfect form – with the exception of those spiritually perfected beings who are the Muḥammadan inheritors. Perfection, in effect, is imprinted upon them, like a seal in wax...'[47]

This preoccupation with subtle or transcendental realities underlying human experience re-occurs throughout the text. Like Plotinus' *Enneads* (though their similarity to the text at hand is easily over-stated), the *Kitāb al-Mawāqif* describes a reality in which the divine absolute is connected to the day-to-day phenomenal world through a many-levelled metaphysical hierarchy. Unlike the (Neo-)Platonists' *One* or *Idea of the Good*, however, the centre of ʿAbd al-Qādir's reality is quite explicitly God Himself as revealed in the Qur'ān.[48]

Rather than logically subdividing Himself according to one conceptual scheme or other, God reveals and manifests Himself through His Divine Names – those epithets contained within the Qur'ān. 'Allah is the Name which unites all of the Names'[49] and from which they flow, at once setting up an ontological equivocation which is characteristic of ʿAbd al-Qādir's view of reality as a whole. God is absolutely one and indivisible, while simultaneously also being what is described by the 99 Qur'ānic[50] epithets which render Him the multifarious source from which all created multiplicity flows:

> 'True Reality [*al-ḥaqq*] – God the Most High – in manifesting Himself to Himself through Himself, is not dependant on the creations, and thus needs not the worlds [of creation]. He needs not [*ghanī ʿan*] even His Names, for to whom shall He be named, and to whom described? But only in his Singularity [*aḥadiyyah*] has he no need of them, for in His manifestation through His Names and attributes, and their effects [*āthārha*], He has need [*muftaqar ilā*] for the creations... in the sense that [the Names] demand their effects, as all that demands has need for that which it demands. So, the heavens and the earth, and all beings illuminated by the name *al-Nūr* [the Light] are the shadows of the Names and [divine] attributes.'[51]

This apparent contradiction – between monism and dualism, unity and multiplicity, transcendence and immanence – is bridged in the *Kitāb al-Mawāqif* by a subtle ontological equivocation. ʿAbd al-Qādir avoids the horns of this dilem-

47 Mawāqif, p. 182–183.
48 Variations on similar ideas have played significant roles in European thought since antiquity (as famously discussed by Arthur Lovejoy [2001, *passim*]), though this need not demand equating them.
49 *Mawāqif*, p. 225.
50 It should be noted that ʿAbd al-Qādir includes the name '*al-Muḍill*', the misleader – present in the passage which opens this chapter – which is inferred from rather than used directly in the Qur'ān.
51 *Mawāqif*, pp. 225–226.

ma by employing a notion of liminality drawn from a Qur'ānic symbol seen as structurally central to the thought of Ibn al-ʿArabī.[52] It is the metaphor of the isthmus or *barzakh*[53] which simultaneously joins and separates two different bodies of water, one sweet and one salty, but which is itself neither essentially one nor the other, nor a thing of its own: '*He has let free the two bodies of flowing water, meeting together. Between them is a Barrier [barzakh] which they do not transgress.*'[54] So,

> 'the *barzakh* is that which joins two things, which is neither identical with them nor different from them, and within which lies the power of each of them. Were it not for the *barzakh*, realities would be mixed up [*ikhṭalaṭat al-ḥaqā'iq*] and all paths confused. It is like the geometric boundary [*al-khaṭṭ al-handasī*] which divides between shade and sun: it is neither shadow nor sunshine, nor is it perceived as other than these two. All the sensoria perceive is shadow and sun – so it [the *barzakh*] is of two kinds: connected to man, and separated from him [*mutaṣṣil bil-insān wa munfaṣṣil ʿanhu*].'[55]

That which separates and differentiates, that is, is the selfsame 'thing' which unites and combines. As a result, ʿAbd al-Qādir is neither a thoroughgoing ontological monist nor dualist but, like his *barzakh*, something in-between which attempts to unite both perspectives without challenging the claims of either. This is a significant point which bears repeating, particularly given the ease of its mischaracterisation. The unity to which he attests is absolutely inclusive of multiplicity, and does not do away with his system of categories, nor with the moral universe of good and bad which it undergirds. Again, it is also worth re-stating that this does not represent a creative innovation on his part, but expresses views common in the mainstream of his Sufi backgrounds – and does so in the most conspicuously conventional of language.

The hierarchy of Being presented by ʿAbd al-Qādir is not only a matter of general or special metaphysics, however. His God, it must be remembered, is the personal deity of the Abrahamic religions, not exclusively an abstract metaphysical principle. God has a will, intentions, likes and dislikes (to which ʿAbd al-Qādir does not take the Muʿtazilite approach of declaring purely metaphorical) – and God has sent a clear Revelation in the words of the Qur'ān. These flow down the hierarchy from divinity to humanity as does Being itself – indeed they are ultimately united as reflections of God's own nature beyond the created world. After the quintessential act of love and mercy [*raḥmah*] in the gratuitous

52 Bashier, 2004, *passim.*
53 For a further discussion of this term's use by Ibn al-ʿArabī, see al-Hakīm, 1981, pp. 191–196.
54 Qur'ān 55:19–10.
55 *Mawāqif*, p. 812.

Creation, ʿAbd al-Qādir describes God's love for mankind [*maḥabbah*] descending from unity to generality to specificity, from Essence to Names to a-temporal archetypes [*aʿyān thābitah*] to every instant of a person's life. His Love manifests and unites all being, and his Love differentiates among beings between the favoured and the blameworthy in the same creative motion.

God 'loves those who keep themselves pure and clean'[56] ʿAbd al-Qādir quotes from the Qur'ān, and 'Truly Allah loves those who fight in His Cause in battle array,'[57] while He 'loveth not those who do wrong.'[58] God's approval applies to classes on the basis of their common behaviours' conformity to his law. On a more specific and individual level, God also loves those who are the subject of a ḥadīth ʿAbd al-Qādir (like so many other Sufis) quotes: 'my servant will not cease in drawing closer to me in supererogation until I love him, and I am that through which his hearing hears, and his seeing sees...'[59] The devoted servant of God must be Godly in his thoughts, actions, and very being – which is nothing apart from God. This is not the apotheosis of certain pantheists or solipsists who might declare themselves God. Ittiḥād, or the undifferentiated union and utter identification of Creator and Creation with the attendant possibility of the 'deification' of the human individual is almost universally considered heretical in Islam, it must be remembered. Rather, ʿAbd al-Qādir insists, he who consciously[60] so much as utters the assertion that they are God 'shall be dealt with by the swords of the sharīʿah and the ḥaqīqah, and their blood will be spilled, as happened to al-Ḥussein bin Manṣūr al-Ḥallāj[61] (may God be pleased with him).'[62] In this, ʿAbd al-Qādir both honours the renowned Sufi martyr (famous for the scandalous ejaculation *'anā al-ḥaqq'*, 'I am Truth' or 'I am God') while simultaneously agreeing with the Malikite judge who sentenced him to death.

This demanding and subtle project forms the core of the Sufi path as understood by ʿAbd al-Qādir. It involves a complete internalisation of God's nature and God's intentions, at once both metaphysical and ethical, spiritual and social:

---

56 *Mawāqif*, p. 229; Qur'ān 2:222

57 *Ibid.*; Qur'ān 61:4

58 *Ibid.*; Qur'ān 3:57 and 3:23.

59 *Ibid.*; *Ṣaḥīḥ* of al-Bukhārī, Volume 8, Book 76, Number 509

60 Uttering this (or any other) sentence while out of one's wits would not constiute a transgression, ʿAbd al-Qādir argues, 'because reason [*al-ʿaql*] is a condition for the apportioning of guily [*taklīf*], and this is absent' – *Mawāqif*, p. 1044.

61 Al-Ḥallāj, the famous 9th-10th century mystic reportedly sentenced to death in Baghdad by a Malikite judge, supposedly for uttering the phrase 'I am God' (*ana al-ḥaqq*). He is most famously discussed by Massignon [1994].

62 *Mawāqif*, p. 1044.

'The Lord has made for his servant two eyes, an exterior and an interior [*ẓāhirah wa bāṭinah*], so as to see the interior by means of the interior [*al-bāṭin bil-bāṭinah*] and the exterior by means of the exterior [*al-zāhir bil-ẓāhirah*]. He is like an isthmus between these two visions [*kal-barzakh bayna al-shuhūdayn*], and neither one of them will benefit him without the other, but would be half-blind.'[63]

The truly accomplished Sufi, according to 'Abd al-Qādir, imitates Muḥammad in his universal capacity (but never his legislative function – a role none other can usurp),[64] becoming the bridging *barzakh* between Heaven and Earth, the Perfect Man[65] in thought and deed. In doing so, he becomes the mirror of God, as 'Abd al-Qādir explains while glossing the Qur'ānic verse '*there is nothing whatever like unto Him* [*laysa ka-mithlihi shay*]':[66]

'the person who unites the Names *al-Ẓāhir* and *al-Bāṭin*[67] is the most noble of creatures, and the most complete. His superiority to other created beings lies in the fact that the Perfect Man is the joining entity [*al-kawn al-jāmi'*] between Heavenly and earthly realities. And he is the likeness of which the Most High said 'there is nothing like my likeness'. For in the word 'like' (*kāf*) there are two ways [of reading the word]: addition, and the absence of addition.... read in terms of addition, the meaning is that nothing is like the Real, the Most High – for He is the source of being and not like being... read as non-addition... the Most High fixed a likeness of Himself, and it is the Perfect Man... for he is a being which unites in itself all the Realities of the Divine Names...[68]

By means of this process of layering metaphysical interpretations of the Qur'ānic text on top of the more generally accepted readings, 'Abd al-Qādir justifies both esoteric interpretations, those requiring specialised explanation, and exoteric ones, drawing only on generally held knowledge,[69] by the same token: the au-

63 *Mawāqif*, p. 815.
64 *Mawāqif*, pp. 769–771 discuss the distinction between the 'general and the legislative prophethoods' of Mūsā (who brings God's law, and is a true prophet) and the mysterious al-Khiḍr (who brings no law, and is a saint). 'Abd al-Qādir takes the mainsteam Islamic view of the finality of Muḥammad's revelation.
65 'Abd al-Qādir's usage of this term, *al-insān al-kāmil*, derives from the eponymous text of al-Jīlī, a descendant of the founder of 'Abd al-Qādir's own Qādiriyyah Sufi order, and it is found throughout the writings of sufis influenced by Ibn al-'Arabī, who employed it himself [al-Ḥakīm, 1981, pp. 158–168].
66 Qur'ān 42:11.
67 These polyvalent terms may be translated as 'The Outer' and 'The Inner', or 'The Visible' and 'The Hidden', or 'The Manifest' and 'The Un-manifest'.
68 *Mawāqif*, pp. 569–575. See also, pp. 230–233, 1379.
69 These strict usages of the terms 'esoteric' and 'exoteric' are distinct from the terms' employment by other writers on 'Abd al-Qādir, most of whom adopt (without specific explanation) var-

thoritative text of the Qur'ān. The unity of the Qur'ānic text becomes the means for reconciling ostensibly mutually contradictory assertions. More than a rhetorical tactic, the centrality of the Qur'ān and the unity of its many messages – spiritual, metaphysical, ethical, moral, historical, social, and political – is the bedrock upon which ʿAbd al-Qādir builds his teaching in the *Kitāb al-Mawāqif.* As in the *Dhikrā*, so in the *Kitāb al-Mawāqif*, ʿAbd al-Qādir's theology is partly apophatic ('negative')[70] in denying that any description of God can encompass Him – save His own inimitable disclosure through the Revelation, which must by the same token (like Him) be subtle and multifarious (and hence not exhaustible by a single human interpretation).[71] 'A man's understanding [*fiqh*][72] is incomplete until he sees that the Qur'ān has many faces,'[73] where to deny one aspect would deny the others, and throw his Qur'ānic worldview into disarray. Similarly, the absence of the Qurʿān, or a rejection of its divine origin, would rad-

---

iants of the terms' more recent usages as designating different worldviews along loosely defined supernatural/natural, magical/empirical, and metaphysical/discursive cleavages. Scholars of 'western Esotericism' Wouter Haanegraaff [1999] and Antoine Faivre [in Faivre and Haanegraaff (eds.), 1998] offer five or four different senses (respectively) of such modern usages. One of these in particular (that related to the school of 'Traditionalist' perrenialist thought inaugurated by René Guénon and identified with writers including Frithjof Schoun and Ananda Coomaraswamy) is typically assumed by writers on ʿAbd al-Qādir's Sufism as part of a (re-)interpretive project which will be discussed in the final section of this chapter.

70 Negative or apophatic theology, the *via negativa* or negating method which forms elements of both most 'mystical' religious writings and of more mainstream writings by the likes of Rabbi Moses Maimonides, Saint Thomas Aquinas, and elements of Ashʿarī *kalām* (*ta'tīl*), approaches the divine through its fundamental incomparability to ordinary human experience and insusceptibility to human analysis, comparison, and delineation. Rather than attempting to define and circumscribe what God is, that is, it addresses what God is not – especially with respect to comparisons with created things. It is consequentially more concerned with exposing the limits imposed by particular human definitions of divinity than with positing its own alternative characterisation. As is the case with both Aquinas and Maimonides, of course, ʿAbd al-Qādir's belief in positive divine revelation provides a moderating counter-point to this approach. For more on this tradition's role in the Islamic tradition, see the Encyclopaedia of Islam, 2nd Edition, entry on *tashbīh wa tanzīh* [van Ess].

71 'The God who is known by the ʿAshʿarīs is other than the God who is known by the Muʿatazilīs, who is other than the God who is known by the Ẓāhirīs, who is other than the God who is known by the wise philosopher. What they claim to be knowledge of God is not knowledge of God, but rather imagination and fancy.' – *Mawāqif*, p. 383.

72 *Fiqh* (*lit.* understanding, comprehension) is the standard term for jurisprudence, and denotes that area of Islamic law and ethics which result from indirect inferences such as argument from analogy (*qiyāṣ*). As distinct from the Sharʿī injunctions found explicitly in the Qur'ān and Sunnah, *fiqh* derivations from these sources are traditionally considered open to legitimate disagreement (hence the co-existence of the various schools of Islamic jurisprudence).

73 *Mawāqif*, p. 26.

ically undermine his approach. The divinity and polysemy of the Qur'ān are for him foundational.

It is by virtue of the resultant process of interpretive palimpsest that ʿAbd al-Qādir can present passages such as that quoted above, which contain elements which might appear scandalous in isolation, while remaining true to the mainstream of his faith. He contrasts this recognition of the polysemy of the divine revelation and the God from whom it comes favourably with the exclusive chauvinisms of squabbling theoreticians. In so doing, he expands his argument beyond a mere apology for his own approach into a universal call for Muslim unity and tolerance:

> 'the factions of the theologians [*mutakallimūn*] curse one another and accuse one another of unbelief [*yukaffir*]! Not so are the people of God the Most High, His Knowers, whose words are one in the unity of the True God [*tawḥīd al-ḥaqq*]. All of their concern is as said by the Most High: "*Remain steadfast in religion, and make no division therein.*"'[74]

While ʿAbd al-Qādir warns against the dangers of factionalism and *takfīr*, the central metaphor of the liminal isthmus or *barzakh* (already seen above) acts to guarantee that his Sufi insights cannot threaten to abnegate the standards of Islamic civilisation and Islamic law. Such abnegation is after all the typical fear of Sufism's Muslim critics, including other Sufis.[75] Rather, it is presented as amplifying those standards through remembrance of their divine origin. The isthmus divides and differentiates as much as it unites, of course, even while binding the clearly differentiated elements in a mutually dependent relationship. It is a barrier, in the very words of the Qur'ān from which the metaphor arises, which the elements it joins '*do not transgress.*'

This fact is perhaps most elegantly and explicitly illustrated, in characteristically Qur'ānic terms, in the following passage from the *Kitāb al-Mawāqif*. In it, ʿAbd al-Qādir quotes passages which alternate between what seem like mutually incompatible divine assertions of monism and dualism, fatalism and free-will, resignation and action, before concluding that they in fact necessitate one another:

> "God the Most High said: 'He has set free the two bodies of flowing water, meeting together: between them is a Barrier [*barzakh*] which they do not transgress.'[76]

---

74 *Mawāqif*, p. 50; Qur'ān 42:13.

75 See for instance the condemnation of non-observant '*soi-disant* Sufis' in Al-Ghazālī's post-*Iḥya... Fayṣal al-Tafriqa* [2003, p.115], or the numerous discussions of this point in Karamustafa's *God's Unruly Friends* [2006].

76 Qur'ān, 55:19–20.

> So, the two seas are the *Sharīʿah* [Law] and the *Ḥaqīqah* [Reality], and the isthmus [*barzakh*] between the two of them is the Knower [*al-ʿārif*]. So, the *Sharīʿah* does not transgress upon the *Ḥaqīqah*, and the *Ḥaqīqah* does not transgress upon the *Sharīʿah*...

[The Knower] witnesses the *Sharīʿah* through the words of God the Most High:

> 'Work (righteousness); soon Allah will observe your work.'[77]

And he witnesses the *Ḥaqīqah* through the words of God the Most High:

> 'They will be able to do nothing with aught they have earned.'[78]

And he witnesses the *Sharīʿah* through the words of God the Most High:

> 'Seize them and slay them.' [79]

And he witnesses the *Ḥaqīqah* through the words of God the Most High:

> 'It is not ye who slew them; it was Allah.'[80]

And he witnesses the *Sharīʿah* through the words of God the Most High:

> 'Not for thee, (but for Allah), is the decision.'[81]

And he witnesses the *Ḥaqīqah* through the words of God the Most High:

> 'Verily those who plight their fealty to thee do no less than plight their fealty to Allah.'[82]
> ...Thus the *Sharīʿah* demands the *Ḥaqīqah* and the *Sharīʿah*, and the *Ḥaqīqah* demands the *Sharīʿah* and the *Ḥaqīqah*."[83]

The crux of ʿAbd al-Qādir's *Kitāb al-Mawāqif*, then, is a call to a project of personal transformation which, while not necessarily altering the individual believer's duties and obligations, fundamentally reshapes their psychological attitudes

77 Qur'ān 9:105
78 Qur'ān 2:264
79 Qur'ān 4:89
80 Qur'ān 8:17
81 Qur'ān 3:128
82 Qur'ān 48:10.
83 *Mawāqif*, pp. 147–148.

and spiritual being. This is not because Shariah-based orthopraxy is irrelevant to such a project (it in fact demands it), but because it is required to persist in its own logic. ʿAbd al-Qādir's image of the accomplished Sufi is to his mind more observant, not less, than his fellow Muslim. None is absolved from obeying God's commandments, as ʿAbd al-Qādir argued since before his *Risālah on Hijrah*, though all are forgiven. By not only doing the right thing, but doing it for the right reasons, the true Sufi becomes the most Muslim of the Muslims, and a worthy inheritor of the Prophet Muḥammad.

Constant awareness of unity in multiplicity through the utter dependence of all phenomena on God is expected to bring about an attitude of worshipful resignation and submission towards God, and humble forgiving amity towards one's fellow human beings. 'Who thanks not the people, thanks not God,' ʿAbd al-Qādir reminds his students, quoting al-Tirmidhī, as there is no absolute duality [*lā ithnayniyyah*][84] and it is ultimately God who acts through us all. Our obligation as God's devoted servants, he maintains in his *Kitāb al-Mawāqif*, is to internalise this fact while scrupulously adhering to His divine commandments and the model of the Prophet Muḥammad.

ʿAbd al-Qādir's Sufi teachings have increasingly come to play a different role in the western secondary literature, however, which has only in the 20th century taken interest in this text. This new interpretation is one which distances this text from the strictures of the Qur'ān and the example of the Prophet. Moreover, it does so in a manner intimately related to the narratives of conversion surrounding ʿAbd al-Qādir's purported transformation from warrior to pacifist, from premodern Islamic theocrat to post-modern religious pluralist. The textual evidence for each of these alleged changes of heart will be discussed in the next sections of this chapter, and systematically compared to the original Arabic sources.

5.2 ʿAbd al-Qādir's Later Life and Politics: Reading Conversion into the *Kitāb al-Mawāqif*

Perhaps the most jarring discontinuity, and clearest evidence for 'conversion', in ʿAbd al-Qādir's biographies is his apparent transformation from an practitioner of politically-engaged religiosity before his imprisonment in France to an advocate of pacifist religious quietism subsequent to it. The erstwhile Algerian political leader is consistently presented as shunning politics by the time of his arrival in Damascus. Meanwhile, very little of the literature is concerned with his final

84 *Mawāqif*, p. 157.

decades from any perspective other than the study of certain aspects of his Sufism. These facts are related through the particular characteristics predicated of what is taken to be his approach to Sufism; he is understood as having embraced so pacific and quietist a variety of Sufism as to motivate, justify, and exemplify his supposed retreat from worldly affairs after his defeat by France. The character of his teachings on Sufism as they are reflected in the west is thus crucial to the maintenance of the 'Road to Damascus' narrative governing his biography. Some pre-eminent examples of this tendency, drawn from the most scholarly and influential of his treatments, must be discussed here. These have been selected both because of the high quality and significant influence of the studies in which they arise, and because of the explicitness with which they attempt to ground their characterisations of ʿAbd al-Qādir on specific texts.

Jacques Berque's excellent account of ʿAbd al-Qādir, for instance, offers a quotation from the *Kitāb al-Mawāqif* to suggest that the erstwhile war-leader transformed into a pacifist after his defeat by France. 'To kill and to destroy what God has made is not His Will,' Berque quotes approvingly from the 74th *Mawqif*,[85] before observing what a 'remarkable proposition [this is] for a man of war in his time'. This would seem to constitute dramatic evidence of a change of heart in ʿAbd al-Qādir – first waging then denouncing warfare. It is certainly true that he wrote the sentence in question. But in its proper context it forms part not of a denunciation of warfare, but an orthodox endorsement of ethical warfare as a religious obligation – one repeatedly recognised throughout the *Kitāb al-Mawāqif*, in fact.[86] This is the case to the extent that he declares elsewhere that

> 'the religion *is jihād* [*al-dīn al-jihād*], even though the religion has other pillars besides *jihād*... God the Most High's love for the *mujāhids* is a special affection [*maḥabbah khāṣah*], which has effects in this world and the next, just as the *mujāhids*' particular love for Him, the Most High, is special and additional [*zā'idah*] to that of other believers who are not *mujāhids*.'[87]

The chapter of the *Kitāb al-Mawāqif* from which the sentence quoted by Berque is taken in fact revolves around the traditional mainstream distinction between the so called *Greater* and *Lesser Jihāds*.[88] The former holy war is the battle against one's own worst inclinations (*jihād al-nafs*), and the latter that against non-Muslim foes (*jihād al-kuffār*). In this chapter, ʿAbd al-Qādir attempts to establish the superiority of the *Greater* over the *Lesser Jihād* – a very conventional

85 Berque, 1978, p. 518.
86 E.g. *Mawāqif*, pp. 27, 155–156, 229.
87 *Mawāqif*, p. 1048.
88 E.g. Khadduri, 1955, pp. 56–7.

project, and not a new departure. He first does this by pointing out that the *Greater Jihād* is a prerequisite for the *Lesser*, and not the other way around. One must be rightly motivated to perform truly righteous actions including just warfare, that is: 'Not all who do battle are true *mujāhids*.'[89] Conversely, one may be a good Muslim in times of peace; the duty to fight only comes about 'from time to time'.[90] Thereafter, ʿAbd al-Qādir contends that the *Greater Jihād* is a good in itself, leading directly to the perfection of the soul and God's favour. The *Lesser Jihād*, by contrast, is a means to an end. It is in this context that the sentence quoted in isolation by Berque arises:

> 'The intention of the Lawgiver [*al-shāriʿ*] was not for combat in itself, *for killing and destroying what God has made is not His Will*... The intention of the Lawgiver [in enjoining warfare] is rather to combat the evil of the unbelievers and to prevent them from doing harm to the Muslims.'[91]

ʿAbd al-Qādir is not asserting that warfare is against God's will, but rather that God's Will requires warfare not as an end in itself but rather in order to bring about other goods (combatting evil and protecting Muslims from harm). This is a perfectly mainstream view, not at all an abnegation or rejection of *jihād*. One must also recognise that this attitude – that one must only kill for a higher purpose and not for the sheer love of killing – is hardly remarkable in ʿAbd al-Qādir's day or any other, among either religious or secular wagers of war. Rather, it is the typical attitude of the conscientious soldier. To suggest otherwise does a deep injustice to all traditions of military ethics, and to the moral characters of many historical persons. This was surely not Berque's intention. Rather, an effort to demonstrate ʿAbd al-Qādir's *volte-face* after his defeat by France seems the motive factor. It is the Road to Damascus narrative which once again distorts our view.

Similarly, Weismann's study of ʿAbd al-Qādir presents him as advocating not just pacifism but total political quietism after his release from captivity in France: a shunning of the moralistic activism which so marked the first half of his life. If accepted at face value, this would constitute a stark dividing line between ʿAbd al-Qādir's Algerian and Damascene biographies. It would arguably even imply an antinomian abnegation of the Qur'ānic politico-religious imperative of *al-amr bil-maʿrūf wa al-nahī ʿan al-munkar*, 'command the good and forbid the wicked' – as it has significantly since been taken to do by Michael Cook in his magisterial

---

89 *Mawāqif* p. 145.
90 *Mawāqif*, p. 27.
91 *Mawāqif*, pp. 145–146, emphasis added.

study of this fundamental injunction.[92] It would certainly go a long way toward justifying the dichotomous narratives of ʿAbd al-Qādir's life, in characterising the Damascene Sufi as promulgating a teaching which rules out many of the actions taken in his Algerian political incarnation. But it must be remembered, this stance would also be incompatible with the most celebrated act of his Damascene decades: his armed defence of the innocent in the face of sectarian violence in the July of 1860, and with the justifications we have seen him give for it.

As in the example taken from Berque, above, this interpretation proceeds by selectively quoting from the *Kitāb al-Mawāqif.* The argument hinges on an interpretation of ʿAbd al-Qādir's gloss on the Prophetic saying that '[H]e among you who observes evil shall remove it by his hand; if this is beyond his power, [he shall remove it] by his tongue; if this is beyond his power, [he shall remove it] in his heart, and this is the minimum in faith.' [It should be noted that Étienne, more appropriately, quotes this same *ḥadīth* while describing ʿAbd al-Qādir's actions during the 1860 sectarian violence.][93] But Weismann reads ʿAbd al-Qādir's discussion of the well-known saying in a way that begs the question against his commitment to Qur'ānic injunctions:

> 'The removal by hand, ʿAbd al Qādir asserts, is incumbent upon the ruler and governors; by tongue, upon the *ʿulemā* who profess to be knowledgeable; and by heart by common believers who recognise the evil. The Sufis, however, do not belong to any of these three categories and, therefore, are not obliged to remove evil at all! ...This is clearly a call to completely shun politics...'[94]

The first, and quite conventional, part of this description is a close paraphrase of ʿAbd al-Qādir's own words (quoting the *ḥadīth*). From 'the Sufis' onward, however, it represents Weismann's own gloss on the text. Rather than discussing the freedom of Sufis from the obligation to combat evil (which is never explicitly stated by ʿAbd al-Qādir), the *Mawqif* is concerned with the impossibility of

92 E.g. Cook, 2002, p. 88: 'Did Sufis exploit the potential of their beliefs to place themselves above forbidding wrong? We do encounter occasional suggestions to this effect. ʿAbd al-Qādir al-Jazā'irī (d. 1883), who settled in Syria after leading the resistance to the French conquest of Algeria, argues that the mystic is not covered by the tripartite division of labour, and is thus not obligated by the duty.' Cook also notes, however [op.cit., p. 95] that 'no consolidated doctrine directed against [the obligation to order the good and forbid the wrong] ever emerges [among the Sufis] bar that of ʿAbd al-Ghanī, which achieved no wider success.' Sufis including the Kitāb al-Mawāqif's greatest influence, Ibn al-ʿArabī, took the view that the obligation to change evil in the world was not affected by one's spiritual acceptance of it as subject to God's will [op.cit. p. 466].

93 Étienne, 2003, p. 281

94 Weismann, 2001a, p. 191.

'change in the heart' for a particular kind of Sufi in a specific spiritual state and station. The Arabic text itself reads as follows:

> 'It is recounted in the *Ṣaḥīḥ* [of Bukhārī] that the Prophet (may God honour him and grant him peace) said:
>
> "He among ye who sees wickedness [*munkaran*] shall change it with his hand, and if he cannot then with his tongue, and if he cannot then in his heart[95] – and this is the least in faith."
>
> Know that change with the hand is for the Sultan and the rulers to do. The change with the tongue is for the religious scholars [*ʿulemā'*], who are knowledgeable and who expound knowledge among the general population. The change in the heart is for the common man who knows of wickedness, and consists in his hating in his heart [*yakrah*] that action or utterance which is wicked in the religion, resultant from his faith in what was brought by Muḥammad (may God honour him and grant him peace). As for him who is not one of these three groups, while being a witness to the True Agent [*wa hūwa shāhid lil-fāʿil al-ḥaqīqī*], he is not obliged to that. That is, the ruler's change by the hand and the scholar's by the tongue produce a benefit for the general population and for the one found doing wickedness, whereas the change in the heart brings no benefit [*lā fā'idah fīhi*] except for the common believer [himself] – in making his faith sound through believing in the forbidden-ness of the wicked such that he does not incline to it. Thus, the absence of change in the heart does not do away with any principle of the *Sharīʿah*, and does not make licit that which is forbidden.'[96]

ʿAbd al-Qādir attempts to prove why the 'least in faith' 'change in the heart' is impossible for a 'witness of the True Agent' – that is to say for the thoroughgoing fatalist (representing a specific stage in the Sufi itinerary of spiritual development) who sees God as the author of all events, the only true agent. He repeatedly makes the point that he is discussing the internal attitudes of a fatalist who happens to be neither a ruler nor a scholar; the text introduces the predicate 'witness to the True Agent' in a *ḥāl* clause, and does not explicitly argue that no rulers or scholars might also occupy such a state (though it might be difficult for some to imagine them doing so while remaining effective in their roles).[97]

---

95 *Bi-qalbihi* – this may be translated 'in the heart' or 'through the heart', and has been variously interpreted according to this ambiguity [e.g. Cook, 2002, pp. 35–38]. ʿAbd al-Qādir, however, clearly reads the *ḥadīth* as referring to change in the heart, and in the heart alone – which 'brings no benefit except for the believer himself'.

96 *Mawāqif*, p. 294.

97 It is worth remarking that even as early as al-Ghazalī [*Iḥyā*, Book 35], the view that *tawakkul* would result in total inaction, 'the body falling like a rag to the ground... what the ignorant believe' was already being repudiated. While the image of the passive fatalist, imobilised by Leibniz's *fatum mahumetanum*, does represent a persistent Orientalist stereotype of 'Eastern Religion' [see for instance King, 2008, *passim*], it is not a solely western preserve.

ʿAbd al-Qādir quotes Ibn al-ʿArabī to the effect of specifying that internal psycho-spiritual events rather than law and politics are in question:

> 'The Foremost Knower [*imām al-ʿārifīn*], Muḥyī al-Dīn [ibn al-ʿArabī] when speaking of the secret of number said: "When a person does battle with the inclinations of his [lower] self [*nafs*], the pair overcomes the singular (that is, the witnessing of Lord and servant overcomes that of the singular, that is of the Lord alone)."'[98]

ʿAbd al-Qādir is no more arguing that the Sufi should 'shun politics' and permit all wickedness than he (or Ibn al-ʿArabī) is arguing that the Sufi should shun the *jihād al-nafs* against their own base inclinations and permit all 'Satanic ideation' [*khawāṭīr shayṭāniyyah*]. Rather, both are analysing a conflict between distinct, and typically transient, spiritual states – the titular topic of the *Kitāb al-Mawāqif* itself. The denial of everything but God and its concommitant fatalism is not presented as exhaustive of Sufi Islam, still less as a political manifesto. It is worth remembering that

> 'God, [Muḥyī al-Dīn Ibn al-ʿArabī] declares, after all, has imposed on us the duty of taking action against wrongs (*izālat al-munkar*) *even if our spiritual perception tells us that the offence is predestined* [by God].'[99]

Furthermore, ʿAbd al-Qādir's text must be read in its context. This is not only true in the sense that it was composed by a self-described 'man of action',[100] famous in both Algeria and Damascus for his actively 'forbidding evil' by both argument and by force, even while presenting himself as a Sufi. Nor should it even be read only in the context of the numerous references to political acts, including Shariah observance and the obligation to *jihād*, in the *Kitāb al-Mawāqif*. Rather, this *mawqif* must be seen as part of ʿAbd al-Qādir's complex and multifaceted account of Sufism itself: the book, like most Sufi practice and certainly like the complex hierarchies and typologies in Ibn al-ʿArabī's writings, is concerned with different 'stopping places' [*mawāqif*] on the path, and not only with the path's ultimate goal. When in this chapter of the *Kitāb al-Mawāqif* ʿAbd al-Qādir writes 'Some of the Knowers have said: whosoever looks upon the disobedient through the gaze of the *sharīʿah* condemns them, and whososever looks upon them with the eye of the *ḥaqīqah* forgives them'[101] before listing Qur'ānic

98 *Ibid.*
99 Quoted in Cook, 2002, p. 466, emphasis added.
100 Outrey to the Ministry of Foreign Affairs, Damas/Consulat/13, 17-04-1861.
101 *Mawāqif*, p. 294.

passages which deny man's agency in lieu of God's,[102] one must recall the other *mawāqif* quoted here. Our survey of the *Kitāb al-Mawāqif*, above, has repeatedly shown ʿAbd al-Qādir to use these twinned categories and the same Qur'ānic verses as part of a single whole, in which each element demands the other and, he insists time and again, cannot function properly alone. We have seen that ʿAbd al-Qādir argues at length that to have only 'the eye of the *ḥaqīqah*' would be half-blind,[103] and to read only those verses of the Qur'ān which denigrate man's agency and responsibility would be impious.[104] He does not refer to the Sufis (in general or as an ideal) as the subject of this *mawqif*, but rather discusses one aspect of one step on the Sufi path – a step he clearly argues elsewhere is insufficient on its own.

Weismann's presentation of this *Mawqif* as evidence for ʿAbd al-Qādir's change of heart after his imprisonment in France, therefore, both confuses a psychological discussion for a political one and mistakes a Sufi account of one mental state for a general account of Sufism. Once more, it may be the narrative pressure of the 'Road to Damascus' which has brought about this confusion, since Weismann's analysis is otherwise precise, accurate, and wary of this very error. It recognises elsewhere that such a deterministic or fatalistic spiritual station [*tawakkul*] as is the subject of the *mawqif* in question above does not exhaust ʿAbd al-Qādir's Sufism, and hence cannot be used to infer his political attitudes. He eloquently describes him as seeing the ideal Sufi as uniting the pure *mutasabbib* [believer in free will]

> 'whose view is limited to the causes and blinded to God, and the pure *mutawakkil* [fatalist] whose view is diverted from the causes and immersed in the vision of God. Between them stands the perfect believer, the outward *mutasabbib* and the inward *mutawakkil*, "whose hand is in the cause while his heart is joined to the creator".'[105]

This equivocal attitude to agency and causation is repeatedly stated by ʿAbd al-Qādir and constantly reflected in his ontology – as we have seen throughout this

102 *Mawāqif*, p. 294–5. In this passage, ʿAbd al-Qādir quotes Qur'ān 37:96 ['But Allah has created you and your handiwork!'], 2: 264 ['They will be able to do nothing with aught they have earned'], 8:17 ['It was not ye who slew them; it was Allah'], 72:30 ['But ye will not, except as Allah wills'], 7:54 ['Is it not His to create and to govern?'], and 4:78 ['Say: all things are from Allah'].
103 *Mawāqif*, p. 815.
104 *Mawāqif*, pp. 147–148; see the passages quoted at the close of the previous section of this chapter, where he quotes many of the same verses as in this *mawqif* as examples of one half of the Qur'ānic whole.
105 Weismann, 2001a, pp. 188–189.

chapter. Yet when interpretation concerns ʿAbd al-Qādir's supposed shunning of politics, this connection has apparently not been drawn. As a consequence, ʿAbd al-Qādir appears to make a dramatic shift toward a privatised understanding of religion and a retirement from public life. Again, it would appear that the narrative pressure to differentiate between the two putative halves of ʿAbd al-Qādir's life (pre- and post-'conversion', soldier and saint, proscriptive and permissive) has undermined an otherwise scrupulous and sensitive reading of his teachings. Maintaining the 'Road to Damascus' narrative, that is, requires us to elide or remove aspects of his life and thought which run counter to it. But we can, once again, be still more specific about the processes which led generations of scholars to perpetuate it.

Both Berque and Weismann, like almost all who have written on the religious aspects of ʿAbd al-Qādir's Damascene period, base their appreciation on the pioneering translations made by scholar, convert, and devotee of Ibn al-ʿArabī, Michel Chodkiewicz. [106] While this translation has been of inestimable help in spreading interest and awareness of ʿAbd al-Qādir's teachings in the west, it is – like any translation or any interpretation – part of a hermeneutic process rather than a final re-statement. It will be contended here that its representation of ʿAbd al-Qādir's views exaggerates certain aspects while understating others, producing a systematically distorted impression which inclines the reader to endorse rather than question the 'Road to Damascus' narratives surrounding ʿAbd al-Qādir. Specifically, Chodkiewicz's presentation of ʿAbd al-Qādir unnecessarily facilitates the view that he advocated a pantheistic monism which undercut his commitment to the Qur'ānic revelation in favour of a post-modern religious pluralism. In so doing, it lays the theological foundations for a strong case in favour of ʿAbd al-Qādir's conversion to a new perspective at dramatic variance with his words and actions as Algerian *amīr al-mu'minīn*.

5.3 ʿAbd al-Qādir's Conversion to Pluralism: Investigating the Evidence

Here we shall focus on a key chapter of the *Mawāqif*, and Michel Chodkiewicz's translation will be compared to the Arabic text of the same edition from which he worked;[107] a line-by-line textual analysis of the entire book is very far beyond the

---

106 Explicitly credited, for example, in Berque, 1978, pp. 506, 520 [while Michel Chodkiewicz was preparing his manuscript for publication]; Weismann, 2001, p. XI; Étienne, 1994, p. 428.
107 Specified by Chodkiewicz 1995, p. 23.

scope of this study. Claims at some kind of interpretive infallibility are similarly beyond its ambition; what concerns us here is precisely the unavoidable limitation of the hermeneutic process, where the interpretation reflects the interpreter. The key chapter has been selected both because of its particular significance to the secondary literature on ʿAbd al-Qādir, and because of the broad gamut of translating artefacts it contains. So significant has it been that Bruno Étienne, in his most influential work on ʿAbd al-Qādir, uses its text as a mystical dialogue between himself and the spirit of ʿAbd al-Qādir he claims appeared to him in Damascus so as to preach religious pluralism and 'the non-existence of error'.[108] Other authors have also identified Chodkiewicz's translation of this *Mawqif* as the clearest evidence for ʿAbd al-Qādir's endorsement of the radically pluralist assertion that 'all ideas are true.'[109]

In terms of clearly identifiable and contestable artefacts introduced through translation, we find in this single text instances of the addition of terms, the deletion of terms, and the substitution of terms. In each case the change has the effect of effacing the mainstream and conventional Islamocentric moralising of the original work in favour of a pan-religious monism. In this, they are consonant with Chodkiewicz's framing attribution to ʿAbd al-Qādir of the maxim that there is 'no state in which saintliness cannot find a place', [110] understood as indicating that 'all ideas are true,'[111] in apparent conflict with the Algerian ʿAbd al-Qādir's evident dedication to the Qur'ān and Shariah as God's own criterion (*furqān*) dividing good from ill in thought and deed. Michel Chodkiewicz's presentation of passages from the *Mawāqif* has been described by his colleague and collaborator on the monumental *Fūtūḥāt Makkiyyah*, James Morris, as highlighting the universal and transcendental aspect of ʿAbd al-Qādir's teaching.[112]

In other words, each instance of problematic translation has the effect of distancing the Damascene ʿAbd al-Qādir further and further from the Algerian ʿAbd al-Qādir who ruled with sword and Qur'ān in hand. That is an impression further encouraged by Chodkiewicz's dismissal of ʿAbd al-Qādir's earlier writings as 'lacking originality...[and] written for a particular situation',[113] with the implication that this in itself renders them second-rate or suspect. Still more so his in-

---

108 Étienne, 2003, pp. 312, 315 – 6.

109 E.g. Kebache in Geoffroy et al., 2010, p. 102.

110 Chodkiewicz, 1995, p.1.

111 This phrase is also frequently used by Michel Chodkiewicz's co-translator of Ibn al-ʿArabī's *Futūḥāt Makkiyyah* [Chodkiewicz, Chittick, and Moris, 2002], William Chittick [e.g. Chittick, 1994, pp. 139, 140, 145, 165].

112 Morris, 1987, pp. 117 – 118.

113 Chodkiewicz, 1995, p. 187.

sistence on the later ʿAbd al-Qādir's 'transcending'[114] his earlier role as a soldier and leader, apparently forced on him in spite of himself.

The text in question is the 254th *Mawqif*, concerned with interpreting the Qur'ānic verse '"*Thy Lord hath decreed that ye worship none but Him.*"[115] As in the case of his exegeses seen in the first half of this chapter, ʿAbd al-Qādir uses the Qur'ānic text to unify apparently mutually exclusive positions without compromising their respective claims. The case will be made here, however, that Michel Chodkiewicz's translation systematically favours one set of claims over the other, and in so doing encourages the narrative of a 'converted ʿAbd al-Qādir'.

In terms of the addition of words in the translated text, we find the dramatic statement that

> 'Those who are destined for perdition are such, therefore, *solely* by reason of their disobedience to the commands and prohibitions which have been brought by the Messengers of Allah, since *no one* is an infidel in every respect.'[116]

The Arabic text from which he translated, however, itself reads quite differently:

> 'Whosoever goes to his ruin [in this life and the next; *halaka*][117] does so as a result of his defiance of such commands and prohibitions as God has sent through His prophets, for he has utterly disbelieved in God [*liannahu kafara billah min kulli wajh*].'[118]

This dramatic alteration of the text is, unlike the others which will be described below, pointed out by its translator himself in an endnote. That endnote reads simply, and in its entirety: 'The negation required by the meaning is omitted in the Arabic text.'[119] The Arabic text itself does contain numerous errors, particularly with regard to typography and punctuation, as Chodkiewicz rightly points out.[120] In this particular instance, though he does not present the Arabic text itself, it seems a simple negation which he is suggesting is absent, presumably an additional '*lam*' or '*mā*' [*not*] before the verb '*kafara*' [*he disbelieved*]. This is plausible – and this first change is certainly the most defensible of those Chodkiewicz brings to the text. It must be pointed out, however, that the translated text also

---

114 Chodkiewicz, 1995, p.5.
115 Qur'ān 17:23.
116 Chodkiewicz, 1995, p. 126.
117 The term used for 'go to one's ruin' here, *halaka/hulk*, is also often read to have connotations of damnation in the hereafter.
118 *Mawāqif*, p. 767.
119 Chodkiewicz, 1995, p. 217, emphasis added.
120 Chodkiewicz, 1995., p. 23.

adds the word 'solely' into the preceding clause, setting the stage for the putatively absent negation and greatly increasing its comprehensibility. This word (or phrase), too, is absent from the Arabic text.

On the basis of the impression of ʿAbd al-Qādir's approach to Qur'ānic exegesis outlined in his own words in the present chapter, a sentence which appears to relate to the public, juridical, orthodox aspect of ʿAbd al-Qādir's thought has been altered in Michel Chodkiewicz's translation so as to reflect the private, spiritual, metaphysical dimension of his thought. *Ḥaqīqah*, in ʿAbd al-Qādir's terms as we have come to recognise them in this chapter, appears to cross the impassable isthmus (*barzakh*) and transgress upon the *Sharīʿah*. This will be the common factor in all three instances of problematic translation addressed here, and is the likely origin of the view in the secondary literature following Chodkiewicz that ʿAbd al-Qādir 'tipped toward the inclusive immanent interpretation of Ibn al-ʿArabī's teaching at the expense of the exclusive transcendental one'.[121] Yet this is an alleged 'tipping' which we have already seen ʿAbd al-Qadir rule out as by definition impossible.

In terms of the deletion of terms from the Arabic text, we find a similar phenomenon, this time without any hint from the translator that it has taken place. Chodkiewicz's translation contains the following striking exposition of an egalitarian, pluralist, and radically subjectivist faith, which does not differentiate between one belief(-system) and another, but relativises them all:

> '*He is that*... Every representation which is made of Him is really Him, and His presence in this representation does not cease if the one who represents Him in this way later represented Him otherwise. He will be *equally present* in this new representation. *He is* limited *for* someone who believes and represents Him as limited, absolute *for* someone who believes Him Absolute. *He is* substance or accident, transcendent or immanent, *He is* pure concept; or He resides in the heavens, or on the earth, and so on, *in conformity* with each of the innumerable beliefs and doctrines.'[122]

This apparently sweeping relativist gesture is, however, more nuanced in the Arabic text – due primarily to the inclusion of a word whose equivocating significance we have seen ʿAbd al-Qādir expound at length during his exegesis of the verse 'There is nothing like me/my likeness', above. The term in question is the word 'like' (*ka*), and the Arabic text is more literally translated as follows:

> 'He is, as we are told by the *Ṣaḥīḥ*, "in the reckoning of every thinker, and on the tongue of every speaker." Contemplation and speech are His creation, and so His Imagining is in the

---

121 Weismann, 2001a, pp. 191–2.

122 Chodkiewicz, 1995, pp. 126–7. Emphasis added.

> imagining[123] of every one who imagines anything, and is the very Being of such imagining. This Being does not cease with the cessation of one conceiver's conception and its transformation into another, but rather it persists in the new conception. Thus when one considers and imagines Him to be limited, He is *like* that [*fa-hūwa ka-dhālik*]. Or imagined as unlimited, He is *like* that [*fa ka-dhālik*]. Or as essence, He is *like* that. Or as accident, He is *like* that. Or as incomparable, He is *like* that. Or as comparable, He is *like* that. Or as [pure] meaning, He is *like* that. Or imagined in the heavens or on the earth, He is *like* that. Or otherwise, of which conceptions and utterances one might scarcely encompass [*aw ghayr dhālik, mimmā lā yukād yunḥaṣir min al-ʿitiqādāt wa al-maqālāt*]'[124]

The omitted word, which brings about a significant shift in the meaning of the text from unambiguous endorsement to a more nuanced and tentative position, occurs in a set phrase which is repeated eight times in succession. Michel Chodkiewicz identified this as the chapter's *Leitmotif*, choosing the phrase 'He is that' as the title of his translation. [125] As in the case of the 'missing negation' above, Chodkiewicz also inserts additional words and phrases into his translation to support his editorial decision: 'he is that *for* someone who... he is *equally* present... [He is] in *conformity* with each...' Each of these (italicised) additions, not reflected in the Arabic text, specify the essential subjectivity of divinity while denying objective differences.

Read as including the term 'like', and the ontological equivocation at the heart of ʿAbd al-Qādir's teaching (and to which we have already seen him explicitly relate it), this does not seem to imply that all ideas are equally valid. Nor is this conclusion encouraged by paying attention to the lexical character of the pairs of terms set out – all of which refer to debates within mainstream Islamic thought, and not to more *outré* theological differences (like theism vs. atheism, or monotheism vs. polytheism, for instance). Rather, ʿAbd al-Qādir seems to suggest that all ideas are equally *real*, through their dependency upon The Real, upon God. It is God's claim upon ideas, rather than the reverse, which is in that respect in question. Moreover, they all contain elements of both truth and untruth, in relation to their respective conformity or otherwise to the accessible but inexhaustible epistemological criterion (the Qur'ān) at the heart of ʿAbd al-Qādir's apophatic critique of interpretive exclusivism.

All true worship, wherever it takes place, is by definition worship of God, ʿAbd al-Qādir asserts. This effectively tautological insight is that expressed by Wilfred Cantwell Smith when he writes that 'no one in the whole history of

---

123 *Taṣawwur* – this may also be rendered 'conception'.

124 Mawāqif, p. 767.

125 Chodkiewicz, 1995, p. 125; '*Il est cela...*' – Chodkiewicz, 1983, p. 127.

man has ever worshipped an idol. Men have worshipped God – or something – in the form of idols. That is what idols are for.'[126] But this does not entail that all who try or claim to worship are equally and absolutely worshipful. ʿAbd al-Qādir is not conflating the devout prayers of Muḥammad with those of hypocrites, or the Meccan polytheists against whom he fought. The abandoning of hypocrisy (*nifāq*) and doubt (*shakk*) for truthfulness (*ṣidq*) and certainty (*yaqīn*) are exalted goals of a lifetime's demanding Sufi practice, not the instantaneous result of embracing relativism as an intellectual position. The struggle to become more truly devoted to God in spite of one's moral, intellectual, and spiritual frailties – the *Greater Jihād*[127] – is as alive in the *Mawāqif* as it was in ʿAbd al-Qādir's Algerian *Risālah on Hijrah*. This tension between perfection and imperfection is evident even in this *mawqif*; its list of conceptions of God both are and are not God; He is with them, but they are not with Him, to paraphrase ʿAbd al-Qādir's related discussion which opens this chapter.[128]

While Michel Chodkiewicz's translation retains the former (ontologically unifying) aspect, it unnecessarily excludes the second (ethically and epistemologically differentiating) dimension. Once more, the inward and unifying *ḥaqīqah* washes over the impassable isthmus, to efface the outward and differentiating *sharīʿah* in defiance of the Arabic text as it stands.

Finally, in terms of the substitution of one term for another, we find an elaboration of the last discussion. So, Michel Chodkiewicz's seminal translation of ʿAbd al-Qādir's teaching reads:

> 'For the author of this saying, Allah is other than that which comes to your mind [not for you, but] for him who professes a belief different from yours: both are in fact *equally* valid. "Difference" here is understood to mean everything which is mutually incompatible, whether it is the incompatibility of contraries, of opposites, of divergent terms or of things that are alike – for, *according to the logicians*, things that are alike are also mutually incompatible.'[129]

Once more, we find in action the same subjective-relativist interpretation of ʿAbd al-Qādir's approach. The passage in question is more literally translated as follows:

> '"Truly He is *like* that which occurs to you, but also on the contrary *unlike* that which occurs to you by virtue of His being *like* the understanding of another whose opinion differs from

126 Smith, 1991, p. 141.
127 *Mawāqif*, p. 144.
128 *Mawāqif*, p. 764.
129 Chodkiewicz, 1995, p. 127. Emphasis added.

> your own." This is to say that He is unfettered by that which occurs to you, which is to say your beliefs, about Him. Nor is He circumscribed by your utterances. What the speaker of this utterance intended was that God is different from that which occurs to one about Him, [for instance] in those whose expressions and convictions differ from one's own, yet all similarly turn out to be true.[130] What is intended here by the word "difference" [*ikhtilāf*] is meant all which is mutually incompatible, from opposites to antitheses to divergences to even similar [positions], as these are recognised as incompatible with one another *by traditionally authoritative scholars of Qur'ān and Sunnah* [*al-uṣūliyyīn*]. The result of all of this is: He is as He occurs in your thoughts and beliefs, and He is otherwise.'

Here we again encounter the distinction between Michel Chodkiewicz's presentation of a teaching which embraces all ideas on an equal basis and the more discerning attitude we have attributed to ʿAbd al-Qādir. Again, this occurs through a hardening of tentative Arabic into emphatic French (and subsequently English). Many of the same observations made directly above are again apposite. What is new, moreover, is the peculiar replacement of the word '*uṣūliyyīn*' (literally 'fundamentalists',[131] in the sense of people concerned with the fundamental bases of the religion and language)[132] with the term 'logicians' (*manāṭiqah*).

To most Sunni Muslims such as ʿAbd al-Qādir, *uṣūl* – and hence *uṣūlī* – will tend to be most associated with the common phrases *uṣūl al-dīn*[133] (credal principles of the Islamic faith) and *uṣūl al-fiqh*[134] (principles of Islamic legal reasoning; literally 'fundamentals of understanding', something between legal theory and moral philosophy).[135] Many of the overt influences on ʿAbd al-Qādir, including al-Ghazālī, use *uṣūlī* in just such a way, signifying the qualified specialist in *uṣūl al-fiqh*.[136] That is, to refer to one accomplished in '"the science of *kalām*... [and] the science of *ḥadīth*... [who] expounds the way in which the Prophet's words indicate juristic norms, whether by explicit or implied meaning of through intellectual analysis and deduction" such as syllogistic analogy'[137] (*qiyās*; the

---

130 *Ka-mā ṣaḥḥa hādha ṣaḥḥa hādha* – the verb in question is often understood to mean 'authenticate', and the clause may be read 'as each is authenticated [by the scriptural sources]'.

131 While this term has now come to be used in the same broad way as the English word 'Fundamentalist' (with its origins in American Protestantism) [Ayubi, 2007, p. 256], such a usage would be anachronistic in ʿAbd al-Qādir's time, and is clearly not what he means.

132 *Encyclopaedia of Islam*, pp. 928–930; the term is used in this sense, and of ʿAbd al-Qādir, by Bū ʿAzīz [1964, p. 132], for example.

133 *Encyclopaedia of Islam*, pp. 930–931

134 *Encyclopaedia of Islam*, pp. 931–934

135 The former gloss is more conventional, while the latter has recently been argued to be more appropriate [e.g. Reinhart, 1995].

136 *Encyclopaedia of Islam*, pp. 931–932.

137 *Ibid.* quoting al-Ghazālī, *Mustaṣfā*, I, pp. 5–6.

dominant mode of inference drawn on by ʿAbd al-Qādir's *Risālah on Hijrah* as shown in Chapter Two of this book). This usage of *uṣūlī* is still found after the time of ʿAbd al-Qādir, for instance in the writing of Rashīd Riḍā.[138] That usage of *uṣūlī* that most Sunni Muslims would recognise is also found in many contemporary western academic treatments of Islamic law[139] and North African Sufism.[140] Vincent Cornell's study of North African Sufism consistently employs the term to mean adherence to *uṣūl al-fiqh* methodology and 'reforming Islamic law by making the regional corpus of juridical precedent conform to the tenets of *uṣūl al-fiqh*'.[141] The *uṣūlī* approach is presented as having 'forever transformed'[142] North African Malikism. He also notes the debt owed to Abū Ḥāmid Al-Ghazālī by the resultant tradition of 'juridical Sufism',[143] and the role of the *uṣūlī* approach in 'draw[ing] mysticism into the fold of normative Islam.'[144] Since he was a North African Sufi of Mālikī persuasion familiar with al-Ghazālī and evidently supportive of 'juridical Sufism', this reading seems entirely appropriate to ʿAbd al-Qādir.

This close-knit family of readings' similarity to one another and distinctness from the term 'logicians' found in Michel Chodkiewicz's translation is quite apparent. The interpretation favoured here, by contrast, has a specifically Islamic and normative, rather than secular and descriptive, sense. This interpretation, it must be stressed, is motivated not by the present author's religious conviction, but on a scrupulous reading of the Arabic text as it stands – both lexically (as shown above) and contextually. Where the reading of *ūṣūlī* suggested here naturally applies to all of the theological differences of opinion ʿAbd al-Qādir lists (and after all, *ikhtilāf* is the conventional Arabic term for a debate among religious scholars), the term 'logicians' must confine itself to the final diad alone. On this book's translation, ʿAbd al-Qādir is recognising the epistemological pre-eminence of trained scholars of the Islamic revelation, even if – as repeated-

138 Riḍā gives: 'A specialist in the science of the *uṣūl al-dīn* or, more predominantly, the science of the *uṣūl al-fiqh.*' *Encyclopaedia of Islam 2*, 2000, vol. X, p. 937.

139 Umar F. Abd-Allah [Winter (ed.), 2008, p. 254], for instance, gives for '*uṣūlī*' 'jurisprudent… a scholar of Islamic legal theory,' while Johansen [1995, p. 135] uses the term to designate a practitioner of Islamic jurispurdential casuistry.

140 Cornell [1998, p. 360], defines *uṣūl* as the tradition of theological legal reasoning [*fiqh*] developed by al-Shāfiʿī, hence *ūṣūlī* as 'a person, doctrine or approach that made use of the methodology of *uṣūl*,' where '[t]he *uṣūlī* approach to Sufism helped to draw mysticism into the fold of *normative Islam.*' [emphasis added].

141 Cornell, 1998, p.16

142 Cornell, 1998, p. 124

143 Cornell, 1998, pp. 17, 62

144 Cornell, 1998, pp. 130, 360.

ly elsewhere in the *Mawāqif*[145] – he questions the claims of interpretive supremacy made by individual schools or scholars. Reading the text as 'the logicians', however, tells us only that 'similar things' are 'incompatible with one another'. This un-edifying assertion, with little connecton to the passage in which it occurs, may be stated as: 'logic dictates that similar objects are non-identical.' Such an observation would be striking both in its banality and in its incompatibility with Chodkiewicz's own editorial decision throughout the chapter to conflate similarity and identity (substituting *He is that* for *He is like that*).

As in each of the cases of problematic translation described here, the (surely unintended) effect of Michel Chodkiewicz's translation is to remove its subject from a traditional Islamic context. ʿAbd al-Qādir's teaching is repositioned through a sidelining of the *Sharīʿah*'s normative specicifities in lieu of the cosmic generality of ontological *Ḥaqīqah*. While Chodkiewicz's translation does not present ʿAbd al-Qādir as an antinomian pantheist or an advocate of relativism, it does move him significantly closer to such positions than the text justifies. Michel Chodkiewicz's exposition of the 'theme of what we might call Akbarian[146] "universality"'[147] in ʿAbd al-Qādir, which is 'unacceptable to Islamic exotericism',[148] has certainly encouraged others to perceive him in such terms, as we have already seen. Where his collaborator on translations from Ibn al-ʿArabī's *Fūtūḥāt Makkiyyah*, James Morris, has praised Chodkiewicz's highlighting the universal and transcendental aspect of ʿAbd al-Qādir's teaching,[149] we should point out that this focus conflicts with the goal of gaining a holistic and lifelike impression of ʿAbd al-Qādir as a historical figure.

Like the earlier, political, accounts of ʿAbd al-Qādir's supposed conversion from parochialism to cosmopolitanism, Chodkiewicz's account presents the ʿAbd al-Qādir who emerged from his war with (and captivity in) France replacing the specific with the general, the local with the global, and the differentiating with the unifying. But whereas this book has maintained that ʿAbd al-Qādir retained a consistently communitarian and Islamocentric attitude as against 'Road to Damascus' narratives, the objection to his putative religious pluralism does

---

145 E.g. Mawāqif, pp. 50, 383.

146 The term 'Akbarian' refers to the thought and following of Muḥyī al-Dīn ibn al-ʿArabī, and is derived from one of his most common sobriquets 'Al-Shaykh al-Akbar'. It follows the pattern of naming a school after its founder (e.g. Qādiriyyah after ʿAbd al-Qādir al-Jīlānī, Tijāniyyah after Aḥmad al-Tījānī etc.), though in ibn al-ʿArabī's case this is understood to be informal, lacking the institutional dimension the term 'Akbariyyah' might imply.

147 Chodkiewicz, 1995, pp. 17–18.

148 Chodkiewicz, 1995, p. 19.

149 Morris, 1987, pp. 117–118.

not rest on the claim that he was religiously parochial. This chapter's opening discussion of the *Kitāb al-Mawāqif* demonstrates the absolutely universal – indeed cosmic – role of in the Qur'ānic revelation to Muḥammad in his view of the world. Rather, ʿAbd al-Qādir adhered to a fundamentally different sort of universalism than that which so many of his sympathetic 20th-century biographers have wished him to espouse. The presumption that normative Islam is necessarily parochial is as natural to the secular observer as the converse is hard to grasp, and its influence on interpretations of ʿAbd al-Qādir is profound. As such, it will be argued that the literature on ʿAbd al-Qādir's Sufi teachings has become the locus for a conspicuously modern clash of universalisms – a clash occasioned largely by the persistence of the idea that ʿAbd al-Qādir underwent a tectonic shift or conversion mid-way through his life. A shift occasioned by, and typically occuring in, France.

5.4 The Western Roots of ʿAbd al-Qādir's Spiritual 'Conversion'

If ʿAbd al-Qādir's biographers, at the very least since Michel Chodkiewicz contributed his translations of several chapters from the *Kitāb al-Mawāqif*, have tended to present him as relativising the Qur'ānic revelation in general and its ethico-legal content in particular, one must ask: why? While the apparent plausibility of the narrative of conversion seems to have played a significant role, it is possible to say more. Apart from the fact that it presented a radically different impression from earlier images of ʿAbd al-Qādir as fanatical Algerian war-leader, why would this new depiction coalesce quite as it has done? Certainly, the motives of 19th-century writers who sought to justify French colonialism through its cultural victory over ʿAbd al-Qādir are not at work here; there is no hint of apology for colonialism in any of the writing of those who have studied the *Mawāqif* in the 20th century. Rather, a different and much more benign form of Eurocentrism is active in distorting our impression of ʿAbd al-Qādir. It is not France which is being made to politically conquer ʿAbd al-Qādir, but ʿAbd al-Qādir who is being repurposed so as to spiritually enrich France.

It is almost a truism that secular Europeans tend to prefer privatised forms of religiosity to the moralising, restrictive, legally and socially demanding forms of religion more commonly found in the rest of the world and in earlier European history.[150] We have repeatedly explored the reformulation of ʿAbd al-Qādir's ideas to

150 This fact has generated a range of 'secularisation theories' within the European social sci-

fit such a context, with the concomitant downplaying of elements which conflict most obviously with it. This is most striking in relation to the austere and exacting Shariah strictures which he imposed in Algeria and which modern westerners most often associate with illiberal theocratic regimes. It is certainly true that 20th-century depictions of the aged ʿAbd al-Qādir seeing God as 'compatible with all beliefs', preaching that 'all ideas are true'[151] and 'abstain[ing] from nothing since he sees God in everything'[152] are appealing in a secular age. The west blooms with New Religious Movements which combine theological pantheism with political and/or moral liberalism, which make few explicit demands but to love and do no harm; such convivially *laissez-faire* ideas are popular commodities in the marketplace of ideas. In a world where religion more often seems to the secular observer as a cause of conflict than reconciliation, and in which governments scrupulously avoid religious interventions out of an understandable horror of repeating past religious oppressions, religion can to many seem best when it is an entirely personal matter. The effort to make ʿAbd al-Qādir sympathetic to a western audience living in more or less secular environments might therefore naturally incline commentators to develop his thought in such directions, however bizarre he himself might have found such a project.[153]

The pre-eminent western writers on ʿAbd al-Qādir's Damascene religious teachings have gone even further than this. ʿAbd al-Qādir is now presented as consciously and deliberately relativising and privatising his conception of religion, and even doing so expressly as to make it more in tune with European tastes. He sought to 'revitalise [Ibn al-ʿArabī's legacy's] immanent bent to facilitate openness toward the west...[154] [T]hese deviations were designed to serve as a means for the integration of Islam within the modern world.'[155] In the same vein, Bruno Étienne insists

---

ences. Prominent examples would include the earlier work of Karel Dobbelaere and David Martin, which were concerned with general declines in (European) religiosity. Following criticisms of such ideas from writers such as Jose Casanova (who points both to New Religious Movements and to the persistence of religiosity in industrialised states outside of Northern Europe), reformulated neo-secularisation theories have been developed by scholars such as David Yamane and Mark Chavez. These lattermost focus more on declines in religious authority structures than upon religiosity *per se*.

151 Geoffroy et al., 2010, p. 102.

152 Weismann, 2001a, pp. 179, 189.

153 ʿAbd al-Qādir, for whom *irreligion* (from that of the Ottomans in Algeria, to the invading French armies, to the lawless rioters of Damascus), not religious extremism, seemed the greatest source of conflict, would not have seen things this way – though we have also seen him criticise the arrogance of some exclusivist theologians.

154 Weismann, 2001a, p. 165.

155 Weismann, 2001a, pp. 191–2.

time and again that ʿAbd al-Qādir's heralding of 'that religious form... beyond the particular form of Islam and superior to it'[156] represents 'an opportunity for Islam and for France',[157] amenable to his own view that 'the waters of Lourdes have the same validity as the ZamZam spring or the waters of Benares... In other words, I fell very early on into the crime of cultural relativism, and did so in utter serenity.'[158] The fact that ʿAbd al-Qādir taught the lessons of the *Mawāqif* in Arabic to his closest students, but did not publish them during his lifetime – still less have them translated into European languages – does not impede this interpretive trend. His message is universal, his biographers consider, and the west remains for many the natural home of universalism.

The interpretive tendency to portray the Damascene ʿAbd al-Qādir as so different from his Algerian incarnation as to demand some dramatic conversion in between can also be related to a more specific cultural movement than that of European secularism, however – to one of its reactions, in fact. One intellectual and spiritual tradition above all others has illuminated ʿAbd al-Qādir's teachings for a western (and, increasingly, Muslim) audience, and in doing so reshaped them in its own image. This school is the so-called 'Traditionalist' movement inaugurated by the French perennialist metaphysician René Guénon, who preached the universality of the mystical experience in all sufficiently ancient religions through their respective initiatic traditions. ʿAbd al-Qādir and René Guénon have increasingly come to 'represent two historical destinies within the very same spiritual itinerary. That spirituality presents itself as a mechanism defending "Tradition" in the face of an alienating and subversive western modernity'.[159] It has come for many followers of Guénon to constitute a 'global strategy for the spiritual renovation of humanity in general and of the west in particular...[which is] contaminated by the process of secularisation.'[160]

Before engaging in greater detail with this school of thought, it must be mentioned that Guénon's ideas draw heavily on the broader post-Renaissance European ideas of *(philo)sophia perennis* (as analysed by Antoine Faivre, among others). To further illustrate the indebtedness of western scholarship on ʿAbd al-Qādir's to 20th-century perennialism, meanwhile, it may be mentioned that several of the articles quoted here are published in the journal (*The Journal of the Muhyiddin Ibn ʿArabī Society*) of a syncretistic European New Religious Move-

156 Étienne, 2008, p. 69.
157 Étienne, 2003, p. 432.
158 Étienne, 1999, p. 32.
159 Djeradi, in Geoffroy et al., 2010, p. 215
160 Djeradi, in Geoffroy et al., 2010, p. 217.

ment, Beshara ['Good News'], whose membership broadly[161] shares such views.[162]

René Guénon, who wrote primarily about (certain forms of Vedantic-) Hinduism, ultimately converted to Islam on the grounds that it was a better fit to his own cultural background in France. 'There is nothing that implies the superiority of one traditional form [of religion] – in itself – over another, but merely what one would call reasons of spiritual convenience,'[163] the subjective attractiveness of a given faith to a given individual, he maintained. While Guénonian interpretations of religion often (but not invariably) encourage the believer to observe the laws and mores of his or her chosen faith,[164] they do not do so because of the objective superiority of one revelation over another. In this, and in spite of the movement's critique of modernity, Guénon's perennialism marks a conspicuously (post-)modern departure from earlier faiths, which typically saw events such as the Sending Down [*tanzīl*] of the Qur'ān or the Incarnation of Christ not as interchangeably inspiring metaphors but as real and axial cosmic events in their own rights. This gap is difficult to bridge. Whereas the 20th-century perennialist interpretation of Ibn al-ʿArabī and ʿAbd al-Qādir's Sufisms presents them as evincing a 'deep resonance with... postmodernism',[165] their fundamental commitment to cosmic tales of creation, meaning, and revelation do not sit easily with a Lyotardian 'rejection of metanarratives'.[166]

Guénon's interest in Sufism focused on Ibn al-ʿArabī rather than ʿAbd al-Qādir. Yet the latter played a significant role in his initiatic chain or *silsilah* –

---

161 In spite of their considerable similarities, and somewhat overlapping associations, acrimonious differences have arisen between proponents of Guénonian ideas who insist on observant adherence to the 'exoteric' rules of whichever 'initiatic Tradition' one adopts and the more permissive and syncretic Beshara movement [e.g Taji-Farouki, 2007, pp. 181, 211–2, 365].

162 This movement encourages a non-denomination and non-sectarian 'spiritual' approach to Sufi texts alongside a broad range of non-Islamic writings, such as those of the Maharishi, Lao Tzu, Meister Eckhart, and Shunryu Suzuki, as well as the Bhagavad Gita, the Nag Hammadi manuscripts, and some Navajo poetry ['Essential Reading' (http://www.beshara.org/essentials/readings.html – accessed 01/04/2009)]. Taji-Farouki describes the Muhyiddin Ibn 'Arabi Society as 'a forum for reinforcing the personal convictions' of Beshara members [Taji-Farouki, 2007, p. 178], 'which endeavours to represent a man whose work is so universal that all sects and creeds can find their truth in it' [Taji-Farouki, 2007, p. 179], and which 'joins its voice with those of certain sufi academics in a projection of the 'influence' of ('role') of Ibn ʿArabī in the contemporary world which is at least in part conviction-driven' [Taji-Farouki, 2007, p. 183].

163 Guénon to Colard, 1938 [Attias *et al.*, 1998, p. 139].

164 This is for instance the view of Michel Vâlsan, *pace* Frithjof Schoun, among his foremost immediate followers.

165 Chittick, 1994, p. 11.

166 E.g. Lyotard, 1989, pp. XXIV and XXV.

a matter of no less significance to the Traditionalist school than to Sufis, who themselves often set great store by such lineages. Guénon had been 'initiated' into Sufism by the Swedish modernist artist and religious pluralist Ivan Aguéli, a former member of the Theosophical Society who traced his connection to Ibn al-ʿArabī through ʿAbd al-Qādir's former student ʿAbd al-Raḥmān ʿIllaysh. Aguéli had met the latter in Cairo while carrying out his own investigations into the unity of religions. [ʿIllaysh has been tellingly described by Étienne as 'an akbarian (i.e. follower of Ibn ʿArabī) of course – very open and modern.'][167]

> 'Ibn al-ʿArabī is important to Sufis; for most Traditionalists, who followed Aguéli's lead, he was to become overwhelmingly significant. The later Traditionalist emphasis on Ibn al-ʿArabī, then, derives ultimately from the Amir Abd al-Qadir.'[168]

While it is unclear if Guénon ever learned to read classical Arabic,[169] many of his followers did so with great proficiency. Quite naturally, they set about studying and translating the great texts of their master's initiatic tradition, and popularising them in the west. The heirs of René Guénon would almost singlehandedly become responsible for introducing ʿAbd al-Qādir's spiritual writings to Europe. The seminal translations of his metaphysics and poetry in European languages – those of Gilis and Chodkiewicz – are both the work of Guénonians, for instance.[170] Meanwhile, references to the French metaphysician and his close associates (particularly Frithjof Schoun and Michel Vâlsan, the latter of whom 'initiated' both Chodkiewicz and Gilis)[171] are very frequent indeed in the 20th-century secondary literature on ʿAbd al-Qādir's later writings.[172]

This French school of 'esotericism' explicitly advocates all of the positions which, we have argued, have been misattributed to ʿAbd al-Qādir. This is by no means limited to a pervasive sense in the secondary literature that ʿAbd al-Qādir is more interested in interpreting Ibn al-ʿArabī than in reading the Qur'ān – not an implausible accusation, even if ʿAbd al-Qādir himself would almost certainly have repudiated it.

---

167 Étienne, 2003, p. 278.
168 Sedgwick, 2004, 62.
169 Sedgwick, 2004, p. 77.
170 Hatina, 2007, p. 403; Sedgwick, 2004, p. 134–6.
171 Sedgwick, 2004, p. 134–5; Michel Chodkiewicz explicitly acknowledges this fact in the foreword to his *Ocean Without Shore* [2003].
172 Direct references to Guénon are for instance be found in the works of Étienne, Gilis, Bouyerdene, Chodkiewicz, Penot, Djeradi, and Gai Eaton referred to in this book – this list is neither exhaustive, nor representative of indirect influences.

Rather, it includes an idiosyncratic reading of the Qur'ānic assertion of the unity of revelation through successive prophets (culminating in Muḥammad's recitation of the perfect Qur'ān) as asserting the equality of Islam and other faiths.[173] This is the same reading which we have seen advanced by secondary sources in our earlier discussion of the reception of ʿAbd al-Qādir's *Dhikrā* as well as his *Kitāb al-Mawāqif* above. The 20th-century French school includes a metaphysical separation between the so-called (and idiosyncratically understood) 'esoteric' and 'exoteric'[174] aspects of religion, while making the latter contingent upon and eclipsed by the former. This is also a view which we have seen several authors suggest was shared by ʿAbd al-Qādir. This European school also makes the consequent claim, reflected in Guénon's words above, for a radically subjective ('esoteric') understanding of religion which relativises all ethical and discursive ('exoteric') 'outward forms' – rendering scriptures and ethical frameworks interchangeable while undermining their respective claims to finality, objectivity, and superiority.[175] Again, these ideas, and their verbal expression in an 'idiosyncratic' exoteric/esoteric binary, have surfaced in our discussion of the western reception of ʿAbd al-Qādir's *Kitāb al-Mawāqif*. Finally, the school in question makes all of these claims in the context of an overarching project of harmonisation between the Orient and the Occident, a project at once political and spiritual.[176] This, too, is a project which we have seen 20th-century writers on ʿAbd al-Qādir's Sufism attribute to him on a slim evidential basis.

In each of these instances, we have explored both the congruence of 20th-century appreciations of ʿAbd al-Qādir's thought with that of 20th-century writers René Guénon and Michel Vâlsan, and a concomitant incongruity between those interpretations and the primary sources. In so far as this is the case, it is clear that the Guénonian approach to religion has systematically re-formed

173 E.g. Vâlsan, 1984, p. 19.

174 The specialised uses of these terms by past scholars of ʿAbd al-Qādir's Sufi thought conform to those predicated of 'Traditionalist' perennialism by Haanegraaff [1999] and Faivre [in Faivre and Haanegraaff (eds.), 1998]. Again, 'Traditionalism' in this instance refers to the school of perrenialist thought inaugurated by René Guénon and identified with writers including Frithjof Schoun and Ananda Coomaraswamy. One might contrast this usage with the more mainstream use of these terms in, for instance, Michael Gilsenan's *Recognizing Islam* [2008, pp. 31–33], where he characterises the activity of the *'ulemā'* as rendering the text *esoteric:* their comprehension dependant upon education within a particular school.

175 E.g. Vâlsan, 1984, p. 24. C.f. Chittick, 1994, p. 173: 'But to make absolute claims for a revelation that by nature can only be one of many brings about a certain imbalance and distortion that modern-day observers quickly sense...'

176 E.g. Vâlsan, 1984, p. 27–28.

our impression of ʿAbd al-Qādir's ideas – particularly those expressed during his later life. In effect it has done so in its own image.

This observation is not intended as a slight against scholars of ʿAbd al-Qādir motivated by Guénonian ideas. It is an unavoidable hermeneutic consequence of that school's dominance in this field, rather than some duplicity or failing. A constrained range of effective histories[177] has been brought to bear on this material – and this is by no means the fault of those who *have* applied themselves to it. This movement and its fellow travellers have contributed immeasurably to western knowledge of ʿAbd al-Qādir's ideas, and of Sufism in general. They have certainly done so, as Ernest Gellner recognises even while criticising[178] (the Guénonian) Martin Lings' tendentiously pantheistic[179] reading of Ibn al-ʿArabī, 'inspired by the most admirable of motives'.[180] It is neither the place nor the intention of this study to dispute Guénonian or perennialist approaches as such; indeed, such groups arguably represent an authentically indigenous 'Far-western Islam'.[181]

To the extent, however, that their particular perspective has exerted a prejudicial influence over the broader reception and reproduction of texts and their author, we are obliged to point to their historicity. By presenting the 19th-century ʿAbd al-Qādir as a spokesman for their 20th-century movement, they both distort the reality of his own life and contribute substantially to the narratives of conversion which divide its course so dramatically in two: by rendering an image of his old age so at odds with the facts about his youth. Whether

177 In Gadamer's [2003, *passim*] sense of all those factors predisposing a particular interpretive stance – a notion not altogether dissimilar in this context to the 'preparedness' (*istiʿdād*) Ibn ʿArabī and ʿAbd al-Qādir frequently use to illustrate the fact that human limitations as contingent beings leave them open to some but not other possible experiences of God, world, and text.
178 '[Lings] has much sympathy with a kind of pan-mystic eclecticism, in which he goes a good deal farther than the subject of his study... Mr. Lings' own attitude is a kind of 'Mystics of all religions, unite' approach' Gellner, 2000, p. 134.
179 Lings' reading, like those taken of ʿAbd al-Qādir above, praise these Sufis for the self-same things which are traditionally seen as among the greatest calumnies against Sufis within the Islamic tradition. This invidious situation is expressed, for instance, in Martin Lings' introduction to Nicholson's translation of a collection of Ibn ʿArabī's poetry: 'the following lines [*laqad ṣāra qalbī qābilan...*]...express the Sufi doctrine that all ways lead to the One God... Much valuable information is contained in a text on Monism by ʿAlī b. Sulṭān Muḥammad al-Qārī al-Harawī – a polemic against [Ibn al-ʿArabī's 'monism']... Of course the offending passages [of Ibn ʿArabī's *Futūḥāt*] admit of more than one interpretation, and *the author would doubtless have repudiated the construction put upon them* [by al-Harawī and his like]... Their pantheistic import, however, *cannot be explained away*' [in Nicholson, 1978, pp. vii-viii. Emphasis added].
180 Gellner, 2000, p. 135.
181 A paraphrasing of Morris' term [Morris, 2001].

those 20th-century religious movements are best described as 'anti-modern'[182] or as 'counter-modern',[183] they simply do not include ʿAbd al-Qādir – who was insufficiently modern to be either. He does not advocate piety in defence against an encroaching *laïcism*, but because he never questioned its centrality. He does not 'reconcile reason and religion' as a critique of secular public reason, but because he never imagined them to be in conflict. His veneration of tradition is of a thoroughly traditional sort, not a critique of novel ideas and ways of life. His nostalgia is a time-worn one for the time of the Prophet Muḥammad and his Rightly Guided successors, not a Romantic's despair at a desiccated, anonymous, and mechanical modernity.

This is not to suggest that the reading of ʿAbd al-Qādir's life presented here is entirely incompatible with perennialists' aim of inter-religious peace – still less that it is opposed to it. Rather, it supports that aim, and attempts to do so on the basis of a relatively disinterested survey of the facts. ʿAbd al-Qādir deserves his place in the history of Muslim-Christian relations. This is true beyond even the fact of his heroic rescue of so many thousands of innocent Christians in the winding streets of old Damascus.

ʿAbd al-Qādir's views are indeed respectful of 'non-Islamic' piety. This is not, however, through a relegation of Islam from religious pre-eminence, nor by recognition of other faiths' equality with Islam, nor indeed by the positing of some post-religious metaphysic or reified 'esotericism'. Rather, ʿAbd al-Qādir's '[echoing of] ibn al-ʿArabi's doctrine of the universality of religious experience and the receptivity of the mystic's soul to all forms and places of worship'[184] is based on a radical openness to seeing Islam reflected in other faiths. While it does not grant them equal value, it insists that they do have value, and value of the same sort as does Islam – a claim which finds its justification in the Qur'ān's text's explicit positioning of itself as the culmination of a process of successive scriptural revelations. As we have seen ʿAbd al-Qādir argue in the *Mawāqif*, and as we have already seen him assert with respect to the Islamic law following the Damascus Riots, its universality is such that it enfolds them all.

ʿAbd al-Qadir's is a universalistic moral monism[185] rather than a moral pluralism or relativism. It is open to the idea that even a non-Muslim can exhibit genuine, and therefore *ipso-facto* genuinely Islamic, virtue of one sort or extent or another. There is in fact an expectation that this will be the case, even if such

---

182 Sedgwick, 2004, *passim*.

183 Wasserstrom, 1999, p. 232.

184 Shinar, 1965, pp. 158–9.

185 N.B. 'monism' is being used here in the sense of moral philosophy, not of ontology (as above).

imperfect believers do not recognise it: *'God will place some truths upon the tongues of people who are unworthy to speak them such that they might be known by those who are worthy,'*[186] after all. Moreover, this is an attitude which, while perhaps particularly common among Sufis, is hardly their sole preserve. It is suggested for instance by the long-standing polysemy of the word '*ḥanīf*', historically applied to Abraham, Muḥammad, the Sufis (*taḥannuf*), and also certain righteous people who had never heard the Qur'ān recited.[187] The famous, if perhaps apocryphal, Prophetic narration *uṭlubū al-ʿilm wa law fī al-ṣīn*, 'search for knowledge even in [distant and unfamiliar] China', is well known among Muslims irrespective of their interest in Sufism. Even Muslims who are suspicious of Sufism may still find ʿAbd al-Qādir's magnanimity inspiring, and there is no need to artificially limit the appeal of his moral example by making it contingent on a particular understanding or experience of 'esotericism'. He has been admired by non-Muslims, as his numerous decorations attest. In this, too, he stands as a true 'bridge between civilisations'. What is more, in all of this he offers his example to a greater rather than a lesser range of persons, and does so more rather than less approachable fashion. His model of tolerance speaks to an audience which is not restricted to those who, like him, spent years in study and meditation, nor endured such dramatic political upheavals and geographic displacements. It may not be either a panacea, nor what all of his readers would hope for, but it is substantive and significant for all that.

Rather than a pluralist or relativist position, ʿAbd al-Qādir's attitude to the status of Islam among religions might be better described in terms such as that of Franz Martin Wimmer's 'integrative centrism' in the field of comparative philosophy. That is to say, a view proceeding from a

> 'conviction about the objective superiority of one's own ways of thinking and living, but [which] may at the same time not try arrogantly to overcome rivals. One's own way could be thought to be attractive to such a degree that it would be self sufficient to attract and integrate others... The task of the centre according to this view consists in the permanent maintenance or

---

186 *Mawāqif*, p. 768.

187 'The word *ḥanīf* is used especially of Abraham as the type of this pure worship of God; II, 135/129; III, 67/60, 95/89; IV, 125/124; VI, 79, 161/162; XVI, 120/121, 123/124; XXII, 31/32. In most of these verses the *ḥanīf* is contrasted with the idolaters (*mushrikūn*). It is also asserted that Abraham was neither a Jew nor a Christian (III, 67/60; cf. II, 135/129), and that the people of the book were originally commanded to worship God as *ḥunafā'* (XCVIII, 5/4). In the remaining two passages where the word is used in the Ḳur'ān (X, 105; XXX, 30/29), Muḥammad and his followers are commanded to worship God as *ḥunafā'*, not idolaters... Further this religion is in accordance with the natural disposition (*fiṭra* [*q.v.*]) created in men by God (XXX, 30)...' [W.M. Watt, *EI2*, entry on *ḥanīf*]

> restoration of what is known to be the right order. No further activity of the centre is thought to be necessary, since the attraction of the centre is so strong that every activity that comes from the periphery aims at adapting itself to the way of the centre.'[188]

Such an attitude is certainly encouraged by the Qur'ān, and has been held by many Muslims before ʿAbd al-Qādir. That scripture, after all, both presents itself as a final part of a continuity including all other genuine revelations and (as ʿAbd al-Qādir was later to assure the Freemasons after they approached him to become a member – though this connection soon lapsed)[189] 'there be no compulsion in religion: Truth stands out clear from Error: whoever rejects evil and believes in Allah hath grasped the most trustworthy handhold.'[190] We should, therefore, reverse Berque's description of ʿAbd al-Qādir as an adherent of ideas which are 'global with an Islamic flavour':[191] ʿAbd al-Qādir's Islam has a global flavour.

It is this universality of the truth of Islam which for ʿAbd al-Qādir makes it the *telos* to which all religiosity inherently inclines, God's final revelation revealed to the ultimate prophet and Perfect Man. In this, it re-iterates a long tradition in Islam, embodied for instance in the (apocryphal) saying of the Prophet that 'whatever is rightly spoken was spoken by me.'[192] Neither in theory nor in practice does ʿAbd al-Qādir's theology exclude a total commitment to Islamic ideas or standards. Rather, it depends on them; faith in the 'inimitable' Qur'ānic revelation is not a negotiable or fungible element of his worldview. Its conviction – rather than giving rise to chauvinism – is precisely that which permits it to be restrained, tolerant, and optimistic towards others. Alexandre Bellemare, whose biography of ʿAbd al-Qādir does not concern itself with his place in the world of Islamic thought, does illustrate this position well with an anecdote. Hearing of the intention of a young *curé* to meet him so as to convert him to Catholicism, ʿAbd al-Qādir replied: 'this must be a good man, for he has good intentions. Write to him and tell him to come. It is I who shall convert him, and it will be a triumph for me to cause a Christian marabout to embrace my religion.'[193]

Recognising this 'integrative centrism' permits us to see ʿAbd al-Qādir both as a self-confidently tolerant man, and as a fervent believer – without necessitating a moment of transformation from one personality to the other. It allows us to

---

188 Wimmer, 2002, pp. 57–58.
189 Geoffroy et al., 2010, p. 110.
190 Qur'ān 2:256.
191 Berque, 1978, p. 517.
192 Discussed in Goldziher, 1981, p. 44.
193 Bellemare, 1863, p. 453.

see the teachings of the Damascene ʿAbd al-Qādir as congruent with rather than conflicting with his considerable political influence, his various martial exploits, and the strictness of his own observance and imposition of Islamic law. It similarly obviates the need for those of us interested in his Sufi spirituality to see the Algerian ʿAbd al-Qādir's political ventures as having taken place 'in spite of rather than because of his religiosity'.[194] It allows us to imagine how the Algerian war-leader, prior to any meaningful exposure to western life, could nonetheless have struck his European prisoners as 'in all circumstances highly tolerant and free from prejudice against those who think differently from himself'.[195] In short, it permits us to perceive ʿAbd al-Qādir's life without the need for Eurocentric 'Road to Damascus' narratives of conversion which cannot be sustained in the light of the evidence.

194 This is a paraphrase of Richard King's critique of modern conceptions of mysticism [King, 2008, p. 24]. The idea that ʿAbd al-Qādir's political involvements were forced upon him in spite of himself, and in spite of his spiritual calling, is common in the secondary literature on ʿAbd al-Qādir's Sufism, and has been evidenced above.
195 Berndt, 1840, p. 63.

6.0 Conclusion

'Imām al-Mālik said:

Whosoever practices Sufism *[taṣawwuf]*
and not jurisprudence *[fiqh]*
will be a heretic.
Whosoever practices jurisprudence *[fiqh]*
and not Sufism *[taṣawwuf]*
will be corrupted.
Whosoever combines the two
will have the truth.[1]

In this concluding chapter, we shall survey the continuous and holistic account of ʿAbd al-Qādir's life and ideas which has been developed throughout this text. An appreciation of his life, ideas, and various careers has been assembled which obviates the need for putative 'Road to Damascus' transformations in ʿAbd al-Qādir's character. In the process, it has exposed the western roots of this artificial and misleading narrative imposition. This continuous account will be summarised in brief as part of this concluding chapter, underlining the consistency of the account we have supplied instead. Its distinctness from alternative versions will be underlined by drawing on each chapter's engagement with the relevant literature and the documentary and archival evidence it has explored. This will allow us to focus on the figure of ʿAbd al-Qādir that a non-fragmented, integrated approach to his biography reveals. Finally, this study will close with some suggestions for future research, both intra- and inter-disciplinary, which might build on the work carried out here.

6.1 Another Road to Damascus

The account of ʿAbd al-Qādir's origins in Chapter One began by showing that, with the exception of a few weeks' experience of an Ottoman school, his upbringing took place in the exclusively Sufi milieu of his family *zāwiyah*. While no material evidence of his childhood education remains, the influences one might expect from such a setting seem very much in evidence in his adult writing. While European secondary sources have often indulged in speculatively Occidentalising his education by imagining him poring over thinkers with the great-

1 Quoted in Ibn ʿAjība, 1972, p. 5–6.

DOI 10.1515/9783110499513-008

est kudos in European philosophy – such as Aristotle, Averroes or Ibn Khaldūn[2] – the conservatively mainstream cast of his life's works suggests more conventional foci in his upbringing. Much of his childhood will have been spent memorising Qur'ānic verses and *ḥadīth* compendia, and studying their various social and spiritual exegeses through the lenses of Qādirī Sufism (influenced, it has been shown in Chapters Three to Five, by figures such as al-Ghazālī and Ibn al-ʿArabī) and the mainstream of Mālikite legal theory we explored in Chapter Two. It is these which would provide him with the conceptual means to interpret, understand, and affect the world around him.

This potential was actuated by ʿAbd al-Qādir's assumption of hard, executive and temporal power via his family's long-standing soft-power influence as prominent Sufis and honoured descendants of the Prophet. The conservative moral and legal appeal of the Islamic virtues his family embodied appealed to a population cast into chaos by the destruction of the Ottoman regime at the hands of the growing French invasion of North Africa. While his status as maraboutic scion of a dominant *ṭarīqah* and as a sharīf delivered the reins of power into his hands, it was the promise of order and justice which made his leadership most compelling, and his ability to conform to social expectations which made it most credible. Correspondingly, his first speech as *amīr al-mu'minīn* promised the proper functioning of Islamic law, and that its pursuit would be characteristic of his rule. The results we have seen are both appealing and unpleasant from a modern perspective; but his fiscal probity, his relatively magnanimous treatment of captives and innocents, and his formalising of previously corrupt and chaotic judicial systems drew on the same wellsprings as his restrictive and punitive social legislation, which saw offences against public morals punished with public beatings and the strictures of *ḥudūd*.

ʿAbd al-Qādir's desire to practise a morally pure Islamic leadership on the model of the pious Muslim forbears repeatedly led him into difficulties, even as it functioned as the pre-eminent legitimating factor of his rule. His inherited contempt for 'immoral' Ottoman mores (which would continue until his death) prevented him from making strategically well-advised alliances with the rump state of Constantine. His horror of Muslim submission to infidel rule led him into interminable and sometimes quixotic raids on tribes and *ṭuruq* friendly to France. His Islamocentric world-view stymied his ill-informed attempts at playing politics with the great powers of the west, compounding his consistently ill-judged selection of western representatives. His few genuine diplomatic successes depended on polyglot Jewish traders and diplomats such as the brilliant

2 E.g. Étienne, 2003, pp. 46–49, 76–77, 94, 97, 124, 134, 142, 179, 260, or Bouyerdene, 2008, p. 293.

Judah Bendraham, called Ben Durand,[3] and upon French incompetence and infighting.

Finally, as he was driven into hiding in the mountains of the Moroccan Rīf, the ever-present tension between his own authority and that of the Moroccan Sultan became increasingly conflicted. Caught between the moral, legal, religious, and political imperative to refrain from fomenting disorder against the Sultan on the one hand, and the occasionally violent war of words waged with him, his position became untenable. Even while launching pre-emptive attacks on the Sultan's agents and denouncing his capitulations to France, ʿAbd al-Qādir refused to challenge the Sultan directly, attempting to the last to maintain the fiction that their relationship was an amicable one of ruler and subject. With the intensification of the Sultan's military manoeuvres against him, the execution and imprisonment of his followers, and the refusal to grant *amān* of safe passage, ʿAbd al-Qādir was forced to attempt to exit the field by the only means remaining to him. The Sultan of Morocco had forced him to accept the unreliable *amān* of the French army.

Chapter Two elucidated ʿAbd al-Qādir's thinking during this chaotic period through the medium of his *Risālah on Hijrah*, a discussion of the obligation to migrate to Muslim lands in the face of infidel conquest. It explored, *in situ*, the moral and juridical traditions which informed ʿAbd al-Qādir's politics. It also revealed the historical precedents out of which those traditions grew, and upon whose symbolism they attempted to draw. The conservative, mainstream Mālikite jurisprudential positions on social and political organisation which he had attempted to implement drew on a history of Islamo-Christian conflict and cohabitation stretching back to the centuries of Muslim Iberia and the Christian *Reconquista*. Largely derivative of al-Wansharīsī's *Miʿyār*, it shows that however expedient his attempts at splitting the Muslims of Algeria away from France may have been, they were also the products of a clearly elaborated tradition in Islamic political thought. The text also establishes the influence of Shāfʿī moral and legal reasoning, particularly that of al-Ghazālī, on whom ʿAbd al-Qādir would continue to draw both as an authoritative Sufi and as a giant of jurisprudential theory. It also offers insight into the rhetorical priority of appeals to Islamic law over more segmentary loyalties in his society; the ethico-legal discourse adopted by ʿAbd al-Qādir in this text cut across tribal, ethnic, and confraternal lines, maximising the resonance of his political message.

Its main political theme was the summoning of Muslims from the French jurisdiction, whose sovereignty ʿAbd al-Qādir never formally recognised, to his

3 Julien, 1964, p. 124.

own. This message would later become pertinent to his own life, however. Its burden in the historical context of its writing, aside from encouraging moral probity in compliance with divine law, was to strengthen his power at the expense of the French colony while simultaneously justifying his raids and reprisals against Muslim groups who failed to submit to him. With the failure of his *jihād* and his increasingly precarious position as *persona non grata* in the Sultanate of Morocco, ʿAbd al-Qādir would find himself put to the same moral tests as those Muslims his *Risālah on Hijrah* had denounced as fools, liars, and hypocrites. His previous statement of principle, therefore, had direct implications for his own comportment in France.

Chapter Three took up the chronological thread of ʿAbd al-Qādir's life at the point of his 'surrender' to the armies of France – a surrender which ʿAbd al-Qādir never regarded as such: he saw it as an agreement to be exiled from the Maghreb in favour of the Islamic eastern Mediterranean and Hejaz. His safe passage was to be bought in exchange for a vow to abandon the struggle in North Africa – a promise he kept until his death. We then explored the hardships and the honours visited upon ʿAbd al-Qādir and his companions when they were brought, not to their expected destination, but to imprisonment in a series of chateaux across France. Challenging the myth that this period ended with ʿAbd al-Qādir's embrace of French civilisation, we found both that his assurances to France remained consistent throughout his imprisonment, irrespective of changes in government, and that he repeatedly refused offers to trade his captivity for a very comfortable life in Europe. The myth of his cultural 'conversion' was deliberately fostered so as to support the interests of the 19th-century French state. Its initial aims were transforming a scandal of duplicity into a triumph of magnanimity, averting an aristocratic plot to further embarass a royal dynasty, assuaging the fears of a wary population, and ultimately symbolising the capitulation of Muslim Algeria to French colonial rule.

Yet this myth belied the reality. Rather than adopting a novel stance, ʿAbd al-Qādir held fast to the obligations he had preached in his wartime *Risālah on Hijrah*, and to the assurances he had originally given to the French army on the plains of North Africa. While on a personal level he developed great affection for certain Frenchmen – notably Eugène Daumas and Louis Napoleon/Napoleon III – his plans went substantially unaltered by his involuntary sojourn in the Loire valley. His great regard for the new Emperor would not extend so far as to deign to live among his subjects, convert to his faith, nor even to learn his language. Rather, ʿAbd al-Qādir would migrate east to Muslim lands and trouble Algeria no more: fulfilling his original solemn promise to Lamoricière and the Duc d'Aumale, and enacting the only practical guarantee of his continued freedom.

There he would resume his family's accustomed roles as scholars, teachers, mediators, and – should propitious circumstances arise – overt political leaders.

Chapter Four detailed ʿAbd al-Qādir's reception in Istanbul, where he comported himself as a hero of the *jihād* while French and Ottoman authorities jockeyed to secure him as a symbol of their respective claims on Algiers. With his move to Bursa, near the Sea of Marmara, he would become head of the largest Algerian community he had led since the dissolution of his depleted *dāʾirah* in North Africa. Here we found evidence of his continued interest in military affairs, in spite of his diplomatic disavowals of martial matters during his imprisonment. We saw him repeating the patterns of his Algerian rule, introducing European technical innovations while practising and patronising traditional Islamic scholarship – all, once more, while minimising contact with the neighbouring Ottoman Turks. Drawing on French and Ottoman pensions while exploiting his anomalous nationality (to which both Empires laid certain claims) ʿAbd al-Qādir established himself as the undisputed head of what amounted to an Algerian colony, while also drawing in and patronising North African Muslims across the wider eastern Mediterranean.

This chapter followed ʿAbd al-Qādir's move to Damascus after Bursa's ruin by a series of earthquakes, and his further establishing himself as a Levantine eminence. It described his tensions with both the French and Ottoman authorities, his manipulation of their obligations towards him, and his repeated slighting of their respective claims over him. We examined his despatch of a didactic text on the inadequacy of reason and the necessity of divine revelation to the French Asiatic Society, and his diplomatic attempts to maintain order among the sectarian tensions of the Levant. When these efforts failed, this chapter described his organising of a sizeable militia, chaos crystallising his soft-power influence into hard-power force once more, his political and military actions followed the trajectory they had taken in Algeria. As in Algeria, ʿAbd al-Qādir found his pursuit of what he regarded as the unambiguous moral right enjoined by Qurʾānic law hampered by his ambivalent submission to a (nominally) Muslim authority he deeply distrusted. Then, during an episode of public disorder, in spite of Ottoman hesitation, ʿAbd al-Qādir succeeded in saving the lives of thousands of innocents. This act would come to be regarded as a service to Islam in the Muslim world, and as a service to the west in the west. He himself repeated his Algerian model and presented himself as upholding the divine law. His profile rising ever higher in Damascus, he repeated his youthful pilgrimage to Mecca. As before, this gesture combined his personal spiritual inclinations with a public expression of both his piety and – on his triumphant return to Damascus at the head of a thousand horsemen – the military and political power he held in potential.

Chapter Five began by outlining the final years of ʿAbd al-Qādir's life, during which he remained head of the North African community, pre-eminent among Arab leaders in the locality, and widely distrusted among Ottoman and European diplomats suspicious of his influence. This was also the time of his greatest literary work, the posthumously published *Kitāb al-Mawāqif*, a collection of lessons on Sufi exegesis of the Qur'ān recorded by his students in Damascus. Through this text, we gain the clearest insight into the internal world of ʿAbd al-Qādir al-Jazā'irī – none of his earlier writings contain so much psychological autobiography. An account was presented of his teachings in that text, exploring their conservative derivation from the mainsprings of the Sufi tradition in general and the complex symbolic lexicon of Muḥyī al-Dīn Ibn al-ʿArabī in particular. Hinging on a subtle ontological equivocation between monism and dualism, this work urges the internalisation of God's truths and laws on scales bridging the personal with the cosmic, and the immanent with the transcendent. It reveals ʿAbd al-Qādir urging openness and moderation as Islamic virtues while demanding utterly scrupulous adherence to Shariah and Sunnah in imitation of Muḥammad, understood as the Perfect Man and embodiment of the eternal metaphysical Muhammadan Reality.

Throughout this entire sequence of acts and writings, a coherent personality emerges – one heavily influenced by the circumstances of his upbringing in his family *zāwiyah*. A legist Sufi until his death, ʿAbd al-Qādir's final metaphysical lessons to his students make the same demands for the primacy of Islamic law as did his *Dhikrā al-ʿĀqil*, presenting it as the only palliative for the inadequacy of reason; and as, earlier still, his *Risālah on Hijrah* and his Algerian rule demanded as the only alternative to anarchy, injustice, and ruin. The political effectiveness of his Algerian and Damascene appeals to Islamic law was closely tied to the special cultural and theological status of the law in most forms of Islam, including those understood by ʿAbd al-Qādir, his followers, and their ancestors who informed them. Internalising what he took to be God's law, verse by verse and action by action, was a goal of both his Sufi practice and his religio-political exhortations, and being seen to do so in ways meaningful to his contemporaries his greatest political strength. His religio-political prestige and considerable self-confidence as *sharīf* and marabout combined with this outlook to provide ʿAbd al-Qādir with both the motive and the means to exert himself politically when situations proved propitious.

ʿAbd al-Qādir did not single-handedly forge history around him, after the fashion of rightly discredited Victorian imaginings of 'Great Men', though he always responded to it to great effect. His political inclination was always more reactionary than radical – in its conservatism, its idealisation of the distant (Prophetic and immediately post-Prophetic) past, and in its responding to changing circumstances rather than attempting to overturn existing order. Both in Morocco and in Syria, he resisted calls to declare himself against Muslim rulers with whom he enjoyed very strained relations. Rather, it was invariably in political vacuums that he asserted himself. During his lifetime ʿAbd al-Qādir found himself in the midst of societal breakdown on only three occasions: the collapse of Ottoman rule from Algiers following the French conquest in 1830, the collapse of the French July Monarchy in 1848, and the 1860 sectarian riots in Damascus, of which he said 'Yet Damascus has a governor; but it is the same thing as if it had not one.'[4] Only on the second occasion – upheaval in an alien nation in which he was held prisoner – did ʿAbd al-Qādir, self-described 'man of action'[5] until his death, fail to take an active stand.

On each occasion, his effective power varied to the degree permitted by his circumstances. Beyond mere opportunism, it has been remarked that his characteristically maraboutic approach to political activism relied upon and demanded such an approach[6] [which may also recall Sufi reactions to the power vacuums of the so-called 'Maraboutic Crisis' of the fifteenth to seventeenth centuries].[7] His claims to Godly conviction and worldly disinterest, to acting out of necessity for others' sakes rather than out of personal ambition, was what empowered him, gained him a following, and permitted him to undertake ambitious projects – while the elaborate ethical content of the traditions in which he grew up provided ample motivation. On a more psychological level, one might also observe that both political leadership and the Sufi path make great demands for conviction and certainty (*yaqīn*): ʿAbd al-Qādir possessed these in abundance.

But we can say more about ʿAbd al-Qādir than that he evinced the confident moralism of a maraboutic upbringing, the pride of a sharifian lineage, and the Shariah-mindedness of a conservative Islamocentric education. He inherited a pronounced dislike for the Turks from his father – an attitude which was widely shared among the North Africans they had ruled and the Syrians they continued to dominate. Had Ottoman rule disintegrated further in Damascus, it is easy to

---

4 Quoted in *The New York Times*, August 20, 1860.

5 Outrey to the Ministry of Foreign Affairs, *Damas/Consulat/13*, 17-04-1861.

6 Seraulky, 1990, pp. 53, 55.

7 Cornell [1983, p. 88]. 'It must be remembered, however, that such support of a *ṭarīqah* for a regime was limited, and lasted only as long as the Shaykh's successors felt that the Saadians upheld the principles with which they had allied themselves. As far as the perceived immorality and duplicity of the Saadian rulers was seen to increase, the passive support of the Sufi shaykhs became vocal resistance, and by the time of the interregnums of the early seventeenth century, we see a few of them in open revolt against the state.'

imagine him taking a leading role in organising the Sunnis of Syria as so many of his contemporaries had predicted, hoped, or feared. Rumours of his involvement in plots to seize power notwithstanding, this was a possibility which has been shown to have been considered plausible by both Ottoman and western political agents until ʿAbd al-Qādir's death. Ottoman rule would muddle along until some decades after his passing, however, and the opportunity did not in the event arise.

Other observations can be made which do not rely on counter-factuals. The formidable intellect which enabled ʿAbd al-Qādir's scholarship also gave him an interest in engineering, though he never received the mathematical education necessary to develop it in himself. A life-long technophile, ʿAbd al-Qādir sought, with varying degrees of success, to introduce the latest technological innovations in Algeria, in Anatolia, and in the Levant. From foundries in Tagdempt to farms in Bursa to canals and railways from Suez to Damascus. His intellectual and spiritual conservatism did not hamper his taste for material novelty. Perhaps the most poignant example of this comes in the course of his *Kitāb al-Mawāqif*, where he embraces the photograph (for several of which he proudly posed) as analogous with the mirror as a spiritual metaphor beloved by centuries of Sufis before him.[8]

There as elsewhere, the substitution of modern tools for ancient ones did not alter the structure or intent of their use one iota; ʿAbd al-Qādir's taste for novelty always comprised putting old wine in new bottles. He never encountered science as a challenge to traditional modes of thought – both because his exposure to it was relatively modest, and because he was never involved in the cultural and religious discourses which gave localised western 'culture wars' their meaning and significance. He never struggled to reconcile science with his faith because he never felt compelled to do so by the very modern belief that they are in need of reconciliation. His conservative Islamic education, as his writings evidence, naturally conceived of knowledge – like politics – as subsisting within a totalising Islamic framework.

Aside from his respect for technical innovation (which at the time derived primarily from Europe, though there may be no need to classify it as an exclusively European cultural preserve – which it certainly is not today), the conventional mythology of ʿAbd al-Qādir's 'conversion' by France finds its truest resonance in his more personal friendships. His affection for his liberator Napoleon III, in particular, seems to have been very genuine, though their contact was extremely limited. As much as the monetary and political advantages

---

8 *Mawāqif*, p. 627.

his adoptive 'citizenship' conferred, it formed the bedrock of his relationship with France. He invariably expressed great warmth towards the Emperor as an individual – however often this was (mis)interpreted as a metonym for France or Frenchness as such. On Napoleon III's death, ʿAbd al-Qādir wasted no time in sending his condolences to his widow,[9] with whom he had also carried on an occasional correspondence. His contacts with the subsequent Third Republic were minimal, by contrast – primarily concerned with guaranteeing clemency for his rebellious son Muḥyī al-Dīn while at the same time continuing to assuage persistent fears that he might breach the bargain struck for his freedom by re-entering the North African scene. According to the French consul in Damascus, reporting on ʿAbd al-Qādir's death, it was for Napoleon III's releasing him, above and beyond any other of his or his countrymen's virtues, that ʿAbd al-Qādir remained thankful to the end of his days.[10] Consistent with his deeply-held beliefs, none of this required a great conversion, no shocking revelation – simply experience and time.

6.2 Reflections on the Road Onward

The continuous and integrative impression of ʿAbd al-Qādir developed here renders implausible the conventional narratives of dramatic transformation and conversion thought to have been occasioned by ʿAbd al-Qādir's defeat by the armies and/or the culture of France. The stark divisions between the Algerian nationalist and the Damascene cosmopolitan, between the Algerian Machiavelli and the Damascene saint, between the Algerian soldier and the Damascene pacifist, between the Algerian Islamist and the Damascene pluralist, cannot be sustained in the light of the evidence; they seem better explained as products of European expectations.

The much more consistent account of ʿAbd al-Qādir presented here therefore seems preferable to the gamut of conventional 'Road to Damascus' narratives previously read into ʿAbd al-Qādir's life. It is preferable in its parsimony in describing one ʿAbd al-Qādir rather than several; in according more consistently with the gamut of historical facts and documentary records; in being a more accurate reflection of his own self-representations throughout his life. It is also preferable in relying less heavily on extra-textual presumptions about the generic essence of his words and actions.

9 Robin to the Ministry of Foreign Affairs, *Damas/Consulat/65*, 01-02-1873.
10 Portalis to the Ministry of Foreign Affairs, *Damas/Consulat/14*, 03-05-1883.

Dispensing with the myth of ʿAbd al-Qādir's conversion relieves us of the need to explain the contradiction between its imagined products and what historically took place. We no longer face the task of defending his putative conversion to French culture, patriotism, or philosophy in light of his failure to learn the French language (so essential to French conceptions of polity), his steadfast refusal to live among the French (preferring even to live under the jurisdiction of the Ottomans he despised), and his shaky and rather mercenary relationship with the French state (resenting and contesting all constraints placed upon him even while soliciting financial and political support). We need not defend his supposed adoption of the Masonic cause, given what we have witnessed, with his failure to produce more than a brief and rather anodyne correspondence with the Freemasons at their instigation, nor need we be perplexed by his failure to attend Masonic meetings – even the un-attended grand convocation needlessly called by the Grand Orient de France on his visit to Paris.[11] (Had he taken his relationship with the movement seriously, this would have constituted a dramatic snub; most likely, it simply seemed to him to be an irrelevance.) We need not grapple with explaining why the supposed Damascene quietist and pacifist bemoaned delays in authorising his thousand-strong armed militia to open fire on the rioting crowds.[12] We no longer face the impossible task of defending his putative pluralist transcending of an Islamocentric religious worldview against the textual evidence of his unshaken faith in the Islamic revelation, with Qur'ān as pure and final word of God and Muḥammad as both ultimate Prophet and archetypical human being.

It remains now to offer some final observations on the structural issues underlying the 'Road to Damascus' accounts. The initial, 19th-century political impetus for this interpretation – demonstrating Algerian submission to the French colonial project while concealing the terms of ʿAbd al-Qādir's 'surrender' – is surely not a motive behind the narrative's continued presence in the latest literature. We may also leave aside the aesthetic possibility that conversion myths are simply inherently attractive, close as they are to the ideal of dramatic fiction found from Aristotle's *Poetics* to Hollywood screenwriting[13] in their tripartite rise and fall of prelude, climax, and denouement.

Certain structural similarities exist between the divided literatures on ʿAbd al-Qādir's pre- and post-imprisonment treatments in the secondary literature. It is through recognising these, and their specifically modern and western char-

11 Kabache in Geoffroy et al., 2010, p. 99.

12 Brant to the Foreign Office, FO 78/1520, 24-07-1860.

13 The latter, of course, has often been argued to be indebted to the former – not least in such recent publications as Michael Tierno's *Aristotle's Poetics for Screenwriters* [2002].

acter, that we may both better understand the process of interpretive imposition to which ʿAbd al-Qādir has been made subject, and problematise the interpretive challenges which have given rise to them. In so doing, we can remove previous distortions and avoid replicating them in the future. Most strikingly, much distortion has arisen from applying to a figure who combines elements of politics, religion, warfare, and mysticism in his actions and ideas, sets of analytic apparatus which are inherently resistant to such combinations. ʿAbd al-Qādir's 'conversion' has increasingly been demanded by the contradictions produced by essentialising the phases of his life – seeing them as fundamentally exclusively political, or exclusively religious – in terms alien to his own worldview, and therefore difficult to reconcile with it.

This problem is largely a hermeneutic one, which can be ameliorated through reflection on the manner in which it has arisen. While secular disciplinary differences have played a detrimental role in the western scholarly interpretation of ʿAbd al-Qādir's life, this situation is not inevitable. Rather, it is the product of specific sub-disciplary schools' dominance in the secondary literature. In contrast, however, both social and political science and religious studies for their parts contain sufficient resources to permit integrative accounts to be deepened in coming decades. We may hope that this integration will continue to be deployed in the case of the life of ʿAbd al-Qādir.

While ʿAbd al-Qādir naturally took no part in 20th-century western 'culture wars', his biography has become their anachronistic battlefield. ʿAbd al-Qādir has been represented as an opponent[14] and as a proponent[15] of a laïcism he never meaningfully encountered and could not easily have comprehended. He has been represented as 'political not religious',[16] and also as 'transcending the categories of a soldier',[17] 'his kingdom not of this world'[18] in spite of his lack of a conceptual lexicon capable of systematically articulating such distinctions. It is only recently, in the idiosyncratic course of western modernity, that essential cleavages between religion and politics have become so evident to us.

> 'As of the late nineteenth century, indeed, we have fully-formed alternatives [between 'naturalistic materialism' and 'faith']. But it is wildly anachronistic to project this very familiar scenario of Victorian times, or today, onto earlier centuries, when the rival outlooks between which we hesitate today were still being forged.'[19]

---

14 Heck *et al.*, 2007, p. 12–13.
15 Sfeir, 2011, p. 9.
16 Danziger, 1977, pp. 183, 212.
17 Chodkiewicz, 1995, p.2.
18 Étienne in Geoffroy *et al.*, 2010, p. 79.
19 Taylor, 2007, p. 28.

Not only does ʿAbd al-Qādir's life largely predate the '*Entstehungsgeschichte* of exclusive humanism'[20] (which it is far from clear he ever encountered), moreover, it also takes place geographically and discursively outside of it. We have seen in detail that ʿAbd al-Qādir's conceptual frame of reference was not significantly aware of nor influenced by the specifically western discourses which gave rise to secular conceptions of politics and religion. This fact must be recognised in spite of the universalising ambitions of modern secular thought if we are to properly understand him. This presents something of an interpretive challenge which has beset much writing on ʿAbd al-Qādir:

> 'The insistence that religion has an autonomous essence – not to be confused with the essence of science, or of politics, or of common sense – invites us to define religion (like any essence) as a transhistorical and transcultural phenomenon. It may be a happy accident that this effort of defining religion converges with the liberal demand in our time that it be kept quite separate from politics, law, and science – spaces in which varieties of power and reason articulate our distinctively modern life. This definition is at once part of a strategy (for secular liberals) of the confinement, and (for liberal Christians) for the defence of religion.'[21]

Beyond the characteristically modern reification of religion – let alone 'the religions'[22] – ʿAbd al-Qādir's biography presents a deeper difficulty. More than anything else, it is his combination of mysticism with political leadership which has been most problematic for western scholarship, as each has respectively come in modern culture to represent extremes of personal individuality and impersonal sociality. This tendency has even been argued to have particularly influenced the western study of Islam, moreover.[23]

'Mysticism' is a term with a particular provenance, coming into limited use in Christianity, Leigh Schmidt informs us, from the 17th century and enjoying some considerable developments by the time in the 20th century that western scholarship became interested in ʿAbd al-Qādir in earnest. For many centuries, the adjectives 'mystic' or 'mystical' (as distinct from the much later substantive 'mysticism') were descriptive of Christian beliefs, practices, and concerns.[24] 'The meanings attached to *mystic* and *mystical* were inextricably woven into a larger

---

20 Taylor, 2007, p. 26; that is, its 'historical coming-into-being' or the '(hi)story of its coming to exist'.

21 Asad, 1993, p. 28.

22 Problematised for instance by Wilfred Cantwell Smith [1991].

23 E.g. Wasserstrom, 1999, p. 240.

24 E.g. Schmidt, 2003; this is not to deny that the word derives from earlier Greek usages (such as the 'Eleusinian Mysteries' or *Μυστήρια*), though these too related to quite specific religious contexts (such as the cults of Demeter and Persephone) rather than an to abstract concept.

system of Christian theology, linked at the level of practice to a recognizable set of devotional and exegetical habits.'[25] The terms did not initially imply an abstract concept or category, let alone its reified 20th-century usages; it seems to have described language more than experience.[26]

This situation has developed considerably (even reversed) by the present day, when 'mystical' has come often to denote something a- or anti-rational, the wordless, a mysterious and magical realm which can only be experienced and never be described. This view is arguably implicit in proto-secular attempts at separating religion and politics by rendering the former private and the later public – such as John Locke's *Letter Concerning Toleration*,[27] or perhaps even certain classical thinkers such as Epicurus. Yet these were always minority voices.[28] It was 20th-century writers like Aldous Huxley, William James, Walter Stace, and René Guénon, who each in their own way developed the concept to refer to a psycho-spiritual phenomenon separate from, underlying, uniting, or perhaps superseding the world's religions.

Essentialising mystical states or mystical tradition entails not only a particular view of mysticism, but a special attitude towards religion as such.[29] It is not our aim to argue for or against such a view – simply to point to its distinctness and the historicity of its formulation. Certainly, Sufisms such as that of ʿAbd al-Qādir (not to mention his 'Greatest Master' Ibn al-ʿArabī) have lent themselves to cross-cultural comparisons: suffice it to note in passing that they have been com-

---

25 Schmidt, 2003, p. 277

26 '[I]n the sixteenth and seventeenth centuries, already existing writings were termed "mystic", and a mystic tradition was fabricated... The isolation of this domain of truth is already apparent linguistically with the change in the status of the word "mystic" from an adjective to a noun. See Michel de Certeau, "Mystique au XVIIe siècle: le problème du langage Mystique," in *L'homme devant Dieu. Mélanges de Lubac* (Paris: Aubier, 1964), vol. 2, pp. 267–281, and Gotthold Müller's comments in "Ueber den Begriff der Mystic," *Neue Zeitschrift für System Theologie*, 13 (1971), pp. 88–98. It should be kept in mind that in the vocabulary of the time "mysti" referred essentially to a way of treating language; 'spirituality" designated the experience.' De Certeau, 2006, pp. 82, 244.

27 Where it was ironically also adduced as part of his anti-Catholic campaign.

28 Taylor, 2007, p. 19: 'This thesis, placing exclusive humanism only within modernity, may seem too bald and exceptionless to be true. And indeed, there are exceptions. By my account, ancient Epicureanism was a self-sufficient humanism... My plea here is that one swallow doesn't make a summer. I'm talking about an age when self-sufficient humanism becomes a widely available option, which it never was in the ancient world, where only a small number of the élite which was itself a minority espoused it.'

29 Argued, for instance, by Haanegraaff, 1999.

pared, *inter alia*, with (Neo-)Platonism,[30] Christianity,[31] Gnosticism,[32] Cynicism,[33] Stoicism,[34] Judaism,[35] Hindu Vedānta,[36] Buddhism,[37] Daoism,[38] Transcendental Meditation,[39] Dante,[40] Deconstruction,[41] Postmodernism in general,[42] Hollywood cinema,[43] epileptic and schizotypal mental disorders,[44] and the altered mental states of the psychoactive drug user.[45]

---

30 E.g. Goldziher, 1981, pp. 135 – 140; 'Ibn 'Arabī's thinking is fundamentally Platonic' – Titus Burckhardt writing in the preface to R.W.J. Austin's translation of Ibn 'Arabī's *Bezels of Wisdom* [1980, p. XIII].

31 Evident in the very title of Asín Palacios' early study of Ibn 'Arabī, *Islam Christianisado.* Meister Eckhart and Nicolas of Cusa are the most common points of comparison. Ian Netton [1994, p. 293] calls Ibn 'Arabī 'the Meister Eckhart of the Islamic tradition'; Michel Chodkiewicz [1995, p. 212] compares Ibn 'Arabī and 'Abd al-Qādir to Meister Eckhart, while the title he gives to chapter 30 (p. 133, 'On Learned Ignorance') of *op. cit.* refers to Cusanus' *De Docta Ignorantia*; see also for instance Almond, 2001; Smirnov, 1993.

32 E.g. Nicholson, quoted in Abun-Nasr, 2007, p. 26

33 E.g. Goldziher, 1981, pp. 149, 150; what is intended is naturally the philosophical school of antiquity connected with Diogenes ('the Cynic').

34 E.g '['Abd al-Qādir's Islam] is not unlike the patient and cheerful stoicism of Epicetus and Marcus Aurelius.' [Clayton, 1975, p. 6]

35 E.g. Bashier [2004, p. 76] refers to suggestions that Ibn 'Arabī's metaphysics was drawn from Philo's *Logos.*

36 E.g. Zaehner, 1969, pp. 86 – 109; Chittick, 1994, p. 11. Comparisons with ('Neo-Vedanta' receptions of) the Advaitavedanta of Shankara and (less frequently) the Visishtadvaita of Ramanuja are generally favoured. See also Addas [1993, p. 110].

37 E.g. Zaehner, 1969, for instance, devotes some effort to parallel parables in Sufi and Buddhist teaching at least since Abū Yazīd al-Bisṭāmī. Also, for example, Goldziher, 1981, pp. 143 – 144; Izutsu, 1971, p. 51; Weismann, 2001a, p. 38.

38 The major text in this regard is naturally Toshihiko Izutsu's *Sufism and Taoism: a comparative study of key philosophical concepts* [1983].

39 E.g. Geoffroy et al., 2010, p. 219.

40 E.g. Gilis, 1996, p. 12.

41 Almond's *Sufism and Deconstruction* [2004], for instance, attempts to draw parallels between Ibn 'Arabī and Derrida.

42 E.g. Chittick, 1994, pp. 11, 139.

43 E.g. Morris, 2001, p. 110 asserts that the films *Field of Dreams*, *Jacob's Ladder*, and *The Fisher King* evince Sufi thought.

44 Asín Palacios, 1931, pp. 68 – 80, 101 – 105. There have also been studies attempting to link 'religious experience' or 'mystical experience' with relatively materially describable neuro-chemical states brought about by hallucinogens, schizophrenia, stroke and some forms of epilepsy in particular. The lattermost 'explanation' (once popular also in strongly atheistic Soviet readings) is for instance popularised by Christopher Hitchen's *God is Not Great* to account for the experiences of the Prophet Muḥammad. Such materialism is also to be found in some of the academic literature drawn on here. Martin [1976, pp. 1 – 2] presents the assertion that ecstatic 'mystical experiences' during Sufi rituals are the products of hyperventilation and consequent oxygen-star-

No matter how appealing such comparisons may make the idea of an essential mysticism, nor how influential in popular culture and among New Religious Movements in it may be, it remains the subject of controversy in the academy. It has been rejected not only by religious believers upset by perceived attacks on their faith, but also from pre-eminent historians of religion such as *Eranos*-participant Gershom Scholem.[46] It has also been questioned by writers on the socio-political expression of mystical religion in general, and as it relates to western-orientalist representations of the 'mystic east' in particular. It is for this reason that Richard King points out that

> 'The narrowly experiential approach [to study of the mystic] occludes or suppresses other aspects of the phenomenon of the mystical that tend to be more important for these figures and the traditions to which they belong – for example, the ethical dimension of the mystical, the link between mysticism and the struggle for authority, or the extent to which statements and activities of mystics may relate to issues of politics and social justice... The mystic, it would seem, can only be a revolutionary in spite of, and not because of, her mystical qualities.'[47]

By contrast, a social-constructivist interpretation which rejects the perennial thesis, [48] often associated with Steven Katz,[49] has increasingly gained academic as-

---

vation of the brain. An example of a more informed (though not uncontroversial) summary of 'mental health' approaches has been offered by the US Group for the Advancement of Psychiatry [GAP; 1976], in a report entitled *Mysticism: Spiritual Quest or Psychic Disorder?*

45 E.g. Zaehner, 1972; Hawi [1974, p. 253] explicitly compares the Sufi's 'going into themselves' to the famous Mescaline experiences of Aldous Huxley's *Doors of Perception.* The parallel between 'mystical states' and drug use (particularly alcohol and ether) is also a major theme in William James' influential discussion in *The Varieties of Religious Experience* [pp. 366–413]. See also the preceding footnote.

46 'There is no such thing as mysticism in the abstract, that is to say, a phenomenon or experience which has no particular relation to other religious phenomena. There is no mysticism as such, there is only the mysticism of a particular religious system, Christian, Islamic, Jewish mysticism and so on' [Scholem, 1974, p. 5].

47 King, 2008, pp. 20, 24.

48 Katz [1978, p. 57] writes that 'mystical' and 'ascetic' practices (among which he explicitly includes Sufism) 'appear, on the face of it, as movements which lead the 'self' from states of 'conditioned' to 'unconditioned' consciousness, from 'contextual' to 'non-contextual' awareness. Moreover, this is the usual way of evaluating them, especially by those seeking some variety of the *philosophia perennis*, the universal common mystical experience... Those who advocate this position, however, are mislead by appearances... Properly understood, yoga, for example, is *not* an *un*conditioning or *de*conitioning of consciousness, but rather it is a *re*conditioning of consciousness, i.e. a substituting of one form of conditioned and/or contextual consciousness for another, albeit a new, unusual, and perhaps altogether more interesting form of conditioned-

cendance over perennialist ideas.[50] It in many respects comes closer to the earliest conceptions of mysticism which tied it directly to one or another set of exegetical or devotional habits; it is particularly helpful in highlighting what one might call the 'conservative'[51] potential of mysticism. Conversely, however, it is by the same token also farther from it than 20th-century perennialism in its relative wariness of attributing its objects to a transcendent or absolute reality. Neither the perennialist nor the constructivist explanatory model should be conflated with the realities they attempt to describe.

The account given here has effectively leaned more towards the constructivist interpretation in that it has privileged ʿAbd al-Qādir's own accounts of his mystical experiences – which are invariably steeped in the Qur'ān and in specific Sufi exegeses – rather than presupposing the contours of an unspeakable reality beyond. In this much, it concurs with Katz's view that '[n]o scholar can get behind the autobiographical fragment [the mystic's report of his or her experience] to the putative "pure experience"... the *only* evidence one has to call upon to support one's analysis, and hence one's description of this relationship, is the given recording of the mystic.'[52] This is the case, at least, in so far as it accords with Vincent Cornell's observation that 'we must assume that our informants tell us the truth as they see it'[53] – rather than making the hermeneutically unjustified claim that our own (potentially mystical in one sense or another) experiences have no bearing whatsoever on our reception of the mystic's report.

In contradistinction to this approach, we have seen that the bulk of writing on ʿAbd al-Qādir's spirituality has typically presumed it to be an independent element in an uneasy balance with his allegedly fungible 'exoteric' commitments. Where this study has focused more upon the slow enculturation of *formation* or *Bildung*, past accounts have preferred the drama of *initiation*. Both differences result from the distinction between our own constructivist bent and those studies' Guénonian 'Traditionalism'. We have attempted throughout to show that the former approach is less problematically applied to ʿAbd al-Qādir's life and writings. This need not constitute a rejection of the perennialist ideal. It is simply a

contextual consciousness.' Against the strength of Katz' constructivism, of course, one might argue that the ideal nature of 'reconditioned' consciousness is wholly or partly constitutive of a perennial truth.

49 E.g. Katz et al., 1978, pp. 1, 8, 22–74, 75, 96.

50 'The social constructivist position of Steven Katz has now become the mainstream philosophical position within the study of mysticism.' King, 2008, p. 169.

51 Katz (et al.), 1984, pp. 3–60.

52 Katz et al., 1984, p. 5.

53 Cornell, 1998, p. xlii.

recognition that, unlike René Guénon, whose shadow has been shown to fall across most western writing on ʿAbd al-Qādir's Sufism, ʿAbd al-Qādir himself did not argue for it. Nor is it the intention here to endorse a strictly constructivist account. Though we have consistently highlighted the constitutive significance of cultural and intellectual, the choice between Katz and Guénon is a false dilemma; 'rejecting Katz's version of constructivism does not force one into a perennialist position.'[54]

Understanding ʿAbd al-Qādir's 'mysticism' as embedded in and relevant to its wider religious, social, and political contexts does not only have the advantage of cohering rather than conflicting with his own repeated insistence that this is the case (see Chapters Four and Five). It also avoids the 'cliché that Sufism is *ab initio* in opposition to the Law'[55] rather than its 'necessary completion, as the interpretation of the law *ab intra*'.[56] It avoids the 'opinion of some scholars that since the object of mysticism is mystical, it is acceptable to mystify it… [presuming it to be] incapable of rational explanation.'[57] Sufism certainly contains unexplainable elements – as does all human experience, sacred or secular. The philosophical problems of *qualia* do not afflict mysticism alone; atheists are often artists, even logical positivists fall in love, and not all poetry is psalmic. Yet the *Kitāb al-Mawāqif* is nothing other than ʿAbd al-Qādir's lengthy and elaborate attempt at explaining himself, while his idol, Muhyī al-Dīn Ibn al-ʿArabī, was himself a quite exceptionally prolific and creative author. Those writings do not take the place of experience, nor exhaust it, but they do inform it, and most certainly permit discussion of it. This is very much their purpose.

A contextualised perspective argued for throughout this monograph, moreover, also permits a greater accessibility of ʿAbd al-Qādir's religio-political thinking to the secular toolset of the social sciences out of which the present study ultimately arises:

> 'A genealogy of "the mystical"… demonstrate[s] that a category that is often conceived to be pre-eminently 'otherworldly', private and apolitical is in fact implicated in a network of power relations in the contexts in which it has been employed… The very fact that 'the mystical' is seen as irrelevant to issues of social justice and political authority itself reflects contemporary, secularised notions of and attitudes toward power. The separation of the mystical from the political is itself a political decision.'[58]

54 King, 2008, p. 183.
55 Radtke, 1992, p.78; Also Radtke, 1994, p. 53
56 Radtke, 1994, p. 53. Also Radtke, 1992, pp. 77–8
57 Radtke, 1992, p. 71.
58 King, 2008, pp. 2, 10.

The converse attempt to relate Sufism to political issues, however,

> 'is not to reduce Sufism, a primarily spiritual venture, to a political phenomenon, nor to suggest a univocal Sufi approach to politics, but [rather] to draw attention to [the fact that] Sufism has been involved in all that we think of as politics: conceptions of authority and power, legitimacy, and contestation of rule, formation of the socio-moral order of a community or nation, competition for patronage, prestige, and control of a society's wealth, the mobilisation of people and resources in support or against the status quo, and so on.'[59]

It was not by religious studies *per se*, but by a specific school of thought within comparative religion that ʿAbd al-Qādir's mysticism has been artificially de-politicised. It was not only a failure to link it to his political life, but a fundamental presumption that the two were essentially discrete which has demanded a 'Road to Damascus' conversion myth to account for the presumed transition from one occupation to the other. Similarly, the tendency in some recent political histories of ʿAbd al-Qādir's Algerian career to substitute form for content by attributing rational-choice logic to political analyses of ʿAbd al-Qādir's own intentions and psychology is not an inevitable result of his study by secular methods. It is one approach among many, and has certainly been questioned and problematised within the academy:

> '...attempts by social scientists at rendering such [religo-political] discourses as instances of local leaders manipulating religious symbols to legitimise their social power should be viewed sceptically. This is not simply because "manipulation" carries a strong sense of cynical motivation, even in cases where evidence for such imputation is not forthcoming, but more broadly because it introduces the notion of a deliberative, rationalistic stance into descriptions of relationships where that notion is not appropriate. For the same reason, the metaphor of 'negotiation' – with its overtones of calculation – seems to me equally suspect. Although these familiar metaphors are central to market transactions everywhere and to politics in liberal societies, this fact does not make them suited to explicating every kind of practice in all societies.'[60]

Yet 'power' can be rhetorical, situational, and spiritual. It can be informal as well as formal. It can be co-operative and consensual as well as coercive. It can be constitutive of reality as well as masterful over given facts. All of this is now widely recognised in the social sciences, and does not present any insuperable

59 Heck et al., 2007, pp. 1–2.
60 Asad, 1993, pp. 210–211.

obstacles to the study of ʿAbd al-Qādir or others like him.[61] 'Capital' may be cultural, symbolic, and social as well as material.[62] Economics is not necessarily to be treated as distinct from culture, nor are material interests often exclusively material.[63] Contemporary social science is quite capable of dealing with such realities. Bearing this in mind should obviate the need to continue disputes as to whether ʿAbd al-Qādir was 'a religious or a political figure'. Recognising the subjective truth and social effectiveness of our subjects' accounts – in this instance those of ʿAbd al-Qādir evidenced through texts such as his *Risālah on Hijrah* or *Kitāb al-Mawāqif* – permits us to integrate them more productively even within our secular models. More recently-developed toolsets of sociology, anthropology, and political theory have much to offer the analysis of ʿAbd al-Qādir's place in history which past attempts have been shown to lack.

Similarly, rather than mystifying the role of religion in ʿAbd al-Qādir's politics through its hyper-secular relegation, its pious transcendence, or its opaque reification as inscrutable 'charisma',[64] 'the process of constituting Sufi identities could be described [for instance], following Michel Foucault and Norbert Elias, as a mechanism of "subjectification", for it aims to produce social actors whose discourses and practices are framed and disciplined by an internalised normative framework.'[65] Such a view would furthermore harmonise with the findings of Vincent Cornell's quantitative studies of hagiographic literatures with respect to the pre-eminent '*sine qua non*' status of orthopraxy in the lives of North African saints.[66] It also points to ʿAbd al-Qādir's culture's discursive political production – chiefly the law and jurisprudence, but also folk moralities and popular beliefs – as fertile ground for political analysis. The ideas people offer to explain, order, and experience their world are a worth the attention of anyone who wishes to understand those people's actions. This seems as true of Sufis as of everyone else.

---

61 All of these 'general perceptions' of power are enumerated for example by Haugaard [2002, p. 4], as well as being central to political writers from Antonio Gramsci [2005] to Joseph Nye [2004].

62 These terms, particularly 'social capital', have become common currency in past two decades' Sociology, from Bourdieu [1986] to Putnam [2000] to Halpern [2005].

63 E.g. Bourdieu, 2005; Gudeman, 1986, *passim*.

64 Christelow, 1980, p. 139.

65 Heck et al., 2007, p. 125. The term subjectification broadly refers to the processes by which a person's subjectivity, their experience of themselves as an individual subject with particular characteristics, capabilities, wants, and needs, is constructed and constrained by their socio-cultural context.

66 This factor has been found to far outnumber indigenous references to miracles, let alone mystically altered states of consciousness (*aḥwāl*) – Cornell, 1998, pp. 110–112.

Such approaches within and between the disciplines relevant to this study permit us to relate ostensibly religious and political facets of ʿAbd al-Qādir's thought and actions without resorting either to mystifying factors such as tautological 'charisma', exclusive materialism, or unsubstantiated attempts to reimagine practical questions as spiritual expressions.[67] They permit us to recognise and contextualise the conservative as well as the radical possibilities of (Sufi) cultures such as that which raised ʿAbd al-Qādir to political prominence. They do this on a basis which makes political considerations of context more, not less significant, and does so without ignoring the content of ideas. The pragmatic, holistic, and integrative approach argued for here permits us to recognise historically common occurrences such as the actions of the Sufi ʿAbd al-Qādir (or his father, or his contemporary Shamyl, or Usman dan Fodio, or great numbers of other Sufi leaders and *mujāhids* past and present) in connection with certain circumstances necessary for the political expression of dynamics already predisposed by a given Sufi orientation and its ideological situation. This is not essentially as a matter of 'politics coming to find Sufism'.[68] It does not require the *deus ex machina* intervention of a 'Road to Damascus' conversion to bridge the relatively routine tensions that such action involves.

Similarly, deeper political analysis can be applied to the recognition of certain Sufis' – such as ʿAbd al-Qādir's – commitment not only to Islamic virtue but also to Islamic law: another dichotomy which comes easier to the modern secular reader than it would have done to ʿAbd al-Qādir himself. We have underlined the necessity for political historians to engage with the political content of Islamic law and jurisprudential theory. This project is far from exhausted by the chapter above on ʿAbd al-Qādir's legal thinking, nor by our later reflection on its place in his metaphysical thought. The current impasse is not an insurmountable one, as we are reassured by broader movements in the academy to recognise and theorise the power of ideas as constitutive of personal and political realities.

The 'Road to Damascus' narrative is not convincing in the light of the evidence. But the increasing divergence in approaches to ʿAbd al-Qādir in the secondary literatures is not unavoidable; it can be overcome, both by critically in-

---

67 The most egregious example comes in the work of Étienne, who attempts to prove that the fairly conventional layout of ʿAbd al-Qādir's Algerian encampment (highest ranks at the well-defended centre, emanating out to the least loyal and most expendable) is not the product of obvious martial concerns, but *rather* an expression of sacred cosmic geometry [Étienne, 2003, pp. 196, 280, 312, 314].

68 This phrase is borrowed from Clancy-Smith (1994, p. 5), but the idea of essentially apolitical Sufism being artificially politicised 'from without' has been shown to run throughout the secondary literatures on ʿAbd al-Qādir throughout this book.

tegrative projects and through the internal resources of the disciplines out of which it has grown. But the single greatest step which can be taken in producing an integrative account of his life and thought consists in abandoning the artificial and Eurocentric myth of ʿAbd al-Qādir's 'Road to Damascus conversion'. No other factor so strongly militates against progress in integrating our various partial readings of the man and his ideas. No other idea more perpetuates the colonial power imbalance between ʿAbd al-Qādir's world and that of France.

A way forward has been suggested here. It is one which allows us to appreciate the seriousness and depth of his commitments to his and to other faiths, to their respective adherents, and to his God. It is an appreciation which urges us – in ʿAbd al-Qādir's words – to move 'from conception to conception before we see the reality of a thing',[69] as 'our understanding will not be complete until we recognise that it has many faces.'[70]

69 *Dhikrā*, p. 38.
70 *Mawāqif*, p. 26.

Afterword

Another Road to Damascus has had the good fortune and great honour to be awarded the British Association of Islamic Studies' De Gruyter Prize in the Study of Islam and the Muslim World. Quite rightly, I have been asked to offer some reflection on the relevance of the book to the times in which we live today. I cannot but agree that the discussion of ʿAbd al-Qādir rewards study in the present. I would scarcely have undertaken this work had I thought otherwise. It is less obvious, however, which lessons to emphasise for a readership already well-equipped to reach their own conclusions. Nevertheless, and without exaggerated claims to finality or authority, I shall suggest some potential connections between this 19th-century subject and our 21st-century situation. These suggestions will be by turns political, interpretive, and moral, and will cover (I hope) a sufficient range to offer the reader some inspiration for exploration, reflection, and discussion.

Though they are far from the least contentious, we might begin with the most materially manifest comparisons: the search for broad political parallels. The argument has been made throughout this text that what might be termed the more political aspects of ʿAbd al-Qādir's worldview expressed themselves most clearly during periods of widespread instability. Anarchy gave birth to his power, as Alexis de Tocqueville remarked. It was during power-vacuums in Algeria and Syria that we find him the most assertive; during periods of relative stability the misleading image of the quietist seems at its most persuasive. When established institutions and power structures were collapsing, moreover, it was to the laws and morals of his Islamic tradition that he turned. In spite of attempts by Western scholars and politicians to claim ʿAbd al-Qādir as a proponent of European universalisms that were in reality culturally and chronologically distant from him, the account he consistently gave of himself remains more parsimonious. The historian's periodisation may place him in the modern era, but his goal was never to re-shape reality in a new mould (nor indeed to understand time and temporality as our historian might). When seeking safety in a sundered world, he reached for what was familiar, time-tested, and reassuring. In his reality, there was nothing so much so as the Holy Qur'an: the Qur'an interpreted, implemented, and internalised by the Sunni, Mālikī, and Qādirī traditions in which he had been raised. The same can evidently be said of a great many of his contemporaries.

It is only natural that, faced with darkest night, people reach for what seems to them the brightest light. It is a matter of sociological fact that the sorts of symbols, ideals, and inclinations we are used to describing as religious have historically filled such a role for the greatest part of humanity. In fact, this observation

DOI 10.1515/9783110499513-009

verges on the tautological. One need not be religious to see why a pious person might aver that 'There are no atheists in a foxhole.' Beyond observing the salience and propinquity of religious ideals in an overwhelmingly religious society, one can in this case say more. As well as embodying what 'Abd al-Qādir understood to be the highest possible ideals, the religious tradition in which he was raised carried within it codified memories of broadly similar events to those which faced him. When he recalls the events of the *Reconquista*, he sees them not only as symbolic but also in terms of their role in the developing history of Islamic thought. The medieval conquest of Muslim states in Iberia by increasingly intolerant Christian kingdoms gave rise not only to movements of population, but to a body of jurisprudence. It occasioned not only metaphors and memories, but also a wide range of practical policy proposals upon which he drew – whether or not 'Abd al-Qādir was himself their ideal interpreter. One might certainly object to this that the political character of imperial France was very different from the tenor of mind of those mediaeval monarchs who drove Jews and Muslims from their lands and launched Inquisitions to erase their vestigial influence. A modern historian advising 'Abd al-Qādir might have warned him that he was indulging in anachronism. But one must recognise how attractive this course was to a man in his position, and how implausible or inaccessible most alternatives. One cannot reasonably deny that it was in point of fact attractive: we have our subject's testimony to that fact, and have no hope of understanding him without giving his testimony credence.

In considering these 19th-century events, the reader might be tempted to make a much shorter temporal leap from 'Abd al-Qādir's time to the present – a scant third of the span which separated the French invasion of Algeria from the surrender of Granada's last Nasrid emir. Such a leap might attract those sensitive to the influence of Sufi orders in Muslim public life, not least that of the Naqshbandiyyah-Khālediyyah from Turkey through Central Asia – one of the *turuq*, indeed, with which 'Abd al-Qādir was himself affiliated. It might do so whether or not one gives credence to the notion of a 'Neo-Sufism' arising in his day. One might be moved by 'Abd al-Qādir's persistent symbolic importance to a range of contemporary movements, Sufi and otherwise, or by contact with younger men who would after his death go on to play a role in the development of the *salafī* movements so salient today. One might, in short, feel moved to see in his experience parallels with contemporary politics in the Muslim world in general and the Arab world in particular. This appeals most particularly to cases in which beleaguered populations are rallied under the banner of the faith and the discipline of divine law.

It has since the 1970s become commonplace to see the apparent revival of religion in regional politics, sometimes described as Islamism, in such a vein – perhaps partly influenced by a Marxian tendency to see faith as a palliative 'sigh of the oppressed'. The predominantly Muslim populations of the Middle East and North Africa have certainly suffered more than have inhabitants of many other regions: more war, more poverty, more suspicion, more humiliation, more despair. The Muslim Brotherhood's slogan 'Islam is the Solution' [*al-islām huwwa al-ḥall*] can only be meaningful if one presumes a problem to be solved. The regionally dominant secular ideologies of ethnic nationalism, consumer capitalism, and authoritarian socialism have experienced many setbacks, even while their 'over-stated' institutions (to borrow Nazih Ayubi's marvellously polysemic phrase) stolidly resisted change. The space between the promise of prosperous dignity and the reality of degraded disillusionment leaves a void: not only in bare cupboards and barren life-prospects but in the imagination. It afflicts not only the poor, but also the affluent. Yet nature abhors a vacuum as an empty stage calls for actors. A thousand years' pious practice and tradition, however developed or degenerated, leave a script already part-written.

Assertions that 'The Qur'an is our Constitution' [*al-qur'ān dustūrnā*] certainly owe much of their popularity to perceived failures of secular formations to deliver the goods they have promised. That same assertion characteristically combines ostensibly religious and secular lexis: holy scripture juxtaposed with the *Grundgesetz* of the Napoleonic Code. The very words of the phrase tell a story of disenchantment and reaction to Eurocentric modernity not all of its utterers may intend, and the subject of this monograph could not have predicted. They are evidence that the resurgence of religion disguises the fact that religion never really went away. Rather, it lived, developed, and changed along with the rest of the culture in which it was embedded. As a result, today's activist Muslims may read the same scripture as ʿAbd al-Qādir and may want to give it the same central role, but each read it in their own way. Josef van Ess once remarked to me that 'Every exegesis is also an eisegesis;' we read *into* texts when we read *from* them. Our own nature is reflected in our interpretations. It is a very different question whether one considers this to be the result of a Gadamerian hermeneutic process, say, or the particular pre-dispositions [*istiʿdād*] of readers' eternal archetypes [*ʿayān thābitah*] to receive knowledge. The fact remains: the imaginations of ʿAbd al-Qādir and the inhabitants of the 21st century flower from different soils, and their differences should not be under-stated. Yet the 'constitutional' slogan's subtext, with its desire for authentic order in the midst of (perceived) hypocrisy and chaos, would have been very familiar to him nonetheless.

Such reflections seem most salient in the catastrophic circumstances of contemporary Iraq and Syria. Warfare and destruction have opened up the most yawning gulfs between the promise of order and the reality of its absence. The so-called Islamic State in Iraq and the Levant is but one of the many armed factions currently active under the banner of faith; groups like *Jabhat al-Nuṣrah*, *Aḥrār al-Shām al-Islamiyyah*, and the members of *Jaysh al-Fataḥ* may wear their claims to religiosity on their sleeves, but religion is not alien even to the formally secular forces arrayed against them. The protean potential of a flexible discourse marshalling symbols ranging from the domestic to the cosmic cannot be understated. This is true even if (like Wael Hallaq) one sees many of the institutions they once sustained as irretrievably consigned to the past and inherently incompatible with the present. Some readers might even recall Karl Marx's *Eighteenth Brumaire of Louis Napoleon* bemoaning the failed revolution which took place outside ʿAbd al-Qādir's French prison walls and the 'bourgeois coup' which would grant him his freedom:

> 'And just when they seem engaged in revolutionising themselves and things, in creating something entirely new, precisely in such epochs of revolutionary crisis they anxiously conjure up the spirits of the past to their service and borrow from them names, battle slogans and costumes in order to present the new scene of world history in this time-honoured disguise and this borrowed language.'

When today's 'borrowers' commit atrocities in opposition both to the mainstreams of Islamic law and the practice of the Prophet's followers, we might almost agree with the essay quoted above that 'the tradition of past generations lies like a nightmare upon the mind of man.' Yet ʿAbd al-Qādir is an example of a wholly different recourse to convention, his borrowings as conscientious as theirs are contentious. Where they might echo him in raising the banner of *jihād*, in their waging of it many modern movements more strongly miror the sectarian rioters against whom he took up arms in the streets of Damascus. The same sensitivity to context which led us to question whether ʿAbd al-Qādir was really a utility-maximising *Realpolitiker* or proponent of a secularised meta-religion must also give us pause when evaluating the claims of modern 'men of action'. Ideas and institutions of recent European provenance will tend to be as natural to them as they were alien to him. He was not raised within the apparatus of a secular nation-state, whereas they generally were. He did not rebel against the notions and the demands of such a state, whereas they often do. Lessons might potentially be drawn here, too, which reflect as much upon the modernity these fighters flee as the antiquity they purportedly seek to revive.

Many readers will be inclined to trace proximal causes of the tragedies in which so many Muslim militants are embroiled to the military adventurism of western powers which devoted more energy to demolishing existing structures than to nurturing new ones. In this respect, too, one might perhaps draw parallels with the experiences of ʿAbd al-Qādir. One might certainly recall the precipitous French decision to overthrow the (undoubtedly corrupt and piratical) Regency of Algiers without any substantive view on what should take its place. Even the later sectarianism of the Levant was not unrelated to increasingly heavy-handed interventions by negligent powers. This is true whether they were pressing the Ottoman Empire to adopt new models of citizenship while undermining that same process, or whether they were globalising trade while abdicating responsibility for the upheavals globalisation caused, or they were actively invading territory by force of arms. The seemingly banal (but sadly unlearned) lesson for domestic and international policy-makers might be that destroying one system of social order without putting an alternative in place may lead to a resurgence and re-imagining of older social forms, symbols, and ideals. Whether the result is constructive or destructive can no more be predicted than can the degree of creativity that participants bring to it.

One might, conversely, recall the observation that ʿAbd al-Qādir's soft, cultural and potential power only crystallised into forceful action once the power-vacuum around him neared completeness. The same conservative moral and cultural frameworks that informed and empowered him also constrained him, inclining him to acquiesce to the authority of weak or questionable powers where possible. Readers inclined to draw speculative parallels with contemporary events may find this more heartening, a sign that when sufficiently flexible, vital, and legitimate social institutions exist, those who follow a similar path to his may be expected to favour co-operation. Their secular critics warn that these stories are far from over, and the worst may still lie ahead. Yet the fact that so many writers have seen in ʿAbd al-Qādir's subtle and sophisticated Sufism an exemplar of the liberal virtues of pluralism and tolerance might be a reminder to these critics that religion may not be their servant, but neither need it be their nemesis.

Readers less inclined to make such speculative leaps might nonetheless take something of value from *Another Road to Damascus* in more methodological terms. The text itself, not least its concluding chapter, speaks explicitly on such a level. It repeatedly identifies and questions cultural and disciplinary chauvinisms. It opposes the Eurocentrism of reducing our understanding of 19th-century Muslims such as ʿAbd al-Qādir to what R.S. O'Fahey describes as an axis of 'accommodation vs. rejection of the West' (a precursor, perhaps, of the binary Mahmood Mamdani calls 'Good Muslim/Bad Muslim'). It rejects both patriarchal Victorian Great Man historiography and the dehumanising excesses of 20th-century structuralisms; it does not seek to find a single social phenomenon, whether personal or societal, to which all others can be reduced. It opposes what Talal Asad calls the 'sociologism' of uncritically privileging scholarly models over the self-representation of our subjects. It problematises both Guénonian Traditionalism's devaluation of aspects of religion which diverge from its essentialist *Perennial Philosophy*, and also a countervailing constructivist reluctance to take our subjects' claims of transcendence seriously. It tries not to take philosophical questions for granted, nor to brush them aside; it tries to match the ambition of its ends with humility in its means. It tries to explain without explaining away. Through the resultant discussions, moreover, it suggests developments within and across disciplines which have been employed to tackle similar interpretive challenges. Each of these conversations may, *mutatis mutandis*, be relevant to debates in the present day. Beyond the specific interpretive issues involved in the task of understanding ʿAbd al-Qādir's life, however, we might offer some still broader reflection.

The text's willingness to draw from multiple sources and perspectives is part of an attack both on interpretive exclusivism and on its concomitant presumptions of total incommensurability between fields of knowledge. It embodies a scepticism about claims that one description can explain everything in our lives, that is – be it as a reflection of the world or the content of our consciousness. It consequently entails a wariness of assertions that such necessarily limited aspects of our world can only exist as microcosms, as little universes isolated unto themselves. We can discuss reality without exhausting it, speak without presuming absolute knowledge – though this fact has troubled some even before Meno debated with Socrates whether one can ever ask a question without already knowing the answer. Our representations need not strive for the 1:1 scale seen in the satirical nation-scale maps imagined in Jorge Louis Borges' *On Exactitude in Science*. And while we must see that the differences between terms we might use to measure a person's height and the depths of their longing are not interchangeable in and of themselves, we must recognise that neither exist in an ideational or material vacuum. Our focused methodologies may try to ignore the world around their targeted problem, but that world does not go away when we are not looking at it. Recognising the limits of our perceptions reveals the hopeful reality that all are enfolded by something greater – whether one understands this in theological or psychological, naturalistic or hermeneutic terms. Only an unlimited field would necessarily preclude contact with any other; only the utterly exhaustive can be truly exclusive. It is the very fact that our descriptions of the world are not universes in themselves that holds out the possibility of bringing them into contact.

In short, this book is an exercise in interdisciplinarity. It surely exhibits many of the shortfalls of such an approach, certainly apparent to sundry of its readers. It cannot equal in any of its multiple disciplinary facets the best of the genera on which it draws. But then it would be quite unreasonable to expect it to do so. The contrary expectation would represent an insult to those scholars who quite properly conduct their research within the bounds of what Thomas

Kuhn called normal science. One interdisciplinary scholar is not the match of two who work within a settled paradigm, and it would be absurd to suggest otherwise. In the end, to undertake such a project as this is to make peace with the reality that one will misunderstand and one will err; it is to make a start on an unfinished work. Nonetheless, it is my hope that this book demonstrates some of the virtues of interdisciplinarity as well as its difficulties.

The contributions such an approach offers to learning are not purely quantitative, not just a stacking up of ostensibly true statements against false ones. There is a particular quality to work across disciplines which by its nature cannot be reached at by any other means. By bringing disparate discussions into dialogue it begins to expose characteristics and consequences of each that would otherwise have been occluded. I often recall a phrase heard during my youth on the west coast of Ireland: *Is maith an scáthán súil charad.* 'A friend's eye is a fine mirror;' it's through one another that we know ourselves. The subject of this book himself might have recognised in this sentiment an echo of the Quranic notion that God divided humanity (into male and female, peoples and tribes) 'so that you might know each other' [*li-taʿarrafū*, Qur'ān 49:13]. Whether one agrees with the view that this fact reflects the dynamics of divine self-disclosure, whether one sees it as a fact of more anthropological significance, or whether like Giambattista Vico one sees in it the workings of principles of poetry governing all expression… is another question entirely. The fact remains, however we make sense of it.

We – and especially those of us who spend much of our lives focused on the world of ideas – can be tempted to see philosophical coherence as a prerequisite for collective action, for living together peaceably. If the many admirable aspects of ʿAbd al-Qādir's life can teach us anything, it is surely that this need not be the case. *Another Road to Damascus* has certainly resisted attempts by earlier writers to include him in the embrace of one totalising ideology or another (whether religious or secular, cynical or utopian). But it has done so without wishing to denigrate all that such ideologies might justify. Proponents of humanistic ideals are in a sense as justified in counting ʿAbd al-Qādir as their comrade as he might be in seeing God's hand at work in their good deeds – though each necessarily entails elevating the perspective they hold over that of the other. Much of *Another Road to Damascus* has been concerned with drawing such moments of elevation (or projection) to the reader's attention. A major role of scholarly monographs is to offer such reminders, and it is my hope that I have succeed in doing so adequately. But that at least up to a point we do indeed understand each other, with all our differences and our misconstructions, is a fact with not only epistemological but moral significance.

It is appropriate in an afterword to reflect broadly upon the project in question. In the most general terms, both this book and its post-script might be understood as questioning the practice of presenting ʿAbd al-Qādir as a 'bridge between civilisations'. They might even be read as an attack on such perspectives – though I would not commend a conclusion that dispensed so finally with the recognition of diversity just applauded. Certainly, the text has been at pains to recognise difference as well as similarity. But the fact that ʿAbd al-Qādir could so often act in apparent conformity with others' ideals he did not himself conceive or articulate only underlines his extraordinary fitness for the role which has fallen to him. A bridge, after all, separates as much as it unites; a bridge which spans no gulf is no bridge at all. It is only by virtue of his distance from his modern admirers that his story can reach out to them. To deny division, on the other hand, precludes unification. Insistence on an identity of views forestalls meaningful dialogue, while having an answer for everything will condemn us to ignorance.

We are left with the question of what might substantively remain to us, after all this is said. Perhaps these reflections don't leave us committed to a Rawlsian search for overlapping consensus, but still less do they support a disregard of the justifications we offer to one another. Intention is part of action, after all. The youthful ʿAbd al-Qādir, memorising the *ḥadīth* collection of al-Bukhārī in his father's *zāwiyah*, knew the Prophet himself to have said as much. But intention encompasses a range of realities, from the discursive traditions which are apt subjects for scholarly monographs to dispositions of the heart which are not. Since we have employed the Damascene Conversion as a literary *Leitmotiv* throughout this text, it may not be entirely inappropriate to offer a last word to the most celebrated of the Pauline epistles. 'Where there are tongues, they will be stilled; where there is knowledge, it will pass away... And now these three remain: faith, hope, and love. But the greatest of these is love.'

Bibliography – Archival Sources

Archives Nationales d'Outre Mer (ANOM), Aix-en-Provence, France

French military and diplomatic correspondence of the Department of Algerian Affairs:

FR ANOM F80

French military and diplomatic correspondence of the General Government of Algeria (including 'Abd al-Qādir's correspondence seized by the French army and the correspondence of 'Abd al-Qādir and his handlers in France):

FR ANOM GGA1E113; FR ANOM GGA1E116; FR ANOM GGA1E117; FR ANOM GGA1E211; FR ANOM GGA1E215; FR ANOM GGA1E217; FR ANOM GGA1E218; FR ANOM GGA1E219; FR ANOM GGA1E235

British National Archives, Kew, London, U.K.

Correspondence of British Foreign Office staff in the Maghreb and Gibraltar:

FO 3/38; FO 3/40; FO 3/42; FO 3/43; FO 3/44; FO 3/45; FO 3/46; FO 3/47; FO 3/48; FO 3/50; FO 52/40; FO 52/41; FO 99/5; FO 99/6; FO 99/7, FO 99/9; FO 99/11; FO 102/7; FO 174/38

Correspondence of British diplomatic staff in Istanbul:

FO 78/928; FO 78/3081; FO 195/381; FO 195/385; FO 195/479; FO 195/519; FO 196/19; FO 146/445

Correspondence of British diplomatic staff in Jerusalem:

FO 78/1217

Correspondence of British diplomatic staff in Damascus:

FO 78/1118; FO 78/1520; FO 195/976; FO 226/131

DOI 10.1515/9783110499513-010

Centre des Archives Diplomatiques de La Courneuve, Paris, France

Correspondence of French Ministry of Foreign Affairs staff in Morocco:

Correspondance Politique/Maroc/4; Correspondance Politique/Maroc/5; Correspondance Politique/Maroc/6; Correspondance Politique/Maroc/7; Correspondance Politique/Maroc/8; Correspondance Politique/Maroc/9; Correspondance Politique/Maroc/10; Correspondance Politique/Maroc/11; Correspondance Politique/Maroc/12; Correspondance Politique/Maroc/13; Correspondance Politique/Maroc/14; Correspondance Politique/Maroc/15; Correspondance Politique/Maroc/16; Correspondance Politique/Maroc/17; Correspondance Politique/Maroc/18; Correspondance Politique/Maroc/19

Correspondence of French diplomatic staff in Portugal:

Correspondance Politique/Portugal/163

Correspondence of French diplomatic staff in Britain:

Correspondance Politique/Angleterre/659

Correspondence of French military and diplomatic staff in Istanbul:

Correspondance Politique/Turquie/305; Correspondance Politique/Turquie/309; Correspondance Politique/Turquie/310; Correspondance Politique/Turquie/311; Correspondance Politique/Turquie/315

Correspondence of French diplomatic staff in Bursa:

Correspondance Politique des Consuls/Turquie/Brousse/1

Centre des Archives Diplomatiques de Nantes (CADN), Nantes, France

Correspondence of the French consulate in Damascus:

Damas/Consulat/8; Damas/Consulat/9; Damas/Consulat/10; Damas/Consulat/11; Damas/Consulat/12; Damas/Consulat/13; Damas/Consulat/14; Damas/Consulat/15; Damas/Consulat/16; Damas/Consulat/17; Damas/Consulat/18; Damas/Consulat/19; Damas/Consulat/21; Damas/Consulat/22; Damas/Consulat/23; Damas/Consulat/24; Damas/Consulat/26; Damas/Consulat/27; Damas/Consulat/28; Damas/Consulat/32;

Damas/Consulat/33; Damas/Consulat/34; Damas/Consulat/35; Damas/Consulat/37; Damas/Consulat/40; Damas/Consulat/65; Damas/Consulat/66; Damas/Consulat/68; Damas/Consulat/69

Correspondence of the French embassy in Istanbul:
Constantinople/Ambassade/C/247

Durham County Records Office, Durham, U.K.

Private correspondence of the Marquess of (later Lord) Londonderry:
D/Lo/C 74; D/Lo/C 137; D/Lo/C 458

Haus-, Hof- und Staatsarchiv, Vienna, Austria

Political correspondence of the Austrian consulate in Beirut:
VII/2; Beirut Konsulararchiven/Politische Korrespondenzen/Karton 1

General correspondence of the Austrian embassy in Istanbul:
PA XIII; Botschaft Konstantinopel/Karton 32

United States National Archives, College Park, Maryland, U.S.A.

Correspondence of American State Department staff in the Maghreb and Gibraltar
A2 Cab. 14/8; A2 Cab. 38/8

Correspondence of American diplomatic staff in Beirut and Damascus:
A2 Cab. 40/9

Texts by ʿAbd al-Qādir al-Jazāʾirī

Chodkiewicz, Michel, 1982. *Emir Abd el-Kader: Écrits Spirituels.* Paris: Éditions du Seuil

Chodkiewicz, Michel, 1995. *The Spiritual Writings of Amir 'Abd al-Kader.* Albany: SUNY
Gilis, Charles-André, 1996. *Émir Abd al-Qâdir l'Algérien: Poèmes Métaphysiques.* Beirut: Dar Al-Bouraq.
al-Jazā'irī, 'Abd al-Qādir (trans. Benmansour, Hacène.), 1995. *Autobiographie, écrite en prison (France) en 1849.* Paris: Dialogues
al-Jazā'irī, 'Abd al-Qādir; Haqqī, Mamdūḥ (ed.), 1966. *Dhikrā' al-'Āqil wa tanbīh al-ghāfil.* Beirut: Dār al-Yaqẓah al-'Arabiyyah
al-Jazā'irī, 'Abd al-Qādir, 1967. *Kitāb al-Mawāqif fī al-taṣawwuf wa al-wa'z wa al-irshād.* Beirut: Dār al-Yaqẓah al-'Arabīah [3 volumes; vol. 1 1966]
Al-Jazā'irī, 'Abd al-Qadir ibn Muḥyī al-Dīn, 1973. *Al-Miqrāḍ al-Ḥādd li-qaṭ' lisān muntaqis dīn al-islām bil-bāṭil wa al-ilhād.* Beirut: Dar Maktabāt al-Ḥayāt
al-Jazā'irī, 'Abd al-Qādir (al-Bannānī, Muḥammad al-Ṣaghīr; Samātī, Maḥfuẓ; and Aljūn, Muḥammad al-Ṣāliḥ, eds.), 2007. *Mudhakkarāt al-amīr 'abd al-qādir: sīrah dhātiyyah kutiba fī al-sijn sannah 1849.* Algiers: Dār al-Ummah
al-Jazā'irī, 'Abd al-Qādir (trans. Patroni, Fernand; ed. Benachenhou, Yacine), 2009. *Règlements et Codes Militaires de l'Armée Musulmane [Wishāḥ al-Katā'ib wa Zīnah al-'Askar al-Muḥammadī al-Ghālib].* Algiers: Éditions Alpha
Lagarde, Michel, 2000, 2001, 2003. *Le Livre Des Haltes (Kitâb al-Mawâqif).* Leiden: Brill [3 volumes]
Penot, Abdallah, 2008. *Le Livre Des Haltes.* Paris: Éditions Dervy
Sfeir, Antoine (ed.), 2011. *Abd el-Kader: Lettre aux Français.* Paris: Libella
Note: several other texts in the literature contain reproductions (original and in translation) from 'Abd al-Qādir's writing – most especially:
al-Jazā'irī, Muḥammad bin 'Abd al-Qādir; Ḥaqqī, Mandūḥ (ed.), 1964. *Tuḥfat al-Zā'ir fī tarīkh al-jazā'ir wa al-amīr 'abd al-qādir.* Beirut: Dār al-Yaqẓah al-'Arabiyyah

Additional Primary Sources

Al-Bayṭār, 'Abd al-Razzāq, 1963. *Ḥilyat al-bashar fī ta'rīkh al-qarn al-thālith 'ashar.* Damascus: Majma' al-Lughah al-'Arabiyyah
Azan, Paul, 1925. *L'Émir Abd el Kader, 1808–1883, du fanatisme musulman au patriotisme français. Paris: Hachette*
Bellemare, Alexandre, 1863. *Abd-el-Kader: sa vie politique et militaire.* Paris: Hachette
Berndt, Johann Carl, 1840. *Abdelkader – oder, Drei jahre eines Deutschen unter den Mauren.* Berlin: Nicolai
Churchill, Charles Henry, 1867. *The Life of Abdel Kader – ex-sultan of the Arabs of Algeria.* London: Chapman and Hall
Daumas, Eugène, 1858. *Les Chevaux du Sahara et les mœurs du désert.* Paris: Lévy
Dupuch, Monseigneur Antoine-Adolphe, 2004. *Abd-el-Kader au Chateau D'Amboise.* Paris: Ibis Press
al-Jazā'irī, Muḥammad bin 'Abd al-Qādir; Ḥaqqī, Mamdūḥ (ed.), 1964. *Tuḥfat al-Zā'ir fī tarīkh al-jazā'ir wa al-amīr 'abd al-qādir.* Beirut: Dār al-Yaqẓah al-'Arabiyyah
al-Murābiṭ, Jawād, 1966. *Al-Taṣawwuf wa al-Amīr 'Abd al-Qādir al-Ḥasanī al-Jazā'irī.* Damascus: Dār al-Yaqẓah al-'Arabiyyah
Roches, Léon, 1904. *Dix Ans à Travers l'Islam.* Paris: Perrin

Scott, Colonel, 2010. *A Journal of a Residence in the Esmailla of Abd-el-Kader and of Travels in Morocco and Algiers.* Memphis: General Books
Tocqueville, Alexis de, (Pitts, Jennifer *trans.*), 2001. *Writings on Empire and Slavery.* Baltimore: Johns Hopkins University Press

Secondary Sources

Abd-Allah, Umar F., 2008. "Theological dimensions of Islamic law" in Tim Winter (ed.), *The Cambridge Companion to Classical Islamic Theology.* Cambridge: CUP, pp. 237–257
Abdel-Jaouad, Hedi, 1999. "The Sands of Rhyme", *Research in African Literatures* – Volume 30, Number 3, Fall 1999, pp. 194–206
ʿAbd al-Karīm, Muḥammad bin, 1981. *Ḥukm al-hijrah min khilāl thalāth rasā'il jazā'iriyyah.* Algiers: al-Sharikah al-Waṭaniyyah lil-Nashr wa al-Tawzīʿ
Abou El Fadl, Khaled, 1994. "Islamic Law and Muslim Minorities: The Juristic Discourse on Muslim Minorities from the Second/Eighth to the Eleventh/Seventeenth Centuries." *Islamic Law and Society,* Vol. 1, No. 2, 1994, pp. 141–187
Abrahamov, Binjamin, 1998. *Islamic Theology: Traditionalism and Rationalism.* Edinburgh; Edinburgh University Press.
Abun-Nasr, Jamil, 2007. *Muslim Communities of Grace.* London: Hurst & Co.
Abun-Nasr, Jamil, 1971. *A History of the Maghrib.* Cambridge: Cambridge University Press
Achrati, Nora, 2007. 'Following the Leader: A History and Evolution of the Amir 'Abd al-Qadir al-Jazairi as Symbol', *The Journal of North African Studies,* 12:2, 2007, pp. 139–152
Addas, Claude, (Kingsley, Peter trans.) 1993. *The Quest for the Red Sulphur: the life of Ibn ʿArabī.* Cambridge: Islamic Texts Society
Akkach, Samer, 2007. *'Abd al-Ghani al-Nabulusi: Islam and the Enlightenment.* Oxford: Oneworld
Almond, Ian, 2001. 'Divine Needs, Divine Illusions: preliminary remarks toward a comparative study of Meister Eckhart and Ibn Arabi,' in *Medieval Philosophy and Theology* , vol. 10, no. 2, 2001, pp. 263–282
Almond, Ian, 2004. *Sufism and deconstruction : a comparative study of Derrida and Ibn 'Arabi.* London: Routledge
Anderson, Benedict, 1991. *Imagined Communities: Reflections on the Origin and Spread of Nationalism.* London: Verso
Aouli, Smaïl; Redjala, Ramdane; Zoummeroff, Philippe, 1994. *Abd el-Kader.* Paris: Fayard
Asad, Talal, 1993. *Genealogies of Religion: discipline and reasons of power in Christianity and Islam.* London: Johns Hopkins University Press
Asín Palacios, Miguel, 1931. *El Islam Cristianizado: estudio del "sufismo" a través de las obras de Abenarabi de Murcia.* Madrid : Editorial Plutarco
Attias, Jean-Christophe (ed.), 1998. *De la Conversion.* Paris: Cerf.
Ayubi, Nazih, 2007. *Political Islam.* Abingdon: Routledge
Ayubi, Nazih, 2001. *Over-Stating the Arab State.* London: I.B. Tauris
Bashier, Salman H., 2004. *Ibn al-ʿArabī's Barzakh: the concept of the Limit and the Relationship between God and the World.* New York: State University of New York Press
Bellemare, Alexandre, 1863. *Abd-el-Kader: sa vie politique et militaire.* Paris: Hachette

Bennison, Amira, 2011. "'Abd al-Qādir's *Jihād* in the Light of the Western Islamic *Jihād* Tradition", *Studia Islamica, nouvelle édition/new series, 2, 2011, pp. 69–90*
Bennison, Amira Katherine, 2000. "'Abd al-Qādir, Morocco and the Sharifian Model," *The Journal of Algerian Studies*, vol. 4–5, 1999/2000, pp. 1–20
Bennison, Amira Katherine, 2002. *Jihad and its Interpretation in Pre-Colonial Morocco: state-society relations during the French conquest of Algeria.* London: RoutledgeCurzon.
Bennison, Amira Katherine, 1998. "Opposition and Accommodation to French Colonialism in Early 19th Century Algeria", *Cambridge Review of International Affairs*, XI, 2, 1998, pp. 99–116
Bennison, Amira Katherine, 1997. "The 1847 Revolt of 'Abd al-Qadir and the Algerians against Mawlay 'Abd al-Rahman, Sultan of Morocco", *Maghreb Review*, 22, 1–2, 1997, pp. 109–123
Bennison, Katherine, 1996. "The Dynamics of Rule and Opposition in 19th Century Morocco", *Journal of North African Studies*, 1, 1996, pp.1–24
Bennison, Amira, 2004. "The 'New Order' and Islamic Order: the introduction of the *Nizāmī* Army in the Western Maghrib and its legitimation, 1830–1873'", *International Journal of Middle Eastern Studies* 36: 4, 2004, pp. 591–612
Berque, Jacques, 1978. *L'Intérieur du Maghreb.* Paris: Gallimard
Binder, Leonard, 1988. *Islamic Liberalism: a critique of development ideologies.* London: University of Chicago Press
Blunt, Wilfred, 1947. *Desert Hawk – Abd el Kader and the French Conquest of Algeria.* London: Methuen & Co.
Bourdieu, Pierre, 1986. "The Forms of Capital," In J. Richardson (Ed.), 1986. *Handbook of Theory and Research for the Sociology of Education.* New York: Greenwood, pp. 241–258
Bourdieu, Pierre, 2005. *The Social Structures of the Economy.* Cambridge: Polity
Bouyerdene, Ahmed, 2008. *Abd el-Kader: l'harmonie des contraires.* Paris: Éditions du Seuil
Brett, Michael, 1978. Review of *Abd al-Qadir and the Algerians: Resistance to the French and Internal Consolidation* by Raphael Danziger. *African Affairs*, Vol. 77, No. 308, (Jul., 1978), pp. 416–416. Oxford: OUP, p. 416
Brower, Benjamin, 2011. "The Amîr 'Abd Al-Qâdir and the "Good War" in Algeria, 1832–1847", *Studia Islamica*, 2, 2011, pp. 35–68
Bū Azīz, Yaḥya, 1964. *Al-Amīr 'Abd al-Qādir: rā'id al-kifāḥ al-jazā'iri.* Dār al-Kitāb al-Jazā'irī
Bū Azīz, Yaḥya, 2004. *Mawḍū'āt wa qaḍāyā min tā'rīkh al-jazā'ir wa al-'arab.* 'Ayn Malīlah: Dār al-Hudā
Burke III, Edmund, 1978. Review of *Abd al-Qadir and the Algerians: Resistance to the French and Internal Consolidation* by Raphael Danziger. *The International Journal of African Historical Studies*, Vol. 11, No. 2, 1978. Boston: Boston University African Studies Center, pp. 292–295
Burke III, Edmund, 1998. "Theorizing the histories of colonialism and nationalism in the Arab Maghrib – Beyond Colonialism and Nationalism in North Africa", *Arab Studies Quarterly*, Spring 1998, pp. 5–19
Chittick, Wiliam C., 1994. *Imaginal Worlds – Ibn al-'Arabi and the Problem of Religious Diversity.* New York: State University of New York Press
Chittick, Wiliam C., 1989. *The Sufi Path to Knowledge.* New York: SUNY
Chodkiewicz, Michel, 1993. *Ocean Without Shore.* Albany: SUNY

Chodkiweicz, Michel; Chittick, William.; Morris, James, 2002. *The Meccan Revelations – volume 1.* New York: Pir Press
Christelow, Allan, 1980. "Saintly Descent and Worldly Affairs in Mid-Nineteenth Century Mascara, Algeria." *International Journal of Middle East Studies*, vol. 12, no. 2, September 1980, pp. 139–155
Clancy-Smith, Julia A., 1997. *Rebel and Saint: Muslim notables, populist protest, colonial encounters (Algeria and Tunisia, 1800–1904).* London: University of California Press
Clayton, Vista, 1975. *The Phantom Caravan – Abd El Kader, Emir of Algeria.* New York: Exposition Press
Commins, David Dean, 1988. "'Abd al-Qādir al-Jazā'irī and Islamic reform," *The Muslim World*, no. 78, 1988, pp. 121–132
Commins, David Dean, 1990. *Islamic Reform: Politics and Social Change in Late Ottoman Damascus.* Oxford: Oxford University Press
Cook, Michael, 2002. *Commanding the Right and Forbidding the Wrong.* Cambridge: Cambridge University Press
Cornell, Vincent, 1998. *Realm of the Saint: power and authority in Moroccan Sufism.* Austin: University of Texas Press
Danziger, Raphael, 1981. "Abd al-Qadir and Abd al-Rahman: religious and political aspects of their confrontation 1843–1847", *Maghreb Review*, 6, 1–2, 1981, pp. 27–35
Danziger, Raphael, 1977. *Abd al-Qadir and the Algerians: resistance to the French and internal consolidation.* London: Holmes & Meier
Danziger, Raphael, 1974. "Abd Al-Qadir's First Overtures to the British and the Americans (1835–1836), *Revue de l'Occident musulman et de la Méditerranée*, Vol.18, No. 18, 1974, pp. 45–63
Danziger, Raphael, 1979. "Diplomatic Deception as Last Resort: Abd al-Qadir's oblique please to the French and the British, 1846–1847", *Maghreb Review*, 14, 4–5, 1979, pp. 126–128
Danziger, Raphael, 1980. "From Alliance to Belligerency: Abd al-Qadir in Morocco, 1843–1847", *The Maghreb Review*, vol. 5, 2–4, 1980, pp. 63–80
Danziger, Raphael, 1983, "The attitude of Morocco's Sultan Abd al-Rahman towards the French as reflected in his internal correspondance 1844–1847", *Revue de l'Occident musulman et Méditerranée*, vol. 36, pp. 41–50
De Certeau, Michel, (trans. Massumi, Brian), 2006. *Heterologies: discourses on the other.* Minneapolis: University of Minnesota Press
De Jong, Frederick and Radtke, Bernd (eds.), 1999. *Islamic Mysticism Contested – thirteen centuries of controversies and polemics.* Leiden: Brill.
Dunn, Ross, 1979. "Review of Abd al-Qadir and the Algerians: Resistance to the French and Internal Consolidation by Raphael Danziger". *ASA Review of Books*, vol. 5., 1979, pp. 188–189
Eaton, Charles le Gai, 1985. *Islam and the Destiny of Man.* London: Islamic Texts Society
Emerit, Marcel, 1947. 'Le Légende de Léon Roches,' *Revue Africaine*, vol. 91, 1947, pp. 81–105
Emerit, Marcel, 2002. *L'Algerie à l'Époque d'Abd-el-Kader. Paris: Editions Bouchen*
Emerit, Marcel, 1951. "Un Problème de distance morale: la résistance algérienne à l'époque d'Abdel-Kader". *L'information Historique*, vol. 13, July-October, 1951, pp. 129–131
Étienne, Bruno, 1999. *Une Grenade Entrouverte.* La Tour d'Aigue: Éditions de L'Aube

Étienne, Bruno, 2003. *Abdelkader – isthme des isthmes (barzakh al-barazikh).* Hachette Littératures

Étienne, Bruno, 2008. *Abdelkader et la Franc-Maçonnerie: suivi de soufisme et franc-maçonnerie.* Paris: Éditions Dervy

Faivre, Antoine, and Haanegraaf, Wouter (eds.), 1998. *Western Esotericism and the Science of Religion.* Louvain: Peeters

Freeden, Michael, 1998. *Ideologies and Political Theory: a conceptual approach.* Oxford: Oxford University Press

Frégosi, Franck (ed.), 2009. *Bruno Étienne, le fait religieux comme fait politique.* La Tour d'Aigue: Éditions de L'Aube

Gadamer, Hans-Georg, 2003. *Truth and Method.* London: Continuum

Geertz, Clifford, 1971. *Islam Observed: religious development in Morocco and Indonesia.* London: University of Chicago Press

Gellner, Ernest, 2000. *Muslim Society.* Cambridge: CUP.

Gellner, Ernest, 1979. "Review of Abd-al-Qadir and the Algerians. Resistance to the French and Internal Consolidation by Raphael Danziger". *Middle Eastern Studies*, vol. 15, no. 1, Jan. 1979, pp. 106–113

Geoffroy, Eric, *et al.*, 2010. *Abd el-Kader: un spirituel dans la modernité.* Beirut: Albouraq

Gilsenan, Michael, 2008. *Recognizing Islam.* London: I.B. Tauris

Al-Ghazālī, Abū Hāmid (Ṣalībā, J. and ʿIyād , K. eds), 1981. *Munqidh min al-ḍalāl wa al-muwaṣṣil ilā dhī al-ʿizza wa al-jalāl.* Beirut: Dār al-Andalus

Al-Ghazālī, Abū Ḥāmid, (Jackson, Sherman, trans. and Nomanul Haq, Syed ed.), 2003. *On the Boundaries of Theological Tolerance in Islam – Abū Ḥāmid al-Ghazālī's Fayṣal al Tafriqa bayna al-Islām wa al-Zandaqa.* Oxford: OUP

Goldziher, Ignaz, 1981. *Introduction to Islamic Law and Theology.* New Jersey: Princeton University Press

Gramsci, Antonio, 2005. *Prison Notebooks: a selection.* King's Lynn: Biddles

Green, Nile and Searle-Chatterjee, Mary, 2008. *Religion, Language, and Power.* London: Routledge

Green, Donald P., and Shapiro, Ian, 1994. *Pathologies of Rational Choice Theory: a critique of applications in political science.* Yale University Press

Gudeman, Stephen, 1986. *Economics as Culture: models and metaphors of livelihood.* London: Routledge

Haanegraaff, Wouter, 1999. "Some remarks on the study of Western Esotericism," *Esoterica*, vol. 1, pp. 3–19

Al-Ḥakīm, Suʿād, 1981. *Al-Muʿjam al-Ṣūfī: al-ḥikmah fī ḥudūd al-kalimah.* Beirut: Dandara

al-Ḥasanī al-Jazāʾirī, Badīʿah, 2000. *Fikr al-Amīr ʿAbd al-Qādir.* Damascus: Dār al-Fikr li-'l Ṭibāʿah wa al-Tawzīʿ wa al-Nashr

Halaq, Wael, 2014. *The Impossible State: Islam, Politics, and Modernity's Moral Predicament.* New York: Columbia University Press

Halpern, David, 2005. *Social Capital.* Cambridge: Polity

Hatina, Meir, 2007. "Where East Meets West: Sufism, cultural rapprochement, and politics," *International Journal of Middle Eastern Studies*, 39, vol. 3, 2007, pp. 389–409

Haugaard, Mark (ed.), 2002. *Power: a reader.* Manchester: Manchester University Press

Hawi, Sami S., 1974. *Islamic Naturalism and Mysticism: a philosophic study of Ibn Ṭufayl's Ḥayy bin Yaqẓān.* Leiden: Brill

Heck, Paul, 2006. "Mysticism as Morality", *Journal of Religious Ethics*, 2006, pp. 253–286

Heck, Paul L. (ed.), 2007. *Sufism and Politics*. Princeton: Markus Wiener
Hourani, Albert, 2008. *Arabic Thought in the Liberal Age, 1798–1939*. Cambridge: CUP
Hulliung, Mark, 1983. *Citizen Machiavelli*. Princeton: Princeton University Press
Ibn al-ʿArabī, Muḥyī al-Dīn, (Nicholson tr.), 1978. *Tarjumān al-ʿAshwāq*. Fletcher and Sons: Norwich
Ibn al-ʿArabī, Muḥyī al-Dīn, (Austin, tr.)., 1980. *The Bezels of Wisdom*. New Jersey: Paulist Press.
Ibn ʿAjība, Aḥmad, 1972. *Īqāẓ al-Himam fī Sharḥ al-Ḥikam*. Cairo: Ḥalabī and Sons
Izutsu, Toshihiko, 2002. *Ethico-religious Concepts in the Qur'ān*. London: McGill
Izutsu, Toshihiko, 1983. *Sufism and Daoism: a comparative study of key philosophical concepts*. Berkley: University of California Press
James, William, 1971. *The Varieties of Religious Experience*. London: Collins
Jantzen, Grace, 1990. "Where two are to become one: mysticism and monism," in Godfrey Vesey (ed.), *The Philosophy of Christianity*. Cambridge: Cambridge University Press, pp. 147–166
Johansen, Baber, 1995. "Casuistry: Between Legal Concept and Social Praxis", *Islamic Law and Society*, Vol. 2, No. 2, 1995, pp. 135–156
Jonsen, Albert, and Toulmin, Stephen, 1989. *The Abuse of Casuistry: a history of moral reasoning*. University of California Press
Julien, Charles-André, 1964. *Histoire de l'Algérie Contemporaine: la conquête et les débuts de la colonisation (1827–1871)*. Paris: Presses Universitaires
Kant, Immanuel, 1784. "Beantwortung der Frage: was ist Aufklärung", *Berlinische Monatsschrift*. December, 1784, pp. 481–494
Karamustafa, Ahmet T., 2006. *God's Unruly Friends*. Oxford: Oneworld
Katz, Steven (ed.), 1978. *Mysticism and Philosophical Analysis*. London: Sheldon
Katz, Steven (ed.), 1984. *Mysticism and Religious Traditions*. Oxford: Oxford University Press
Kedourie, Elie, 1980. *Islam in the Modern World*. London: Mansell
Kenny, Anthony, 2005. *Medieval Philosophy*. Oxford: Clarendon
Khadduri, Majid, 1955. *War and Peace in the Law of Islam*. Baltimore: Johns Hopkins Press
King, John, 1997. "Abd al-Qadir: nationalist or theocrat?", in the *Journal of Algerian Studies*, vol. 2, 1997, pp. 62–80
King, Richard, 2008. *Orientalism and Religion*. New York: Routledge
Kiser, John, 2008. *Commander of the Faithful*. Cambridge: Archetype
Knysh, Alexander D., 1999. *Ibn Arabi in the Later Islamic Tradition: the making of a polemical image in Medieval Islam*. Albany: State University of New York Press
Koslowski, Peter (ed.), 1988. *Gnosis und Mystik in der Geschichte der Philosophie*. Munich: Artemis
Kugle, Scott, 2006. *Rebel Between Spirit and Law*. Bloomington: Indiana University Press
Kuhn, Thomas, 1996. *The Structure of Scientific Revolutions*. London: University of Chicago Press
Lakoff, George, and Johnson, Mark, 1999. *Philosophy in the Flesh: the embodied mind and its challenge to Western thought*. New York: Basic Books
Lovejoy, Arthur Oncken, 2001. *The Great Chain of Being*. Cambridge, Mass.: Harvard University Press
Lowe, Edward Jonathan, 2004. *The Possibility of Metaphysics: substance, identity and time*. Oxford: Clarendon
Lukes, Steven, 2004. *Power: a radical view*. Basingstoke: Palgrave Macmillan

Lyotard, Jean François (*trans.* Bennington, Goeff and Massumi, Brian), 1989. *The Postmodern Condition: a report on knowledge.* Minneapolis: University of Minnesota Press
MacDougall, James, 2006. *History and the Culture of Nationalism in Algeria.* Cambridge: CUP
MacIntyre, Alasdair, 2004. *After Virtue.* King's Lynn: Biddles
Maidstone, Viscount, 1851. *Abd-El-Kader: a poem in six cantos.* London: Chapman and Hall.
Makdisi, Ussama, 2000. *The Culture of Sectarianism: Community, History, and Violence in Nineteenth-Century Ottoman Lebanon.* University of California Press: Berkley
Ma'oz, Moshe, 1969. *Ottoman Reform in Syria and Palestine, 1840–1861: the impact of the Tanzimat on Politics and Society.* Oxford: OUP
Martin, Bradford G., 1976. *Muslim Brotherhoods in 19th Century Africa.* Cambridge: CUP
Massignon, Louis, 1994. *Hallāj: mystic and martyr.* Princeton: Princeton University Press
Masters, Bruce, 1990. "The 1850 Events in Aleppo: an aftershock of Syria's incorporation into the capitalist world system." *International Journal of Middle East Studies* 22, 1990, pp. 3–20
Michot, Yahya, 2006. *Muslims Under Non-Muslim Rule: Ibn Taymiyya.* Oxford: Interface.
Miller, Kathryn, 2000. "Muslim Minorities and the Obligation to Emigrate to Islamic Territory: Two fatwas from fifteenth century Granada." *Islamic Law and Society,* Vol. 7, No. 2, *Islamic Law in Al-Andalus* (2000), pp. 256–288
Moosa, Ebrahim, 1998. "Allegory of the Rule (*Ḥukm*): Law as Simulacrum in Islam", *History of Religions,* Vol. 38, No. 1, 1998, pp. 1–24
Morris, James W., 2001. "Ibn 'Arabī and the 'Far West' – visible and invisible influences", *Journal of the Muhyiddin Ibn 'Arabi Society,* vol. XXIX, 2001, pp. 87–121
Morris, James W., 1987. "Ibn Arabi and His Interpreters Part II (Conclusion): Influences and Interpretations", *Journal of the American Oriental Society,* Vol. 107, No. 1, 1987, pp. 101–119
Munson, Henry, 1993. *Religion and Power in Morocco.* New Haven: Yale University Press.
Nettler, Ronald, 2003. *Sufi Metaphysics and Qur'ānic Prophets.* Cambridge: Islamic Texts Society
Netton, Ian, 1994. *Allah Transcendent: studies in the structure and semiotics of Islamic philosophy, theology and cosmology.* Richmond: Curzon Press
Nicholson, Reynold, 2003. *Studies in Islamic Mysticism.* London: RoutledgeCurzon
Nye, Joseph, 2004. *Soft Power: the means to success in world politics.* New York: PublicAffairs
O'Fahey, Rex Sean, 1990. *Enigmatic Saint: Ahmad Ibn Idris and the Idrisi Tradition.* Evanston: Northwestern University Press
O'Fahey, Rex Sean and Radke, Bernd, 1993. "Neo-Sufism Reconsidered." *Der Islam,* vol. 70, issue 1, pp. 52–87
Pinto, Paulo, 2007. "Sufism and the political economy of morality in Syria", in Paul Heck (ed.), *Sufism and Politics.* Princeton: Markus Wiener, pp. 103–136
Parekh, Bhikhu, 2000. *Rethinking Multiculturalism: cultural diversity and political theory.* Basingstoke: Palgrave
Plattner, Stuart, 1989. *Economic Anthropology.* Stanford: Stanford University Press
Polanyi, Karl, 2001. *The Great Transformation: the political and economic origins of our time.* Boston: Beacon Press
Putnam, Robert, 2000. *Bowling Alone: The Collapse and Revival of American Community* New York: Simon & Schuster

Quine, Wilard Van Orman, 1980. *From a Logical Point of View.* Cambridge, Mass.: Harvard University Press

Radtke, Bernd, 1992. "Between Projection and Suppression – some considerations concerning the study of Sufism", in De Jong, F. (ed.), 1992. *Shīʿa Islam, Sects and Sufism – historical dimensions, religious practices and methodological considerations.* Utrecht, pp. 70–82

Radtke, Bernd, 1994. "Erleuchtung und Aufklärung: Islamische Mystik und europäischer Rationalismus," *Die Welt des Islams*, New Ser., Vol. 34, Issue 1, 1994, pp. 48–66

Rafeq, Abdul-Karim, 1988. "New Light on the 1860 Riots in Ottoman Damascus." *Die Welt Des Islams*, XXVIII, 1988

Reinhart, A. Kevin, 1995. *Before Revelation: the boundaries of Muslim moral thought.* Albany: State University of New York Press

Rogan, Eugene, 2004. "Sectarianism and Social Conflict in Damascus: the 1860 events reconsidered." *Arabica*, 51, 2004, pp. 493–511

Said, Edward, 1978. *Orientalism.* New York: Vintage

Sahli, Mohamed, 1988. *L'émir AbdelKader, mythes français et réalités Algériennes.* Algiers: ANEP

Sahli, Mohamed, 2007. *L'émir AbdelKader: Chevalier de la foi.* Algiers: ANEP

Schatkowski Schilcher, Linda., 1981. "The Hauran Conflicts of the 1860s A Chapter in the Rural History of Modern Syria," in *International Journal of Middle East Studies*, Vol. 13 No. 2, 1981, pp. 159–179

Schimmel, Annemarie, 1975. *Mystical Dimensions of Islam.* Chapel Hill: University of North Carolina Press

Schmidt, Leigh Eric, 2003. 'The Making of Modern "Mysticism",' *Journal of the American Academy of Religion*, June 2003, Vol. 71, No. 2, 2003, pp. 273–302

Scholem, Gershom, 1995. *Major Trends in Jewish Mysticism.* New York: Schocken Press

Sedgwick, Mark, 2004. *Against the Modern World.* Oxford: Oxford University Press

Serauky, Eberhard, 1990. "Zu einigen religiös-politischen vorstellungen ʿAbd al-Qādirs," *Hallesche Beiträge zur Orientwissenschaft*, 13.14. Halle (Saale): Martin-Luther-Universität Halle-Wittenberg Wissenschaftliche Beiträge, pp. 51–57

Shinar, Pessah, 1965. "Abd el-Kader and 'Abd al-Krim: religious influences on their thought and action,' *Asian and African Studies*, vol. 1, 1965, pp. 139–174

Skinner, Quentin, 1969. "Meaning and Understanding in the History of Ideas," *History and Theory*, 8, 1969, pp. 3–53

Smirnov, Andrey V., 1993. "Nicholas of Cusa and Ibn ʿArabī: Two Philosophies of Mysticism," *Philosophy East and West*, vol. 43, no. 1, 1993, pp. 65–85

Smith, Wilfred Cantwell, 1977. *Islam in Modern History.* Princeton: Princeton University Press

Smith, Wilfred Cantwell, 1991. *The Meaning and End of Religion.* Minneapolis: Augsburg Fortress

Stelzer, Steffen A., 2008. "Ethics" in Tim Winter (ed.), The Cambridge Companion to Classical Islamic Theology. Cambridge: CUP, pp.161–179

Taji-Farouki, Suha, 2007. *Beshara and Ibn ʿArabī.* Oxford: Anqa Publishing

Tarakci, Muhammet, and Sayar, S.ulayman, 2005. "The Qur'ānic view of the corruption of the Torah and the Gospels", *The Islamic Quarterly*, vol. 49, no 3, 2005, pp. 227–245

Taylor, Charles, 2007. *A Secular Age.* London: Harvard University Press

Toulmin, Stephen, 2001. *Return to Reason.* Cambridge, Massachusetts: Harvard University Press

Tierno, Michael, 2002. *Aristotle's Poetics for Screenwriters.* New York: Hyperion
US Group for the Advancement of Psychiatry, 1976. *Mysticism: Spiritual Quest or Psychic Disorder?* New York: Group for the Advancement of Psychiatry
Vâlsan, Michel, 1984. *L'Islam et la fonction de René Guénon.* Paris: Éditions De L'œuvre
Van Ess, Josef, 2006. *The Flowering of Islamic Theology.* London: Harvard
Volpi, Frederic, 2010. *Political Islam Observed.* London: Hurst and Co.
Waardenburg, Jacques, 2003. *Muslims and Others.* Berlin: Walter De Gruyter.
Wansbrough, John, 1968. "The Decolonisation of North African History", in *The Journal of African History*, vol. 9, no. 4., 1968, pp. 643–650
Ward Gwynne, Rosalind, 2004. *Logic, Rhetoric, and Legal Reasoning in the Qur'an: God's Arguments.* London: RoutledgeCurzon
Wasserstrom, Steven, 1999. *Religion After Religion: Gershom Scholem, Henry Corbin, and Mircea Eliade at Eranos.* Princeton: Princeton University Press
Weismann, Itzchak, 2001a. *Taste of Modernity: Sufism, Salafiyya, and Arabism in Late Ottoman Damascus.* Leiden: Brill
Weismann, Itzchak, 2001b. "God and the Perfect Man in the Experience of ʿAbd al-Qādir al-Jaza'irī", *Journal of the Muhyiddin Ibn 'Arabi Society*, vol. XXX 2001, pp. 55–72
Weismann, Itzchak, 2001c. "Between Ṣūfī Reformism and Modernist Rationalism: A Reappraisal of the Origins of the Salafiyya from the Damascene Angle," *Die Welt des Islams*, New Ser., Vol. 41, Issue 2. 2001, pp. 206–237.
Westerlund, David (ed.), 2004. *Sufism in Europe and North America.* London: Routledge
Wimmer, Franz Martin, 2002. *Essays on Intercultural Philosophy.* Chennai-Madras: Satya Nilayam.
Winter, Tim, (ed.), 2008. *The Cambridge Companion to Classical Islamic Theology.* Cambridge: CUP
Wolfson, Harry, 1976. *The Philosophy of the Kalām.* London: Harvard University Press
Zaehner, Robert Charles, 1972. *Drugs, Mysticism and Make-Believe.* London: Collins
Zaehner, Robert Charles, 1969. *Hindu and Muslim Mysticism.* New York: Schocken Press

Newspapers and websites: *Al-Quds al-ʿArabī*; *The Times*; *Illustrated London News*; *Le Monde Diplomatique*; *le-Mubacher*; *Moniteur Universel*; *La Presse*; *New York Times*; *www.beshara.org*

Reference: *Ṣaḥīḥ* of Bukhārī; *Sunan Abī Dāwūd*; *al-Muʿjam al-Mufahris Alfāẓ al-Qur'ān al-Karīm* of ʿAbd al-Bāqī; *Encyclopaedia of Islam* (2nd Edition); *Encyclopaedia of the Qur'ān*; Hans Wehr *Dictionary of Modern Written Arabic* (4th edition).

Appendix A – ʿAbd al-Qādir's Risālah on Hijrah

٤١١

ذكر ما كتبه الأمير جواباً عن سؤال قدّمه اليه
بعض الأعيان من خواصه

الحمد لله ، حمداً يوافي نعمه ، ويكافيءُ مزيده . وصلى الله : على سيّدنا محمد ، وآله ومَن تبعه ، وجرى على منواله .

اللهم ! ! إني أعوذ بك من معضلات الفتن . ما ظهرَ منها وما بطن ونضرع إليك . يا مقلّب القلوب ! ! أن تثبّت قلوبنا ، على ديننا المحبوب .

أما بعد ، يا أخي ! ! فإني رأيتك متعطّشاً ، إلى سماع ما لا عَنّا من الكلام ، في هؤلاء ، الذين ركنوا للعدوّ . فأحببت أن أذكر لك ؛ ماروي عنهم في ذلك . ولولا أني رأيت شدّة تعطشك وأوامك ؛ ماذكرت لك شيئاً . ممّا هنالك . إذ ربّما تفني ، في نصيحة أولئك الجهلة ، باقي أيامك من غير طائل ويكون تعبك في علاجهم ؛ كتعب مَن رام إصلاح الفاسد . أو حياة الهالك . وهل يصلح العطّار ما أفسد الدهرُ ؟ !

وأعلم : أن الراكن إلى الكفّار ، الداخل تحت ذمّة أهل البوار ، أحد رجلين ، إمّا رجل ، كذب الله في ضمانه لرزقه — نعوذ بالله من كفره وحمقه — وقال : إن هاجرت متّ جوعاً ، وازداد — بذلك — هلوعاً ، واعتقد أن وطنه ؛ هو رازقه . لا أن الذي يرزقه ؛ هو موجده وخالقه . ولما خطر هذا ، في قلوب جماعة من المؤمنين ، في زمانه — صلى الله عليه وسلم — بعد أن نزل قوله تعالي ، آمراً بالهجرة : يا عبادي ! ! إنّ أرضي واسعة فإيّاي فاعبدون » أنزل الله قوله « وكأيّن من دابّة لاتحمل رزقها ، الله يرزقها وإياكم « قال المفسرون : في هذه الآية ؛ تحريض على الهجرة لأن بعض المؤمنين ؛ فكّر في الجوع والفقر ، اللذين يلحقانه في الهجرة . وقال : غربةٌ في دار ، لا مال فيه ، ولا عقار ولا مَن يطعم الجار ؟ ! ! فضرب الله لهم المثل ، بحال الدوابّ ، التي لا تسعى في تحصيل قوت ولا تدّخره . . . وإمّا رجلٌ ، متكالب على الدنيا ، أصمّه وأعماه حبّها . يريد الظفر بها سواء كان ذلك : بالإسلام أو بالكفر . وكلا هذين الرجلين ؛ لا يرجى صلاحها . ولا يؤمل نجاحها . ومَن يرد الله فتنته ؛ فلن تملك له ، من الله ، شيئاً . أولئك الذين ، لم يرد الله أن

DOI 10.1515/9783110499513-011

٤١٢

يطهّر قلوبهم. لهم في الدنيا خزيٌ. ولهم في الآخرة عذابٌ عظيم. إن هي إلاّ فتنتك. تضلّ بها مَن تشاءُ وتهدي مَن تشاءُ.. إن الله لا يهدي مَن يضلّ. وهذه الفتن، جرت بها سنة الله، التي قد خلت في عباده. وحكمته الجارية في أرضه وبلاده؛ ليتبيّن الصادق من المدّعي. ومَن تحلّى بحلية ليست له؛ فضحته شواهد الامتحان. أم حسب الناس أن يتركوا أن يقولوا: آمنا. وهم لا يفتنون؟ ولقد فتنّا الذين من قبلهم. فليعلمنّ الله الذين صدقوا. وليعلمنّ الكاذبين. أم حسبتم أن تتركوا؛ ولما يعلم الله الذين جاهدوا منكم؟! يعني إن الله – تعالى – يختبر عباده. ويمتحنهم؛ حتى يتبيّن للناس، الذي لم يتّخذ وليّاً ولا نصيراً، من دون: الله ورسوله والمؤمنين؛ من الذي يتّخذ، نعوذ بالله من المهالك. أم حسبتم أن تدخلوا الجنّة؛ ولمّا يعلم الله الذين جاهدوا منكم. ويعلم الصابرين؟! ولعلّ هذا هو الزمان، الذي أخبر به رسول الله – ﷺ – بقوله: «تأتي في آخر الزمان فتنٌ، يصبح الرجل مؤمناً. ويمسي كافراً. إلاّ مَن أجاره الله بالعلم». وفي رواية: «بعلمه» ولقد ظهر في أهل هذا الزمان؛ مصداق قوله – ﷺ – لتتبعُنّ سنن مَن قبلكم شبراً بشبرٍ، وذراعاً بذراع. حتى، لو دخلوا جحر ضبّ لدخلتموه. قالوا: اليهود والنصارى؟ يا رسول الله!! قال: فمن؟! رواه البخاري في صحيحه. لأن أهل هذا الوقت؛ كانوا يطلبون الجهاد. ويتمنّون مجيء النصارى. فلمّا ظهر الجهاد؛ نكصوا على أعقابهم. فهم في هذا؛ كبني إسرائيل، إذ قالوا لنبيٍ لهم: ابعث لنا ملكاً، نقاتل في سبيل الله. قال: هل عسيتم إن كتب عليكم القتال؛ ألا تقاتلوا؟ قالوا: ومالنا ألاّ نقاتل في سبيل الله؟ وقد أخرجنا من ديارنا وأبنائنا؟! فلمّا كتب عليهم القتال؛ تولّوا، إلاّ قليلاً منهم. والله عليم بالظالمين. فلمّا كتب عليهم القتال؛ إذا فريق منهم يخشون الناس، كخشية الله، أو أشدّ خشية. وقالوا: ربّنا لِمَ كتبتَ علينا القتال؟! لولا أخّرتنا إلى أجلٍ قريب؟! ثم، بعد هذا؛ أرادوا من سلطانهم، أن يجاهد وحده. ويتكفّل بردع العدوّ. ويعرّفه حدّه. فهم في هذا؛ كبني إسرائيل أيضاً. إذ قالوا لموسى – عليه السلام – اذهب. أنت وربّك فقاتلا. إنّا ههنا قاعدون. ثم بعد هذا؛ صاروا ردءاً للكفّار ومعينين لهم بالأنفس والأموال، على مَن بقي مستمسكاً بعروة الإسلام. وأعظم

هؤلاء ذنباً ، وأشدّهم هلاكاً ، وأبعدهم نجاةً ، وأكثرهم في الأمر سقوطاً ؛ رجلان:

أحدهما ؛ رجل عرف الحق وعاند . وهو أوّل مَن تسعّر به النار ، إذ هو عالم ، لم ينفعه الله بعلمه وجحد الحقّ مع معرفته به ، أنه حقّ وهذا ؛ أصل مِن أصول الكفر الستة . ومنه ؛ كفر الموجودين في زمانه ـ ﷺ ـ المشاهدين لمعجزاته . قال ـ تعالى ـ فيهم : إنهم لايكذبونك . ولكن الظالمين ؛ بآيات الله يجحدون . وهذا ؛ أعظم الضلال ، والداءِ العضال ، أضلّه الله على علمٍ . وختم على سمعه وقلبه . وجعل على بصره غشاوةً . فبعد الختم ؛ لاترجى زيادة ، ولا نقصان في الشيء المختوم عليه .

والآخر ؛ رجل قرأ بعض أبواب الفقه ، فعلم بعض أحكام الصلاة والنكاح والبيوع ؛ فظنّ أنه وصل إلى غاية ، استحق أن يسمى بها عالماً . فصار يقول في دين الله ؛ ما ليس له به علم . ويفتري على الله الكذب ، ومَن أظلم ممن افترى على الله كذبا ؟ أو كذّب بآياته ؟ إنه لايفلح الظالمون . ويستدلّ : بآياتٍ ، وأحاديث وكلام الائمة . . وهو ـ مع هذا ـ لايحسن النطق ، والتلفّظ بمبانيها فكيف له الغوص على معانيها ؟ فالحمار أحسن حالاً مِن هذا . إذ جهل الحمار بسيط . وجهل هذا مركّب .

قال حمارُ الحكيم توما لو أنصف الدهر ؛ كنت أركب
لأن جهلي ؛ جهلٌ بسيطٌ وصاحبي ؛ جهله مركّب

والجهل المركّب ؛ أصل مِن أصول الكفر الستة . فجميع هذا الصنف ـ مع قبح ماهم عليه ، مِن الدخول تحت ذمّة الكافر ـ استحلّوا ماحرّم الله مِن ذلك . والمستحلّ لما حرم الله ؛ كافر . وخرقوا الإجماع ؛ وهو منعقد على وجوب الهجرة . ومخالف الإجماع ؛ كافرٌ .. وجعلوا ، ماورد في القرآن والسنّة ، مِن ذكر الهجرة ومدحها ، والأمر بها ؛ عبثاً ومنسوخاً . وذلك ؛ باب لميلهم ، وأقوالهم الكاذبة . كيف ؟ ! والقرآن مملوءٌ بذكر الهجرة ، ومدحها ، وذمّ تاركها . وقد قال ـ عليه الصلاة والسلام ـ : لاتنقطع الهجرة ؛ حتى يغلق باب التوبة . ولا يغلق باب التوبة ؛ حتى تطلع الشمس مِن مغربها !! وقال ـ عليه الصلاة والسلام ـ أنا بريءٌ مِن كلّ

٤١٤

مسلم ، مقيم بين أظهر الكافرين رواه أصحاب الصحيح ، ماعدا البخاري . وقال آخر ـ وهو ممّن بلغ رتبة الاجتهاد ، الحافظ السيوطي ، في : « حسن المحاضرة ، في في أخبار مصر القاهرة » لمّا ساق هذا الحديث : ما تبّرأ منهم ـ ﷺ ـ إلاّ لكفرهم وفي الصحيح : مَن جامعهم ، أو ساكنهم ؛ فهو منهم !! قالوا : لِمَ يا رسول الله ؟ قال : ألا تترايا نارهما ؟ وقال مالك ـ رضي الله عنه ـ : تجب الهجرة مِن أرض الظلم والعدوان . فكيف ببلدٍ يكفر فيه بالرحمن ؟ وتعبد ـ من دونه ـ الأوثان ؟ وقال تعالى : قالوا : فيمَ كنتم ؟ قالوا : كنّا مستضعفين في الأرض ، قالوا : ألم تكن أرض الله واسعة ؛ فتهاجروا فيها ؟! قال أبو السعود : في الآية ؛ دليل على أنه لاعذر في ترك الهجرة ، إلاّ عدم اتّساع الأرض ، وقد وسّعها الله . ولو كان هناك عذرٌ يقبل في ترك الهجرة ، ما كان في الآية ؛ تبكيتٌ لتاركيها . . إذ ربّما يعتذرون بعذرٍ آخر فلمّا ذكر الله اتّساع الأرض ؛ دلّ على أنه لا عذر غيره . وقال الوانشريسي ، في كتابه . « المعيار » : الواجب ؛ الفرار مِن دارٍ غاب عليه الشرك والخسران ، إلى دار الأمن والإيمان . ولذلك ؛ قوبلوا بالجواب ، عند الاعتذار : ألم تكن أرض الله واسعة ؟ فلاعذر المستطيع بوجهٍ ، وإن كان بمشقّة : في العمل ، أو الحيلة ، أو اكتساب الرزق . في ضيق المعيشة ؛ إلاّ المستضعف رأساً ، الذي لايجد حيلةً . ولا يهتدي سبيلًا . وعجز المسلم ، عن حمل أهل بيته وولده ؛ لا يبيح له التخلّف عن الهجره . بل يهاجر بنفسه وقد هاجر ـ ﷺ ـ لما تعذّر عليه إخراج أهله معه . ومالحقوابه ؛ إلاّ بعد حين . وكذا إن خاف ، إن هاجر ؛ يسلب ماله . فإن مفارقة الوطن ، أو سلب المال ليس بعذر ، في ترك الهجرة . نصّ على ذلك صاحب المعيار . وقد ذكر أهل الأحوال ؛ أنّ الضرورات ، التي تجب المحافظة عليها ، خمسة : الدين ، والنفس والعقل ، والنسب ، والمال . فكلٌّ واحدٍ من هؤلاء ؛ يجب حفظه ، مـا لم يعارضه ، حفظ ماقبله . فالمال ؛ هو آخر المراتب . والدين ؛ أولها . فهو مقدّم على غيره . وكذا ؛ تجب الهجرة على المرأة . إذا لم يهاجر زوجها . وقد هاجر كثيرٌ من المسلمات إلى الحبشة ، قبـــل هجرته ﷺ ـ وفيهن أنزل الله ـ تعالى ـ قوله : يا أيها الذين آمنوا ؟ إذا جاءكم المؤمنات مهاجرات فامتحنوهن

الآية . ولم يعذر الله – تعالى في المقام ، تحت ذمّة الكافر ؛ إلا الذي لايستطيع حيلةً . ولا يهتدي سبيلًا ، كالأعمى الذي لايجد قائداً . والزمن الذي لا يجد حاملًا . مع نيّتهما : أنهما متى وجدا ذلك ؛ هاجرا . فإن تركا النيّة ، وماتا ؛ ماتا على غير سبيل المؤمنين . نصّ على ذلك ؛ غيرُ واحدٍ . والكتاب العزيز الذى لايأتيه الباطل من بين يديه ، ولا من خلفه – محذّر من مخالطة الكفّار ، وموالاتهم ، وموادتهم . قال – تعالى – : يا أيها الذين آمنوا لاتتخذوا عدوّي وعدوّكم أولياء ، تلقون إليهم بالمودة . ، إلى قوله : ومن يفعله . منكم ؛ فقد ضلّ سواءَ السبيل . وقال : إنما ينهاكم الله عن الذين قاتلوكم في الدين . وأخرجوكم من دياركم ، وظاهروا على إخراجكم أن تولّوهم . ومَن يتولّهم ؛ فأولئك هم الظالمون . وقال : بشّر المنافقين ، بأنّ لهم عذاباً أليما ... إلى قوله فإن العزّة لله جميعاً . فعيّن الله – تعالى – مراده في المنافقين ، في الآية بقوله : الذين يتّخذون الكافرين ؛ أولياء من دون المؤمنين . فالذي يتّخذ الكافر وليّاً ؛ منافق . إلى غير ذلك من الآيات ، والأحاديث القاطعة الصريحة الصحيحة ، التي لاتحتمل تأولًا . وقد ذكر صاحب المعيار ، في باب الجهاد : أنّ هؤلاء المقيمين تحت ذمّة النصارى لاتصحُّ لهم صلاةٌ ، ولا صيامٌ ، ولا حجٌ ، ولا جهادٌ ؛ بوجهٍ من الوجوه . فانظره ، فإنه قد طال عهدي به . ومما ذكره : أنّ الزكاة ؛ شرطها أن تدفع للامام . يعني سلطان المسلمين . فاذا دفعها للنصارى ليتقوّوا بها على المسلمين ؛ كانت المصيبة أشدّ . ومنها ؛ أنّ شهر رمضان – في الغالب – لايثبت إلا برؤية عدلين ، إبتداءً وانتهاءً . والعدالة إنما تثبتُ عند الإمام ، وقاضيه . وحيث أنه لا إمام ولا قاضي ؛ فيكون رمضان ؛ مشكوك الأول والآخر؛ إلى غير دلك من الوجوه . ولا تجوز شهادة المقيمين ، تحت ذمّة النصارى إلا من له عذرٌ مقبول شرعاً . ولا تنفّذ أحكام قضاتهم . قال بعض العلماء هم أشدُّ من أهل الأهواء . وقد ردّت شهادتهم وأحكامهم . قال ابن عرفة : شرط قبول خطاب القاضي؛ صحّة ولايةِ ، ممّن تصحُّ ولايته ، بوجه الشرع ، احترازاً

من أهل الدجن . كقضاة مسلمي : بلنسية ومرسية وقوصـــرة ،من الأندلس .
ومرادهم بالدجن ؛ المسلمون الداخلون تحت ذمـّـة النصـارى وأهل الجزائر ؛
يسمّونهم المنافقين . وسئل المازري عن أحكام ، تأتي ،من صقلية ، ،من عنـــد
قاضيها . فأجاب : القادح في هذا ؛ وجهان : الأول ؛ ،من جهة القاضي ،من
حيث العدالة. فلا يباح له المقام في دار الحرب ، في قيد أهل الكفر .

والثاني ،من جهة الولاية، إذ القاضي ، مولـّى ،من قبل أهل الكفر . ومَن كان هذا
حاله ؛ فلا يعتبر حكمه في الشرع . وقد بلغني عن هؤلاء الرؤساء الجهـال ،
الذين أفتوا بغير علم ؛ فضـّلوا وأضلوا" . المعنيين بقوله – ﷺ وعلى آله – يأتي
على الناس زمان ؛ عالمهم أنتن ،من جيفة حمار . أنهم يستدلون بقوله ﷺ لا هجرة
بعد الفتح » وهذا الحديث ، في صحيح البخاري وغيره . ولا حجـّة لهم فيـه
لأنّ النبي ﷺ قاله لسائل سأله عن الهجرة ،من مكة إلى المدينة بعد الفتح ؛
فأجابه : بأنّ الهجرة ، التي كانت واجبة ، ،من مكة إلى المدينة ؛ قد انقطعت
بالفتح ، ونسخت كما نسخت حرمة رجوع المهاجر إلى وطنه ، إذ عاد دار إسلام
وأمّا وجوب الهجرة ، ،من دار الكفر إلى دار الإسلام ؛ فهو باقٍ إلى طلوع
الشمس ،من مغربها. قال ابن العربي : الهجرة أقسام . منها ؛ الهجرة ،من الخوف على الدين والنفس
كهجرة النبي ﷺ وهجرة أصحابه المكـّيين . فإنها كانت عليهـــم فريضة . ولا
يجزىء إيمان بدونها . ومنها ؛ الهجرة إلى النبي – ﷺ – في داره التي استقرّ فيها
فقد – بايع (ﷺ) مَن قصده ، على الهجرة كما بايع آخرين ؛ على الإسلام
وهاتان الهجرتان انقطعتا بفتح مكـّة . وأمّا الهجرة ،من أرض الكفر ؛ فهي باقيةٌ
إلى يوم القيامة . وكذا الهجرة ، ،من أرض الباطل والحرام . والهجرة ،من أرض
الفتنة . وروى أشهب عن مالك : لا يقيم أحدٌ ، في موضعٍ ، يعمل فيه بغير
الحقّ . وقال البرزالي في بعض أجوبته : الإجماع على وجوب الهجرة ؛ إن
وجد المسلمُ إليها سبيلاً . وكذا يستدلون بقوله تعالى : إلاّ أن تتـّقوا منهم تقاةً
وهذه الآية منسوخة . روى البخاري ، في صحيحه ، ،من كتاب التفسير ،
عن ابن عباس – رضي الله عنهما – أنه قال : لا تقيّة اليوم ، لاتساع البـلاد

الإسلامية ، وكذا يستدلون بقوله تعالى : « إلا من أكره ، وقلبه مطمئن بالإيمان » . والآية : إنما وردت فيمن يظفر به الكافر ، من غير اختيار ، كالأسير فإذا حملوه على معصية ، أو نطق بكفر ؛ يسوغ له ذلك ، لخوف القتل .. والصبر أجمل . أما كونه متمكناً من الفرار ، ويبقى تحت حكمهم ؛ فلم يقل به مسلم . وكذا يستدلون بما ذكره البيضاوي ، في تفسير قوله – تعالى – على خزائن الأرض ، إني حفيظ عليم . فانه قال : في الآية ؛ دليل على جواز التولية ، على يد الكافر . ولا حجة لهم في هذا فإن البيضاوي قال بعد هذا ؛ إذا علم أنه لا سبيل إلى إقامة الحق ، وسياسة الخلق ، إلا بالاستظهار به . وهذا الشرط ؛ معدوم اليوم . وقد قال غير واحد : إن الملك ؛ كان أسلم قبل ذلك . على أنه ؛ إنما يكون . ما ذكره البيضاوي ؛ على تقدير صحته ، فيمن كان تحت أسرهم ، فإنه يجوز له أن يطلب منهم ذلك في التولية . إذ بعض الشر أهون من بعض . ويوسف – عليه السلام – جده الخليل – عليه السلام – وهو أول من سن الهجرة . قال الله – تعالى – حاكياً عنه ، وقال : إني مهاجر إلى ربي . ومعه سارا . فدخل قرية ، فيها جبار من الجبابرة ...(الحديث بطوله) وكذلك ؛ يستدلون بما نقل عن : النووي والرافعي : أن المسلم ؛ إذا كانت له عشيرة تحميه ، أو له جاه ؛ لا تجب عليه الهجرة . ولكن ؛ تستحب في حقه . نقل ذلك ؛ ابن النحاس « في مشارع الأشواق ، إلى مصارع العشاق » . وهذا أيضاً ؛ لا دليل فيه لأن كلام النووي والرافعي ، فيمن كان كافراً في دار الحرب ؛ ثم أسلم . وكان لا يخاف الفتنة في دينه ، لحماية عشيرته ، وتوفر عصابته ، أو جاهه ، بحيث لو أراد الكفار ذلك ؛ لا يقدرون . فيأمن لذلك من الفتنة . وقد وقع ، من هذا النمط ، كثير في الصدر الأول . كما ذكر ذلك : أهل السير والأخباريون . أما من كان مسلماً ، في دار الإسلام ودخل عليه الكفار ، بالقهر والغلبة ؛ فلا يتصور أن تكون له عشيرة تحميه أو جاه يأمن بها من الفتنة في دينه ، مهما أرادهما الكفار منه . وهل يوجد واحد ، من هذه الشعوب والقبائل ، الداخلة تحت ذمة الكفار ؛ من له عشيرة

٤١٨

تحميه من الكفّار ، إذا أرادوا إجراء حكمٍ من الاحكام عليه ؟! أو يأمن الفتنة
بواحدٍ من هذين الوجهين ، اللذين ذكرهما الرافعي والنووي ؟! اللهم !! إلا أن
يكون أحمق ضعيف العقل والإيمان ؛ فيأمنهم ، ويثق بعهودهم ومواثيقهم . وإن
الشارع الحكيم ، لا يقبل شهادتهم وأقوالهم ، بالإضافة إلينا . وكأن هذا الأحمق
لم يصل إليه خبر الأندلس !! خصوصاً أهل قرطبة . فإنهم تعاقدوا مع الكافر
– لمّا غلبهم – على نيفٍ وستين شرطاً ، اشترطوها عليه . فلم يحل الحول عليها ،
حتى نقضوها عروةً عروةً !! وآخر الأمر ، صار الكافر ، يأتي إلى المسلم
فيقول له : إن جدّك ، أو جدّ أبيك ، وأباك أو جدّك ، كان كافراً . فارجع
إلى الكفر ، الذي كان عليه جدّك . واترك دين الإسلام !!! إلى غير ذلك ...
فالنصارى ، لا يوفون بعهدٍ ، إلاّ إذا كانت كلمة الإسلام ، هي العليا . وشوكته
قائمة . كيف ؟! والله – تعالى – يقول : لا يزالون يقاتلونكم ؛ حتى يردّوكم
عن دينكم ، إن استطاعوا . وقال : كيف ؟! وإن يظهروا عليكم ، لا يرقبوا
فيكم إلاًّ ولا ذمّة (والإلّ : القرابة) وأولئك هم المعتدون . أي المتجاوزن .
أي لا يقفون عند شرطٍ ولا عهدٍ . ومِن شنيع حمق هؤلاءِ ، وضعف عقولهم
ومرض إيمانهم ، أنهم يسمّون طاعتهم للكافر مهادنة !! وهل يسوغ ؟ لمن له أدنى
عقلٍ وتمييز ، أن يتلفّظ بهذا ؟! كيف ؟! وأحكام الكافر وشرائعه وتصرّفاته ؛
جارية على شريفهم ووضيعهم . ويؤدّون إليه المغارم . ويحملون أثقاله ؛ إذا
أراد الغزو على المسلمين . ويقاتلونهم معه ، في جملة عساكره وجيوشه . هذا
– والله – الهذيان ، الذي لا يُعقل . على أن المهادنة ، خاصّة بالإمام ، ونائبه .
فلا يعقدها سواهما . قال خليل : وللامام ؛ المهادنة . يعني : لا لغيره فقدّم
الخبر ، مع جرّه باللام ، وكلاهما ، يفيد : الحصر والاختصاص . واعلم : أن
هذه المصيبة ، التي هي ، ظهور الكفّار على المسلمين ، حتى دخلوا تحت ذمتهم
لم تكن في القرن الأوّل . ولا في الثاني ، ولا في الثالث ، ولا في الرابع ،
وإنما حدثت ، في الخامس وبعده . ولذا ، لم يوجد فيها قولٌ ، ولا نصٌ ، لواحد
من الأئمة ، (رضي الله عنهم) . ولمّا حدثت . ووقع السؤال عنها ، قاسها ساداتنا

٤١٩

أهل النظر ، والاجتهاد المذهبي ، على مسألة : مَن أسلم ؛ ولم يهاجر . قال ابن رشد : وهو قياسٌ صحيح . وقد اختلف الأئمة ، فيمن أسلم ؛ ولم يهاجر !! وأقام تحت ذمّة الكفار ، مِن غير أن تحصل منه إعانةٌ لهم : لا بالنفس ، ولا بالمال . أما إن أعانهم بماله ، طوعاً أو كرهاً ، بأن أخذوه منه مغرماً أو بايعهم . أو شاراهم ، ولو في أقلّ شيء ؛ فقال القاضي ابن الحاج التجيني الأندلسي : مِن القواعد ؛ أن الإعانة بالمال ؛ تبيح المال . والإعانة بالنفس ؛ تبيح النفس . وقال الإمام المغيلي ، في كتابٍ له ، سمّاه : « مصابيح الفلاح » : إن هؤلاء المؤمنين (يعني : الذين طلبوا الأمان مِن الكفار . وأمّنوهم ، وأقاموا تحت ذمتهم . ودانوا بطاعتهم) تؤخذ أموالهم . ويقتلون ، ولو كانوا يقرؤون القرآن . وقال ابن القاسم : والصحيح في مال المسلم ، المقيم في دار الحرب ؛ أنه مباح . وأنّه لا يدَ لصاحبه . وإنما اليد ؛ للكافر . وقد حرّره في هذه المسألة : الإمام ابن عباد ، شارح الحكم ، في جواب له . ونصّه : حالُ المتنصّرة ؛ على حسب فرقهم . فإنّ منهم ؛ مَن يلجأ لحصون العدوّ ، ليدافع بها عن نفسه . ومنهم ؛ مَن يكون معيناً له : بنفسه وماله (بمعنى : أنهم يقاتلون مع العدوّ . ويدافعون عنه . ويغيرون على المسلمين) فهؤلاء ؛ أشدُّ ضرراً على المسلمين . وحكمهم حكم أهل دار الحرب : في قتلهم ، وسلب مالهم ... وأما أولادهم ؛ فلا يقتلون . ولا يكونون فيئاً . وإنما أبيح قتل البالغين ؛ لكونهم ردءاً للعدوّ الحربيّ . معينين لهم بأنفسهم . وحكم الرده ، إذا لم يقاتل مع العدوّ ، حكم المقاتل . فأحرى ؛ إذا قاتل !! قال بعض المحققين ، مِن علماء تونس ، في جوابٍ عن أهل حصنٍ ؛ كانوا ردءاً للكافرين المحاربين ، ما نصّه : وقول هرقل : لو كنت أرجو أن أخلص إليه ؛ لتجشّمت لقيه . يعني : دون خلعٍ مِن ملكه . وهذا التجشم ؛ هو الهجرة . وكانت فرضاً على كلّ مسلم ، قبل فتح مكة . فإن قيل : إن النجاشي ؛ لم يهاجر ، قبل فتح مكة ؟! وهو مؤمن !! فكيف سقط عنه فرض الهجرة ؟ قلنا : إنه هو في مملكة أغنى عن : الله ورسوله وعن جماعة المسلمين ؛ منه لو هاجر بنفسه فرداً . لأن أوّل غنائه ؛ أنه حبس الحبشة كلهم

٤٢٠

عن مقاتلة النبي (ﷺ) مع طوائف الكفّار . هذا ؛ مع أنـه كان ملجأ لمن أوذي ، من أصحاب رسول الله (ﷺ) ورِدءاً لجماعة المسلمين ، وحكم الرِدء في جميع الأحوال ؛ حكم مَن كان ردءاً له . وكذلك ردءُ اللصوص والمحاربين عند مالك والكوفيين ؛ يقتل بقتلهم . ويجب عليه ؛ ما يجب عليهم . وإن كانوا لم يحضروا الفعل . ومثله في المساواة : تخلّف عثمان وطلحة وسعد بن زيد ـ رضي الله عنهم ـ عن بدر . وضرب لهم النبي ـ صلى الله عليه وسلم ـ بسهامهم ، مِن غنيمة بدر . قالوا : وأجرنا يا رسول الله ! ! قال : وأجركم (انتهى) فانظر قوله : وحكم الردءِ ... إلى آخر كلامه ؛ ففيه الكفاية ، في تبيّن ما يجب العمل به . ومنه ؛ تعلم : أن مَن يدخل تحت جوارهم وأمانهم ، من غير إعانةٍ لهم بنفسه ولا بماله ، وأنه لم يكن لهم عيناً ، ولا ردءاً دونهم ؛ لا يباح قتله وإنما هو عاص ، لا يباح ماعصمه الإسلام مِن دمه وماله ؛ وإنما يباح سلبُ مالِ ، مَن يكون معيناً للعدوّ به ، على قتال المسلمين ، ومقاومتهم ، ومناهضتهم . وقد أفتى العلماء : بإباحة أخذ مالِ قومٍ ؛ كانوا بقرب حصن العدّو . وهم قادرون على منازلته ، بذلك المال ، ولم يفعلوا ! . فجوّزوا : للقيام بالحقّ المتعيّن ؛ أن يأخذ الإمام القدر الزائد على كفايتهم . ويصرفه في منازلة ذلك الحصن . لا سيّما ؛ إذا علم : أنهـم ينفعونه ويعينونه به ، مثل هؤُلاء ، الذين نتكلم في أمرهم . وإنما لم يبح قتل أولادهم ، ولا سبيُ نسائهم ؛ فلعدم تعلّق الاثم بهم . لصغر الأولاد ، وضعف النساء ، وأصالة إسلامهم بخلاف الحربيّ ؛ إذا أسلم ، وأقام بدار الحرب ، حتى أخذ . فولده وماله ؛ فيءٌ مطلقاً ـ ولا يقاس المسلم ـ بالأصالة ـ عليه . خلافاً لابن الحجاج . هذا ؛ هو التحقيق ، في هـذه المسألة . ومنهم ؛ من لجأ للمسلمين . وصار يقاتل العدوّ معهم . وهو ـ مع ذلك ـ يعين العدوّ خفيةً . ويعلمه بأحوال المسلمين . ويطلعه على عوراتهم . وكذلك : إن أطلعهم على كتب يكتبونها . فإن حكم هؤلاء ؛ حكم الزنادقة . إن اطلع عليهم ؛ قتلوا : وإلاّ ؛ فأمرهم إلى الله (انتهى كلام ابن عبّاد) وقال القاضي ابن الحاج : الأرجح ؛ سبي ذراري هؤُلاء ليعيشوا في دار الإسلام ، آمنينِ من الفتنة في الدين . يعني : لا ليُملكوا ! ! وأما الذين يستجيشون بالكفّار ويطلبون منهم الغزو على المسلمين ؛ فهم مرتدّون . قال البرزلي ، في نوازله : احفظ : أن أمير المسلمين ، يوسف بن تاشفين ؛ استفتى علماءَ العدوة ، في المعتمد

٤٢١

ابن عباد . فاتفقت فتياهم : على أن مجرّد الاستجاشة على المسلمين ، بالكفار ، ردّة .
مقصودهم بذلك : ولو لم يحصل المطلوب ! ! والمعتمد بن عباد هذا ، كان من ملوك
الاندلس . واستجاش بالطاغية ، على يوسف المذكور ، ونصر الله المسلمين ، فظفر به
يوسف . وقال بعض شرّاح (رسالة ابن أبي زيد القيرواني) : الفرار من دار الإسلام ، إلى
دار الحرب ، ردّة . وقال الحطّاب ، في باب الردّة : إدخال السرور على الكفّار ، ردّة
ولا يخفى على كل مميّز ، ما يدخل على الكافر من السرور ، عند دخول من يدخل
تحت ذمّته . قال الأجهري ، في حاشيته على المختصر : جعل البرنيطة ، على الرأس ، ردّة !!
وهؤلاء المتعضدّون بالنصارى ، الداخلون تحت ذمّتهم ، يحبّون نصرة الكفّار على المسلمين
الذين يغيرون عليهم ، ويفرحون بذلك - كلّهم - رجالاً ونساءً . وهذه ، ردّة .
نسأل الله السلامة . . والمرأة ، إذا ارتدّت ، قال كثير من الفقهاء : تقتل ، كالرجل .
وقال أشهب : تسترقّ ولا تقتل . نقله التلمساني ، في حاشيته . على الشفا ، لعياض . قال
القاضي أبو بكر بن العربي : ومنشأ الخلاف في ذلك ، أنّ قتل الكافر ، هل هو لكفره ؟
أو لحرابته ؟ فأمّا من قال : لكفره ، قال : تقتل المرأة . وأمّا من قال : لحرابته ، قال :
لا تقتل ، لأنها لا تحارب . وإذا تاب أحدٌ ، ممّن ارتدّ - والعياذ بالله - فالمشهور ، أنّ
ماله يردّ عليه . ونقل ابن عرفه . في مختصره ، عن ابن شعبان : أنه لا يردّ عليه . بل
يبقى فيئاً ، كما كان في حال ارتداده ، كما أفتى به بعض العلماء . ففي سبي نسائهم وذراريهم
خلاف . فالذي ذهب إليه كثير من الفقهاء : أنه لا سبيَ ، في نسائهم وذراريهم . والذي
ذهب إليه خليل ، حيث قال : وإن ارتدّ جماعةٌ . وحاربوا ، فكالزنديق . يعني : يقتل ، ولا تسبى
إمرأته ولا ولده . وقال ابن وهب ، من المالكية . وجمهور الشافعية : المرتدّ ، يسبى
كالكافر الأصلي . وهو حكم أبي بكر الصديق - رضي الله عنه - في أهل الردّة . فإنه
حكم بسبيهم . وأعطى عليّاً بن أبي طالب - رضي الله عنه - أمّ محمد بن الحنفية ، وكانت
سبيت ، يوم حرب أهلها ، بني حنيفة ، وقتل مسيلمة الكذّاب . ووطئها عليٌّ - رضي الله
عنه - بملك اليمين . قال ابن حجر ، في شرح الأربعين : قول : ابن بطّال : الإجماع :
على أن المرتدّ ، لا يسبى ؛ منقوض بما ذهب إليه ابن وهب ، من المالكية . وبما ذهب
إليه جمهور الشافعية . وخالف عمرُ بن الخطاب أبا بكر - رضي الله عنهما - فإنه أطلق

سراح المرتدين ، بعد موت أبي بكر – رضي الله عنه – وقد كانوا في أسره . وقال بعض العلماء كما نقله الشيخ سالم : لاخـلافَ بين أبي بكر وعمر – رضي الله عنهما – في سبي المرتدّين . إذ الإمام ؛ مخيرٌ ، بـين الاسترقاق والمنّ !! فأبو بكر – رضـي الله عنه – اختار استرقاقهم . وعمر – رضي الله عنه – مَنّ عليهم . ولا تناقض في ذلك . وإذا قتل الغزاةُ ، نساءَ هؤلاءِ المتنصّرة ، الذين تحت ذمّـة النصارى ، وصبيانهم ؛ فلا حرج على قاتلهم . ولا إثم !! وقد عقد البخاري لذلك ، باباً في صحيحه . قال : باب أهل دار الحرب يسبون . وفيهم النساء والصبيان . ثم ساق الحديث : على أنه – صلى الله عليه وسلم – سئل عن ذلك ؛ فقال : هم منهم . وذكر في آخـر الباب : لا حمى إلاّ لله ولرسوله .

(انتهى) المقصود ، بحمد الله ، وحسن عونه ، من جواب سؤال المحبّين ، قطعاً لشبه المرتدّين . ونحن في الثغر مرابطون . ولا كتبَ عندنا . ولا موادّ . في ذي الحجة سنة ثمان وخمسين ومائتين وألف ١٢٥٨ ، من هجرة حائز الفخر والشرف ، صلى الله عليه وسلم .

وعندما تغلّب العدوّ على الجهة الغربيّة من الوطن ؛ هاجر إخوان الأمير إلى المغرب الأقصى . وبقي الأمير بأهله وجيوشه ، في الجهة الشرقية ؛ لمدافعة العدوّ . ولما طالت المدّة ؛ كتب الأمير إلى إخوانه ، يتشوّق اليهم . وذكرهم بأسمائهم . فقال :

يا سوادَ العين ! يا روحَ الجسد ! يا ربيـعَ القلب ! يا نعمَ السندْ !!
كنتَ لي قرّةَ عين . وبهـا راح قلبي . لا بمـالٍ وولدْ
فرمى الدهـر بعيني أسهماً مذ نأيتم ؛ لا أرى فيها أحـد
أيروق الطرفَ شيءٌ بعـدكم ؟! لا وربّ البيت ، في هزل وجدّ
مُـذ ترحّلتم ؛ أذبتم مهجتي ودموعي ؛ فائضـات من كمد
قد فني صبري . ولم يفنَ الجوى مـا أراه فانيـاً ؛ حتى الأبد
وانزوى ؛ ما كان رطباً يانعاً . ووهى العظم . ولم يبقَ الجلد
مـذ تواريتم ؛ توارى فرحي ما يسرّ القلب في أخـذ وردّ
فحياتي – بعدكم – مـذ غبتمُ ؛ من مجازٍ مرسلٍ – عنـدي – يعدّ
طال ليلي ، يا أحبّـائي !! ولا يعلم الحال ؛ سوى الفرد الصمد
كم أنادي – حين يبدو صبحه – يا سعيدُ !! هل خيالٌ لي يُردّ ؟

Appendix B – ʿAbd al-Qādir's Mawqif #254 ('He Is [Like] That')

طوراً يمان اذا لقيتُ ذا يمن   وان لقيتُ مَعَدّياً فعدنان(١)

ولا غرو ، فانهما حالتان كانتا له ــ صلى الله عليه وسلم ــ أخبر عنهما بلفظ واحد يؤدي المعنيين ، فانه ــ صلى الله عليه وسلم ــ أُعطي جوامع الكلم ، وينابيع الحكم ، وكل أُناس يعلمون مشربهم ، فيسلكون مذهبهم ، وربما في الغيب معان أخر لهذا الحديث ، يلقيها الله على مَن يشاء مِن عباده .

الموقف

ـ ٢٥٤ ـ

قال تعالى :

« وَإِلَٰهُكُمْ إِلَٰهٌ وَاحِدٌ لَا إِلَٰهَ إِلَّا هُوَ(٢) » .

وقال :

« قُلْ إِنَّمَا يُوحَىٰ إِلَيَّ أَنَّمَا إِلَٰهُكُمْ إِلَٰهٌ وَاحِدٌ(٣) » .

وقال :

« قُلْ إِنَّمَا أَنَا بَشَرٌ مِثْلُكُمْ يُوحَىٰ إِلَيَّ أَنَّمَا إِلَٰهُكُمْ إِلَٰهٌ وَاحِدٌ(٤) » ؛

وقال :

« أَنَّهُ أَنَا لَا إِلَٰهَ إِلَّا أَنَا(٥) » .

ونحو هذه مِن الآيات ، خاطب بها تعالى كلَّ مَن بلغه القرآن الكريم .

---

(١) كذا بالاصل والبيت كما في الكامل للمبرد ٨٩٩ و ٩٠٢ :

يوماً يمان اذا لاقيت ذا يمن   وان لقيت معديا فعدناني

والشعر لعمران بن حطان . وانظر خبر البيت مع أبيات آخر في الكامل . (تعليق : احمد طافر كوجان) .

(٢) ٢/١٦٣ البقرة . (٣) ٢١/١٠٨ الأنبياء . (٤) ١٨/١١٠ الكهف . (٥) ١٦/٢ النحل .

DOI 10.1515/9783110499513-012

والكلام القديم من يهودي ونصراني ومجوسي ووثني وصنمي ومنوي وغيرهم من الأجناس والأصناف المختلفي العقائد والمقالات • في الحق تعالى ، أخبرهم أن الههم واحد ، وان اختلفت مذاهبهم وعقائدهم فيه • فهو واحد العين ، ولا يلزم من اختلافهم فيه اختلاف في عينه وحقيقته ، فانها كالأسماء له • ولا يلزم من تعدّد الأسماء تعدّد في المسمّى • وان له تعالى أسماء في كلّ لغة من اللغات التي لاتحصى كثيرة ،وليس ذلك بقادح في وحدة عينه ، ففي الآيات المتقدّمة اشارة الى ما تقوله الطائفة العلية ، طائفة الصوفية ، من وحدة الوجود وانه تعالى عين كل معبود ، وانّ كلّ عابد انمّا عبد الحق من وجه ، ببرهان هذه الآيات وبقوله :

« وَقَضَى رَبُّكَ أَلَا تَعْبُدُوا إلاَّ إيَّاهُ[(١)] » .

حكم تعالى أن لايعبد عابد الاّ اياه ، فمحال أن يعبد غيره ، لأن وقوع خلاف قضائه محال • وانما هلك من هلك ، من جهة مخالفته لما جاءت به رسل الله من أوامر ونواهيه ، لأنه كفر بالله من كلّ وجه ، فهو تعالى عين كلّ معقول ومتخيّل ومحسوس بوجوده ، الواحد الذي لايتعدّد ولا يتبعّض ، عين النقيضين والضدين والخلافين والمثلين ، وليس في الوجود الاّ هذه ، وهو الأوّل والآخر والظاهر والباطن ، وليس في العالم الاّ هذه ، فلا تقيده المظاهر ولا تحصره المقالات والاعتقادات من الأوائل والأواخر ، فهو كما أخبر في الصحيح : « عند ظنّ كلّ معتقد ، ولسان كلّ قائل » والظن والقول خلقه ، فتصوّره في تصوّر كلّ متصوّر عين وجوده ، ووجوده في تصوّر من تصوّره لايزول بزوال تصوّر من تصوّره الى تصوّر آخر ، بل يكون له وجود في ذلك التصور الآخر ، فمن اعتقده وتصوره مقيداً فهو كذلك ، أو مطلقاً فكذلك ، أو جوهراً ؛ فكذلك ، أو عرضاً ؛ فكذلك ، أو منزّهاً ؛ فكذلك ، أو مشبهاً ؛ فكذلك ، أو معنى ؛ فكذلك ، أو في السماء أو الأرض ؛ فكذلك ، أو غير ذلك ، ممّا لايكاد ينحصر من الاعتقادات والمقالات• ولهذا قال بعضهم : كل

---

(١) ٢٣/١٧ الاسراء •

ما يخطر ببالك فالله بخلاف ذلك . فهذه القولة لها وقع عظيم في باب الحقائق، فان صدرت من عارف فهو أهل لها ، وأن صدرت من غير عارف فقد يجري الله بعض الحقائق على ألسنة غير أهلها فيعرفها اهلها، والمتكلمون القائلون بالتنزيه المطلق العقلي غير الشرعي يتداولون هذه المقالة بينهم ، لظنّهم أنها دليل لهم على تنزيههم المطلق ، وليس الأمر كما توهموا ، بل معناها عدم حصر الحق تعالى في قولة قائل ، واعتقاد معتقد ، وأنه تعالى كما اعتقده كلُّ معتقد من وجه ، كما قال كلُّ قائل من وجه . فكل ما يخطر ببالك في الحق تعالى ، من حيث الذات والصفات فالله كذلك ، وبخلاف ذلك فليس مراد القائل أنه ليس كما خطر ببالك ؛ بل مراده : أنه كما خطر ببالك ، وبخلاف ذلك عند مخالفك، أي غير مقيَّد بما خطر ببالك ، بمعنى اعتقادك ، ولا منحصر في مقالتك . فان هذا القائل حكم أنه تعالى بخلاف ما خطر ببالك ، عند مخالفك في عقدك وقولك ، وهو كما خطر ببالك ، فكما صحّ هذا صحّ هذا . فالمراد من الخلاف ؛ كلُّ مناف ، سواء كان من تنافي الضّدين والنقيضين ، أو الخلافين ، أو المثلين فان المثلين متنافيان ، عند الأصوليين . والحاصل : انه ان خطر ببالك واعتقادك كذلك ، وبخلاف ذلك تعالى ، كما قال أهل السنة ، فهو كذلك وبخلاف ذلك، وان خطر ببالك وأعتقادك أنه تعالى كما قالت واعتقدت جميع الفرق الاسلامية؛ فهو كذلك وبخلاف ذلك . وان خطر ببالك أنه تعالى كما قالت واعتقدت جميع الطوائف من اسلام ونصارى ، ويهود ومجوس ، ومشركين وغيرهم ؛ فهو كذلك ، وبخلاف ذلك . وان خطر ببالك واعتقادك أنه كما يقول العارفون المحققون من الأنبياء والأولياء والملائكة ؛ فهو كذلك، وبخلاف ذلك. فما عبده أحد من خلقه من كلّ وجه ، ولا كفر به أحد من كلّ وجه ، ولا عرفه أحد من خلقه من كلّ وجه ، ولا جهله أحد من كل وجه . قال الذين هم من أعلم الخلق بالله تعالى :

« سُبْحَانَكَ لاَ عِلْمَ لَنَا إلاَّ مَا عَلَّمْتَنَا[(١)] » .

فهو المعبود لكلّ مخلوق من وجه ، المعروف لكل مخلوق من وجه ،

(١) ٢/٣٢ البقرة .

المجهول لكل مخلوق مِن وجه . فما خلق الخلق الاّ ليعرفوه فيعبدوه ، فلابدّ أن يعرفوه من وجه ، فيعبدوه من ذلك الوجه . فلا خطأ في العالم ؟ الاّ بالنسبة ومع هذا ، مَن خالف ما جاءت به الرسل – عليهم الصلاة والسلام – هلك ولابدّ ، ومَن وافقهم نجا ولابدّ .

« وَاللّٰهُ وَاسِعٌ عَلِيمٌ » .

وسع اعتقادات جميع مخلوقاته كما وسعتهم رحمته ، وسع كلّ شيء رحمة وعلماً ، عزيز منيع ، ان يعرفه أحد مِن مخلوقاته كما يعرف نفسه ،أو يعبده عابد كما تستحق عظمته وجلاله ، لطيف ظهر بما به بطن ، وبطن بما به ظهر ، لا اله الاّ هو ، حيرة الحيرات ، لايحيط هو تعالى بذاته ، فكيف يحيط به عجز المخلوقات ؟!

الموقف

– ٢٥٥ –

قال تعالى ، حكاية عن موسى انه قال للخضر – عليهما السلام – :

« هَلْ أَتَّبِعُكَ عَلَىٰ أَنْ تُعَلِّمَنِ مِمَّا عُلِّمْتَ رُشْداً(١) » ؟!

في الآية اشارة الى أن الكبير قد لايعلم بعض العلوم التي تكون عند الصغير . وذلك فيما يتعلق بالكوائن وحوادث العالم ، لا في العلم بالله – تعالى – فان الأنبياء ، أعني أصحاب النبُوة الخاصة أعلم بالله من الأولياء . ولو كان الوليُ مِن أنبياء الأولياء ، والخضر مختلف في نبوته عند الفقهاء ، حتى قال الحافظ بن حجر : « ينبغي أن يكون الخضر نبياً ، لئلا يكون غير النبي أعلم من النبي » وأما أهل طريقنا – رضوان الله عليهم – فلا خلاف بينهم انه غير نبيّ ، النبوّة الخاصة ، نبوّة التشريع . وانما هو من الأفراد الذين لهم نبوّة الولاية

(١) ١٨/٦٧ الكهف .

Index

ʿAbd al-Raḥmān, Sultan of Morocco 15, 26, 31, 37, 41, 44 f., 49 – 56, 58, 191
'Abdulrahman Husni Bey' 157
ʿĀdil al-Ṣulḥ 156
aḥadiyyah 164
ʿAin Māḍī 31 f, 63, 76, 114
Aḥmad Bey 27, 43
al-Bayṭār, ʿAbd al-Razzāq 2 f., 8 f., 21, 24, 26, 139, 143, 150, 153 f., 160
al-Fāsī, Shaykh Muḥammad 153
Algeria 2 f., 5 f., 8 – 10, 12 f., 15, 17 – 28, 30, 37 f., 41, 43, 47 – 50, 52, 57 – 59, 61 – 63, 65, 69, 77 f., 81, 85, 89, 94 – 97, 101 – 105, 107 f., 110, 112 – 116, 118, 120 – 122, 124, 139, 141, 145 f., 150 – 153, 158 – 160, 171, 173 f., 176, 178 f., 183, 187 – 189, 197, 200 – 203, 205 – 207, 215, 217, 219 f., 227
al-Ghazālī, Abū Ḥāmid 62, 71, 74, 76, 125 – 127, 136, 140, 160, 169, 184 f., 199 f.
al-Hāshimī (son of ʿAbd al Qādir) 159
al-Ḥussein bin Manṣūr al-Ḥallāj (al-Ḥallāj, al-Ḥussein) 11, 166
al-insān al-kāmil 128, 167
al-Jazā'irī, Tāhir 143
al-Jīlānī, ʿAbd al-Qādir 22, 160, 186
al-Jīlī, ʿAbd al-Karīm 88, 167
al-Khānī, Moḥammad 160
al-Muʿaskar/Mascara 21, 23, 28 f., 31, 39, 102, 107, 116
al-Naqshbandī, Shaykh Khaled 24, 160
al-Qayṭanah 21 f.
al-Qayrawānī, Ibn Abī Zayd 97
al-Sanūsī, Yūsuf 70, 97
al-Suyuti, Jalāl al-Dīn 69, 74
al-Ṭanṭawī, Muḥammad 160
al-Ṭahṭāwī, Rifāʿah 117, 136
Althusser, Louis 61
al-Tijānī, Muḥammad al-Ṣaghīr 31 f., 44
al-Tirmidhī (al-Ḥakīm) 171
al-Wansharīsī (Aḥmad) 69 f., 82, 200
Amboise 49, 70, 95, 102, 106, 109, 112, 130, 132, 230
amīr al-mu'minīn 12, 15, 25 f., 49, 178, 199
Andalusian 68 f., 71, 81 f., 113, 163
anti-modern 152, 194
ʿāqil 8, 13, 97, 120, 122, 125 – 127, 129, 137, 160, 203
ʿaql 126 – 128, 130, 134, 136 f., 166
Aquinas, Thomas 68, 137, 168
Aristotle 68, 134, 136, 199, 207
aʿyān thābitah 166

Bāb Tūmā 146, 148
Barbotan, Countess 102 f.
barzakh / isthmus 165, 167, 169 f., 181, 183
Bayʿah 25
Bendraham, Judah, a.k.a. Ben Durand 200
Boissonet, Estève 102, 118 – 120
Brougham, Lord 103
Bugeaud, Thomas Robert 36, 39 – 42, 46, 48, 52 f., 55 – 57, 63, 83, 90, 112
Bursa 13, 118, 120 – 124, 142, 202, 205, 228
Burton, Richard 157

Carlyle, Thomas 18
Chaouche, Muḥammad 152
Chishtiyyah 22
Churchill, Charles Henry 9, 38, 111, 115
Constantine 27, 43, 49, 199
Crimean War 123 f.

Dā'irah 39, 202
Damascus 3 – 6, 8, 12 – 14, 16, 20 f., 24, 27, 29, 48 f., 58 f., 61, 68, 94 f., 106 f., 109 f., 115, 120, 122, 124 f., 129 f., 132, 139 f., 143 – 147, 151 – 157, 159, 162, 171 – 173, 176 – 179, 186, 188, 194, 197 f., 202 – 207, 215, 217 – 219, 222 f., 225, 227 – 229
Damrémont, Charles-Marie Denys de 39, 41, 63
Dan Fodio, Usman 70, 217
Dante (Alighieri, Dante) 68, 211
Darqāwiyyah 23 f.
Daumas, Eugène 8, 25 – 28, 31 f., 42, 76, 89, 97 f., 100 – 102, 105, 111 f., 115 f., 201

deism 115
de Lesseps, Ferdinand 142, 156
Descartes, René 133, 136 f.
Desmichels, Louis Alexis 37 f., 40, 50, 93, 95
De Tocqueville, Alexis 10, 15, 27, 30, 43, 45 f., 63, 81, 102, 219
dhimmī /ahl al-dhimmah 83, 139, 142, 149–151
d'Orléans, Henri, duc d'Aumale 43, 100, 103, 153, 201
d'Orsay, Count 12, 103 f.
dualist, dualism 164 f., 169, 203
Dumas, Alexandre 103
Dupuch, Monseigneur Antoine-Adolphe, also Bishop 102 f., 108, 111

Engels, Friedrich 48
Elias, Norbert 216
Enlightenment 129, 132–134, 136 f.
enlightenment 98, 109
Epicurus 210
esotericism 109, 115, 161, 167 f., 191–5

Faivre, Antoine 168, 189, 192
fatalism 169, 176
Fez 54 f., 68, 72
fiqh 68, 71, 97, 168, 184 f., 198
Foucault, Michel 61 85 216
Franco-Prussian War 158
Freemasonry, Freemasons 11, 115, 196, 207
Fuad Pasha 147 f.

Geertz, Clifford 19, 45, 86
Gellner, Ernest 29, 81, 193
Gibraltar 54, 227, 229
'Great Man' theory of history 18, 152, 203, 223
Grotius, Hugo 42, 46
Guénon, René 168, 189–193, 210, 213 f.

Ḥanafism 69
ḥaqīqah 91, 163, 166, 170, 176 f., 181, 183, 186
Hassan Bey (a.k.a. Colonel O'Reilly) 156
Herder, Johann Gottfried von 134
hijrah 13, 36, ch.2 passim, 95 f., 98, 101, 108, 116, 120, 130, 138 f., 150, 160, 171, 183, 185, 200 f., 203, 216, Appendix A passim
Ḥudaybiyyah, Ṣulḥ of 34, 84
Hugo, Victor 103
Huxley, Aldous 210, 212

Ibn al-ʿArabī (Muḥyī al-Dīn Ibn al-ʿArabī) 12, 72, 74, 82, 88, 111, 113 f., 122, 129, 131, 143, 159–161, 163, 165, 167, 174, 176, 178, 181, 186, 188, 190 f., 193, 199, 203, 210 f., 214
Ibn Khaldūn 71, 134, 199
Ibn Rushd/Averroes 67 f., 82, 199
ijāzahs 22
Iron Gates/Bībān 43, 51
Istanbul 13, 119 f., 124, 140, 144, 157, 159, 202, 227–229
isthmus/*barzakh* 165, 167, 169 f., 181, 183
ithnayniyyah 171

James, William 210, 212
Jerusalem 120, 140, 143 f., 227
jihād 2, 20, 30, 32, 34, 43–45, 55, 58, 78, 85–87, 107, 172 f., 176, 183, 201 f., 222

Kant, Kantian 129, 133
Khomeini, Ayatollah Ruhollah 113
Kubrawiyyah 224 f.
Kuhn, Thomas 224

laïcité 7, 79, 93, 187–189
Lamoricière, Louis Juchault de 12, 55, 57, 95, 97, 99, 103, 106, 153, 201
Lanusse, Acting Consul 145 f., 148 f., 153
Leibniz, Wilhelm von 134, 162, 175
Lesseps, Ferdinand de 142, 156
Locke, John 133, 210
Londonderry, Marquess/Lord 10, 103 f., 229
Louis Napoleon/Napoleon III 38, 94, 102–106, 108, 111, 115, 117, 120–124, 143, 151, 158, 201, 205 f., 221 f.
Louis Philippe 95 f., 98 f., 101, 117

MacIntyre, Alasdair 132
Macta, battle of 38
madhdhāhib 36, 68, 129 f.

Mahmoud Pasha 141
Maidstone, Viscount (George William Winchilsea) 103
Maimonedes, Moses 168
makhzan 28 f., 44, 58
Malikite/Mālikī 45, 62 f., 67–70, 72 f., 78, 81 f., 84, 87, 97, 129 f., 142, 159, 166, 185, 199 f., 219
Maraboutism 15, 19, 23, 30–32, 45, 51, 53, 56 f., 74–76, 79, 88–91, 108, 114, 149, 160, 196, 199, 203 f.
Marseilles 102, 118
modernity 2, 7, 35, 109, 113, 132 f., 189 f., 194, 208, 210, 221 f.
monism (ethical or ontological) 164, 169, 178 f., 193 f., 203
Morocco 9 f., 13, 15, 23, 26, 28, 34, 37, 40, 48–58, 61, 89, 95, 100, 200 f., 204, 228
Mostaganem 41
muḥammadī/muḥammadiyyah 91 f., 114, 163
mujāhid 2, 45, 51, 55, 144, 172 f., 217
Muḥyī al-Dīn (father of ʿAbd al Qādir) 22 f., 25 f., 37, 50, 153
Muḥyī al-Dīn (son of ʿAbd al Qādir) 158, 206
munāfiq 64–66, 73, 75, 77 f., 108, 183, 201, 221
Mustapha Bey 147
Muʿtazilites 165
mysticism 11, 34, 109, 131, 185, 197, 208–210, 212–215

Naqshbandiyyah 22, 220
nasab 21
negative (apophatic) theology 168, 182

Oued Khadra 43

pacific, pacifism 35, 99, 109, 113, 123, 171–173, 206 f.
pantheistic 161, 166, 178, 186, 188, 193
Paris 9, 105, 118, 123 f., 207, 210, 228
Pascal, Blaise 87
Pau 49, 95
pluralism 71, 138 f., 151 f., 178 f., 186, 194, 223
Plato, Platonic 134, 136, 211
Plotinus 134, 164
Porphyry 134
postmodernism 190, 211

Qādirī/Qādiriyyah 22–24, 30 f., 70, 87, 91 f., 113, 160, 167, 186, 199, 219
qiyāṣ 68, 71, 168, 184 f.
quietism 171, 173
Qūnawī, Ṣadr al-Dīn 161

Radtke, Bernd 11, 67, 92, 214
Raḥmāniyyah 23, 92
rationalism 131–137
Reconquista 36, 68, 70 f., 78, 81, 200, 220
relativism 7, 183, 186, 189, 194
ribāṭ 45 f.
Rīf 30, 48, 51 f., 55–57, 200
riots, rioters 2, 14, 145–153, 157, 188, 194, 204, 222
Roches, Léon 9, 31, 48, 55 f., 100, 114 f.

Said, Edward 6, 132
Sadra, Mullah 113
ṣaffs 30
Scott, Colonel 36, 53 f., 83, 150
Shādhilī 153, 163
Shāfiʿism 62, 68 f., 73, 76, 78, 130, 185
Shāmil (Shamyl), Imam 2, 181
sharīf, sharifianism 20–26, 31, 51, 79, 88–90, 105, 141, 199, 203 f.
ṣidq 76 f., 126, 183
Sokoto Caliphate 70
Spain 45, 53, 77, 108
Spinoza, Baruch 134, 136, 162
Stace, Walter 211
Suez 142, 156, 205
Suhrawardiyyah 22

Tafna 39, 41 f., 50 f., 54, 63
Tafna, treaty of 39, 41 f., 51, 54, 63
Tagdempt 32, 36, 122, 205
taḥrīf 83, 130, 139
takfīr 169
Tangiers 50
Taqī-al-Dīn al-Ḥusnī, Mufti Hassan 156
taqlīd 129 f.

ṭarīqah(s), ṭuruq 22, 30–32, 91f., 114, 153, 199, 204
tawakkul 111, 175, 177
Taylor, Charles 7, 93, 208–210
Thackeray, William Makepeace 48, 103
theocratic 80, 93, 171, 188
Tijaniyyah 23f., 31, 63, 75, 92, 186
Toulon 49, 95, 97, 100, 112

universalisms, clash of 187, 194–197

Valée, Governor-General Sylvain Charles, comte de 43
Vâlsan, Michel 190–192
Van Ess, Josef 137, 168, 221

waḥdat al-wujūd 161
Wellington, Arthur Wellesley, Duke of 103
Westphalia, Peace of 42, 84

zāwiyah 22f., 114, 198, 203, 226
Zmala 39

Author Index

Abd-Allah, Umar F. 185
Abdel-Jaouad, Hedi 48, 103, 106
ʿAbd al-Karīm, Muḥammad bin 64, 69
Abou El Fadl, Khaled 68–70, 72, 82
Abrahamov, Binyamin 134
Abun-Nasr, Jamil 3, 22, 24, 30f., 33, 39, 45, 47f., 64, 70, 84, 91, 139, 211
Achrati, Nora 6, 19, 107, 110, 151
Addas, Claude 211
al-Ḥakīm, Suʿād 62, 88, 163, 165, 169
al-Ḥasanī al-Jazāʾirī, Badīʿah 2, 63, 153
Almond, Ian 211
Asad, Talal 7, 19, 21, 59–61, 86, 209, 215, 223
Asín Palacios, Miguel 211
Attias, Jean-Christophe 190
Ayubi, Nazih 33, 184, 221
Azan, Paul 10, 16, 138f
Bashier, Salman H. 165, 211
Bennison, Amira (Katherine) 9–11, 16, 20f., 23, 26, 28, 30, 34, 39, 43–45, 47–50, 53, 56, 60f., 79, 86, 89, 91f., 112
Berndt, Johan Carl 10, 35, 47, 197
Berque, Jacques 12, 80, 172–4, 178, 196
Blunt, Wilfred 12, 26–28, 36, 39f., 83, 89, 117
Borges, Jorge Louis 224
Bourdieu, Pierre 86, 216
Bouyerdene, Ahmed 12, 101, 138, 150, 154, 191, 199
Brower, Benjamin 8
Burke III, Edmund 44–46, 87
Chittick, Wiliam C. 179, 190, 192, 211
Chodkiewicz, Michel 2, 5, 11f., 13, 113, 131f., 151, 160, 163, 178–187, 191, 208, 211
Christelow, Allan 64, 89f., 216
Clancy-Smith, Julia A. 80, 92, 217
Clayton, Vista 12, 23, 26, 38, 47, 89, 115f., 138, 211
Commins, David Dean 4, 11f., 24, 36, 98, 129, 131f., 143, 155
Cook, Michael 173–176
Cornell, Vincent 69, 74, 89, 126, 185, 204, 213, 216
Danziger, Raphael 2, 5, 10, 16f., 19f., 22–30, 32–35, 37–41, 43–46, 50, 53f., 73, 79, 81, 83, 85, 89–92, 110, 112, 151, 208
De Certeau, Michel 210
De Jong, Frederick 67
Eaton, Charles le Gai 151, 192
Emerit, Marcel 9
Étienne, Bruno 2, 6, 10–12, 16, 122, 124, 138, 141f., 144, 149, 156, 158, 174, 178f., 188f., 191, 199, 208, 219
Faivre, Antoine 168, 189, 192
Freeden, Michael 90
Gadamer, Hans-Georg 3, 193, 221
Geertz, Clifford 19, 45, 86
Gellner, Ernest 29, 81, 193
Geoffroy, Eric 11, 109, 179, 188f., 196, 207f., 211
Gilsenan, Michael 192
Gilis, Charles-André 191, 211
Goldziher, Ignaz 68, 87, 130, 142, 150, 159, 196, 211
Gramsci, Antonio 47, 216
Green, Donald P. 60
Group for the Advancement of Psychiatry 211f.
Gudeman, Stephen 86, 216
Haanegraaf, Wouter 168, 192, 210
al-Ḥakīm, Suʿād 62, 88, 163, 165, 169
al-Ḥasanī al-Jazāʾirī, Badīʿah 2, 63, 153
Halpern, David 216
Hatina, Meir 191,
Haugaard, Mark 216
Hawi, Sami S. 212
Heck, Paul L. 77, 93, 110, 208, 215f.
Heidegger, Martin 133
Hourani, Albert 80, 117, 134, 136
Hulliung, Mark 3
Ibn ʿAjība, Aḥmad 198
Izutsu, Toshihiko 77, 211
James, William 210, 212

Johansen, Baber 87, 185
Johnson, Mark 133
Jonsen, Albert 87
Julien, Charles-André 9, 22–29, 31, 36, 38, 43, 45–49, 51f., 81, 89, 101–103, 115f., 121, 150, 200
Kant, Immanuel 129, 133
Karamustafa, Ahmet T. 76, 169
Katz, Steven 212–214
Kedourie, Elie 84
Khadduri, Majid 34, 45f., 82, 84, 87, 90, 172
King, John 3, 23, 29, 34f., 89, 142, 153, 156
King, Richard 6, 8, 175, 197, 212–214
Kiser, John 2, 12, 138, 161
Knysh, Alexander D. 161
Kugle, Scott 69, 76
Kuhn, Thomas 224f.
Lakoff, George 133
Lagarde, Michel 12
Lovejoy, Arthur Oncken 164
Lyotard, Jean François 190
MacIntyre, Alasdair 132
Makdisi, Ussama 145, 148, 152
Martin, Bradford G. 31, 63, 67, 92, 114, 211f.
Massignon, Louis 11, 166
Masters, Bruce 145
Michot, Yahya 31
Miller, Kathryn 70
Morris, James W. 179, 186, 193, 212
Munson, Henry 8, 26, 45, 68, 86, 89
Netton, Ian 211
Nicholson, Reynold 88, 193, 211, 234
Nye, Joseph 216
O'Fahey, Rex Sean 89, 109, 114, 223
Penot, Abdallah 92, 124, 191
Pinto, Paulo 76–77
Plattner, Stuart 86
Polanyi, Karl 86
Putnam, Robert 216
Quine, Wilard Van Orman 133
Radtke, Bernd 11, 67, 92, 214
Reinhart, A. Kevin 184
Rogan, Eugene 12, 145, 148
Said, Edward 6, 132
Ṣalībā, J. 234
Schatkowski Schilcher, Linda 12, 142
Schmidt, Leigh Eric 209f.
Scholem, Gershom 212
Scott, Colonel 36
Sedgwick, Mark 191, 194
Serauky, Eberhard 22f., 34, 48
Sfeir, Antoine 138, 208
Shapiro, Ian 60
Shinar, Pessah 2, 5, 10f., 22, 24–26, 32–35, 80f., 92, 97, 113f., 160, 194
Skinner, Quentin 3
Smirnov, Andrey V. 211
Smith, Wilfred Cantwell 62, 182f., 209
Stelzer, Steffen A. 126f., 129
Taji-Farouki, Suha 190
Tarakci, Muhammet 130
Sayar, Sulayman 130
Taylor, Charles 7, 93, 208–210
Tocqueville, Alexis de 10, 15, 17, 27, 30, 43, 45f., 63, 81, 102, 219
Toulmin, Stephen 87, 127, 132
Tierno, Michael 207
Vâlsan, Michel 190–192
Van Ess, Josef 137, 168, 221
Waardenburg, Jacques 93
Ward Gwynne, Rosalind 71
Wasserstrom, Steven 194, 209
Weismann, Itzchak 2, 12, 24, 110f., 113, 117, 131–138, 142f., 154, 173f., 177f., 181, 188, 211
Wimmer, Franz Martin 195f.
Winter, Tim 126f., 129, 135
Wolfson, Harry 62, 71
Zaehner, Robert Charles 211f.

www.ingramcontent.com/pod-product-compliance
Lightning Source LLC
Chambersburg PA
CBHW031725230426
43669CB00007B/250
* 9 7 8 3 1 1 0 5 0 0 5 5 4 *